A CONCORDANCE OF THE POETICAL WORKS
OF EDGAR ALLAN POE

A CONCORDANCE OF THE POETICAL WORKS OF EDGAR ALLAN POE

By

BRADFORD A. BOOTH

AND

CLAUDE E. JONES

GLOUCESTER, MASS.

PETER SMITH

1967

INTRODUCTION

Dr. Johnson thundered from his tavern chair, and there was none with the temerity to oppose him. Yet his position was not always tenable, for he was sometimes a capriciously impressionistic critic, given to uttering personal whims and prejudices that are the antithesis of sound criticism. Still, if he chose to cut across the well-marked but circuitous path of scholars, by trusting to the validity of his own perceptions, it must not be thought that he would have scorned the mechanics of scholarship. What he might have thought of a concordance to poetry, we do not definitely know, for he never saw one. His choice of illustrative material for the dictionary, however, and his general attitude toward poetic diction make it pretty evident that he would have welcomed such an aid to serious study. But Dr. Johnson had a delicious sense of humor, and it would be surprising if in his well-proportioned mind concordance-makers would not have been lumped together with lexicographers and other harmless drudges.

A concordance is a handy book we should like somebody else to compile. The present editors are fully aware of the small respect which many of their contemporaries have for the tedious and uninspiring labor, for the infinite and often dreary patience, and for the painstaking exactness which must be the chief constituents of any concordance. They justify themselves with thinking that a volume for which they have long felt a personal need may find ready acceptance by others who are interested in the poetry of the American Romantic movement, tongue clackers and head waggers to the contrary notwithstanding. They were heartened in overcoming many practical difficulties by the realization that they were engaged on what must be a standard work. The poet's exhortation that "a man's reach should exceed his grasp" may be an admirable rule of conduct, but it bears no reference to scholarship. Accuracy is the only criterion of excellence by which a concordance may be judged. In that, we trust we have not failed.

The scholarly journals today are bulging with studies of Poe's sources, his aesthetic theories, his metrics, his rhymes. But there has never been any investigation of his diction. It is not easy to understand why, for even the most superficial reader is struck by the iteration of certain key words, such as " shadow," " dream " and " angel." Poe was meticulous in diction, and his vocabulary is as characteristic as his metrics. The effects in his mood-pictures are not the result of happy chance, but of carefully conceived and exquisitely modulated tones. These he achieved through onomatopoeia, judicious use of liquids, long open vowels, and the selection of only-such words as by sound or association contributed directly to the desired effect. However distrustful we may be of " The Philosophy of Composition," it is patent that Poe put a great deal of effort into finding the exact word.

A concordance is of no significance in itself. It is simply an indispensable tool for the study of poetic diction. The compilers of this concordance feel an intangible personal satisfaction in having come to know with some thoroughness Poe's works. It is their hope that through it others will join them in the careful study of one of our finest poets.

METHOD

This concordance was compiled by the following method:

1. Twelve copies of the text (*The Poems of Edgar Allan Poe.* Edited by Killis Campbell. . . . Ginn and Company, Boston [etc., 1917]) were marked with key-word and line number—six for the odd pages, and six for the even.
2. Beginning with the odd pages, the first concordanceable word was marked in each line in one copy; the second word in another copy; and so until all concordanceable words had been marked in red.
3. The copies were then cut, each line containing a word marked in red being mounted on a 3″ x 5″ card.
4. These cards were arranged alphabetically according to marked words.
5. The concordance was then typed from the cards so arranged, and the copy was checked against the cards for collation.
6. The cards were then rearranged alphabetically according to poems, and numerically by lines within the individual poems.
7. The cards so arranged were checked against a key copy of the text to insure against omissions, and dropped lines were added in the typed copy.

The poems not included in our basic (*i. e.*, the Campbell) text were copied into the first draft of the concordance, and carefully checked. We wish to express our gratitude to Thomas Ollive Mabbott for information and suggestions concerning elusive fragments.

KEY WORDS [1]

Acrostic	An Acrostic, from ms. copy, where it lacks title.
Al Aaraaf i-ii	Al Aaraaf; from 1845 coll.
Al Aaraaf i-ii (1829)	Same, from 1829 coll.
Al Aaraaf i-ii (Yankee)	Same, from *B.Y.*, Dec., 1829.

[1] In the legend of key-words these abbreviations are used:

A.W.R.	*The American Whig Review*, New York.
B.G.M.	*Burton's Gentleman's Magazine*, Philadelphia.
B.J.	*The Broadway Journal*, New York.
B.M.	*The Baltimore Museum.*
B.Y.	*The Boston Yankee and Literary Gazette.*
E.M.	*The Evening Mirror*, New York.
F.O.U.	*The Flag of Our Union*, Boston.

Al Aaraaf i-ii (1831)	Same, from *Poems*, 1831.
Al Aaraaf i-ii (1843)	Same from *S.M.*, March 4, 1843.
Alone	Alone, from *Scribner's Monthly,* Sept., 1875.
Annabel Lee	Annabel Lee, from *S.L.M.*, Nov. 1849.
Annabel Lee (1849)	Same, from New York *Tribune*, Oct. 9, 1849.
Annabel Lee (1850)	As Annabel Lee. A Ballad, from *U.M.*, Jan., 1850.
Annie	For Annie, from Griswold ed. *Works*, II, 1850.
Annie (1849)	Same, from *F.O.U.*, April 28, 1849.
Ballad	Ballad ("They have giv'n her to another"), from *S.L.M.*, Aug., 1835.
(Ballad	See *Bridal Ballad* below.)
(Beautiful Physician	See *Physician* below.)
Bells	The Bells, from *U.M.*, Nov., 1849.
Bells (1849)	As The Bells.—A Song, from *U.M.*, Dec., 1849.
Bridal Ballad	Bridal Ballad ("The ring is on my hand"), from Graham copy of 1845 coll.
Bridal Ballad (1837)	As Ballad, from *S.L.M.*, Jan., 1837.
Campaign	Fragment of a Campaign Song, from *New York Times Saturday Review,* March 4, 1899.
(Catholic Hymn	See *Hymn* below.)
City	The City in the Sea, from 1845 coll.
City (1831)	As The Doomed City, from *Poems*, 1831.
City (1836)	As The City of Sin, from *S.L.M.*, Aug., 1836.
City (1845)	As The City in the Sea, A Prophecy, from *A.W.R.*, April, 1845.
Coliseum	The Coliseum, from 1845 coll.
Coliseum (1833)	Same, from *S.M.V.*, Oct. 26, 1833.
Coliseum (1841)	As A Prize Poem, from *S.E.P.*, June 12, 1841.

G.L.B.	*Godey's Lady's Book,* Philadelphia.
G.M.	*Graham's Magazine*, Philadelphia.
H.J.	*The Home Journal,* New York.
M.M.	*The Missionary Memorial,* New York.
Mabbott	*Selected Poems of Edgar Allan Poe.* Ed. Thomas Ollive Mabbott. The Macmillan Company, New York, 1928. (The Modern Readers Series.)
N.Q.	*Notes and Queries.* London.
Pioneer	*The Pioneer,* Boston.
R.E.	*The Richmond Examiner.*
R.W.	*The Richmond Whig.*
S.E.P.	*The Saturday Evening Post,* Philadelphia.
S.L.M.	*The Southern Literary Messenger*, Richmond.
S.M.	*The Saturday Museum,* Philadelphia.
S.M.V.	*The Saturday Morning Visiter,* Baltimore.
U.M.	*The Union Magazine,* New York and Philadelphia.
1827 coll.	*Tamerlane and Other Poems.* Boston, 1827.
1829 coll.	*Al Aaraaf, Tamerlane, and Minor Poems.* Baltimore, 1829.
1845 coll.	*The Raven and Other Poems.* New York, 1845.

Coliseum (1842)	As Coliseum, from Griswold's *The Poets and Poetry of America*, 1842.
(Conqueror Worm	See *Worm* below.)
Departed	The Departed, from *B.J.*, July 12, 1845.
Divine Right	The Divine Right of Kings, from *G.M.*, Oct., 1845.
(Doomed City	See *City* above.)
Dream	A Dream, from *B.J.*, Aug. 16, 1845.
Dream (1827)	Title omitted, from 1827 coll.
Dream-Land	Dream-Land, from Graham copy of 1845 coll.
Dream-Land (1844)	Same, from *G.M.*, June, 1844.
Dream-Land (1845)	Same, from *B.J.*, June 28, 1845.
Dream w. Dream	A Dream within a Dream, from *F.O.U.*, March 31, 1849.
Dream w. Dream (1829)	Same, from *B.Y.*, Dec., 1829.
Dream w. Dream (1831)	Same, from *Poems*, 1831.
(Dream w. Dream	See *Imitation* below.)
(Dream w. Dream	See *To⁴* below.)
Dreams	Dreams, from 1827 coll.
Eldorado	Eldorado, from Griswold ed. *Works*, II, 1850.
Elizabeth	Elizabeth, from ms.
Enigma	An Enigma, from Griswold ed. *Works*, II, 1850.
Enigma (1848)	As Sonnet, from *U.M.*, March, 1848.
Eulalie	Eulalie—A Song, from Graham copy of 1845 coll.
Eulalie (1845)	Same, from *A.W.R.*, July, 1845.
(Evening Star	See *Star* below.)
Experiments	Metrical Experiments, from *S.L.M.*, Nov., 1848 (Mabbott).
Fairy-Land	Fairy-Land, from 1845 coll.
Fairy-Land (1829)	Same, from 1829 coll.
Fairy-Land (1831)	Same, from *Poems*, 1831.
(For Annie	See *Annie* above.)
(Fragment	See *Campaign* above.)
(Fragments	See *Physician* below.)
Happiest Day	Title omitted ("The happiest day, the happiest hour), from 1827 coll.
(Haunted Palace	See *Palace* below.)
Helen¹	To Helen ("Helen thy beauty is to me "), from 1845 coll.
Helen¹ (1831)	Same, from *Poems*, 1831.
Helen¹ (1841)	Same, from *G.M.*, Sept., 1841.
Helen²	To Helen ("I saw thee once—once only—years ago "), from Griswold ed. *Works*, II, 1850.
Helen²	As To —, from *U.M.*, Nov., 1848.
Hymn	Hymn, from Graham copy of 1845 coll.
Hymn (1835)	Title omitted, from *S.L.M.*, April, 1835.

(Hymn	As Catholic Hymn in *B.J.*, Aug. 16, 1845. No variations from *Hymn*.)
Hymn (1835)	Without title, from *S.L.M.*, April, 1835.
Imitation	Imitation, from 1827 coll. (Variant of *Dream w. Dream*, above.)
Impromptu	Impromptu to Kate Carol, from *B.J.*, April 26, 1845.
(Introduction	See *Romance* below.)
Irene	Irene, from *Poems*, 1831.
Irene (1836)	Same, from *S.L.M.*, May, 1836.
Israfel	Israfel, from Graham copy of 1845 coll.
Israfel (1831)	Same, from *Poems*, 1831.
Israfel (1841)	Same, from *G.M.*, Oct., 1841.
Israfel (1843)	Same, from *S.M.*, March 4, 1843.
Lake	The Lake: To—, from 1845 coll.
Lake (1827)	As The Lake, from 1827 coll.
Lake (1829)	As The Lake: To —, from 1829 coll.
Lake (1831)	Title omitted, from *Poems,* 1831.
Lake (1845)	Same, from *M.M.*, 1845.
Lampoon	A West Point Lampoon, from *S.M.*, Feb. 25, 1843.
Latin Hymn	Latin Hymn, from *B.J.*, Dec. 6, 1845.
Lenore	Lenore, from *R.W.,* Sept. 18, 1849.
Lenore (1843)	Same, from *Pioneer*, Feb., 1843.
Lenore (Museum)	Same, from *S.M.*, March 4, 1843.
Lenore (1845)	Same, from *G.M.*, Feb., 1845.
(Lenore	See *Paean* below.)
(Life	See *Louisa* below.)
(Lines	See *Louisa* below.)
(Lines	See *Manuscript* below.)
(Lines	See *To F.S.O.* below.)
Louisa	Lines to Louisa, from ms. (As Life's Vital Stream, in New York *Sun*, Nov. 21, 1915. No variation.)
Manuscript	Lines Written on a Manuscript of Eulalie, from *Bull. N. Y. Pub. Library*, Dec., 1914 (Mabbott).
(Metrical Experiments	See *Experiments* above.)
Mother	To My Mother, from Griswold ed. *Works,* II, 1850.
Mother (1849)	As Sonnet—To My Mother, from *F.O.U.*, July 7, 1849.
Mother (1850)	Same, from *Leaflets of Memory*, 1850.
Nis	The Valley Nis, from *Poems*, 1831. (Variant of *Valley* below.)

Nis (1836)	Same, from *S.L.M.*, Feb., 1836. (Variant of *Valley* below.)
Octavia	[To Octavia] (" When wit, and wine, and friends have met.") Kindness of T. O. Mabbott, who assigns this title.
(Oh, Tempora	See *Tempora* below.)
Paean	A Paean, from *Poems,* 1831. (Variant of *Lenore* above.)
Paean (1836)	Same, from *S.L.M.*, Jan., 1836. (Variant of *Lenore* above.)
Palace	The Haunted Palace, from Graham copy of 1845 coll.
Palace (1839)	Same, from *B.M.*, April, 1839.
Palace (Burton's)	Title omitted, from *B.G.M.*, Sept., 1839.
Paradise	To One in Paradise, from Graham copy of 1845 coll.
	(As To Ianthe in Heaven, in *B.G.M.*, July, 1839. No variation.)
Paradise (1834)	Title omitted, from *G.L.B.*, Jan., 1834.
Paradise (1835)	Same, from *S.L.M.*, July, 1835.
Parody	Parody on Lines by Drake, from *S.L.M.*, April, 1836 (Mabbott).
Physician	Fragments of The Beautiful Physician, from N. Y. *Bookman*, Jan., 1909 (Mabbott).
Poetry	Poetry by Edgar A. Poe, from ms. (Mabbott).
Politian i-v	Scenes from " Politian," an Unpublished Drama, from Graham copy of 1845 coll.
Politian i-v (1835)	As Scenes from an Unpublished Drama, from *S.L.M.*, Dec., 1835, and Jan., 1836.
Politian ii (1845)	As Scenes from " Politian," an Unpublished Drama, from *B.J.*, March 29, 1845.
(Preface	See *Romance* below.)
(Prize Poem	See *Coliseum* above.)
Raven	The Raven, from *R.E.*, Sept. 25, 1849.
Raven (1845)	Same, from *E.M.*, Jan. 29, 1845.
Raven (A. W. R.)	Same, from *A.W.R.*, Feb., 1845.
Raven (B. J.)	Same, from *B.J.*, Feb. 8, 1845.
Raven (Critic)	Same, from London *Critic*, June 14, 1845.
Raven (S. L. M.)	Same, from *S.L.M.*, March, 1845.
Raven (1846)	Same, from *G.M.*, April, 1846.
Raven (1850)	Same, from Griswold ed. *Works*, II, 1850.
River	To the River, from 1845 coll.
River (1829)	Same, from 1829 coll.
Romance	Romance, from 1845 coll.
Romance (1829)	As Preface, from 1829 coll.

Romance (1831)	As Introduction, from *Poems*, 1831.
Romance (1843)	Romance, from *S. M.*, March 4, 1843.
Sarah	To Sarah, from *S.L.M.*, Aug., 1835.
(Scenes	See *Politian* above.)
(Science	See *To Science* below.)
Serenade	Serenade, from *S.M.V.*, April 20, 1833.
Silence	Sonnet—Silence, from 1845 coll.
Silence (1840)	As Silence. A Sonnet, from *B.G.M.*, April, 1840.
Sleeper	The sleeper, from Graham copy of 1845 coll.
Sleeper (1842)	Same, from Griswold's *Poets and Poetry of America*, 1842.
Sleeper (1843)	Same, from the *S.M.*, March 4, 1843.
(Sleeper	See *Irene* above.)
Song	Song, from *B.J.*, Sept. 20, 1845.
Song (1827)	As *To —*, from 1827 coll.
(Song	See *Triumph* below.)
(Sonnet	See *Enigma* above.)
(Sonnet	See *Science* above.)
(Sonnet	See *Silence* above.)
(Sonnet	See *Zante* below.)
Spirits	Spirits of the Dead, from *B.G.M.*, July, 1839.
Spirits (1827)	As Visit of the Dead, from 1827 coll.
Stanzas[1]	Title omitted (" In youth I have known one with whom the Earth "), from 1827 coll.
Stanzas[2]	Stanzas (" Lady! I would that verse of mine "), from *G.M.*, Dec., 1845.
Star	Evening Star, from 1827 coll.
Tamerlane	Tamerlane, from 1845 coll.
Tamerlane (1827)	Same, from 1827 coll.
Tamerlane (1829)	Same, from *B.Y.*, Dec., 1829.
Tamerlane (1831)	Same, from 1831 coll.
Tempora	Oh, Tempora! Oh, Mores!, from *No Name Magazine*, Oct., 1889 (Mabbott).
To[1]	To — (" The bowers whereat, in dreams, I see "), from *B.J.*, Sept. 20, 1845.
To[1] (1829)	Same, from 1829 coll.
To[2]	To — (" I heed not that my earthly lot "), from Griswold ed. *Works*, II, 1850.
To[3]	To — (" Not long ago, the writer of these lines "), from *Columbian Magazine*, March, 1848.
To[3] (1850)	Same, from Griswold ed. *Works*, II, 1850.
To[4]	To — (" Should my early life seem "), from 1829 coll. (Variant of *Dream w. dream* above.)
(To —	See *Song* above.)

(To —	See *To F.S.O.* below.)
(To —	See *To M* below.)
To F	To F — ("Beloved! amid the earnest woes"), from 1845 coll.
To F (1835)	As To Mary, from *S.L.M.*, July, 1835.
To F (1842)	As To One Departed, from *G.M.*, March, 1842.
(To F	See *To F.S.O.* below.)
To FSO	To F—s S. O—d, from 1845 coll. As To F. in *B.J.*, Sept. 13, 1845. (No variants.)
To FSO (1835)	As Lines written in an album, from *S.L.M.*, Sept. 1835.
To FSO (1839)	As To —, from *B.G.M.*, Aug., 1839.
(To Helen	See *Helen*[1] and *Helen*[2] above.)
(To Her	See *Valentine* below.)
To Hunter	To Miss Louise Olivia Hunter, from *N.Q.* CLXII (Apr. 9, 1932), 261.
To M	To M—, from 1829 coll.
To MLS	To M. L. S—, from *H.J.*, March 13, 1847.
To Margaret	To Margaret, from *N.Q.* CLXI (Nov. 28, 1931), 358.
(To Mary	See *To F* above.)
(To Miss Louise Olivia Hunter	See *To Hunter* above.)
(To Octavia	See *Octavia* above.)
(To One Departed	See *To F* above.)
(To One in Paradise	See *Paradise* above.)
(To Sarah	See *Sarah* above.)
To Science	Sonnet—To Science, from 1845 coll.
To Science (1829)	Title omitted, from 1829 coll.
To Science (1830)	As Sonnet, *S.E.P.*, Sept. 11, 1830.
To Science (1841)	Title omitted, from *G.M.*, June, 1841.
(To the River	See *River* above.)
Triumph	Song of Triumph, from *B.J.*, Dec. 6, 1845.
Ulalume	Ulalume, from ms.
Ulalume (1847)	As To —, Ulalume: A Ballad, from *A.W.R.*, Dec., 1847.
Ulalume (1848)	As Ulalume from *The Providence Daily Journal*, Nov. 22, 1848.
Valentine	A Valentine, from *F.O.U.*, March 3, 1849.
Valentine (1846)	As To Her whose Name is Written Below, from *E.M.*, Feb. 21, 1846.
Valentine (1849)	As A Valentine. To —, from *U.M.*, March, 1849.
Valley	The Valley of Unrest, from 1845 coll.
Valley (1845)	Same, from *A.W.R.*, April, 1845.
(Valley	See *Nis* above.)

(Visit of the Dead   See *Spirits* above.)
(West Point   See *Lampoon* above.)
Worm   The Conqueror Worm, from Graham copy of
                         1845 coll.
Worm (1845)   Same, from *G.M.*, Jan., 1843.
Zante   Sonnet—To Zante, from 1845 coll.

OMISSIONS

The following words and their abbreviated forms (*i. e.*, e'er, 'tis, we're, etc.) have been omitted from this concordance:

a	ever	of	through
about	for	off	thy
above	from	oh	thyself
after	had	on	to
again	has	or	under
against	have	other	up
ah	he	ought	upon
along	her	our	us
also	here	ours	was
am	hers	ourselves	we
among	herself	out	were
an	him	own (adj.)	what
and	himself	said	when
any	his	same	where
are	how	say	which
art (vb.)	I	says	while
as	if	shall	who
at	in	she	whom
be	into	should	whose
been	is	so	why
before	it	some	will (vb.)
behind	its	that	with
being	itself	the	within
below	may (vb.)	thee	without
between	me	their	would
but	might (vb.)	theirs	yes
by	mine	them	yet
can	must	themselves	you
cannot	my	there	your
could	myself	these	yours
did	no	they	yourself
do	nor	thine	yourselves
does	not	this	
done	now	those	
else	o	thou	

We omit, in addition to these words: (1) titles of poems; (2) division numbers; (3) stage directions (in *Politian*); (4) speakers' tags (also in *Politian*); (5) in *Politian* all sentences and fragments not containing the line's concordanced word; (6) in variant lines, all entries except concordanceable variants; (7) terminal and initial punctuation unless (a) initial punctuation is closed within the lines, or (b) terminal punctuation (exclusive of the dash) originates within the line.

In conclusion we may add that we are not concerned with the problems of identification surrounding the Poe canon. We include all the lines printed by Killis Campbell, as well as the short poems from *Notes and Queries* and Mabbott's edition of *The Selected Poems* without inquiring into the validity of the ascriptions in our sources.

B. A. B.

C. E. J.

CONCORDANCE

Aaraaf
When first Al Aaraaf knew her course
to be   Al Aaraaf ii 255

Abandon'd
I sought my long-abandon'd land
                    Tamerlane (1827) 361

Abashed
Abash'd, amid the lilies there to seek
                    Al Aaraaf i 119

Abhor
I hate—I loathe the name; I do abhor
                    Politian iv 31

Abide
Could the dishonored Lalage abide
                    Politian iv 26

Able
And take the matter up when I'm more
able   Tempora 24

Abroad
But now, abroad on the wide earth
                    Dream (1827) 3

Absence
Of all to whom thine absence is the night
                    To MLS 2

Absolve
Shall then absolve thee of all farther
duties   Politian iii 37

Abstruse
So deep abstruse he has not mastered it
                    Politian i 55

Abyss
From Balbec, and the stilly, clear abyss
                    Al Aaraaf ii 37
Nodding above the dim abyss   Irene 21

Abysses
Have stirred from out the abysses of his
heart   To³ 11

Accept
Cannot accept the challenge   Politian v 22

Accompaniment
Shall be the accompaniment   Paean 32

Accursed
Alas! for that accursed time
                    Paradise (1835) 27
Ev'n such as from th' accursed time
                    Tamerlane (1827) 145
Thy memory no more! Accursed ground
                    Zante 11

Accurst
Of Passion accurst   Annie 36

Achaian
It lit on hills Achaian, and there dwelt
                    Al Aaraaf i 34
Achaian statues in a world so rich
                    Al Aaraaf ii 35

Aching
Was all on Earth my aching sight
                    Song 7
With which this aching, breast is fraught
                    Tamerlane (1837) 184

Across
Swift dart across her brain; Louisa 10

Ada
Nor Love—Ada! tho, it were thine
                    Lake (1831) 17
My Ada. In that peaceful hour
                    Tamerlane (1837) 286
In mine own Ada's matted bow'r
                    Tamerlane (1827) 358
Nor love, Ada! tho' it were thine
                    Tamerlane (1831) 95

Adder
On bed of moss lies gloating the foul
adder   Coliseum (1833) 25

Address
Thereby, in heat of anger to address
                    Politian v 50

Adeline
Enthralling love, my Adeline   Serenade 17

Adjure
Followed fast and followed faster so,
when Hope he would adjure
                    Raven (1845) 64
Stern Despair returned, instead of the
sweet Hope he dared adjure
                    Raven (1845) 65

Adjust
I would adjust   Politian v 43

Admire
And more I admire   Star 21

Adonis
The "beau ideal" fancied for Adonis
                    Tempora 72

Adore
Our faith to one love—and one moon
adore—   Al Aaraaf i 153
By that Heaven that bends above us—
by that God we both adore   Raven 92

Adoring
Died in the arms of the adoring airs
                    Helen² 35

Adorn
Adorn yon world afar, afar
                    Al Aaraaf i 14

Adorning
Adorning then the dwellings of the sky
                    Al Aaraaf ii 19

Adown
While pettish tears adown her petals run
                    Al Aaraaf i 69
Gazing, entranced, adown the gorgeous
vista   To³ 23

Adrift
Why did I leave it, and, adrift
                    Tamerlane 94

Advance
And, with bold advance, now meeting
                    Departed 7

1

Afar
Adorn yon world afar, afar
Al Aaraaf i 14
Like woman's hair 'mid pearls, until, afar
Al Aaraaf i 33
Meantime from afar Al Aaraaf i (1831) 7
That fell, refracted, thro' thy bounds, afar
Al Aaraaf ii 160
So trembled from afar   Dream 14
Stay! turn thine eyes afar
Israfel (1831) 25
In thy glory afar   Star 16
Afar from its proud natural towers
Tamerlane 141
In the morning light afar
Spirits (1827) 20
From regions of the blest afar
Tamerlane 224
I look not up afar   To⁴ 5

Affairs
With whom affairs of a most private
nature   Politian v 42

Affirm
Uprising, unveiling, affirm   Worm 38

Affright
How they scream out their affright!
Bells 40
How we shiver with affright   Bells 74
Thy raiments and thy ebony cross affright
me   Politian ii 102

Agate
The agate lamp within thy hand
Helen¹ 13

Age
Vastness! and Age! and Memories of Eld
Coliseum 10
From Love to titled age and crime
Paradise (1835) 29
Lustrous in youth, undimmed in age
Stanzas² 20
We grew in age—and love—together
Tamerlane 96
Redoubling age! and more, I ween
Tamerlane (1827) 336
With the weight of an age of snows
To M 16

Ages
And spite all dogmas current in all ages
Tempora 77

Aghast
There the traveller meets, aghast
Dream-Land 33
Mute, motionless, aghast   Paradise 13

Agitations
Its old agitations   Annie 57

Ago
To many a wild star gazer long ago
Al Aaraaf ii 43
It was many and many a year ago
Annabel Lee 1
And this was the reason that, long ago
Annabel Lee 13
I saw thee once—once only—years ago
Helen² 1
Time long ago   Palace 12
Not long ago, the writer of these lines
To³ 1

Agony
In agony, to the Earth—and Heaven
Dream-Land 38
See—see—my soul, her agony Louisa 5
It is but agony of desire   Tamerlane 8
Which is but agony of desire
Tamerlane (1827) 3
The proud heart burst in agony
Tamerlane (1827) 200
There is of earth an agony
Tamerlane (1827) 303
A more than agony to him
Tamerlane (1827) 315
In agony sobbed, letting sink her
Ulalume 58

Agreeable
So pat, agreeable, and vastly proper
Tempora 47

Agreeing
For we cannot help agreeing that no living
human being   Raven 51

Ai
Ai! ai! alas!—alas   Irene 55

Aid
Can I do aught?—is there no farther aid
Politian ii 45
Is there no farther aid   Politian ii 46

Aidenn
Tell this soul with sorrow laden if, within
the distant Aidenn   Raven 93

Ails
Thy happiness!—what ails thee, cousin
of mine   Politian i 6
What ails thee, sir   Politian i 34
What ails thee, Early Politian
Politian iii 90

Air
Her world lay lolling on the golden air
Al Aaraaf i 17
And all the opal'd air in color bound
Al Aaraaf i 41
Heaving her white breast to the balmy
air   Al Aaraaf i 64
How solemnly pervading the calm air
Al Aaraaf i 123
On the sweetest air doth float
Al Aaraaf i (1831) 20
Of georgeous columns on th' unburthen'd
air   Al Aaraaf i 12
Thro' the ebon air, besilvering the pall
Al Aaraaf ii 17
Look'd out above into the purple air
Al Aaraaf ii 23
As she on the air   Al Aaraaf ii 109
But, list, Ianthe! when the air so soft
Al Aaraaf ii 231
In the icy air of night   Bells 5
Through the balmy air of night Bells 18
On the bosom of the palpitating air
Bells 56
That all seem pendulous in the air
City 27
But lo, a stir is in the air   City 42
Nor with too calm an air   Paean 36
And every gentle air that dallied
Palace 13

Dreamy maidens all the day
　　　　　　Al Aaraaf i (1831) 13
And hallow'd all the beauty twice again
　　　　　　Al Aaraaf ii 25
She paus'd and panted, Zantne! all
　beneath,　　　　　Al Aaraaf ii 57
All softly in ear,　　Al Aaraaf ii 145
Seraphs in all but " Knowledge," the keen
　light　　　　　　Al Aaraaf ii 159
For nearest of all stars was thine to our
　　　　　　Al Aaraaf ii 242
All hindering things
　　　　　　Al Aaraaf ii (1843) 93
And all I lov'd—I lov'd alone　Alone 8
Yes! that was the reason (as all men
　know　　　　　Annabel Lee 23
And so, all the night-tide, I lie down by
　the side　　　　Annabel Lee 38
And oh! of all tortures　　Annie 31
That quenches all thirst　　Annie 38
Than all of the many　　Annie 96
All the heavens, seem to twinkle　Bells 7
And all in tune　　　　Bells 21
All alone　　　　　　Bells 81
And all at my command　Bridal Ballad 4
And my friends are all delighted
　　　　　　Bridal Ballad (1837) 21
That all seem pendulous in air　City 27
In a strange city all alone　City (1831) 2
Such dreariness a heaven at all
　　　　　　City (1831) 19
All Hades from a thousand thrones
　　　　　　City (1836) 52
These stones—alas! these gray stones—
　are they all　　　　Coliseum 30
All of the famed and the colossal left
　　　　　　Coliseum 31
" Not all "—the Echoes answer me—" not
　all　　　　　　Coliseum 33
From us, and from all Ruin, unto the
　wise　　　　　Coliseum 35
With a despotic sway all giant minds
　　　　　　Coliseum 38
Not all our power is gone—not all our
　fame　　　　　Coliseum 40
Not all the magic of our high renown
　　　　　　Coliseum 41
Not all the wonder that encircles us
　　　　　　Coliseum 42
Not all the mysteries that in us lie
　　　　　　Coliseum 43
Not all the memories that hang upon
　　　　　　Coliseum 44
And hold this maxim all life long
　　　　　　Divine Right 11
While all the world were chiding
　　　　　　Dream 10
Of Paradise and Love—and all our own
　　　　　　Dream 33
For the tears that drip all over
　　　　　　Dream-Land 12
All that we see or seem
　　　　　　Dream w. Dream 10
Is all that we see or seem
　　　　　　Dream w. Dream 25
Through all the flimsy things we see at
　once　　　　　Enigma 3

Trash of all trash!—how can a lady don it
　　　　　　Enigma 5
Stable, opaque, immortal—all by dint
　　　　　　Enigma 13
And all day long　　　Eulalie 17
For the tears that drip all over
　　　　　　Fairy-Land 4
Or is it all but a dream, my dear
　　　　　　Fairy-Land (1831) 10
Be all ingratitude requited
　　　　　　Fairy-Land (1831) 19
In my own country all the way
　　　　　　Fairy-Land (1831) 30
Clad all in white, upon a violet bank
　　　　　　Helen ^{2} 17
No footstep stirred: the hated world all
　slept,　　　　　Helen^2 25
And in an instant all things disappeared.
　　　　　　Helen^2 29
All—all expired save thee—save less than
　thou:　　　　　Helen^2 36
All my Present and my Past
　　　　　　Hymn (1835) 14
Then, for thin own all radiant sake
　　　　　　Irene (1836) 39
Of his voice, all mute　　Israfel 7
Imbued with all the beauty　Israfel 27
And all the listening things
　　　　　　Israfel (1831) 15
Upon that spot, as upon all　Lake 8
As for Locke, he is all in my eye
　　　　　　Lampoon 1
Than all Syria can furnish of wine
　　　　　　Latin Hymn 12
For her most wrong'd of all the dead
　　　　　　Lenore (1843) 26
All things lovely—are not they　Nis 5
All about unhappy things　Nis 14
Or the sun ray dripp'd all red　Nis 23
One and all, too far away　Nis (1836) 6
All banner-like, above a grave
　　　　　　Nis (1836) 44
My heart, of all that soothes its pain
　　　　　　Octavia 7
That I should not sing at all　Paean 16
All perfum'd there　　Paean 26
To join the all-hallowed mirth
　　　　　　Paean (1836) 35
This—all this—was in the olden
　　　　　　Palace 11
And all with pearl and ruby glowing
　　　　　　Palace 25
All wanderers in that happy valley
　　　　　　Palace (1839) 17
Thou wast that all to me, love
　　　　　　Paradise 1
All wreathed with fairy fruits and flowers
　　　　　　Paradise 5
And all the flowers were mine　Paradise 6
Ambition—all is o'er　Paradise (1834) 15
And all my days are trances　Paradise 21
And all my nightly dreams　Paradise 22
No branch, they say, of all philosophy
　　　　　　Politian i 54
She has any more jewels—no—no—she
　gave me all　　　Politian ii 41
After all　　　　　Politian ii 51

Compose a sound delighting all to hear
Valentine (1846) 18
In the midst of which all day   Valley 7
Out—out are the lights—out all   Worm 33
While the angels, all pallid and wan
Worm 37
Fair isle, that from the fairest of all
flowers   Zante 1
Thy gentlest of all gentle names dost take
Zante 2
Transforming all! Thy charms shall please
no more   Zante 10

Alley
Here once, through an alley Titanic
Ulalume 10

Alloy
For on its wing was dark alloy
Happiest Day 21

Almost
Like—almost any thing   Fairy-Land 33
Were almost passionate sometimes
Romance (1831) 22
Why really, sir, I almost had forgot
Tempora 30

Aloft
Fail'd, as my pennon'd spirit leapt aloft
Al Aaraaf ii 232
See the White Eagle soaring aloft to the
sky   Campaign 1

Alone
In thought that can alone Al Aaraaf i 111
And sound alone, that from the spirit
sprang   Al Aaraaf ii 66
Alone could see the phantom in the skies
Al Aaraaf ii 254
And all I lov'd—I lov'd alone   Alone 8
All alone   Bells 81
In a strange city lying alone   City 2
She, whose voice alone had power
Departed 19
Where tyrant virtue reigns alone
Divine Right 76
I dwelt alone   Eulalie 1
And I must weep alone   Manuscript 2
Yet should I swear I mean alone
Romance (1831) 58
When melancholy and alone   Sarah 1
Some sepulchre, remote, alone Sleeper 54
Thy soul shall find itself alone Spirits 1
Alone of all on earth—unknown
Spirits (1827) 2
In beauty by our God, to those alone
Stanzas¹ 26
When, on the mountain peak, alone
Tamerlane 114
Light in the wilderness alone
Tamerlane 154
Stands she not nobly and alone
Tamerlane 170
To mind—not flow'rs alone—but more
Tamerlane (1827) 142
Peacefully happy—yet alone
Tamerlane (1927) 223
I cannot be, lady, alone   To M 20

Aloud
They lie—they lie aloud   To⁴ 30

Alphabet
Taught me my alphabet to say
Romance 7

Already
Will ruin thee! thou art already altered
Politian i 14

Altar
Not on God's altar, in any time or clime
Politian iv 18

Altered
I kneel, an altered and an humble man
Coliseum 7
Will ruin thee! thou art already altered
Politian i 14

Alterest
Who alterest all things with thy peering
eyes   To Science 2

Although
Nor Love—although the Love were thine
Lake 17
And as for times, although 'tis said by
many   Tempora 5
For he does think, although I'm oft in
doubt   Tempora 79
Its letters, although naturally lying
Valentine 17

Always
Always write first things uppermost in
the heart   Elizabeth 16
Be always throwing those jewels in my
teeth   Politian ii 48
His pleasures always turn'd to pain
Romance (1831) 24
I have not always been as now
Tamerlane 27
And always keep from laughing when I
can   Tempora 62

A. M.
Complete at night what he began A. M.
Tempora 53

Ambition
How daring an ambition! yet how deep
Helen² 46
Ambition—all is o'er   Paradise (1834) 15
Ambition lent it a new tone
Tamerlane 115
Lion ambition is chain'd down
Tamerlane 160
How was it that Ambition crept
Tamerlane 240

Ambitious
I was ambitious—have you known
Tamerlane 128

Amend
I will amend   Politian i 19

Amid
And, amid incense and high spiritual
hymns   Al Aaraaf i 28
Abash'd, amid the lilies there, to seek
Al Aaraaf i 119
Dread star! that came, amid a night of
mirth   Al Aaraaf ii 243
And when, amid no earthly moans
City 50
Amid thy shadows, and so drink within
Coliseum 8
I stand amid the roar Dream w. Dream 12

For it sparkles with Annie   Annie 98
Of the love of my Annie   Annie 100
Of the eyes of my Annie   Annie 102

Another
And wing to other worlds another light
         Al Aaraaf i 146
They have giv'n her to another   Ballad 1
They have giv'n her to another   Ballad 3
They have giv'n thee to another
         Ballad 13
They have giv'n her to another   Ballad 25
Another brow may ev'n inherit
         Happiest Day 10
Like music of another sphere
         Irene (1836) 27
The angels, whispering to one another
         Mother 2
" It in another climate," so he said
         Politian ii 6
Form in the deep another seven
         Serenade 8
Another proof of thought, I'm not mis-
taken   Tempora 86

Answer
" Not all "—the Echoes answer me—" not
all   Coliseum 35
" She died full young "—one Bossola
answers him   Politian ii 18
Thou askest me that—and thus I answer
thee   Politian iv 12
Thus on my bended knee I answer thee
         Politian iv 13
What answer was it you brought me, good
Baldazzar   Politian v 14
Though its answer little meaning—little
relevancy bore   Raven 50
That sad answer, ' Nevermore '
        Raven (1845) 66

Answers
It answers me   Politian ii 64

Anthem
An anthem for the queenliest dead that
ever died so young   Lenore 6

Antique
Type of the antique Rome! Rich reliquary
         Coliseum 1

Anything
Are—not like anything of ours
         City (1831) 7
Call anything, its meaning is the same
         Elizabeth 15
Like—almost anything   Fairy-land 33
Father, this zeal is anything but well
         Politian ii 97
Those won't turn on anything like men
         Tempora 68

Apart
Apart—like fire-flies in Sicilian night
         Al Aaraaf i 145
Her cheeks were flushing, and her lips
apart   Al Aaraaf ii 53
O! leave them apart   Al Aaraaf ii 97
Apart from Heaven's Eternity—and yet
how far from Hell   Al Aaraaf ii 173
Sprang from her station, on the winds
apart   Al Aaraaf ii 235

In climes of mine imagining, apart
         Dream 16
When, from our little cares apart
         Tamerlane 104

Apathy
Will start, which lately slept in apathy
         Stanzas[1] 19

Apes
Who would be men by imitating apes
         Tempora 34

Apology
Apology unto the Duke for me
         Politian iii 112

Appealing
In a clamorous appealing to the mercy
of the fire   Bells 44

Appear
Or so appear—or so appear
         Irene (1836) 29

Appearances
Upon appearances   Politian i 26

Appeared
Appeared to my half-closing eye
         Tamerlane 46

Appears
And, with sweet lovliness, appears
         Tamerlane (1827) 138

Approaches
Approaches, and the Hours are breathing
low   Politian iii 40

Apt
I'm apt to be discursive in my style
         Tempora 37

Aptly
Startled at the stillness broken by reply
so aptly spoken   Raven 61
That have a double life, life aptly made
         Silence (1840) 2

Arabesque
On th' Arabesque carving of a gilded hall
         Al Aaraaf ii 204

Areades
But stay! these walls—these ivy-clad
areades   Coliseum 26

Arching
And crystal lakes, and over-arching forests
         Politian iv 70

Architrave
Lurk'd in each cornice, round each
architrave   Al Aaraaf ii 31

Argument
I will not write: upon this argument
         To Margaret 6

Aright
Heard I aright   Politian i 31
And be sure it will lead us aright
         Ulalume 68
That cannot but guide us aright
         Ulalume 70

Arise
Ah! if that language from thy heart arise
         Acrostic 5
Arise! from your dreaming
         Al Aaraaf ii 80
But the strains still arise
         Al Aaraaf ii 118

Prophetic sounds and loud, arise forever
Coliseum 34
In the morning they arise Fairy-Land 29
Ah, starry Hope! that didst arise
Paradise 8
Arise together, Lalage, and roam
Politian iv 47
Scoundrel!—arise and die Politian v 75

Arisen
Hath without doubt arisen: thou hast
been urged Politian v 49
Lying down to die, have suddenly arisen
To MLS 9

Arms
Died in the arms of the adoring airs
Helen² 35
Pre-eminent in arts and arms, and wealth
Politian i 49

Arose
Uprear'd upon such height arose a pile
Al Aaraaf ii 11
A thought arose within the human brain
To³ 4
Arose with a duplicate horn Ulalume 36

Around
A wreath that twined each starry form
around Al Aaraaf i 40
So eagerly around about to hang
Al Aaraaf i 45
Uprear'd its purple stem around her knees
Al Aaraaf i 49
And zone that clung around her gentle
waist Al Aaraaf ii 54
More beauty clung around her column'd
wall Al Aaraaf ii 216
We came, my love; around, above, below
Al Aaraaf ii 247
Around, by lifting winds forgot City 9
Around the mournful waters lie
City (1845) 25
And cling around about us as a garment
Coliseum 45
On things around him with a ray
Dream 7
Wrapping the fog around their breast
Irene 12
And the tall pines that towered around
Lake 6
All wreathed around about with flowers
Paradise (1835) 5
And mountains, around whose towering
summits the winds Politian iv 71
In every tuneful thing around Sarah 5
Though happiness around thee lay Song 3
Though happiness around thee lay
Song 15
In death around thee—and their will
Spirits 9
Idea! which bindest life around
Tamerlane 183
Grows dim around me—death is near
Tamerlane (1827) 16
A demon-light around my throne
Tamerlane (1827) 27
Her own fair hand had rear'd around
Tamerlane (1827) 219

That loveliness around: the sun
Tamerlane (1827) 318
And the sultan-like pines that tower'd
around Tamerlane (1831) 84
That crowd around my earthly path
To F 2
Around the misty Hebrides Valley 16

Arouse
Arouse them, my maiden
Al Aaraaf ii 142
Arouse thee now, Politian Politian iii 1
Arouse thee! and remember
Politian iii 98

Arrant
The general tuckermanities are arrant
Enigma 10

Art
Thou art now his gentle bride Ballad 14
Endued with neither soul, nor sense, nor
art Elizabeth 11
Now thou art dress'd for paradise
Fairy-Land (1831) 4
Therefore, thou art not wrong Israfel 29
And thou art wild Lenore (1843) 35
Thou art sad, Castiglione Politian i 1
Thou art not well Politian i 11
Will ruin thee! thou art already altered
Politian i 14
Sir count! what art thou dreaming
Politian i 33
Art thou not Lalage and I Politian
Politian iv 33
Do I not love—art thou not beautiful
Politian iv 34
My Lalage—my love! why art thou moved
Politian iv 54
Thou art not gone—thou art not gone,
Politian Politian iv 91
I feel thou art not gone—yet dare not
look Politian iv 92
To say thou art not gone,—one little
sentence Politian iv 96
Ha! ha! thou art not gone
Politian iv 98
Villain, thou art not gone—thou mockest
me Politian iv 101
Thou art my friend, Baldazzar
Politian v 31
"Though thy crest be shorn and shaven
thou," I said, art sure no craven
Raven 45
Thou art an emblem of the glow
River 3
The playful maziness of art River 5
Why and what art thou dreaming here
Sleeper 31
Sure thou art come o'er far-off seas
Sleeper 32
Be nothing which thou art not
To FSO 4
Being everything which now thou art
To FSO 3
I am spelled by art To Hunter 7
Science! true daughter of Old Time thou
art To Science 1

Arts
Pre-eminent in arts and arms, and wealth
Politian i 49

Ascend
Ascend thy empire and so be
Al Aaraaf i 112

Ashen
The skies they were ashen and sober
Ulalume 1
Then my heart it grew ashen and sober
Ulalume 82

Ashore
Whether Temper sent, or whether tempest
tossed thee here ashore   Raven 86

Aside
She throws aside the sceptre—leaves the
helm   Al Aaraaf i 27
As if the towers had thrust aside
City 44

Ask
Nor ask a reason save the angel-nod
Al Aaraaf ii 249
Why ask? Who ever yet saw money made
out of a fat old   Experiments 9
She did not ask the reason why
Tamerlane (1827) 135

Asked
Of her—who ask'd no reason why
Tamerlane 110

Askest
Thou askest me that—and thus I answer
thee   Politian iv 12

Aspersions
Nor deal in flattery or aspersions foul
Tempora 27

Asphodel
On the quiet Asphodel   Nis 26

Aspire
Seas that restlessly aspire
Dream-Land 15

Aspiring
And that aspiring flower that sprang on
Earth   Al Aaraaf i 70

Aspiringly
Aspiringly, are damned, and die
Romance (1831) 57

Ass
And let him see himself a proper ass
Tempora 88

Assailed
Assailed the monarch's high estate
Palace 34

Assailing
Yet are they my heart assailing
Departed 23

Astarte
Astarte within the sky   Eulalie 19
Astarte's debiamonded crescent
Ulalume 37

Astonished
Whom the astonished people saw
Tamerlane 174

Astonishment
Her silent, deep astonishment
Tamerlane (1827) 267

Astray
Astray from reason—Among men
Tamerlane (1827) 251

Athwart
With all thy train, athwart the moony
sky   Al Aaraaf i 144
Beetling it bends athwart the solemn sky
Al Aaraaf ii 192
And roll'd, a flame, the fiery Heaven
athwart   Al Aaraaf ii 236

Atomies
Its atomies, however   Fairy-Land 39

Attempt
Now would I now attempt to trace
Tamerlane 77

Attend
Ceasing their hymns, attend the spell
Israfel 6
Attend thou also more   Politian i 23
Attend thee ever; and I will kneel to thee
Politian iv 82
For that the power of thought attend the
latter   Tempora 75

Attended
Shall be attended to   Politian iii 114

Attention
Then see to it!—pay more attention, sir
Politian i 27

Auber
It was hard by the dim lake of Auber
Ulalume 6
It was down by the dank tarn of Auber
Ulalume 8
We noted not the dim lake of Auber
Ulalume 26
We remembered not the dank tarn of
Auber   Ulalume 28
Well I know, now, this dim lake of Auber
Ulalume 91
Well I know, now, this dank tarn of Auber
Ulalume 93

Audible
Low, sad, and solemn, but most audible
Politian ii 69

Aught
Have I done aught   Politian ii 37
Can I do aught?—is there no farther aid
Politian ii 45
Had deem'd him, in compassion, aught
Tamerlane (1827) 249

August
A Power August, benignant and supreme
Politian iii 36

Autumn
She seemed not thus upon that autumn
eve   Al Aaraaf ii 200
In its autumn tint of gold   Alone 16
Stirred by the autumn wind
Politian iv 58

Availeth
For what (to them) availeth it to know
Al Aaraaf ii 166

Avaunt
"Avaunt:—avaunt! to friends from
fiends the indignant ghost is riven
Lenore 20

Avenging
Hold off—thy sacred hand—avaunt I say
                  Politian v 62
Avaunt—I will not frighten thee—indeed
    I dare not   Politian v 63

Avenging
Like an avenging spirit I'll follow thee
                  Politian v 88
Most righteous, and most just, avenging
    Heaven   Politian v 93

Avow
Thus much let me avow
           Dream w. Dream 3

Awaits
Befit thee—Fame awaits thee—Glory calls
                  Politian iii 22
The hour is growing late—The Duke
    awaits us   Politian iii 88

Awake
Lady, awake! lady awake   Irene 37
Then—ah, then—I would awake Lake 11
That, scarce awake, thy soul shall deem
                  Serenade 20
And would not, for the world, awake
                  Sleeper 15
T' awake us—'T is a symbol and a token
                  Stanzas¹ 24
T' awake her, and a falsehood tell
         Tamerlane (1827) 289
Awake, that I had held a thought
         Tamerlane (1827) 295
My infant spirit would awake
         Tamerlane (1831) 89
At sight of thee and thine at once awake
                  Zante 4

Awaken
For what can awaken   Al Aaraaf ii 148
My sorrow—I could not awaken
                  Alone 6
Would God I could awaken
          Bridal Ballad 28

Awak'ning
My spirit not awak'ning till the beam
                  Dreams 2

Aware
That he, Castiglione, not being aware
                  Politian v 19
Baldazzar, Duke of Surrey, I am aware
                  Politian v 53

Away
Away—away—'mid seas of rays that roll
               Al Aaraaf i 20
On violet couches faint away
        Al Aaraaf (1831) i 15
Of rosy head, that towering far away
               Al Aaraaf ii 7
The moonbeam away Al Aaraaf ii 71
Away then, my dearest Al Aaraaf ii 128
O! hie thee away   Al Aaraaf ii 129
How lovely 't is to look so far away
               Al Aaraaf ii 199
And bore her away from me
           Annabel Lee 18
Yet if Hope has flown away
         Dream w. Dream 6
Went gloriously away
     Dream w. Dream (1829) 12

And over the wet grass rippled away
           Fairy-Land (1831) 28
Didst glide away. Only thine eyes re-
    mained   Helen² 51
Far away—far away   Nis 1, 6
Far away—as far at least   Nis 2
Over the hills and far away   Nis 4
A winged odor went away   Palace 16
Thy looks are haggard—nothing so wears
    away   Politian i 15
Wears it away like evil hours and wine
                  Politian i 18
To while away—forbidden things
                  Romance 19
And quiet all away in jest
          Romance (1831) 30
And all the fires are fading away
          Romance (1831) 49
To dream my very life away
          Romance (1831) 55
And I turn'd away to thee   Star 14
My wilder'd heart was far away
         Tamerlane (1827) 356
If my peace hath flown away
         Tamerlane (1831) 245
Went gloriously away
         Tamerlane (1831) 256
Amid empurpled vapors, far away
                   To³ 26
Went gloriously away   To⁴ 24

Awe
With horror and awe   Politian ii 83

Awhile
Bear with me yet awhile Politian iii 31
O Azrael, yet awhile!—Prince of the
    Powers   Politian v 4

Awoke
Awoke that slept—or knew that he was
    there   Al Aaraaf ii 213
The storm had ceas'd—and I awoke
         Tamerlane (1827) 70

Aye
Aye I did inherit Tamerlane (1827) 24
Aye—the same heritage hath giv'n
         Tamerlane (1827) 33

Azrael
O Azrael, yet awhile!—Prince of the
    Powers   Politian v 4

Azure
Nightly, from their azure towers
                  Valley 5

Babylon
Up fanes—up Babylon-like walls City 18

Back
(Thrown back from flowers) of Beauty's
    eye   Al Aaraaf i 2
Turned back upon the past   Dream 8
Stand back! I have a crucifix myself
                  Politian ii 103
This I whispered, and an echo murmured
    back the word, "Lenore!" Raven 29
Back into the chamber turning, all my
    soul within me burning   Raven 31
Get thee back into the tempest and the
    Night's Plutonian shore Raven 98
And winged pannels fluttering back
                  Sleeper 51

Now
Now as I look back, the strife
                    Tamerlane (1827) 192
Toss back his fine curls from their fore-
head fair   Tempora 51

Bad
Where the good and the bad and the
worst and the best   City 4
The good, the bad, the ideal
                    Tamerlane (1831) 143
For men have none at all, or bad at least
                    Tempora 4

Bade
That bade me pause before the garden
gate   Helen² 23
Chimed in with my desires and bade me
stay   Politian iii 108
And bade it first to dream of crime
                    Tamerlane (1827) 149

Baffled
Shall I be baffled thus?—now this is well
                    Politian v 65

Bajazel
A rebel or a Bajazel
                    Tamerlane (1831) 178

Balbec
From Balbec, and the stilly, clear abyss
                    Al Aaraaf ii 37

Baldazzar
Not so, Baldazzar   Politian iii 5
Baldazzar, it doth grieve me
                    Politian iii 7
Thou heardst it not!—Baldazzar speak no
more   Politian iii 27
And dazzle me, Baldazzar
                    Politian iii 42
Thou heardst not now, Baldazzar
                    Politian iii 51
Baldazzar, it oppresses me like a spell
                    Politian iii 55
Go down, Baldazzar, go   Politian iii 87
Baldazzar, make   Politian iii 111
Baldazzar! oh, I would give
                    Politian iii (1835) 100
What answer was it you brought me,
good Baldazzar   Politian v 14
When saw you now, Baldazzar, in the
frigid   Politian v 24
Thou art my friend, Baldazzar
                    Politian v 31
Baldazzar, Duke of Surrey   Politian v 53

Ball
For at a ball what fair one can escape
                    Tempora 55

Balls
See how her eye-balls glare   Louisa 6

Balm
If there be balm   Politian ii 31
Is there—is there balm in Gilead?—tell
me,—tell me I implore   Raven 89

Balmy
Heaving her white breast to the balmy
air   Al Aaraaf i 64
Through the balmy air of night
                    Bells 18
When from thy balmy lips I drew
                    Sarah 16

Ban
To ev'ry heart a barrier and a ban
                    Al Aaraaf i 149
To bar up our way and to ban it
                    Ulalume 98

Banish
Now are thoughts thou shalt not banish
                    Spirits 19

Banished
So banished from true wisdom to prefer
                    To Margaret 3

Bank
Clad all in white, upon a violet bank
                    Helen² 17

Banks
The mossy banks and the meandering
paths   Helen² 32

Banner
Like a banner o'er thy dreaming eye
                    Irene 36
All banner-like, above a grave
                    Nis (1836) 44

Banners
Banners, yellow, glorious, golden
                    Palace 9
From clouds that hung, like banners, o'er
                    Tamerlane 45

Bar
Of thy barrier and thy bar
                    Al Aaraaf i 89
To bar up our way and to ban it
                    Ulalume 98

Bard
Best bard, because the wisest
                    Israfel 33
Stored with the wealth of bard and sage
                    Stanzas² 18

Bare
Lay bare, thro' vistas thunder-riven
                    Romance (1831) 15

Barely
But barely shelter'd—and the wind
                    Tamerlane (1827) 61

Barks
Like those Nicean barks of yore
                    Helen¹ 2

Barrier
Of thy barrier and thy bar
                    Al Aaraaf i 89
Of the barrier overgone
                    Al Aaraaf i 90
To ev'ry heart a barrier and a ban
                    Al Aaraaf i 149

Bat
A midnight vigil holds the swarthy bat
                    Coliseum 19
Despair, the fabled vampire bat
                    Tamerlane (1831) 27

Bath
Drowned in a bath   Annie 71

Bathe
Bathe me in light Al Aaraaf i (1831) 8
To bathe in the pure element   Irene 50
Let us bathe in this crystalline light
                    Ulalume 63

Bathing
Bathing in many   Annie 63

Battle
In the battle down the dell
     Bridal Ballad 11
Wakening the broad welkin with his loud
 battle cry   Campaign 2
Why in the battle did not I
    Dream w. Dream (1831) 14
Of human battle, where my voice
      Tamerlane 50
The battle-cry of Victory
      Tamerlane 54
Why in the battle did not I
    Tamerlane (1831) 258

Baubles
Of the baubles that it may To[1] 12

Beak
Take thy beak from out my heart, and
 take thy form from off my door
      Raven 101

Beam
Hath cheered me as a lovely beam
      Dream 11
My spirit not awak'ning till the beam
      Dreams 2
And a glittering beam from a maiden's
 eye   Parody 9
But their red orbs, without beam
      Spirits 15
His heart which trembles at the beam
      River 13
Her beam on the waves Star 8
And dearer thy beam shall be Star 17
My own had past, did not the beam
     Tamerlane 135
Her smile is chilly—and her beam
     Tamerlane 203

Beaming
Its Sibyllic splendor is beaming
     Ulalume 64

Beams
For the moon never beams without bringing me dreams Annabel Lee 34

Bear
To bear the Goddess' song, in odors, up to
 Heaven   Al Aaraaf i 81
To bear my secrets thro' the upper
 Heaven   Al Aaraaf i 142
Ah, bear in mind this garden was en-
 chanted   Helen[2] 30
Of the populous Earth! Bear with me yet
 awhile   Politian iii 31

Bearer
To me, Castiglione; the bearer being
     Politian v 52

Bearest
Thou bearest in Heav'n at night Star 20

Bearing
Your bearing lately savored much of
 rudeness   Politian iii 97

Beast
Bird or beast upon the sculptured bust
 above his chamber door Raven 53

Beaten
Of a wind-beaten shore
   Dream w. Dream (1831) 11
With desp'rate energy 't hath beaten
 down   Stanzas[1] 31

Of a wind-beaten shore
    Tamerlane (1831) 250
Of a weather-beaten shore To[4] 18

Beating
To those who hear not for their beating
 hearts   Al Aaraaf ii 177
Who hear not for the beating of their
 hearts   Al Aaraaf ii 264
My thick pulses hastily beating
     Departed 5
So that now, to still the beating of my
 heart, I stood repeating Raven 15

Beats
Than ev'n thy glowing bosom beats withal
    Al Aaraaf ii 217
How my heart beats in coupling those two
 words   Helen[2] 27
The pulse beats ten and intermits
     Physician 1
My bosom beats with shame To[4] 31

Beau
One of these fish, par excellence the beau
     Tempora 59
The " beau ideal " fancied for Adonis
     Tempora 72
My friend, the beau, hath made a settled
 matter   Tempora 76

Beauteous
Told of a beauteous dame beyond the sea
     Politian ii 16

Beautiful
Of beautiful Gomorrah! O, the wave
    Al Aaraaf ii 38
My beautiful one Al Aaraaf ii 101
Of the beautiful Annabel Lee
    Annabel Lee 33, 35, 37
My beautiful Annabel Lee
    Annabel Lee (1849) 16
With rue and the beautiful Annie 65
Beautiful   Experiments 4
Oh, beautiful!—most beautiful!—how
 like   Politian ii 11
So keen a relish for the beautiful
     Politian iii 44
And beautiful Lalage!—turn here thine
 eyes   Politian iv 9
Do I not love—art thou not beautiful
     Politian iv 34
My own, my beautiful, my love, my wife
     Politian iv 84
Fearfully beautiful! the real
    Tamerlane (1827) 169
The wild, the beautiful, conspire
    Tamerlane (1827) 254

Beauty
(Thrown back from flowers) of Beauty's
 eye   Al Aaraaf i 2
Yet all the beauty—all the flowers
    Al Aaraaf i 12
Whence sprang the "Idea of Beauty"
 into birth Al Aaraaf i 31
Seen but in beauty—not impeding sight
    Al Aaraaf i 38
Of other beauty glittering thro' the light
    Al Aaraaf i 39
Like guilty beauty, chasten'd, and more
 fair   Al Aaraaf i 65

In beauty vie   Al Aaraaf i 85
The birth-place of young Beauty had no
more   Al Aaraaf i 154
Beauty's eye is here the bluest
     Al Aaraaf i (1831) 18
And hallow'd all the beauty twice again
     Al Aaraaf ii 25
That Nature loves the best for Beauty's
grave   Al Aaraaf ii 30
And looks so sweetly down on Beauty's
hair   Al Aaraaf ii 187
More beauty clung around her column'd
wall   Al Aaraaf ii 216
Ianthe, beauty crowded on me then
     Al Aaraaf ii 225
As glowing Beauty's bust beneath man's
eye   Al Aaraaf ii 258
And thy star trembled—as doth beauty
then   Al Aaraaf ii 260
Thy luridness of beauty—and of sin
     Al Aaraaf (1827) 43
And the beauty of Annie   Annie 70
Helen, thy beauty is to me   Helen¹ 1
To the beauty of fair Greece
     Helen¹ (1831) 9
They fill my soul with Beauty (which is
Hope)   Helen² 61
Lazily upon beauty's eye   Irene 4
Imbued with all the beauty   Israfel 27
Dead beauty with a tear   Paean 8
In voices of a surpassing beauty
     Palace 31
And Beauty long deceased—remembers me
     Politian ii 66
Thy beauty and thy woes
     Politian iv 22
Of beauty—the unhidden heart
     River 4
Was mingling his with Beauty's breath
     Romance (1831) 32
All Beauty sleeps!—and lo! where lie
     Sleeper 16
In daylight, and in beauty from his birth
     Stanza¹ 3
In beauty by our God, to those alone
     Stanzas¹ 26
The more than beauty of a face
     Tamerlane 78
Of beauty which did while it thro'
     Tamerlane 136
And beauty of so wild a birth
     Tamerlane 185
With the noon-day beauty—which is all
     Tamerlane 212
And happy beauty (for to me
     Tamerlane (1827) 161
With thine unearthly beauty fraught
     Tamerlane (1827) 177
Shed all the beauty of her noon
     Tamerlane (1831) 214
Thy grace, thy more than beauty
     To FSO 6
From the pure well of Beauty undefiled
     To Margaret 2
With Hope and in Beauty to-night
     Ulalume 65

Became
Till the fair and gentle Eulalie became my
blushing bride   Eulalie 4
Till the yellow-haired young Eulalie be-
came my smiling bride   Eulalie 5
And, so, confusedly became
     Tamerlane 125

Because
Because I feel that, in the Heavens above
     Mother 1
Because divided it may chance to be
shaken   Tempora 46
Because to his cat's eye I hold a glass
     Tempora 87

Become
Seem'd to become a queenly throne
     Tamerlane 152
That any should become " great " born
     Tamerlane (1827) 259
The mimes become its food   Worm 30

Becomes
His form once seen becomes a part of
sight   Tempora 70

Becoming
To a becoming carriage—much thou wantest   Politian i 28

Bed
All hurriedly she knelt upon a bed
     Al Aaraaf i 42
Such as the drowsy shepherd on his bed
     Al Aaraaf i 2
Now, in my bed   Annie 14, 86, 90
And narrow my bed   Annie 48
In a different bed   Annie 50
In just such a bed   Annie 52
Tempt the waters from their bed
     City 35
On bed of moss lies gloating the foul
adder   Coliseum (1833) 25
In bed at a reveille roll-call
     Lampoon 4
This bed for one more melancholy
     Sleeper 41
This bed, being for one more holy
     Sleeper (1842) 40
Is grace to its heav'nly bed of blue
     Tamerlane (1827) 321
Of all who, on Despair's unhallowed bed
     To MLS 8

Bedecks
A rarer loveliness bedecks the earth
     Politian iii 48

Bediamonded
Astaste's bediamonded crescent
     Ulalume 37

Bedight
Gaily bedight   Eldorado 1
An angel throng, bewinged, bedight
     Worm 3

Beds
On beds of fire than burn below
     Tamerlane 220

Bee
It still remaineth, torturing the bee
     Al Aaraaf i 58
Have slept with the bee
     Al Aaraaf ii 141

The Sephalica, budding with young bees
Al Aaraaf i 48

Beetling
Beetling it bends athwart the solemn sky
Al Aaraaf ii 192

Befit
Befit thee—Fame awaits thee—Glory calls
Politian iii 22

Befitting
In state his glory well befitting
Palace 23

Beg
Let me beg you, sir   Politian iii 104
I beg your pardon, reader, for the oath
Tempora 35

Began
Complete at night what he began A. M.
Tempora 53

Begirt
The dwindled hills! begirt with bowers
Tamerlane 143

Begone
Of my unspeakable misery!—begone
Politian ii 90

Begotten
Of lip-begotten words   To¹ 4

Beguil'd
And thy trusting heart beguil'd
Ballad 18

Beguiling
Then this ebony bird beguiling my sad
fancy into smiling   Raven 43
But the Raven still beguiling my sad
fancy into smiling   Raven 67
Wins the bird, beguiling   To Hunter 10

Behest
At thy behest I will shake off that nature   Politian iii 10

Behold
Behold the golden token
Bridal Ballad 26
Behold the cross wherewith a vow like
mine   Politian ii 107
Lest I behold thee not; thou couldst not
go   Politian iv 93

Beholder
That any beholder   Annie 15

Beholding
Might start at beholding me   Annie 17

Beholds
Beholds it but through darkened glasses
Dream-Land 50

Being
A wilder'd being from my birth
Dream (1827) 1
For we cannot help agreeing that no liv-
ing human being   Raven 51
I had no being—but in thee
Tamerlane 116

Beings
Tho' the beings whom thy Nesace
Al Aaraaf i 102
Bright beings! that ponder
Al Aaraaf ii 72
From mine own home, with beings that
have been   Dreams 17
Of beings that have been   Imitation 7

There are beings, and have been
To⁴ 8

Believe
I can't believe   Politian ii 40
Believe me, I would give
Politian iii 100
I do believe thee!—coward, I do believe
thee   Politian v 70
But I will half believe that wild light
fraught   Stanzas¹ 11
And, I believe, the winged strife
Tamerlane 38
Father, I firmly do believe
Tamerlane 222
I do believe that Eblis hath
Tamerlane 229
Which knows (believe me at this time
Tamerlane (1827) 189
In their own sphere—will not believe
Tamerlane (1827) 260
Of which sound doctrine I believe each
tittle   Tempora 7

Bell
'Neath blue-bell or streamer
Al Aaraaf ii 68
With a tinkling like a bell
Fairy-Land (1831) 29
Let the bell toll!—a saintly soul floats
on the Stygian river   Lenore 2
Let no bell toll, then, lest her soul, amid
its hallowed mirth   Lenore 23
His blue-bell helmet, we have heard
Parody 1
From the depth of each pallid lily-bell
Valley (1845) 29

Bells
Hear the sledges with the bells Bells 1
Silver Bells   Bells 2
From the bells, bells, bells, bells Bells 12
From the jingling and the tinkling of the
bells   Bells 14
Hear the mellow wedding bells Bells 15
Golden Bells   Bells 16
Of the bells, bells, bells
Bells 32, 103, 109
Of the bells, bells, bells, bells
Bells 33, 67, 111
Bells, bells, bells   Bells 13, 34, 112
To the rhyming and the chiming of the
bells   Bells 35
Hear the loud alarum bells   Bells 36
Brazen bells   Bells 37
Oh, the bells, bells, bells   Bells 51
By the sinking or the swelling in the
anger of the bells   Bells 65
Of the bells   Bells 66, 98, 99
In the clamor and the clangor of the
bells   Bells 69
Hear the tolling of the bells Bells 70
Iron bells   Bells 71
A paean from the bells   Bells 82
With the paean of the bells Bells 94
To the paean of the bells   Bells 98
Of the bells   Bells 99
To the throbbing of the bells Bells 102
To the sobbing of the bells Bells 104
To the rolling of the bells Bells 108

Belong

To the tolling of the bells   Bells 110
To the moaning and the groaning of the
bells   Bells 113
The bells!—hear the bells
                          Bells (1849) 1
The bells!—ah, the bells
                          Bells (1849) 8

Belong
To thee the laurels belong   Israfel 32

Belongs
Very plainly through the window—it
belongs   Politian iii 63

Beloved
Of life—beloved, and fair
                          Paean (1836) 34
And worship thee, and call thee my
beloved   Politian iv 83
Hold off thy hand—with that beloved
name   Politian v 67
Beloved! amid the earnest woes   To F 1

Bended
Thus on my bended knee I answer thee
                          Politian iv 13
Thus on my bended knee. It were most
fitting   Politian v 77

Bendeth
When each pale star earthward bendeth
                          Departed 14

Bends
Beetling it bends athwart the solemn sky
                          Al Aaraaf ii 192
By that Heaven that bends above us—
by that God we both adore   Raven 92

Beneath
Beneath thy burning eye
                          Al Aaraaf i 109
Had burst beneath the heaving of her
heart   Al Aaraaf ii 55
She paus'd and panted, Zanthe! all be-
neath   Al Aaraaf ii 57
Beneath the moon-ray   Al Aaraaf ii 131
Beneath the cold moon
                          Al Aaraaf ii 151
And scowls on starry worlds that down
beneath it lie   Al Aaraaf ii 193
Resignedly beneath the sky   City 10, 24
The singer is undoubtedly beneath
                          Politian iii 65
I stand beneath the mystic moon
                          Sleeper 2
Beneath the eternal sky of Thought
                          Stanzas² 24
The summer dream beneath the tamarind
tree   To Science 14

Benighted
And my mind is much benighted
                          Bridal Ballad (1837) 23

Benignant
A Power august, benignant and supreme
                          Politian iii 36

Bent
And bent o'er sheeny mountain and dim
plain   Al Aaraaf i 157
Here sate he with his love—his dark eye
bent   Al Aaraaf ii 194
His pinions were bent droopingly
                          Tamerlane 189

Beseeming
To duty beseeming   Al Aaraaf 82

Beset
Shake off the idle fancies that beset thee
                          Politian iii 4
Some lake beset as lake can be
                          To F (1835) 11

Beside
To cure his love, was cured of all beside
                          Acrostic 8
Sit down beside me, Isabel
                          Fairy-Land (1831) 1
The sweet Lenore hath gone before, with
Hope that flew beside   Lenore 15
From moan and groan to a golden throne
beside the King of Heaven   Lenore 22
Beside a murm'ring stream   Sarah 3
That she might deem it nought beside
                          Tamerlane 147
Their destinies? in all beside
                          Tamerlane 168

Besides
Besides my innate love of contradiction
                          Elizabeth 6

Besilvering
Thro' the ebon air, besilvering the pall
                          Al Aaraaf ii 317

Best
That Nature loves the best for Beauty's
grave   Al Aaraaf ii 30
Where the good and the bad and the worst
and the best   City 4
They have found to be the best
                          Fairy-Land 14
Best bard, because the wisest
                          Israfel 33
But " the valley Nis " at best
                          Nis 15
And at the best I'm certain, Madam, you
cannot   Politian ii 55
What matters it, my fairest, and my best
                          Politian iv 42
I've been a thinking, whether it were best.
                          Tempora 11
You will not read the riddle though you
do the best you can do   Valentine 20

Bestow
So oft perverted, will bestow
                          Tamerlane (1827) 197

Bethink
Now I bethink me   Poltian ii 42

Betook
Then, upon the velvet sinking, I betook
myself to thinking   Raven 69

Betrothed
As the betrothed of Castiglione
                          Politian iii 68

Better
I am better at length   Annie 12
'Twere better than the cold reality
                          Dreams 5
It had seen better days, he said
                          Tamerlane (1827) 400
One settled fact is better than ten sages
                          Tempora 78

Bewinged
An angel throng, bewinged, bedight
Worm 3
Beyond
Beyond the line of blue
Al Aaraaf i 86
Beyond that death no immortality
Al Aaraff ii 170
Told of a beauteous dame beyond the sea
Politian ii 16
Beyond this bounded earthly clime
Stanzas² 10
No cliff beyond him in the sky
Tamerlane 188
Beyond the utterance of the human tongue
To³ 5
Bid
Each hour before us—but then only, bid
Stanzas¹ 22
Bidden
With thy dear name as text, though bid-
den by thee To³ 18
Bidding
Be given our lady's bidding to discuss
Al Aaraaf ii 246
At bidding of vast formless things
Worm 13
Bier
See! on yon drear and rigid bier low lies
thy love, Lenore Lenore 4
Billow
They bore thee o'er the billow
Paradise (1835) 28
No billow breaking into foam
Stanzas² 11
Billows
The soul that scarce (the billows are so
dense) Al Aaraaf i 22
Bindest
Idea! which bindest life around
Tamerlane 183
Binds
The mystery which binds my still
Alone 12
Bird
Was plumed with the down of the hum-
ming-bird Parody 2
Then this ebony bird beguiling my sad
fancy into smiling Raven 43
Ever yet was blessed with seeing bird
above his chamber door Raven 52
Bird or beast upon the sculptured bust
above his chamber door Raven 53
Then the bird said, "Nevermore"
Raven 60
Straight I wheeled a cushioned seat in
front of bird and bust and door
Raven 68
Fancy unto fancy, thinking what this
ominous bird of yore Raven 70
What this grim, ungainly, ghastly, gaunt,
and ominous bird of yore Raven 71
Prophet!" said I, "thing of evil!—
prophet still, if bird or devil
Raven 85, 91

Be that word our sign of parting, bird or
fiend!" I shrieked upstarting
Raven 97
Hath been—a most familiar bird
Romance 6
The mock-bird chirping on the thorn
Sarah 8
Wins the bird, beguiling
To Hunter 10
Like that bird the lover To Hunter 12
Birds
The wantonest singing birds To¹ 2
Birth
Whence sprang the "Idea of Beauty"
into birth Al Aaraaf i 31
And died, ere scarce exalted into birth
Al Aaraaf i 71
The birth-place of young Beauty had no
more Al Aaraaf i 154
A wilder'd being from my birth
Dream (1827) 1
A Chaos of deep passion, from his birth
Dreams 8
In daylight, and in beauty from his birth
Stanzas¹ 3
And beauty of so wild a birth
Tamerlane 185
Bitter
Dew in the night-time of my bitter trouble
Politian ii 33
Weep not! oh, sob not thus!—thy bitter
tears Politian iv 5
Black
On a black throne reigns upright
Dream-Land 4, 54
Of a wild lake, with black rock bound
Lake 5
And the black wind murmur'd by
Lake (1829) 9
Leave no black plume as a token of that
lie thy soul hath spoken Raven 99
The black hath mellow'd into grey
Romance (1831) 48
Some vault that oft hath flung its black
Sleeper 50
Of a wild lake with black rock bound
Tamerlane (1831) 83
And the black wind murmur'd by
Tamerlane (1831) 87
Blackened
These mouldering plinths—these sad and
blackened shafts Coliseum 27
Blackness
The blackness of the general Heaven
Romance (1831) 16
That very blackness yet doth fling
Romance (1831) 17
Blade
So that the blade be keen—the blow be
sure Politian iv 104
Bland
An Eden of bland repose To F 7
Blandly
Here blandly reposes Annie 54
Blasted
Shall bloom the thunder-blasted tree
Paradise 19

Wither'd and blasted; who had gone
Tamerlane (1827) 276

Blazes
Which blazes upon Edis' shrine
Tamerlane (1827) 156

Bleak
Ah, distinctly I remember it was in the
bleak December   Raven 7

Blend
So blend the turrets and the shadows
there   City 26

Bless
And, failing in thy power to bless
Tamerlane 181
Of her wond'rous ways, and telling bless
Tamerlane (1827) 313
The sacred sun—of all who, weeping,
bless thee   To MLS 4

Blessed
Ever yet was blessed with seeing bird
above his chamber door   Raven 52
And, when she fell in feeble health, ye
blessed her—that she died
Lenore 9

Blessing
While the mute earth sheds her blessing
Departed 30

Blest
An oasis in desert of the blest
Al Aaraaf i 19
Could angels be blest   Al Aaraaf ii 89
The starry and quiet dwellings of the blest
Politian iv 48
Blest with all bliss that earth can yield
Stanzas² 27
From regions of the blest afar
Tamerlane 224

Blew
The wind blew out of a cloud by night
Annabel Lee 15
Today (the wind blew, and) it swung
Fairy-Land (1831) 14

Blighted
My sear'd and blighted heart hath known
Happiest Day 2
My seared and blighted name, how would
it tally   Politian iv 28

Blind
Was Love, the blind, near sober Duty
known   Al Aaraaf ii 180
Which Error's glitter canot blind
Stanzas³ 19
Rendered me mad and deaf and blind
Tamerlane 57

Bliss
That Truth is Falsehood—or that Bliss is
Woe   Al Aaraaf ii 167
To the lone oak that reels with bliss
Irene 20
And the shadow of thy perfect bliss
Israfel 43
Recalls the hour of bliss   Sarah 15
Blest with all bliss that earth can yield
Stanzas² 27
'Tis bliss, in its own reality
Tamerlane (1827) 306
It is not that my founts of bliss To M 9

How many scenes of what departed bliss
Zante 5

Blood
Thou Horror with blood-chilling cries
Louisa 11
A blood-red thing that writhes from out
Worm 27

Bloom
Shall bloom the thunder-blasted tree
Paradise 19

Bloomed
That blushed and bloomed   Palace 38

Blossom
And blossom of the fairy plant, in grief
Al Aaraaf i 61

Blossoms
Where the moon-lit blossoms quiver
Departed 10
Where the nightly blossoms shiver
Departed 39

Blotting
The blotting utterly from out high heaven
To MLS 3

Blow
So that the blade be keen—the blow be
sure   Politian iv 104
Till the blow is over   To Hunter 14

Blown
By notes so very shrilly blown
Romance (1831) 59

Blue
'Neath blue-bell or streamer
Al Aaraaf ii 68
Beyond the line of blue
Al Aaraaf i 86
When the rest of Heaven was blue
Alone 21
His blue-bell helmet, we have heard
Parody 1
The blue sky—the misty light
Tamerlane (1827) 319
Is grace to its heav'nly bed of blue
Tamerlane (1827) 321

Bluest
Beauty's eye is here the bluest
Al Aaraaf (1831) i 18

Blush
When a burning blush came o'er thee
Song 2
That blush, perhaps, was maidens shame
Song 9
When that deep blush would come o'er
thee   Song 14

Blushed
That blushed and bloomed   Palace 38

Blushes
Blushes with love   Israfel 11

Blushing
Till the fair and gentle Eulalie became my
blushing bride   Eulalie 4

Boast
And now, as if in mockery of that boast
To³ 6

Bodied
Which I felt not—its bodied forms
Tamerlane (1827) 164

Bodiless
The bodiless airs, a wizard rout
Sleeper 22
The bodiless spirits of the storms
Tamerlane (1827) 166
Body
Body and soul. One dwells in lonely
places Silence 6
Bold
And, with bold advance, now meeting
Departed 7
This knight so bold Eldorado 8
The corslet on his bosom bold
Parody 3
Till growing bold, he laughed and leapt
Tamerlane 242
Bolder
While a bolder note than his might swell
Israfel 50
Boldly
Ride, boldly ride Eldorado 22
That things should stare us boldly in the
face Tempora 32
Bonnet
As easily as through a Naples bonnet
Enigma 4
Book
In thy own book that first thy name be
writ Elizabeth 3
There, ma'am, 's the book. Indeed she is
very troublesome Politian ii 36
Connivingly my dreaming-book
Romance (1831) 66
Books
From my books surcease of sorrow—sor-
row for the lost Lenore Raven 10
Boots
It boots me not, good friar, to tell
Tamerlane (1827) 348
Bore
Bore burthen to the charm the maiden
sang Al Aaraaf ii 67
And bore her away from me
Annabel Lee 18
And to the church-yard bore me
Bridal Ballad 16
They bore thee o'er the billow
Paradise (1835) 28
Bore a bright golden flower, but not i'
this soil Politian ii 7
Though its answer little meaning—little
relevancy bore Raven 50
Followed fast and followed faster till his
songs one burden bore Raven 64
Till the dirges of his Hope that melan-
choly burden bore Raven 65
That bore me from my home, more gay
Tamerlane (1827) 302
The weary way-worn wanderer bore
To Helen¹ 4
Boreal
In the realms of the Boreal Pole
Ulalume 19
Born
Born and brought up with their snouts
deep in the mud of the Frog-Pond
Experiments 8

The hour when we were born
Louisa 16
The riotous company, too—fellows low-
born Politian i 20
Not mother, with her first-born on her
knee Politian iv 16
That any should become "great" born
Tamerlane (1827) 259
And nebulous lustre was born
Ulalume 34
Borrow
Eagerly I wished the morrow;—vainly I
had sought to borrow Raven 9
Bosom
Than ev'n thy glowing bosom beats withal
Al Aaraaf ii 217
On the bosom of the palpitating air
Bells 56
And his merry bosom swells Bells 93
I felt my bosom swell Bridal Ballad 8
Her bosom is an ivory throne
Divine Right 5
The corslet on his bosom bold
Parody 3
To the fowl whose fiery eyes now burned
into my bosom's core Raven 74
My phrenzy to her bosom taught
Tamerlane (1827) 150
Of a young peasant's bosom then
Tamerlane (1827) 248
Hath long upon my bosom sat
Tamerlane (1831) 28
My bosom beats with shame To⁴ 31
Bossola
She died full young—one Bossola answers
him Politian ii 18
Both
I've news for you both Politian i 41
By that Heaven that bends above us—by
that God we both Raven 92
To leave her while we both were young
Tamerlane (1827) 236
Bother
And in the meantime, to prevent all
bother Tempora 25
Bottomless
Bottomless vales and boundless floods
Dream-Land 9
Bough
I was mistaken—'t was but a giant bough
Politian iv 57
Boughs
Is chilly—and these melancholy boughs
Politian iv 63
Bound
And all the opal'd air in color bound
Al Aaraaf i 41
Thou hast bound my eyes
Al Aaraaf ii 116
Or spell had bound me—'t was the chilly
wind Dreams 21
Of a wild lake, with black rock bound
Lake 5
Which as it were, in fairy bound
Tamerlane (1827) 221
Of a wild lake with black rock bound
Tamerlane (1831) 83

Boundary
  The boundary of the star
                              Al Aaraaf i 87
Bounded
  Beyond this bounded earthly clime
                              Stanzas² 10
Boundless
  Bottomless vales and boundless floods
                              Dream-Land 9
Bounds
  That fell, refracted, thro' thy bounds,
    afar   Al Aaraaf ii 160
  What time upon her airy bounds I hung
                              Al Aaraaf ii 221
Bow
  Why do the people bow the knee
                              Tamerlane (1831) 181
Bowed
  Bow'd from its wild pride into shame
                              Tamerlane 14
  Bow'd down with its own glory grows
                              Tamerlane (1831) 222
Bower
  Spirit, cooped in mortal bower
                              Departed 18
  Up like a dog-star in this bower
                              Fairy-Land (1831) 13
Bow'r
  I pass'd from out the matted bow'r
                              Tamerlane (1827) 284
  I went from out the matted bow'r
                              Tamerlane (1827) 299
  In mine own Ada's matted bow'r
                              Tamerlane (1827) 358
Bowers
  That list our Love, and deck our bowers
                              Al Aaraaf i 13
  In violet bowers   Al Aaraaf ii 81
  Up shadowy long-forgotten bowers
                              City 19
  The muses thro' their bowers of Truth or
    Fiction   Elizabeth 8
  Laden from yonder bowers!—a fairer day
                              Politian v 16
  The dwindled hills! begirt with bowers
                              Tamerlane 143
  Whose pleasant bowers are yet so riven
                              Tamerlane 236
  The bowers whereat, in dreams, I see
                              To² 1
Bowl
  Ah, broken is the golden bowl!—the spirit
    flown forever   Lenore 1
  Succeeds the glories of the bowl
                              Romance (1831) 53
Bows
  And daily strut the street with bows and
    scrapes   Tempora 33
  The soft head bows, the sweet eyes close
                              Physician 5
Boy
  For, being an idle boy lang syne
                              Romance (1831) 19
Boyhood
  In my young boyhood—should it thus be
    giv'n   Dream 11

Then—in my boyhood—when their fire
                              Tamerlane 70
And boyhood is a summer sun
                              Tamerlane 207
Of our boyhood, his course hath run
                              Tamerlane (1827) 385
Boys
  We have been boys together—school-
    fellows   Politian iii 32
Brain
  Perhaps my brain grew dizzy—but the
    world   Al Aaraaf ii 233
  That maddened my brain   Annie 28
  That burned in my brain Annie 30
  Swift dart across her brain   Louisa 10
  And by strange alchemy of brain
                              Romance (1831) 23
  And my brain drank their venom then
                              Tamerlane (1827) 41
  A thought arose within the human brain
                              To³ 4
Branch
  No branch, they say, of all philosophy
                              Politian i 54
Bravo
  Bravo!—bravo   Triumph 4
Brazen
  Light, brazen rays, this golden star unto
                              Al Aaraaf ii 240
  Brazen bells   Bells 37
Break
  Will make it break for thee
                              Octavia 9
  Thou hast no end to gain—no heart to
    break   Politian ii 72
  To break upon Time's monotone
                              Romance (1831) 60
Breaking
  Such language holds the breaking sea
                              Paradise (1834) 17
  No billow breaking into foam
                              Stanzas² 11
Breast
  Heaving her white breast to the balmy
    air   Al Aaraaf i 64
  That enjewel its breast
                              Al Aaraaf ii 135
  To sleep on her breast   Annie 76
  From the heaven of her breast Annie 78
  With her love at my breast Annie 91
  Wrapping the frog about its breast
                              Sleeper 11
  In the breast of him, alas   Song 12
  My breast her shield in wintry weather
                              Tamerlane 98
  I'd throw me on her throbbing breast
                              Tamerlane 106
  Dwell in a seraph's breast than thine
                              Tamerlane (1827) 152
  With which this aching, breast is fraught
                              Tamerlane (1827) 184
  With her own image, my fond breast
                              Tamerlane (1827) 246
  Of many with a breast as light
                              Tamerlane (1827) 341
  Too real, to his breast who lives
                              Tamerlane (1831) 307

Breath
The breath of those kisses
                    Al Aaraaf ii 86
Sweet was that error—ev'n with us the
    breath   Al Aaraaf ii 163
With the breath from their pale faces
                    Fairy-Land 10
Like flowers by the low breath of June
                    Fairy-Land (1831) 8
Was mingling his with Beauty's breath
                    Romance (1831) 32
The breeze—the breath of God—is still
                    Spirits 23
So like you gather in your breath
                    Tamerlane 205
With their own breath to fan his fire
                    Tamerlane 164

Breathe
Within the centre of that hall to breathe
                    Al Aaraaf ii 56
Go! breathe on their slumber
                    Al Aaraaf ii 144
Breathe it less gently forth,—and veil
    thine eyes   Acrostic 6
To breathe the incense of those slumbering
    roses   Helen² 24
Of Heaven untrammelled flow—which air
    to breathe   Politian iv 72

Breathed
She stirr'd not—breath'd not—for a voice
    was there   Al Aaraaf i 12

Breathed
But, when first he breathed his vow
                    Bridal Ballad 7
Pure as the wishes breathed in prayer
                    Stanzas 14

Breathes
Breathes the shrill spirit of the western
    wind   Politian ii 10
Say, holy father, breathes there yet
                    Tamerlane (1831) 177
While the orchestra breathes fitfully
                    Worm 7

Breathing
The hours are breathing faint and low
                    City 49
Approaches, and the Hours are breathing
    low   Politian iii 40
The breathing beauty of a face
                    Tamerlane (1827) 91

Breeze
Do roll like seas in northern breeze
                    Nis 36
The breeze—the breath of God—is still
                    Spirits 23
By that summer breeze unbrok'n
                    Spirits (1827) 25

Breezes
On the breezes to toss
                    Al Aaraaf ii 105

Bribe
Could teach or bribe me to define
                    Lake 16
Could ever bribe me to define
                    Tamerlane (1831) 94

Bridal
I saw thee on thy bridal day   Song 1
Who saw thee on that bridal day
                    Song 13

Bride
Of my darling, my darling, my life and
    my bride   Annabel Lee 99
Thou art now his gentle bride   Ballad 14
Till the fair and gentle Eulalie became my
    blushing bride   Eulalie 4
Till the yellow-haired young Eulalie be-
    came my smiling bride   Eulalie 5
Leaving thee wild for the dear child that
    should have been thy bride
                    Lenore 16
The bride and queen of Tamerlane
                    Tamerlane (1827) 282

Bright
Near four bright suns—a temporary rest
                    Al Aaraaf i 13
Fair flowers, bright waterfalls, and angel
    wings   Al Aaraaf ii 65
Bright beings! that ponder
                    Al Aaraaf ii 72
And the stars never rise but I see the
    bright eyes   Annabel Lee 36
Joys too bright to last   Departed 16
She, earth's bright and loveliest flower
                    Departed 17
What could there be more purely bright
                    Dreams 15
How bright! and yet to creep
                    Dream w. Dream (1831) 9
For I have revell'd, when the sun was
    bright   Dreams 13
Ah, less—less bright   Eulalie 6
Can compare with the bright-eyed Eula-
    lie's most humble and careless curl
                    Eulalie 13
Shines, bright and strong   Eulalie 18
My duty, to be saved by their bright light
                    Helen² 58
For that bright hope at last
                    Imitation 15
The bright i-dea, or bright dear-eye
                    Impromptu 4
And million bright pines to and fro
                    Irene 18
Ah, dream too bright to last
                    Paradise 7
Bore a bright golden flower, but not i'
    this soil   Politian ii 7
Fair river! in thy bright, clear flow
                    River 1
Oh, lady bright! can it be right
                    Sleeper 18
Bright with all hopes that Heaven can
    give   Stanzas² 28
The flush on her bright cheek, to me
                    Tamerlane 151
The world with all its train of bright
                    Tamerlane (1827) 160
One noon of a bright summer's day
                    Tamerlane (1827) 283
Dim! tho' looking on all bright
                    Tamerlane (1827) 322

How bright! and yet to creep
                    Tamerlane (1831) 253
Just o'er that one bright island smile
                    To F 14
Their bright eyes on his Tom and Jerry
    brim   Tempora 66
Thus the bright snake coiling
                    To Hunter 8
To shine on us with her bright eyes
                    Ulalume 48
Bright and expressive as the stars of
    Leoda   Valentine (1846) 2
Brighter
A brighter dwelling-place is here for thee
                    Al Aaraaf ii 228
But my heart it is brighter   Annie 95
Of the brighter, cold moon   Star 5
Brightest
The brightest glance of pride or power
                    Happiest Day 15
Ev'n then I felt—that brightest hour
                    Happiest Day 19
Look at me, brightest   Politian iv 8
Brightly
When the hours flew brightly by
                    Hymn 5
Brightly expressive as the twins of Loeda
                    Valentine 2
Brilliant
The brilliant light that kiss'd her golden
    hair   Al Aaraaf ii (1843) 58
Lo! in yon brilliant window-niche
                    Helen[1] 11
At rest on ocean's brilliant dyes
                    Serenade 5
In the tangles of love's brilliant hair
                    Tamerlane (1829) 243
Brim
Their bright eyes on his Tom and Jerry
    brim   Tempora 66
Bring
As others saw—I could not bring
                    Alone 3
Of an Eternity should bring the morrow
                    Dreams 3
For him who thence could solace bring
                    Lake 20
As go down in the library and bring me
                    Politian ii 30
Bring thee to meet his shadow (nameless
    elf)   Silence 13
How could I from that water bring
                    Tamerlane (1831) 96
Bringing
For the moon never beams without bring-
    ing me dreams   Annabel Lee 34

But what is this?—it cometh—and it
    brings   Al Aaraaf ii 48
Of semblance with reality brings
                    Dreams 31
Brink
Which ev'n upon this perilous brink
                    Tamerlane (1847) 105
Britain
Of Britain, Earl of Leicester
                    Politian i 45

Ungenial Britain which we left so lately
                    Politian v 25
Broad
Wakening the broad welkin with his loud
    battle cry   Campaign 2
Freely would give the broad lands of my
    earldom   Politian iii 101
Broglio's
Ill suit the like with old Di Broglio's heir
                    Politian i 21
Broider'd
Of her " costly broider'd pall "
                    Paean 14
Broke
And as it pass'd me by, there broke
                    Tamerlane (1827) 72
Broken
If with thee be broken hearts
                    Al Aaraaf (1831) i 22
And tho' my poor heart be broken
                    Ballad 31
And, tho' my faith be broken
                    Bridal Ballad 22
And, though my heart be broken
                    Bridal Ballad 23
These vague entablatures—this broken
    frieze   Coliseum (1833) 32
Hath left me broken-hearted   Dream 4
Ah, broken is the golden bowl!—the
    spirit flown forever   Lenore 1
Much about a broken heart   Nis 13
Startled at the stillness broken by reply
    so aptly spoken   Raven 61
With a strange sound, as of a harp-string
    broken   Stanza[1] 23
That the proud spirit had been broken
                    Tamerlane (1827) 199
A kingdom for a broken—heart
                    Tamerlane (1827) 406
Could hope to utter. And I! my spells are
    broken   To[3] 16
Brood
Nothing saves the airs that brood
                    Valley 12
Brooks
Why, then, the prettiest of brooks
                    River 89
Brother
Had I lov'd thee as a brother   Ballad 15
Brought
The night that waned and waned and
    brought no day   Al Aaraaf ii 262
Born and brought up with their snouts
    deep down in the mud of the Frog Pond
                    Experiments 8
Have brought a specimen   Fairy-Land 45
Thy Naiad airs have brought me home
                    Helen[1] 8
What answer was it you brought me, good
    Baldazzar   Politian v 14
That I brought a dread burden down here
                    Ulalume 88
Brow
But the shadow of whose brow
                    Al Aaraaf i 100
Come down to your brow
                    Al Aaraaf ii 77

And the wreath is on my brow
Bridal Ballad 2
And he kissed my pallid brow
Bridal Ballad 14
Take this kiss upon the brow
Dream w. Dream 1
Another brow may ev'n inherit
Happiest Day 10
Or worse—upon her brow to dance
Irene 5
Wreathing for its transparent brow
Irene 82
The fever'd diadem on my brow
Tamerlane 28
Thou hast not seen my brow   To⁴ 28

Brown
Within the valleys dim and brown
Serenade 11

Brute
They are neither brute nor human
Bells 87
As to the seat of thought in man and
brute   Tempora 74

Bubbles
Bubbles—ephemeral and so transparent
Enigma 11

Bud
And the Nelumbo bud that floats for ever
Al Aaraaf i 78

Budding
The Sephalica, budding with young bees
Al Aaraaf i 48
In the budding of my Paradisal Hope
Politian v 7

Build
Yet I build no faith upon   To⁴ 3

Burden
Followed fast and followed faster till his
songs one burden bore   Raven 64
Till the dirges of his Hope that melan-
choly burden bore   Raven 65
That I brought a dread burden down here
Ulalume 88

Burial
Come, let the burial rite be read—the
funeral song be sung   Lenore 5

Buried
She ceas'd—and buried then her burning
cheek   Al Aaraaf i 118
By buried centuries of pomp and power
Coliseum 3
For the resurrection of deep buried faith
To MLS 6

Buries
And buries them up quite
Fairy-Land 25

Burn
On beds of fire that burn below
Tamerlane 220

Burned
That burned in my brain   Annie 30
Burned there a holier fire than burneth
now   Politian iv 19
To the fowl whose fiery eyes now burned
into my bosom's core   Raven 74
Burn'd with a still intenser glow
Tamerlane 71

Burneth
Burned there a holier fire than burneth
now   Politian iv 19

Burning
Beneath thy burning eye
Al Aaraaf i 109
She ceas'd—and buried then her burning
cheek   Al Aaraaf i 115
Of weary pilgrimage and burning thirst
Coliseum 5
With thy burning measures suit
Israfel 36
Can find, among their burning terms of
love   Mother 3
Back into the chamber turning, all my
soul within me burning   Raven 31
When a burning blush came o'er thee
Song 2
As a burning and a fever   Spirits 17

Burnt
With incense of burnt offerings
Tamerlane 234

Bursting
Bursting its odorous heart in spirit to
wing   Al Aaraaf i 72

Burst
Had burst beneath the heaving of her
heart   Al Aaraaf ii 55
A thousand seraphs burst th' Empyrean
thro'   Al Aaraaf ii 157
The proud heart burst in agony
Tamerlane (1827) 200
Will burst upon him, and alas
Tamerlane (1827) 324

Burthen
Bore burthen to the charm the maiden
sang   Al Aaraaf ii 67

Bust
As glowing Beauty's bust beneath man's
eye   Al Aaraaf ii 251
Perched upon a bust of Pallas just above
my chamber door   Raven 41
Bird of beast upon the sculptured bust
above his chamber door   Raven 53
But the Raven, sitting lonely on the
placid bust, spoke only   Raven 55
Straight I wheeled a cushioned seat in
front of bird and bust and door
Raven 68
Leave my loneliness unbroken!—quit the
bust above my door   Raven 100
On the pallid bust of Pallas just above
my chamber door   Raven 104

Busy
With which all tongues are busy—a land
new found   Politian iv 65

Butterflies
Of which those butterflies
Fairy-Land 41

Buy
Of the truth that gold can never buy
To¹ 11

Caesar
Here, where on ivory couch the Caesar
sate   Coliseum (1833) 23
Rome to the Caesar—this to me
Tamerlane 31

Call

Ours is a world of words: Quiet we call
                    Al Aaraaf i 126
It would be mockery to call
                    City (1831) 18
That rose—that what do ye call it—that
    hung   Fairy-Land (1831) 12
May the d—l right soon for his soul call
                    Lampoon 2
In bed at a reveille roll call
                    Lampoon 4
And worship thee, and call thee my be-
    loved   Politian iv 83
You call it hope—that fire of fire
                    Tamerlane 7
I would not call thee fool, old man
                    Tamerlane 11

Called

Was a proud temple called the Parthenon
                    Al Aaraaf ii 215
And the fever called " Living "
                    Annie 5
With the fever called " Living "
                    Annie 29
Called—I forget the heathenish Greek
    name   Elizabeth 14
Called anything, its meaning is the same
                    Elizabeth 15
Therefore by that dear name I long have
    called you   Mother 5
It is called the valley Nis   Nis 7
That I have called thee at this hour
                    Tamerlane (1827) 6

Callous

Or who so cold, so callous to refuse
                    Tempora 57

Calls

Who calls on you now   Al Aaraaf ii 79
Befit thee—Fame awaits thee—Glory
    calls   Politian iii 22

Calm

How solemnly pervading the calm air
                    Al Aaraaf i 123
Forever with as calm an eye   Irene 64
Nor with too calm an air   Paean 36
In calm or storm that ne'er forgets
                    Physician 2
A heaven so calm as this—so utterly free
                    Politian v 26
So sweet the hour, so calm the time
                    Serenade 1
The sunshine, and the calm—the ideal
                    Tamerlane (1827) 167
A calm from his unearthly wings
                    Tamerlane (1831) 30

Calmer

Is calmer now than it was wont to be
                    Politian iii 46
And when an hour with calmer wings
                    Romance 16
But then a gentler, calmer spell
                    Tamerlane (1831) 100

Came

Yet silence came upon material things
                    Al Aaraaf ii 64
Dread star! that came, amid a night of
    mirth   Al Aaraaf ii 243

We came—and to thy Earth—but not to
    us   Al Aaraaf ii 245
We came, my love; around, above, below
                    Al Aaraaf ii 247
So that her highborn kinsman came
                    Annabel Lee 17
That the wind came out of the cloud,
    chilling   Annabel Lee 25
While a reverie came over me
                    Bridal Ballad 15
Came over me in the night, and left
    behind   Dreams 22
Sit down, sit down—how came we here
                    Fairy-Land (1831) 9
Through which came flowing, flowing,
    flowing   Palace 27
While I nodded, nearly napping, suddenly
    there came a tapping   Raven 1
But the fact is I was napping, and so
    gently you came rapping   Raven 21
And so faintly you came tapping, tap-
    ping at my chamber door   Raven 22
When a burning blush came over thee
                    Song 2
Came hurriedly upon me, telling
                    Tamerlane 49
The rain came down upon my head
                    Tamerlane 55
A voice came from the threshold stone
                    Tamerlane 217
There—in that hour—a thought came over
                    Tamerlane (1827) 234

Camest

O lady sweet. How camest thou here
                    Irene 26

Camp

Give not thy soul to dreams: the camp—
    the court   Politian iii 21

Camps

To me, Politian, of thy camps and courts
                    Politian iii 28

Canopy

And wave the curtain canopy
                    Sleeper 24

Canopies

Rich clouds, for canopies, about her curled
                    Al Aaraaf i 36

Canst

Now tell me (for thou canst)
                    Politian ii 62
Hist! hist! thou canst not say
                    Politian iii 50
But its thought thou canst not banish
                    Spirits (1827) 22
Thou canst not—wouldst not dare to
    think   Tamerlane (1827) 103

Capacity

How fathomless a capacity for love
                    Helen² 47

Captives

Of empires—with the captive's prayer
                    Tamerlane 62

Capo

On the fair Capo Deucato, and sprang
                    Al Aaraaf i 44

Capriciously

Or, capriciously still   Al Aaraaf ii 106

Car
Hast thou not dragged Diana from her car
To Science 9

Care
Fair flowers, and fairy! to whose care is
given Al Aaraaf i 80
I care not tho' it perish Imitation 19
There Care shall be forgotten
Politian iv 76
The child of Nature, without care
Tamerlane (1827) 76
O! I care not that my earthly lot
To M² 1

Career
Of peril in my wild career
Tamerlane (1827) 242

Careless
Can compare with the bright-eyed Eula-
lie's most humble and careless curl
Eulalie 13

Carelessly
I read, perhaps too carelessly
Tamerlane 149

Cares
Last night with my cares and toils
oppress'd Poetry 1
I have no time for idle cares
Romance 14
The world, its cares, and my own lot
Sarah 20
Enduring joys and fleeting cares
Stanzas² 6
When, from our little cares apart
Tamerlane 104
As though he'd say, "Why who the devil
cares?" Tempora 18
Mary, amid the cares—the woes
To F (1835) 1
For 'mid the earnest cares and woes
To F (1842) 1

Caressed
She fondly caressed Annie 74

Caresses
And true love caresses
Al Aaraaf ii 96

Caressing
And we wander on, caressing
Departed 29

Carriage
To a becoming carriage—much thou wantest Politian i 28

Carriers
To be carriers of fire Al Aaraaf i 94

Cartel
He doth decline your cartel
Politian v 13

Carving
On the Arabesque carving of a gilded hall
Al Aaraaf ii 204

Casement
With casement open to the skies
Irene 23
Her casement open to the skies
Sleeper 16
With casement open to the skies
Sleeper (1831) 17

Cast
By the comets who were cast
Al Aaraaf i 91
To him whose eyes are cast
Dreams 6

Castiglione
Thou art sad, Castiglione Politian i 1
Late hours and wine, Castiglione,—these
Politian i 13
Kiss her, Castiglione! kiss her
Politian i 39
For he's sure the Count Castiglione never
Politian ii 53
Castiglione lied who said he loved
Politian ii 73
As the betrothed of Castiglione
Politian iii 68
Castiglione lives Politian iv 87
Castiglione die Politian iv 89
That he, Castiglione, not being aware
Politian v 19
The Count Castiglione will not fight
Politian v 29
To me, Castiglione; the bearer being
Politian v 52

Cat
Because to his cat's eyes I hold a glass
Tempora 87

Cataract
Above yon cataract of Serangs
Irene (1836) 22

Catch
Should catch the note as it doth float up
from the damned Earth Lenore 24

Caught
Into the sunlit ether, caught the ray
Al Aaraaf ii 8
Caught from some unhappy master whom
unmerciful Disaster Raven 63

Cause
To give thee cause for grief, my honored
friend Politian iii 8
Than in thy cause to scoff at this same
glory Politian iv 40
That knowing no cause of quarrel or of
feud Politian v 11
Of any feud existing, or any cause
Politian v 20
Having no cause for quarrel
Politian v 30
He should have cause for quarrel
Politian v 37
In such a cause Politian v 72
The cause—but none are near to pry
Spirits (1827) 3

Cavern
From a cavern not very far Annie 43

Caves
And chasms, and caves, and Titan woods
Dream-Land 10

Cease
Still form a synonym for truth. Cease
trying Valentine 19

Ceased
She ceased——and buried then her burning cheek Al Aaraaf i 118

Methought, my sweet one, then I ceased to
soar   Al Aaraaf ii 237
Have ceased, with the fever   Annie 27
The storm had ceased—and I awoke
                        Tamerlane (1827) 70
I mean the reign of manners hath long
ceased.   .   Tempora 3

Ceasing
Ceasing their hymns, attend the spell
                        Israfel 6

Cedars
And million cedars to and fro
                        Irene (1836) 12

Celestial
Upon those crystalline, celestial spheres
                        Helen² 43

Cells
Oh, from out the sounding cells   Bells 25

Censer
Then, methought, the air grew denser,
perfumed from an unseen censer
                        Raven 79

Centre
Within the centre of that hall to breathe
                        Al Aaraaf ii 56
With its centre on the crown
                        Fairy-Land 16

Centuries
By buried centuries of pomp and power
                        Coliseum 3

Certain
And at the best I'm certain, Madame, you
cannot   Politian ii 55

Chain
And rays from God shot down that meteor
chain   Al Aaraaf ii 24

Chained
Was all on earth my chained sight
                        Song (1827) 7
Lion ambition is chain'd down
                        Tamerlane 160

Chains
But hug the glorious chains I wore
                        Divine Right 4
Which hangs like chains of pearl on Her-
mon hill   Politian ii 35
That hangs like chains of pearl on Her-
mon hill   To² 10

Challenge
Cannot accept the challenge
                        Politian v 22
Virtues that challenge envy's praise
                        Stanzas² 7

Chamber
Through the gray chamber to my song
                        Paean 31
As of some one gently rapping, rapping at
my chamber door   Raven 4
" 'Tis some visitor," I muttered, "tap-
ping at my chamber door   Raven 5
'Tis some visitor entreating entrance at
my chamber door   Raven 16
Some late visitor entreating at my cham-
ber door;—This it is and nothing more
                        Raven 17
And so faintly you came tapping, tapping
at my chamber door   Raven 22

Back into the chamber turning, all my
soul within me burning   Raven 31
But, with mien of lord or lady, perched
above my chamber door   Raven 40
Perched upon a bust of Pallas just above
my chamber door—Perched, and sat,
and nothing more   Raven 41
Ever yet was blessed with seeing bird
above his chamber door   Raven 52
Bird or beast upon the sculptured bust
above his chamber door   Raven 53
On the pallid bust of Pallas just above
my chamber door   Raven 104
Flit through thy chamber in and out
                        Sleeper 23
This chamber changed for one more holy
                        Sleeper 40

Chamois
With chamois, I would seize his den
                        Tamerlane (1827) 43

Chance
Because divided it may chance be shaken
                        Tempora 46

Change
Will change me, and as politicians do
                        Tempora 39

Changed
The sands of Time are changed to golden
grains   Politian iii 41
This chamber changed for one more holy
                        Sleeper 40

Changing
Forever changing places   Fairy-Land 8
That you are changing sadly your do-
minion   Tempora 2

Chaos
I left so late was into chaos hurled
                        Al Aaraaf ii 234
A chaos of deep passion, from his birth
                        Dreams 8

Charm
Bore burthen to the charm the maiden
sang   Al Aaraaf ii 67
Shall charm thee—as a token
                        Spirits (1827) 26

Charmion
With gentle names—Eiros and Charmion
                        Politian ii 27

Charms
O charms more potent than the rapt Chaldee   Coliseum 15
Transforming all! Thy charms shall
please no more   Zante 10

Chart
Unrolling as a chart unto my view
                        Al Aaraaf ii 223

Chased
With its phantom chased for evermore
                        Worm 19

Chasms
And chasms, and caves, and Titan woods
                        Dream-Land 10

Chastened
Like guilty beauty, chastened, and more
fair   Al Aaraaf i 65

Check
To check the power that governs here
Divine Right 8

Cheated
And having cheated ladies, dance with
them Tempora 54

Cheek
She ceased—and buried then her burning
cheek Al Aaraaf i 118
Her cheek was flushing and her lips apart
Al Aaraaf (1829) 53
The flush on her bright cheek, to me
Tamerlane 151

Cheeks
Her cheeks were flushing, and her lips
apart Al Aaraaf ii 53
Yon heir, whose cheeks of pallid hue
Lenore (1843) 15
It speaks of sunken eyes, and wasted
cheeks Politian ii 65
These cheeks, where the worm never dies
Ulalume 43

Cheered
Hath cheered me as a lovely beam
Dream 11

Cherish
With a thought I then did cherish
Imitation 20

Cherished
Whom thou hast cherished to sting thee to
the soul Politian ii 59

Cherub
And every sculptured cherub thereabout
Al Aaraaf ii 32

Chide
If her memory do not chide her
Ballad 27

Chiding
While all the world were chiding
Dream 10

Child
She was a child and I was a child
Annabel Lee 7
For she knew I loved her child
Ballad 20
Leaving thee wild for the dear child that
should have been thy bride
Lenore 16
A child—with a most knowing eye
Romance 10
Thrilling to think, poor child of sin
Sleeper 59
My own voice, silly child! was swelling
Tamerlane 51
The child of Nature, without care
Tamerlane (1827) 76

Childhood
From childhood's hour I have not been
Alone 1
Then—in my childhood—in the dawn
Alone 9
In childhood, many an idle stone
Sleeper 56
Even childhood knows the human heart
Tamerlane (1827) 126
In childhood but he knew me not
Tamerlane (1827) 398

Childish
For they were childish and upright
Tamerlane 92

Children
Children, we disagree Politian i 64

Chill
That palpitate like the chill seas
Valley 15

Chilling
Chilling my Annabel Lee
Annabel Lee 16
That the wind came out of the cloud,
chilling Annabel Lee 25
A wind blew out of a cloud chilling
Annabel Lee (1849) 15
Chilling and killing my Annabel Lee
Annabel Lee (1849) 26
Thou Horror with blood-chilling cries
Louisa 11

Chilly
Their still waters, still and chilly
Dream-Land 19
Their sad waters, sad and chilly
Dream-Land 23
Or spell had bound me—it was the chilly
wind Dreams 21
Is chilly—and these melancholy boughs
Politian iv 63
The torrent of the chilly air
Tamerlane 60
Her smile if chilly—and her beam
Tamerlane 203

Chime
With its interminable chime
Tamerlane 24

Chimed
Chimed in with my desires and bade me
stay Politian iii 108

Chiming
To the rhyming and the chiming of the
bells Bells 35

Chirping
The mock-bird chirping on the thorn
Sarah 8

Choir
And they say the starry choir
Israfel 16

Chokes
And the light laughter chokes the sigh
Irene 46

Chorus
In chorus to my pensive sigh Sarah 14

Church
And to the church-yard bore me
Bridal Ballad 16

Circassy
Springs from the gems of Circassy
Al Aaraaf i 4
While the silver winds of Circassy
Al Aaraaf i (1831) 14

Circle
Through a circle that ever returneth in
Worm 21

Circular
A window of one circular diamond, there
Al Aaraaf ii 22

Circumference
While its wide circumference
                              Fairy-Land 18
Cities
Tenantless cities of the desert too
                              Al Aaraaf ii 224
Above all cities? in her hand
                              Tamerlane 167
Of all the cities, and I've seen no few
                              Tempora 41
Citizens
The eyes of the citizens   Politian v 87
City
In a strange city lying alone   City 2
To the imperial city   Politian i 44
For in the eternal city thou shalt do me
                              Politian iii 34
Clad
But stay! these walls—these ivy-clad
    arcades   Coliseum 26
Clad all in white, upon a violet bank
                              Helen² 17
Claim'd
I claim'd and won usurpingly
                              Tamerlane 29
Clambered
I clambered to the tottering height
                              Tamerlane (1827) 352
Clamor
In the clamor and the elangor of the bells
                              Bells 69
Clamorous
In a clamorous appealing to the mercy
    of the fire   Bells 44
Clang
How they clang, and clash, and roar
                              Bells 54
Clanging
And the clanging   Bells 59
Clangor
In the clamor and the clangor of the bells
                              Bells 69
Clash
How they clang, and clash, and roar
                              Bells 54
Clasp
Them with a tighter clasp
                              Dream w. Dream 20
It shall clasp a sainted maiden whom the
    angels name Lenore   Raven 94
Clasp a rare and radiant maiden whom
    the angels name Lenore   Raven 95
Classic
Thy hyacinth hair, thy classic face
                              Helen² 7
Claw
The luckless query from a Member's Claw
                              Tempora 20
Clay
Soon would turn to clay   Departed 36
Clear
By this clear stream
                              Al Aaraaf i (1831) 5
From Balbec, and the stilly, clear abyss
                              Al Aaraaf ii 37
On the clear waters there that flow
                              Irene 57

And hark the sounds so low yet clear
                              Irene (1836) 26
Fair river! in thy bright, clear flow
                              River 1
The night, tho' clear, shall frown
                              Spirits 11
Clearest
To springs that lie clearest
                              Al Aaraaf ii 130
Cliff
From the red cliff of the mountain
                              Alone 14
No cliff beyond him in the sky
                              Tamerlane 188
Climate
It in another climate," so he said
                              Politian ii 6
Clime
And Death to some more happy clime
                              City (1836) 55
From a wild weird clime that lieth, sub-
    lime   Dream-Land 7
From love, and from our misty clime
                              Paradise (1834) 31
From me, and from our misty clime
                              Paradise (1835) 31
Not on God's altar, in any time or clime
                              Politian iv 18
Beyond this bounded earthly clime
                              Stanzas² 10
Climes
In climes of mine imagining, apart
                              Dreams 16
In the ultimate climes of the Pole
                              Ulalume 17
Cling
And cling around about us as a garment
                              Coliseum 45
Which would cling to thee for ever
                              Spirits 18
Cloak
As she threw off her cloak, yon moon
                              Fairy-Land (1831) 22
His cloak, of a thousand mingled hues
                              Parody 5
Close
The soft head bows, the sweet eyes close
                              Physician 5
I close the portrait with the name of Pitts
                              Tempora 92
Closed
Above the closed and fringed lid
                              Sleeper 26
Closing
With half closing eyes
                              Al Aaraaf ii 73
Appeared to my half-closing eye
                              Tamerlane 46
Clothe
And clothe us in a robe of more than
    glory   Coliseum (1833) 50
Clothing
Clothing us in a robe of more than glory
                              Coliseum 46
Cloud
Still think my terrors but the thunder
    cloud   Al Aaraaf i 136

And sees the darkness coming as a cloud
Al Aaraaf ii 46
And the cloud that took the form
Alone 20
A wind blew out of a cloud by night
Annabel Lee 15
That the wind came out of the cloud,
chilling Annabel Lee 25
Into a western couch of thunder-cloud
Helen² 49
And not a cloud obscured the sky
Hymn 6
A fleecy cloud Star 13
Flashing from cloud that hovered over
Tamerlane (1827) 50
Of the pale cloud therein, whose hue
Tamerlane (1827) 320

Clouds
Rich clouds, for canopies, about her curled
Al Aaraaf i 36
Now, when clouds of Fate overcast
Hymn (1835) 13
From the evil taint of clouds?—and he
did say Politian v 27
From clouds that hung, like banners, over
Tamerlane 45
Ah, by no wind those clouds are driven
Valley 17

Cloudy
And cloudy-looking woods Fairy-Land 2

Clung
And zone that clung around her gentle
waist Al Aaraaf ii 54
More beauty clung around her columned
wall Al Aaraaf ii 216

Clutch
And thus I clutch thee—thus
Politian iv 102

Clytia
And Clytia pondering between many a sun
Al Aaraaf i 68

Coat
Was once the locust's coat of gold
Parody 4
And dove-tailed coat, obtained at cost;
while then Tempora 67

Coffin
Thus on the coffin loud and long
Paean 29

Coiling
Thus the bright snake coiling
To Hunter 8

Cold
Beneath the cold moon Al Aaraaf ii 151
'T were better than the cold reality
Dreams 5
Of the brighter, cold moon Star 5
On her cold smile Star 10
Too cold—too cold for me Star 11
Or who so cold, so callous to refuse
Tempora 57

Colder
Than that colder, lowly light Star 23

Coldly
Too coldly—or the stars—howe'er it was
Dreams 25

Coliseum
Lone amphitheatre! Grey Coliseum
Coliseum (1833) 1

Collar
In short his shirt-collar, his look, his tone
is Tempora 71

Color
And all the opal'd air in color bound
Al Aaraaf i 41

Coloring
Dreams! in their vivid coloring of life
Dreams 29

Colossal
All of the famed and the colossal left
Coliseum 31

Column
Here, where a hero fell, a column falls
Coliseum 17

Columned
More beauty clung around her column'd
wall Al Aaraaf ii 216

Columns
Of gorgeous columns on th' unburthen'd
air Al Aaraaf ii 12
Sat gently on these columns as a crown
Al Aaraaf ii 21

Combine
With which they dare combine
To⁴ 33

Come
Come down to your brow
Al Aaraaf ii 77
Gay fire-fly of the night we come and go
Al Aaraaf ii 248
No rays from the holy heaven come down
City 12
Things past and to come Departed 28
Come never again Eulalie 15
And so come down again Fairy-Land 43
O, when will come the morrow
Fairy-Land (1831) 38
Come, let the burial rite be read—the
funeral song be sung Lenore 5
Eternal dews come down in gems
Nis (1836) 48
Poor Lalage!—and is it come to this
Politian ii 57
In days that are to come Politian iv 74
Now prythee, leave me—hither doth come
a person Politian v 41
Sure thou art come o'er far-off seas
Sleeper 32
When that deep blush would come o'er
thee Song 14
To come down and see To Hunter 11
And has come past the stars of the Lion
Ulalume 44
Come up, in despite of the Lion
Ulalume 47
Come up through the lair of the Lion
Ulalume 49
Eternal dews come down in drops
Valley 25
Mere puppets they, who come and go
Worm 12

Comes
Sometimes comes she to me, showing
　　　　　Departed 27
Comes down—still down—and down
　　　　　Fairy-Land 15
Be still!—it comes again
　　　　　Politian iii 69
Hist! hist! it comes again
　　　　　Politian iii 79
With what excessive fragrance the zephyr
　comes　　　Politian v 15
'T is he—he comes himself
　　　　　Politian v 38
There comes a sullenness of heart
　　　　　Tamerlane 192
I know—for Death who comes for me
　　　　　Tamerlane 223
Comes o'er me in these lonely hours
　　　　　Tamerlane (1827) 137
Comes o'er me, with the mingled voice
　　　　　Tamerlane (1827) 340
Comes down with the rush of a storm
　　　　　Worm 36

Cometh
But what is this?—it cometh—and it
　brings　　　Al Aaraaf ii 48

Comets
By the comet who were cast
　　　　　Al Aaraaf i 91

Comforted
Be comforted　　　Politian iv 7

Coming
And sees the darkness coming as a cloud
　　　　　Al Aaraaf ii 46
Lo! one is coming down
　　　　　Fairy-Land (1831) 51
To the sound of the coming darkness
　known　　　Tamerlane 197

Command
Are all at my command
　　　　　Bridal Ballad 4
Command me, sir! what wouldst thou
　have me do　　　Politian iii 9
Command me, sir,　　Politian iii 14
With thoughts such feeling can command
　　　　　Tamerlane (1827) 256

Commanding
Logic and common usage so commanding
　　　　　Elizabeth 2

Commend
No foot of man, commend thyself to God
　　　　　Silence 15

Commingled
Commingled with pansies　　Annie 64

Common
My passions from a common spring
　　　　　Alone 4
Logic and common usage so commanding
　　　　　Elizabeth 2
From common passions　Politian i 64
From us in life—but common—which
　doth lie　　　Stanzas[1] 21
In common sequence set, the letters lying
　　　　　Valentine 17

Communing
In secret, communing held—as he with it
　　　　　Stanzas[1] 2

His spirit is communing with an angel's
　　　　　To MLS 18

Company
Thy riotous company, too—fellows low-
　born　　　Politian i 20
And sought his company　Politian i 58

Compare
Can compare with the bright-eyed Eu-
　lalie's most humble and careless curl
　　　　　Eulalie 13

Compassion
Had deem'd him, in compassion, aught
　　　　　Tamerlane (1827) 249

Compels
What a world of solemn thought their
　monody compels　　　Bells 72

Complete
Complete at night what he began A. M.
　　　　　Tempora 53

Compose
Compose a sound delighting all to hear
　　　　　Valentine (1846) 18

Composedly
And I rest so composedly, Now in my
　bed　　　Annie 13
And I lie so composedly　　Annie 85

Comprehend
If one could merely comprehend the plot
　　　　　Valentine (1846) 12

Con
Twirls into trunk-paper the while you con
　it　　　Enigma 8

Concealed
Of the dear names that lie concealed
　within 't　　　Enigma (1848) 14

Conceive
Of those, who hardly will conceive
　　　　　Tamerlane (1827) 258

Condor
Of late, eternal Condor years
　　　　　Romance 11
Flapping from out their Condor wings
　　　　　Worm 15

Confess
Still does my heart confess thy power
　　　　　Octavia 4
Now each visitor shall confess
　　　　　Valley 9

Confidence
And confidence—his vows—my ruin—
　think—think　　　Politian ii 89

Confused
Crowding, confused became
　　　　　Tamerlane (1827) 176

Confusedly
And, so, confusedly, became
　　　　　Tamerlane 125

Connivingly
Connivingly my dreaming-book
　　　　　Romance (1831) 66

Conquered
Is conquered at last　　Annie 6
And conquered her scruples and gloom
　　　　　Ulalume 74

Conquerer
Had gilded wih a conquerer's name
　　　　　Tamerlane (1827) 272

And its hero, the Conqueror Worm
                      Worm 40

Conscience
Like the grim shadow Conscience, solemn
  and noiseless   Politian iv 56
Not Conscience' self   Politian iv 60

Conscious
I was not conscious of it   Politian i 8
A conscious slumber seems to take
                  Sleeper 14

Conspire
The wild—the terrible conspire
              Tamerlane 163

Constant
It trembled to one constant star again
        Al Aaraaf ii (1829) 197

Constitution
The constitution as late hours and wine
            Politian i 16

Contain
The world, and all it did contain
            Tamerlane 117
Of varied being, which contain
        Tamerlane (1827) 165

Contemn
A heaven that God doth not contemn
            City (1831) 14

Contemplation
Of lofty contemplation left to Time
            Coliseum 2

Content
Here may he revel to his heart's content
            Tempora 49

Contented
Never-contented things   Fairy-Land 44

Contentedly
And I rest so contentedly   Annie 89

Continually
Serenest skies continually   To F 13

Continuing
Continuing—as dreams have been to me
            Dreams 10

Contradiction
Besides my innate love of contradiction
            Elizabeth 6

Control
My spirit spurn'd control
            Dream (1827) 2

Controul
Those thoughts I would controul
            Imitation 13

Converse
The moment's converse; in her eyes
            Tamerlane 148

Cool
Some have left the cool glade, and
            Al Aaraaf ii 140

Cooped
Spirit, cooped in mortal bower
            Departed 18

Cope
To shun the fate, with which to cope
           Tamerlane (1827) 4

Core
Its own core my wild heart eating
            Departed 35

To the fowl whose fiery eyes now burned
  into my bosom's core   Raven 74

Cornice
Lurk'd in each cornice, round each architrave   Al Aaraaf ii 31

Cornices
These shattered cornices—this wreck—
  this ruin   Coliseum 29

Coronet
A vacant coronet   Lenore (1843) 19

Corporate
He is the corporate Silence: dread him
  not   Silence 10

Corrosive
By the corrosive Hours to Fate and me
            Coliseum 32

Corslet
The corslet on his bosom bold Parody 3

Cost
And dove-tailed coat, obtained at cost;
  while then   Tempora 67

Costly
Of her " costly broider'd pall " Paean 14

Cot
Something he spoke of the old cot
        Tamerlane (1827) 399

Cottager
A cottager, I mark'd a throne
           Tamerlane 130

Couch
Here, where on ivory couch the Caesar
  sate   Coliseum (1833) 23
Into a western couch of thunder-cloud
           Helen² 49
Weary—I laid me on a couch to rest
           Poetry 2

Couches
On violet couches faint away
        Al Aaraaf i (1831) 15

Couldst
Thou couldst not so deceive me
        Ballad 10, 22, 34
O still more happy maiden who couldst
  die   Politian ii 14
Lest I behold thee not; thou couldst not
  go   Politian iv 93
I knew thou wouldst not, couldst not,
  durst not go   Politian iv 100

Count
Sir Count! what art thou dreaming? he's
  not well   Politian i 33
For he's sure the Count Castiglione never
           Politian ii 53
Demanded but to die!—what sayeth the
  Count   Politian v 9
No mortal eyes have seen!—what said the
  Count   Politian v 18
The Count Castiglione will not fight
           Politian v 29
Unto the Count—it is exceeding just
           Politian v 36
Thou wilt not fight with me didst say,
  Sir Count   Politian v 64
Thou wilt not fight with me didst say,
  Sir Count   Politian v 65

Countenance
By the grave and stern decorum of the
countenance it wore   Raven 44

Counter
As this for a neat, frisky counter-hopper
Tempora 48

Counters
And hops o'er counters with a Vestris air
Tempora 52

Country
In my own country all the way
Fairy-Land   (1831) 30

Coupling
How my heart beats in coupling those two
words   Helen² 27

Courage
Thy servant maid!—but courage!—'t is
but a viper   Politian ii 58

Course
When first Al Aaraaf knew her course to
be   Al Aaraaf ii 255
Thy life's free course should ever roam
Stanzas² 9
Of our boyhood, his course hath run
Tamerlane (1827) 385
He then, of course, must shake his foot
instead   Tempora 84

Court
Give not thy soul to dreams: the camp—
the court   Politian iii 21

Courts
To me, Politian, of thy camps and courts
Politian iii 28

Cousin
Thy happiness!—what ails thee, cousin of
mine   Politian i 6
Nothing, fair cousin, nothing—not even
deep sorrow   Politian i 17
Cousin! fair cousin!—madam
Politian i 34

Covered
She covered me warm   Annie 80
I sit on some moss-covered stone
Sarah 2

Covering
And their moony covering
Fairy-Land 30

Crept
How was it that Ambition crept
Tamerlane 240

Crescent
His target was the crescent shell
Parody 7
Out of which miraculous crescent
Ulalume 35
Astarte's bediamonded crescent
Ulalume 37

Crest
Though they crest be shorn and shaven,
thou," I said, "art sure no craven
Raven 45

Crested
Triumphant, o'er the crested palls
Sleeper 52

Cried
Wretch," I cried, " thy God hath lent thee
—by these angels he hath sent thee
Raven 81
And I cried: " It was surely October
Ulalume 85

Cries
Thou Horror with blood-chilling cries
Louisa 11
A voice from out the Future cries
Paradise 10

Crime
From Love to titled age and crime
Paradise (1835) 29
My heart would feel to be a crime
Romance 20
I feel it more than half a crime
Serenade 2
Is more than crime may dare to dream
Tamerlane (1827) 5
And bade it first to dream of crime
Tamerlane (1827) 149
When falsehood wore a ten-fold crime
Tamerlane (1827) 190

Crimson
And wave this crimson canopy   Irene 35
Ye crimson life-drops, stay   Louisa 2

Crisis
Thank Heaven! the crisis   Annie 1

Crisped
The leaves they were crisped and sere
Ulalume 2
As the leaves that were crisped and sere
Ulalume 83

Croaking
Meant in croaking " Nevermore
Raven 72

Crocodile
Their crocodile dew   Lenore (1843) 18

Cross
Ah! will they cross me in my angrier
path   Al Aaraaf i 138
Thy raiments and thy ebony cross affright
me   Politian ii 102
Behold the cross wherewith a vow like
mine   Politian ii 107

Crouched
Low crouched on Earth, some violets lie
Nis (1836) 42

Crouches
And crouches to a keeper's hand
Tamerlane 161

Crowd
Where all my love is folly, and the crowd
Al Aaraaf i 135
Not one, of all the crowd, to pry
Spirits 3
That crowd around my earthly path
To F 2
By a crowd that seize it not   Worm 20

Crowded
Ianthe, beauty crowded on me then
Al Aaraaf ii 225

Crowding
Crowding, confused became
Tamerlane (1827) 176

Crowding around my earthly path
　　　　　To F (1835) 2
Crown
Sat gently on these columns as a crown
　　　　　Al Aaraaf ii 21
With its centre on the crown
　　　　　Fairy-Land 16
And on the spectral mountain's crown
　　　　　Serenade 12
Wearing its own deep feeling as a crown
　　　　　Stanzas¹ 32
We walk'd together on the crown
　　　　　Tamerlane 139
And donn'd a visionary crown
　　　　　Tamerlane 156
As nuptial dowry—a queen's crown
　　　　　Tamerlane (1827) 244
Crowns
And laughter crowns the festive hour
　　　　　Octavia 2
Crucifix
Fills me with dread—thy ebony crucifix
　　　　　Politian ii 82
Hast thou a crucifix fit for this thing
　　　　　Politian ii 98
A crucifix where on to register
　　　　　Politian ii 99
I have a crucifix myself
　　　　　Politian ii 103
I have a crucifix　　　Politian ii 104
Crumbling
These vague entablatures—this crumbling
　　frieze　　　　Coliseum 28
These crumbling walls; these tottering
　　arcades　　　Coliseum (1833) 31
Crush
Gurgled within my ear the crush
　　　　　Tamerlane 61
Cry
Wakening the broad welkin with his loud
　　battle cry　　　　Campaign 2
And leap within me at the cry
　　　　　Tamerlane 53
The battle-cry of Victory　Tamerlane 54
I'll neither laugh with one or cry with
　　t'other　　　　Tempora 26
Crystal
Leave tenantless thy crystal home, and
　　fly　　　　Al Aaraaf i 143
Far down within the crystal of the lake
　　　　　Al Aaraaf ii (1829) 40
And crystal lakes, and over-arching
　　forests　　　Politian iv 70
Of crystal, wandering water　River 2
Crystalline
With a crystalline delight　　Bells 8
Upon those crystalline, celestial spheres
　　　　　Helen² 43
Let us bathe in this crystalline light
　　　　　Ulalume 63
Cultured
The fullness of a cultured mind
　　　　　Stanzas² 17
Cumber
That cumber them too　Al Aaraaf ii 87

Cup
Drinking the cup of pleasure to the dregs
　　　　　Politian i 60
Cupid
With Indian Cupid down the holy river
　　　　　Al Aaraaf i 79
Cure
To cure his love, was cured of all beside
　　　　　Acrostic 8
Cured
To cure his love, was cured of all beside
　　　　　Acrostic 8
Curious
Over many a quaint and curious volume of
　　forgotten lore　　　Raven 2
Curl
For no ripples curl, alas　　City 36
Can vie with the modest Eulalie's most
　　unregarded curl　　　Eulalie 12
Can compare with the bright-eyed Eula-
　　lie's most humble and careless curl
　　　　　Eulalie 13
Curled
Rich clouds for canopies, about her curled
　　　　　Al Aaraaf i 36
Curls
Toss back his fine curls from their fore-
　　head fair　　　Tempora 51
Current
And spite all dogmas current in all ages
　　　　　Tempora 77
Currents
Their sulphurous currents down Yaanek
　　　　　Ulalume 16
Cursed
Curs'd was the hour that saw us meet
　　　　　Louisa 15
Curtain
Which thro' some tatter'd curtain pries
　　　　　Fairy-Land (1831) 32
And the silken, sad, uncertain rustling of
　　each purple curtain　　Raven 13
And wave the curtain canopy
　　　　　Sleeper 24
The curtain, a funeral pall　Worm 35
Cushion
On the cushion's velvet lining that the
　　lamp-light gloated o'er　Raven 76
Cushioned
Straight I wheeled a cushioned seat of
　　bird and bust and door　Raven 68
Cut
The youth who cut the ribbon for her
　　shoes　　　　Tempora 58
Cycles
What tho' in worlds which sightless cycles
　　run　　　Al Aaraaf i 133
Cypress
Of cypress, I roamed with my Soul
　　　　　Ulalume 11
Of cypress, with Psyche, my Soul
　　　　　Ulalume 12
Daedalion
A red Daedalion on the timid Earth
　　　　　Al Aaraaf ii 244

Daily
Who daily scents his snowy wings
                 Tamerlane 233
Whom daily thou art wont to see
             Tamerlane (1827) 262
And daily strut the street with bows and
    scrapes   Tempora 33

Dainty
The elfin from the grasse? the dainty fay
             To Science (1841) 13

Dallied
And every gentle air that dallied
                    Palace 13

Dame
Told of a beauteous dame beyond the sea
                Politian ii 16

Dames
Here, where the dames of Rome their
    gilded hair   Coliseum 20

Damn
But damn it, sir, I deem it a disgrace
                 Tempora 31

Damned
Should catch the note as it doth float up
    from the damned Earth   Lenore 24
Aspiringly, are damned, and die
              Romance (1831) 57

Dance
Or worse—upon her brow to dance
                   Irene 5
And having cheated ladies, dance with
    them   Tempora 54

Danced
While the moon danc'd with the fair
    stranger light   Al Aaraaf ii 10

Dances
And dances again   Al Aaraaf ii 122
And he dances, and he yells   Bells 95
In what ethereal dances   Paradise 25

Danger
The danger, is past   Annie 2
How the danger ebbs and flows   Bells 60
How the danger sinks and swells
                     Bells 64
But cannot from a danger nigh
                Tamerlane 200

Dank
It was down by the dank tarn of Auber
                   Ulalume 8
We remembered not the dank tarn of
    Auber   Ulalume 28
Well I know, now, this dank tarn of
    Auber   Ulalume 93

Dare
No subject vice dare interfere
               Divine Right 7
May not—dare not openly view it
              Dream-Land 44
I feel thou art not gone—yet dare not look
               Politian iv 92
Avaunt—I will not fight thee—indeed I
    dare not   Politian v 63
I dare not—dare not   Politian v 66
I cannot—dare not   Politian v 69
Is more than crime may dare to dream
              Tamerlane (1827) 5

Nor would I dare attempt to trace
             Tamerlane (1827) 90
Thou can'st not—would'st not dare to
    think   Tamerlane (1827) 103
With which they dare combine   To⁴ 33

Dared
Where no wind dared to stir, unless on
    tiptoe   Helen² 10
Doubting, dreaming dreams no mortal
    ever dared to dream before   Raven 26
Stern Despair returned instead of the
    sweet Hope he dared adjure
              Raven (Mirror) 65

Darest
Didst say thou darest not
                  Politian v 66
Thou darest not fight with me
             Politian v (1835) 66
Thou darest not   Politian v (1835) 75

Daring
Then here's the White Eagle, full daring
    is he   Campaign 3
How daring an ambition! yet how deep
                  Helen² 46

Dark
Here sate he with his love—his dark eye
    bent   Al Aaraaf ii 194
But hold!—these dark, these perishing
    arcades   Coliseum (1842) 31
Were it not for that dark greeting
                 Departed 34
Dark and sad as they   Departed 40
In visions of the dark night   Dream 1
For on its wing was dark alloy
               Happiest Day 21
How dark a wo! yet how sublime a hope
                  Helen² 44
A dark, unfathom'd tide   Imitation 1
To this dark imagining Lake (1827) 21
Are where thy dark eye glances
              Paradise (1824) 23
'Mid dark thoughts of the gray tombstone
                  Spirits 2
From their thrones, in the dark heav'n
              Spirits (1827) 13
A light in the dark wild, alone
             Tamerlane (1827) 233

Darkened
Beholds it but through darkened glasses
              Dream-Land 50
Springing from a darken'd mind
              Lake (1827) 16

Darkly
Darkly my Present and my Past
                  Hymn 10

Darkness
And sees the darkness coming as a cloud
              Al Aaraaf ii 46
Into the darkness of a room
             Fairy-Land (1831) 33
Of Darkness and the Tomb, O pity me
               Politian v 5
Darkness there and nothing more
                Raven 24
Deep into that darkness peering, long I
    stood there wondering, fearing
                  Raven 25

A dirge for her the doubly dead in that
  she died so young   Lenore 7
Go up to God so solemnly the dead may
  feel no wrong   Lenore 14
For her most wrong'd of·all the dead
                        Lenore (1843) 26
Are mother to the dead I loved so dearly
                        Mother (1850) 11
Dead beauty with a tear   Paean 8
That the dead may feel no wrong
                               Paean 20
Of the dead, who is my bride   Paean 24
Of the dead—dead who lies   Paean 25
It was the dead who groaned within
                             Sleeper 60
The spirits of the dead who stood
                              Spirits 7
The undying voice of that dead time
                            Tamerlane 23
But she who rear'd them was long dead
                     Tamerlane (1827) 405
Lie dead on my heart-strings
                               To M 15
But that, while I am dead yet alive
                               To M 19

Deaf
In a mad expostulation with the deaf and
  frantic fire   Bells 45
Rendered me mad and deaf and blind
                           Tamerlane 57

Deal
Nor deal in flattery or asperisons foul
                            Tempora 27

Dear
Of the dear names that lie concealed
  within't   Enigma 14
While ever to her dear Eulalie upturns
  her matron eye   Eulalie 20
Or is it all but a dream, my dear
                     Fairy-Land (1831) 10
The bright i-dea, or bright dear eye
                           Impromptu 4
Leaving thee wild for the dear child that
  should have been thy bride
                             Lenore 16
Therefore by that dear name I long have
  called you   Mother 5
Oh, lady dear, hast thou no fear
                             Sleeper 30
With thy dear name as text, though bid-
  den by thee   To³ 18
Were you not something of a dunce, my
  dear   Valentine (1846) 20

Dearer
And thus are dearer than the mother I
  knew   Mother 12
Was dearer to my soul than its soul-life
                             Mother 14
And dearer thy beam shall be   Star 17

Dearest
Away, then, my dearest
                        Al Aaraaf ii 128
Ianthe, dearest, see! how dim that ray
                        Al Aaraaf ii 198
Here, dearest, where the moonbeam fell
                     Fairy-Land (1831) 2

Dearly
Are mother to the one I loved so dearly
                             Mother 11

Death
O Death! from eye of God upon that star
                        Al Aaraaf ii 161
Sweet was that error—sweeter still that
  death   Al Aaraaf ii 162
Sweet was their death—with them to die
  was rife   Al Aaraaf ii 168
Beyond that death no immortality
                        Al Aaraaf ii 170
But O that light!—I slumber'd—Death,
  the while   Al Aaraaf ii 210
Lo! Death has reared himself a throne
                               City 1
Death looks gigantically down   City 29
And Death is to some more happy clime
                          City (1836) 55
Their odorous souls in an ecstatic death
                              Helen² 13
Death was in that poisonous wave
                              Lake 18
That did to death the innocence that died,
  and died so young   Lenore 12
The life still there upon her hair, the
  death upon her eyes   Lenore 19
And fill my heart of hearts, where Death
  installed you   Mother 7
I am sick, sick, sick, even unto death
                          Politian iii 29
Now's Death and Hell   Politian v 82
Even unto death   Politian v 89
I could not love except where Death
                        Romance (1831) 31
In death around thee—and their will
                              Spirits 9
A portrait taken after death
                          Tamerlane 206
I know—for Death who comes for me
                          Tamerlane 223
Grows dim around me—death is near
                     Tamerlane (1827) 16

Debate
Each fit to furnish forth four hours'
  debate   Tempora 22

Debonair
For her, the fair and debonair, that now
  so lowly lies   Lenore 17

Deceased
And Beauty long deceased—remembers
  me   Politian ii 66

Deceive
Thou couldst not so deceive me
                       Ballad 10, 22, 32
In earlier days—a friend will not deceive
  thee   Politian ii 61
Where there is nothing to deceive
                          Tamerlane 225

December
Ah, distinctly I remember it was in the
  bleak December   Raven 7

Deck
That list our Love, and deck our bowers
                        Al Aaraaf i 13

Decline
He doth decline your cartel
Politian v 13

Decorum
By the grave and stern decorum of the
countenance it wore Raven 44

Deed
The deed—the vow—the symbol of the
deed Politian ii 105
And the deed's register should tally,
father! Politian ii 106
There is no deed I would more glory in
Politian iv 39
A deed is to be done Politian iv 86
In every deed shall mingle, love
Serenade 25

Deeds
How by what hidden deeds of might
Tamerlane (1827) 351

Deem
You are not wrong, who deem
Dream w dream 4
That, scarce awake, thy soul shall deem
Serenade 20
I will not madly deem that power
Tamerlane 3
That she might deem it nought beside
Tamerlane 147
But damn it, sir, I deem it a disgrace
Tempora 31
How should he love thee? or how deem
these wise To Science 5

Deemed
Have deem'd since I have reach'd to
power Tamerlane 67
Ev'n then, who deem'd this iron heat
Tamerlane (1827) 86
Had deem'd him, in compassion, aught
Tamerlane (1827) 249
Whom she had deem'd in his own fire
Tamerlane (1827) 275
Of long delight, nor yet had deem'd
Tamerlane (1827) 294

Deep
Upon the flying footsteps of—deep pride
Al Aaraaf i 46
In the deep sky Al Aaraaf i 83
In its dream of deep rest
Al Aaraaf ii 133
In a deep dreamy sleep
Al Aaraaf ii (1843) 117
From their deep-toned throats!
Bells (1899) 14
Light from the lurid, deep sea
City (1831) 22
Fierce deep grief is unavailing
Departed 22
Through my fingers to the deep
Dream w Dream 17
A chaos of deep passion, from his birth
Dreams 8
Born and brought up with their snouts
deep down in the mud of the Frog-
Pond Experiments 8
And then, how deep!—O, deep
Fairy-Land 27

How daring an ambition! yet how deep
Helen² 46
Where deep thoughts are a duty
Israfel 24
Proclaim her deep despair Louisa 8
Deep in earth my love is lying
Manuscript 1
Nothing, fair cousin, nothing—not even
deep sorrow Politian i 17
So deep abstruse he has not mastered it
Politian i 55
That in this deep humiliation I perish
Politian v 18
Deep into that darkness peering, long I
stood there wondering fearing
Raven 25
My draught of passion has been deep
Romance (1831) 50
Form in the deep another seven
Serenade 8
Which is enduring, so be deep!
Sleeper 38
As it is lasting, so be deep!
Sleeper 46
When that deep blush would come o'er
thee Song 14
Wearing its own deep feeling as a crown
Stanzas¹ 32
And the deep trumpet-thunder's roar
Tamerlane 48
Her silent, deep astonishment
Tamerlane (1827) 267
Where in a deep, still slumber lay
Tamerlane (1827) 285
Thro' my fingers to the deep!
Tamerlane (1831) 254
For the resurrection of deep-buried faith
To MLS 6

Deeper
An humbler heart—a deeper wo
Tamerlane 221

Deeply
Deeply to sleep Annie 77
Why didst thou sigh so deeply?
Politian i 7
Her image deeply lies River 12
And deeply felt the silent tone
Tamerlane (1827) 180

Define
Could teach or bribe me to define
Lake 16
Could ever bribe me to define
Tamerlane (1831) 94

Defy
O, I defy thee, Hell, to snow
Tamerlane 219
Endure!—no—no—defy To⁴ 40

Degree
Lowly—and of their own degree
Tamerlane (1827) 265

Deign
O! would she deign to rule my fate
Divine Right 9

Deity
For the stars trembled at the Deity
Al Aaraaf i 121

Can it be fancied that Deity ever vindictively   Experiments 5

Delicate
They weep:—from off their delicate stems
               Valley 26

Delight
To keep watch with delight
               Al Aaraaf ii 110
With a crystalline delight   Bells 8
How they ring out their delight
               Bells 19
But a tremulous delight   Lake 14
Some object of delight upon
               Tamerlane (1827) 95
All was an undefin'd delight
               Tamerlane (1827) 162
And raise his infancy's delight
               Tamerlane (1827) 281
Of long delight, nor yet had deem'd
               Tamerlane (1827) 294
But a tremulous delight
               Tamerlane (1831) 92
His very voice is musical delight
               Tempora 69

Delighted
And my friends are all delighted
               Bridal Ballad (1837) 21
The winds ran off with it delighted
               Fairy-Land (1831) 20

Delightful
Those shrieks, delightful harmony
               Louisa 7

Delighting
Compose a sound delighting all to hear
               Valentine (1846) 18

Delirious
To the delirious eye, more lovely things
               Dreams 32

Deliriously
Deliriously sweet, was dropp'd from
Heaven   Al Aaraaf i 54

Dell
In many a star-lit grove, or moonlit dell
               Al Aaraaf ii 63
In the battle down the dell
               Bridal Ballad 11
Once it smiled a silent dell   Valley 1

D'Elormie
Thinking him dead D'Elormie
               Bridal Ballad 18

Demanded
Demanded but to die!—what sayeth the
Count?   Politian v 10

Democritus
Democritus of Thrace, who used to toss
over   Tempora 16

Demon
Of a demon in my view   Alone 22
And his eyes have all the seeming of a
demon that is dreaming
               Raven (1845) 105
A demon-light around my throne
               Tamerlane (1827) 27
Of some ill demon, with a power
               Tamerlane (1827) 173
Ah, what demon hath tempted me here?
               Ulalume 90

Demons
Nor the demons down under the sea
               Annabel Lee 31
And his eyes have all the seeming of a
demon's that is dreaming   Raven 105

Den
With chamois, I would seize his den
               Tamerlane (1827) 43

Denied
Maintained "the power of words"—
denied that ever   To³ 3

Dense
The soul that scarce (the billows are so
dense)   Al Aaraaf i 22

Denser
Then, methought, the air grew denser,
perfumed from an unseen censer
               Raven 79

Depart
I cannot depart   To Hunter 2

Departed
Joy's voice so peacefully departed
               Al Aaraaf i 8
I have dreamed of joy departed
               Dream 2
Of Joy departed   Politian ii 67
How many scenes of what departed bliss!
               Zante 5

Departs
Joy so peacefully departs
               Al Aaraaf (1831) i 23

Depend
But this is, now,—you may depend upon
it   Enigma 12

Depends
For thy lofty rank and fashion—much
depends   Politian i 25

Depth
From ev'ry depth of good and ill
               Alone 11
From the depth of each pallid lily-bell
               Valley (1845) 29

Descend
Let us descend!—'tis time
               Politian iii 95
Let us descend   Politian iii 100
Descend with me—the Duke may be
offended   Politian iii 105
Still will I not descend   Politian iii 111
Into the dust—so we descend together
               Politian iv 44
Descend together—and then—and then
perchance   Politian iv 45
Perennial tears descend in gems
               Valley 27

Descendeth
When the weary moon descendeth
               Departed 13

Descent
And high descent. We'll have him at the
wedding   Politian i 50

Descrying
Ah, this you'd have no trouble in descrying   Valentine (1846) 19

Desert
An oasis in the desert of the blest
               Al Aaraaf i 19

Was the velvet violet, wet with dews
　　　　　　　　　　Parody 6
Nightly their dews upon my head
　　　　　　　　　　Tamerlane 37
Eternal dews come down in drops
　　　　　　　　　　Valley 25

Dewy
An opiate vapor, dewy, dim　　Sleeper 3

Diadem
With stars is like a diadem
　　　　　　　　　　City (1831) 15
The fever'd diadem on my brow
　　　　　　　　　　Tamerlane 28

Diademmed
A diadem'd outlaw!　　Tamerlane 176

Dial
About twelve by the moon-dial
　　　　　　　　　　Fairy-Land 11

Dials
And star-dials pointed to morn
　　　　　　　　　　Ulalume 31
As the star-dials hinted of morn
　　　　　　　　　　Ulalume 32

Diamond
A window of one circular diamond, there
　　　　　　　　　　Al Aaraaf ii 22
In each idol's diamond eye　　City 33
Would have given a real diamond to such
　　as you　　　　Politian ii 54

Dian
But now, at length, dear Dian sank from
　　sight　　　　　　Helen² 48
And I said: " She is warmer than Dian
　　　　　　　　　　Ulalume 39

Diana
Hast thou not dragged Diana from her car
　　　　　　　　　　To Science 9

Did
On its roof did float and flow
　　　　　　　　　　Palace 10

Didst
Didst glide away. Only thine eyes re-
　　mained　　　　　Helen³ 51
But thou did'st not die too fair
　　　　　　　　　　Paean 34
Thou did'st not die too soon　　Paean 35
Ah, starry Hope! that didst arise
　　　　　　　　　　Paradise 8
Why didst thou sigh so deeply? Did I
　　sigh　　　　　　Politian i 7
Thou didst. Thou hast indulged
　　　　　　　　　　Politian i 11
What didst thou say, Jacinta
　　　　　　　　　　Politian ii 37, 42
Didst thou not speak of faith
　　　　　　　　　　Politian ii 92
Didst thou not hear it then
　　　　　　　　　　Politian iii 26
What didst thou say?　　Politian v 13
Thou wilt not fight with me didst say, Sir
　　Count　　　　　Politian v 64
Didst say thou darest not
　　　　　　　　　　Politian v 66
As thou didst when the stars above
　　　　　　　　　　Sarah 11

Die
Of their own dissolution, while they die
　　　　　　　　　　Al Aaraaf ii 18
Sweet was their death—with them to die
　　was rife　　　　Al Aaraaf ii 168
But thou did'st not die too fair
　　　　　　　　　　Paean 34
Thou did'st not die too soon　　Paean 35
O still more happy maiden who couldst
　　die!　　　　　Politian ii 14
I cannot die, having within my heart
　　　　　　　　　　Politian iii 43
And he shall die!　　Politian iv 87
And—he—shall—die!—alas!
　　　　　　　　　　Politian iv 88
Castiglione die　　Politian iv 89
To die ere I have lived　　Politian v 3
Demanded but to die!—what sayeth the
　　Count?　　　　Politian v 10
Scoundrel!—arise and die!
　　　　　　　　　　Politian v 75
O let me die　　　Politian v 76
Aspiringly, are damned, and die
　　　　　　　　　　Romance (1831) 57
Lying down to die, have suddenly arisen
　　　　　　　　　　To MLS 9

Died
His folly—pride—and passion—for he
　　died　　　　　　Acrostic 9
Of her who lov'd a mortal—and so died
　　　　　　　　　　Al Aaraaf i 47
And died, ere scarce exalted into birth
　　　　　　　　　　Al Aaraaf i 71
That smiled and died in this parterre,
　　enchanted　　　　Helen² 15
Died in the arms of the adoring airs
　　　　　　　　　　Helen² 35
An anthem for the queenliest dead that
　　ever died so young　　Lenore 6
A dirge for her the double dead in that
　　she died so young　　Lenore 7
And, when she fell in feeble health, ye
　　blessed her that she died　Lenore 9
That did to death the innocence that died,
　　and died so young?　　Lenore 12
My mother—my own mother, who died
　　early　　　　　　Mother 9
In June she died—in June
　　　　　　　　　　Paean (1836) 33
She died!—the maiden died!
　　　　　　　　　　Politian ii 13
" She died full young "—one Bossola
　　answers him　　Politian ii 18
She died　　　　　Politian ii 25

Dieds't
Thou died'st in thy life's June　Paean 33

Dies
These cheeks, where the worm never dies
　　　　　　　　　　Ulalume 43
At rest on ocean's brilliant dies
　　　　　　　　　　Serenade (1833) 5

Diest
And live, for now thou diest!
　　　　　　　　　　Politian iii 5

Different
In a different bed　　　Annie 50

Dignity
In dignity   Politian i 29
In proper dignity   Politian i 30

Dim
And bent o'er sheny mountain and dim
  plain   Al Aaraaf i 157
Who, musing, gazeth on the distance dim
                         Al Aaraaf ii 45
What guilty spirit, in what shrubbery
  dim   Al Aaraaf ii 174
Ianthe, dearest, see! how dim that ray!
                         Al Aaraaf ii 198
Dim was its little disk, and angel eyes
                         Al Aaraaf ii 253
Far down within the dim West   City 3
Silence; and Desolation! and dim Night
                         Coliseum 11
Happy in that dim possessing
                         Departed 31
Were it not for that dim meeting
                         Departed 33
From an ultimate dim Thule
                         Dream-Land 6
From this ultimate dim Thule
                         Dream-Land 56
Dim vales—and shadowy floods
                         Fairy-Land 1
At morn—at noon—at twilight dim
                         Hymn 1
Nodding above the dim abyss   Irene 21
An Eden of that dim lake   Lake 23
Is but a dim-remembered story
                         Palace 39
(Dim gulf!) my spirit hovering lies
                         Paradise 12
Within the valleys dim and brown
                         Serenade 11
Who haunteth the dim regions where hath
  trod   Silence (1840) 14
An opiate vapor, dewy, dim   Sleeper 3
While the dim sheeted ghosts go by
                         Sleeper (1843) 44
Far in the forest, dim and old
                         Sleeper 48
Dim, vanities of dreams by night
                         Tamerlane 121
Grows dim around me—death is near
                         Tamerlane (1827) 16
Whose failing sight will grow dim
                         Tamerlane (1827) 316
Dim! tho' looking on all bright!
                         Tamerlane (1827) 322
An Eden of that dim lake?
                         Tamerlane (1831) 99
It was hard by the dim lake of Auber
                         Ulalume 6
We noted not the dim lake of Auber
                         Ulalume 26
Well I know, now, this dim lake of Auber
                         Ulalume 91

Dimly
So dimly shone from afar
                         Dream (1827) 18

Dimmer
The sands of Time grow dimmer as they
  run   Al Aaraaf i 140

And dimmer nothings which were real
                         Tamerlane 122

Dimness
The dimness of this world: that greyish
  green   Al Aaraaf ii 29

Dims
Of Science dims the mirror of our joy
                         Al Aaraaf ii 164

Dint
Stable, opaque, immortal—all by dint
                         Enigma 13

Dipt
And so, being young and dipt in folly
                         Romance (1831) 27

Dirge
A dirge for her the doubly dead in that
  she died so young   Lenore 7
In a dirge of melody   Lake (1829) 10
In a dirge-like melody   Lake (1845) 10
And I—to-night my heart is light:—no
  dirge will I upraise   Lenore 25
In a dirge of melody
                         Tamerlane (1831) 88

Dirges
Till the dirges of his Hope that melancholy burden bore   Raven 65

Disagree
Children, we disagree
                         Politian i 64

Disappeared
And in an instant all things disappeared
                         Helen 29

Disaster
Caught from some unhappy master whom
  unmerciful Disaster   Raven 63

Disconsolate
Disconsolate linger—grief that hangs her
  head   Al Aaraaf 62

Discordant
To a discordant melody   Palace 44

Discourse
Thus, in discourse, the lovers whiled away
                         Al Aaraaf ii 261
Much I marvelled this ungainly fowl to
  hear discourse so plainly   Raven 49

Discover
With forms that no man can discover
                         Dream-Land 11
Whose forms we can't discover
                         Fairy-Land 3
We can discover a moon-ray
                         Fairy-Land (1831) 31

Discursive
I'm apt to be discursive in my style
                         Tempora 37

Discuss
Be given our lady's bidding to discuss
                         Al Aaraaf ii 246

Disenthral
And when old Time my wing did disenthral   Al Aaraaf ii 218

Disgrace
But damn it, sir, I deem it a disgrace
                         Tempora 31

Dishonor
And weep!—oh! to dishonor
                         Paean 7

Dishonored
Could the dishonored Lalage abide?
                              Politian iv 26

Disk
Dim was its little disk, and angel eyes
                              Al Aaraaf ii 253

Dismal
By the dismal tarns and pools
                              Dream-Land 29

Dispute
Philosophers have often held dispute
                              Tempora 73

Dissever
Into a shower dissever   Fairy-Land 40
Can ever dissever my soul from the soul
                              Annabel Lee 32

Dissolution
Of their own dissolution, while they die
                              Al Aaraaf ii 18

Dissyllables
Two words—two foreign soft dissyllables
                              To³ 7

Distance
Who, amusing, gazeth on the distance dim
                              Al Aaraaf ii 45

Distant
To distant spheres, from time to time, she
   rode   Al Aaraaf i 24
Tell this soul with sorrow laden if, within
   the distant Aidenn   Raven 93
Thy distant fire   Star 22

Distinct
Distinct with its duplicate horn
                              Ulalume 38

Distinctly
Yet the ear distinctly tells   Bells 61
Ah, distinctly I remember it was in the
   bleak December   Raven 67

Disturb
Disturb my senses—go   Politian ii 79

Ditty
What a liquid ditty floats   Bells 22

Divided
Because divided it may chance be shaken
                              Tempora 46

Divine
The only king by right divine
                              Divine Right 1
Save only the divine light in thine eyes
                              Helen² 37
Thine eyes are wild—tempt not the wrath
   divine   Politian ii 110
Its fount is holier—more divine
                              Tamerlane 10
For passionate love is still divine
                              Tamerlane (1827) 153
To write is human—not to write divine
                              To Margaret 7
Divine—a talisman—an amulet
                              Valentine 6

Diviner
Richer, far wilder, far diviner visions
                              To³ 13

Divining
This and more I sat divining, with my
   head at ease reclining   Raven 75

Divulge
Divulge the secrets of thy embassy
                              Al Aaraaf 147

Dizzy
Perhaps my brain grew dizzy—but the
   world   Al Aaraaf ii 233

Do
And I have not forgotten it—thou'lt do
   me   Politian v 32
You will not read the riddle though you
   do the best you can do
                              Valentine (1846) 20

Doctrine
Of which sound doctrine I believe each
   tittle   Tempora 7

Does
Does it not? unto this palace of the Duke
                              Politian iii 64

Dog
Up like a dog-star in this bower
                              Fairy-Land (1831) 13
You dog   Politian i 40
The page of life and grin at the dog-ears
                              Tempora 17

Dogmas
And spite all dogmas current in all ages
                              Tempora 77

Doing
And I have other reasons for so doing
                              Elizabeth 5

Dome
A dome, by linked light from Heaven let
   down   Al Aaraaf ii 20

Domes
Up domes—up spires—up kingly halls
                              City 17

Dominion
In the monarch Thought's dominion
                              Palace 5
That you are changing sadly your do-
   minion   Tempora 2

Don
"Seldom we find," says Solomon Don
   Dunce   Enigma 1
Trash of all trash!—how can a lady don
   it   Enigma 5

Donn'd
And donn'd a visionary crown
                              Tamerlane 156

Door
Against whose sounding door she hath
   thrown   Irene 69
Was the fair palace door   Palace 26
Through the pale door   Palace 46
And the rivulet that ran before the door
                              Politian ii 86
As of some one gently rapping, rapping at
   my chamber door   Raven 4
" 'Tis some visitor," I muttered, " tap-
   ping at my chamber door   Raven 5
" 'Tis some visitor entreating entrance at
   my chamber door   Raven 16
Some late visitor entreating entrance at
   my chamber door   Raven 17
And so faintly you came tapping, tapping
   at my chamber door   Raven 22

It would weigh down your flight
                    Al Aaraaf ii 95
Which leaps down to the flower
                    Al Aaraaf ii 121
And looks so sweetly down on Beauty's
    hair   Al Aaraaf ii 187
And scowls on starry worlds that down
    beneath it lie   Al Aaraaf ii 193
Far down within the crystal of the lake
                Al Aaraaf ii (1829) 40
Nor the demons down under the sea
                    Annabel Lee 31
And so, all the night-tide, I lie down by
    the side   Annabel Lee 38
Down under the ground   Annie 44
In the battle down the dell
                   Bridal Ballad 11
Far down within the dim West   City 3
No rays from the holy heaven come down
                        City 12
Death looks gigantically down   City 29
Down, down that town shall settle hence
                        City 51
Ever drew down from out the quiet
    stars!   Coliseum 16
Down the Valley of the Shadow
                      Eldorado 21
Born and brought up with their snouts
    deep down in the mud of the Frog-
    Pond   Experiments 8
Comes down—still down—and down
                   Fairy-Land 15
And so come down again
                   Fairy-Land 43
Sit down beside me, Isabel
                Fairy-Land (1831) 1
Sit down, sit down—how came we here?
                Fairy-Land (1831) 9
Has sent a ray down with a tune
               Fairy-Land (1831) 23
Saw only them until the moon went down
                       Helen² 41
Then sinks within (weigh'd down by wo)
                       Irene 59
Glides down the Stygian river!
                    Lenore (1843) 4
Down within the golden east   Nis 4
Eternal dews come down in gems!
                    Nis (1836) 48
Was plumed with the down of the
    humming-bird   Parody 2
Sit down!—let not my presence trouble
    you   Politian ii 3
Sit down!—for I am humble, most
    humble   Politian ii 4
As go down in the library and bring me
                    Politian ii 30
Let us go down   Politian iii 87
Let us go down, I pray you
                    Politian iii 106
I go not down to-night Politian iii 113
That we go down unhonored and forgot-
    ten   Politian iv 43
Far down within some shadowy lake
                       Romance 4
Its down upon my spirit flings
                      Romance 17

The wearied light is dying down
                      Serenade 13
That, o'er the floor and down the wall
                       Sleeper 28
And the stars shall look not down
                       Spirits 12
With desp'rate energy 't hath beaten
    down   Stanzas¹ 31
The rain came down upon my head
                     Tamerlane 55
Of a high mountain which look'd down
                    Tamerlane 140
Lion ambition is chain'd down—
                    Tamerlane 160
Bow'd down in sorrow, and in shame
                Tamerlane (1827) 23
Bow'd down with its own glory grows
               Tamerlane (1831) 222
To gain an empire, and throw down
               Tamerlane (1827) 243
Lying down to die, have suddenly arisen
                       To MLS 9
To come down and see   To Hunter 11
So tear down the temples   Triumph 7
It was down by the dank tarn of Auber
                      Ulalume 8
Their sulphurous currents down Yaanek
                      Ulalume 16
That groan as they roll down Mount
    Yaanek   Ulalume 18
(Though once we had journeyed down
    here)   Ulalume 27
That I journeyed—I journeyed down
    here!   Ulalume 87
That I brought a dread burden down here
                      Ulalume 88
Eternal dews come down in drops
                      Valley 25
Comes down with the rush of a storm
                       Worm 36

Downright
Jew, or downright upright nutmegs out of
    a pine-knot   Experiments 10

Downward
But with a downward, tremulous motion
    thro'   Al Aaraaf ii 239

Downy
As sprang that yellow star from downy
    hours   Al Aaraaf i 155
Owl-downy nonsense that the faintest puff
                       Enigma 7

Dowry
As nuptial dowry—a queen's crown
               Tamerlane (1827) 244

Dragged
Has thou not dragged Diana from her car
                    To Science 9

Drama
That motley drama—oh, be sure
                       Worm 17

Drank
I have drank of a water   Annie 37
Who read Anacreon, and drank wine
                  Romance (1831) 20
And my brain drank their venom then
                Tamerlane (1827) 41

Dreams
Young dreams still hovering on their
  drowsy flight   Al Aaraaf ii 158
For the moon never beams without bring-
  ing me dreams   Annabel Lee 34
Continuing—as dreams have been to me
                              Dreams 10
I' the summer sky, in dreams of living
  light   Dreams 14
Dreams! in their vivid coloring of life
                              Dreams 29
And all my nightly dreams   Paradise 22
Give not thy soul to dreams: the camp—
  the court   Politian iii 21
Doubting, dreaming dreams no mortal
  eved dared to dream before   Raven 26
But dreams—of those who dream as I
                    Romance (1831) 56
('Mid dreams of an unholy night)
                          Tamerlane 42
Dim, vanities of dreams by night
                         Tamerlanc 121
The bowers whereat, in dreams I see
                               To¹ 1
Threshold of the wide open gate of dreams
                              To³ 22
In dreams of thee, and therein knows
                              To F 6
While, on dreams relying   To Hunter 6

Dreamy
Which dreamy poets name " the music of
  the sphere "   Al Aaraaf i 125
In dreamy gardens, where do lie
                    Al Aaraaf i (1831) 12
Dreamy maidens all the day
                    Al Aaraaf i (1831) 13
In a dreamy sleep   Al Aaraaf ii 117
There the vague and dreamy trees
                              Nis 35

Drear
See! on yon drear and rigid bier low lies
  thy love, Lenore!   Lenore 4
Drear path, alas! where grows   To F 3

Dreariest
Whose waning is the dreariest one
                          Tamerlane 208

Dreariness
Such dreariness a heaven at all
                        City (1831) 19
In that time of dreariness, will seem
                          Tamerlane 204

Dreary
Once upon a midnight dreary, while I
  pondered, weak and weary   Raven 1

Dregs
Drinking the cup of pleasure to the dregs
                          Politian i 60

Dress
To thy dress and equipage—they are over
  plain   Politian i 24
Strange is thy pallor! strange thy dress!
                           Sleeper 34

Dressed
Now thou art dress'd for Paradise
                    Fairy-Land (1831) 4

Drew
Even drew down from out the quiet stars!
                            Coliseum 16
When from thy balmy lips I drew
                              Sarah 16
On mountain soil I first drew life
                          Tamerlane 35

Drink
Amid thy shadows, and so drink within
                            Coliseum 8

Drinking
Drinking the cup of pleasure to the dregs
                            Politian i 60

Drip
For the tears that drip all over
                          Fairy-Land 4

Dripped
Or the sun ray dripp'd all red   Nis 23

Dripping
Is dripping from that golden rim
                              Irene 10
And softly dripping, drop by drop
                            Sleeper 5

Driven
And driven the Hamadryad from the
  wood   To Science 10
Ah, by no wind those clouds are driven
                            Valley 17

Droopingly
His pinions were bent droopingly
                          Tamerlane 189

Drop
There the eternal dews do drop   Nis 34
I would have thee drop   Politian i 19
I will drop them   Politian i 22
And softly dripping, drop by drop
                            Sleeper 5
Laughingly through the lattice drop
                           Sleeper 21
No more—like dew-drop from the grass
                           Spirits 22

Dropped
Deliriously sweet, was dropp'd from
  Heaven   Al Aaraaf i 54
The sun-ray dropp'd, in Lemnos, with a
  spell   Al Aaraaf ii 203

Drops
Ye crimson life-drops, stay   Louisa 2
Eternal dews come down in drops
                            Valley 25

Dross
Oh, nothing of the dross of ours
                          Al Aaraaf i 11

Drowned
Drowned in a bath   Annie 71
In veils, and drowned in tears   Worm 4

Drowsily
How drowsily it weigh'd them into night!
                          Al Aaraaf ii 207
Drowsily over halls
                    Fairy-Land (1831) 59
Steals drowsily and musically
                           Sleeper 7

Drowsy
Such as the drowsy shepherd on his bed
                          Al Aaraaf ii 2

Drowsy

Young dreams still hovering on their drowsy flight   Al Aaraaf ii 158
Over every drowsy thing   Fairy-Land 24
An influence dewy, drowsy, dim   Irene 9
With drowsy head and folded wing
Romance 2

Drudges

To be drudges to the last
Al Aaraaf i 93

Drunk

And I am drunk with love   Paean 23

Drunken

But 't was not with the drunken hope
Tamerlane (1827) 2

Drunkenness

And after-drunkenness of soul
Romance (1831) 42

Dry

She has seen that the tears are not dry on
Ulalume 42

Due

Is due unto thy lyre   Israfel (1841) 19

Duke

Madam—the Duke!   Politian i 37
Does it not? unto this palace of the Duke
Politian iii 64
The hour is growing late—the Duke awaits us   Politian iii 88
Unto the Duke   Politian iii 98
Descend with me—the Duke may be offended   Politian iii 105
Apology unto the Duke for me
Politian iii 112
Baldazzar, Duke of Surrey
Politian v 53

Dull

In slightly sinking, the dull tide   City 45
Vulture whose wings are dull realities?
To Science 4

Dunce

"Seldom we find," says Solomon Don Dunce   Enigma 1
Were you not something of a dunce, my dear   Valentine (1846) 20

Duplicate

Arose with a duplicate horn   Ulalume 36
Distinct with its duplicate horn
Ulalume 38

Durst

I knew thou wouldst not, couldst not, durst not go   Politian iv 100

Dusky

Some eager spirit flapp'd his dusky wing
Al Aaraaf ii 27
In dusky grandeur to my eyes
Tamerlane (1827) 363

Dust

The motes, and dust, and flies
Fairy-Land (1831) 35
Into the dust—so we descend together
Politian iv 44
Wings till they trailed in the dust
Ulalume 57
Plumes till they trailed in the dust
Ulalume 59
Till they sorrowfully trailed in the dust
Ulalume 60

Duties

Shall then absolve thee of all farther duties   Politian iii 37

Dutifull

Virginal Lillian, rigidly, humblily dutiful
Experiments 1

Duty

To duty beseeming   Al Aaraaf ii 82
Was Love, the blind, near sober Duty known?   Al Aaraaf ii 180
My duty, to be saved by their bright light
Helen² 58
Where deep thoughts are a duty
Israfel 24
A troop of Echoes, whose sweet duty
Palace 29
And love—a simple duty   To FSO 8

Dwell

Its echo dwelleth and will dwell
Al Aaraaf i 10
That its echo still doth dwell
Al Aaraaf i (1831) 24
And there—oh! may my weary spirit dwell   Al Aaraaf ii 172
They that dwell up in the steeple
Bells 80
Where swell the Ghouls   Dream-Land 30
In Heaven a spirit doth dwell   Israfel 1
If I could dwell   Israfel 45
Dwell in a seraph's breast than thine
Tamerlane (1827) 152
To him, whose loving spirit will dwell
Tamerlane (1827) 311
Where the people did not dwell
Valley 2

Dwellest

Spirit! that dwellest where
Al Aaraaf i 82

Dwelleth

Its echo dwelleth and will dwell
Al Aaraaf i 10

Dwelling

That from his marble dwelling peered out
Al Aaraaf ii 33
A brighter dwelling-place is here for thee
Al Aaraaf ii 228

Dwellings

Adorning then the dwellings of the sky
Al Aaraaf ii 19
The starry and quiet dwellings of the blest   Politian iv 48

Dwells

Little—oh! little dwells in thee
Al Aaraaf i (1831) 16
How it dwells   Bells 28
One dwells in lonely places   Silence 6

Dwelt

It lit on hills Achaian, and there dwelt
Al Aaraaf i 34
I dwelt alone   Eulalie 1
Hath dwelt, and he where   Israfel 47
Thus I remember having dwelt
Tamerlane 81
I dwelt not long in Samarcand
Tamerlane (1827) 359

Dwindled
The dwindled hills! begirt with bowers
Tamerlane 143

Dyes
At rest on ocean's brilliant dyes
Serenade 5

Dying
And each separate dying ember wrought
its ghost upon the floor   Raven 8
Dying along the troubled sky
Romance (1831) 14
The wearied light is dying down
Serenade 13
Kind solace in a dying hour!
Tamerlane 1
As if 't were not the dying hour
Tamerlane (1827) 342
And my hopes are dying   To Hunter 5
And, over each dying form
Worm (1834) 34

Each
A wreath that twined each starry form
around   Al Aaraaf i 40
Lurk'd in each cornice, round each archi-
trave   Al Aaraaf ii 31
Each hindering thing   Al Aaraaf ii 93
What wonder? for each star is eye-like
there   Al Aaraaf ii 186
In each idol's diamond eye   City 33
Where each star most faintly gloweth
Departed 3
When each pale star earthward bendeth
Departed 14
By each spot the most unholy
Dream-Land 31
In each nook most melancholy
Dream-Land 32
Each poet—if a poet—in pursuing
Elizabeth 7
And the like upon each tress
Paean (1836) 28
And the silken, sad, uncertain rustling of
each purple curtain   Raven 13
And each separate dying ember wrought
its ghost upon the floor   Raven 18
But 't will leave thee, as each star
Spirits (1827) 19
Each hour before us—but then only, bid
Stanzas[1] 22
Of which sound doctrine I believe each
tittle   Tempora 7
Each fit to furnish forth four hours' de-
bate   Tempora 22
But, taking one by each hand, merely
groul   Tempora 28
Hast thou not spoilt a story in each star?
To Science (1831) 11
Now each visitor shall confess
Valley 9
From the depth of each pallid lily-bell
Valley (1845) 29
And, over each quivering form
Worm 34

Eager
Some eager spirit flapp'd his dusky wing
Al Aaraaf ii 27

Such eager eyes, there lies, I say, perdu
Valentine 14

Eagerly
So eagerly around about to hang
Al Aaraaf i 45
Eagerly I wished the morrow:—vainly I
had sought to borrow   Raven 13

Eagle
With eagle gaze along the firmament
Al Aaraaf ii 195
Thence sprang I—as the eagle from his
tower   Al Aaraaf ii 219
See the White Eagle soaring aloft to the
sky   Campaign 1
Then here's the White Eagle, full daring
is he   Campaign 3
Here, where the mimic eagle glared in
gold   Coliseum 18
Or the stricken eagle soar!
Paradise 20
When Hope, the eagle that tower'd, could
see   Tamerlane 187
The light'ning of his eagle eye
Tamerlane 239

Ear
A sound of silence on the startled ear
Al Aaraaf i 124
That stole upon the ear, in Eyraco
Al Aaraaf ii 42
That stealeth ever on the ear of him
Al Aaraaf ii 44
All softly in ear   Al Aaraaf ii 145
In the startled ear of night   Bells 39
Yet the ear, it fully knows   Bells 57
Yet the ear distinctly tells   Bells 61
Thus hums the moon within the ear
Irene 25
Which steal within the slumberer's ear
Irene (1836) 28
And yet the sweetest that ear ever heard!
Politian iii 53
Gurgled within my ear the crush
Tamerlane 61
When passing from the earth, that ear
Tamerlane (1829) 18
Now sounded to her heedless ear
Tamerlane (1827) 240

Ears
The page of life and grin at the dog-ears
Tempora 17

Earl
Politian, Earl of Leicester!
Politian i 42
Of Britain, Earl of Leicester?
Politian i 45
What ails thee, Earl Politian?
Politian iii 90
Alas, proud Earl   Politian iv 50
Now, Earl of Leicester   Politian iv 50
Between the Earl Politian and himself
Politian v 12
Unto this man, that I, the Earl of Lei-
cester   Politian v 34
The Earl of Leicester here!
Politian v 45
I am the Earl of Leicester, and thou seest
Politian v 46

Earthward
When each pale star earthward bendeth
                              Departed 14

Ease
Of giant pasturage lying at his ease
                              Al Aaraaf ii 3
This and more I sat divining, with my
    head at ease reclining   Raven 75

Easily
As easily as through a Naples bonnet
                              Enigma 4
Of that Egyptian queen, winning so easily
                              Politian ii 23

East
Down within the golden east   Nis 4

Easy
In easy drapery falls   Fairy-Land 19

Eaten
Time-eaten towers that tremble not!
                              City 7

Eating
Its own core my wild heart eating
                              Departed 35

Ebbs
How the danger ebbs and flows
                              Bells 60

Eblis
I do not believe that Eblis hath
                              Tamerlane 229

Ebon
Thro' the ebon air, besilvering the pall
                              Al Aaraaf ii 17
Then this ebon bird beguiling my sad
    fancy into smiling   Raven (1848) 43

Ebony
Fills me with dread—thy ebony crucifix
                              Politian ii 82
Thy raiments and thy ebony cross affright
    me!   Politian ii 102
Then this ebony bird beguiling my sad
    fancy into smiling   Raven 43

Echo
Its echo dwelleth and will dwell
                              Al Aaraaf i 10
That its echo still doth dwell
                              Al Aaraaf i (1831) 24
And the echo of thine own
                              Politian iii 20
This I whispered, and an echo murmured
    back the word, " Lenore! "   Raven 29
She ne'er shall force an echo more
                              Sleeper 58

Echoes
" Not all "—the Echoes answer me—" not
    all!   Coliseum 33
A troop of Echoes, whose sweet duty
                              Palace 29

Echoing
And the deep thunder's echoing roar
                              Tamerlane (1827) 53

Ecstasies
The ecstasies above   Israfel 35

Ecstasy
With the last ecstasy of satiate life
                              Al Aaraaf ii 169

Ecstatic
Their odorous souls in an ecstatic death
                              Helen² 13

Eden
An Eden of that dim lake
            Lake 23; Tamerlane (1831) 99
An Eden of bland repose   To F 7

Edis
Which blazes upon Edis' Shrine.
                    Tamerlane (1827) 156

E'en
E'en then who knew this iron heart
                              Tamerlane 73

Egyptian
Of that Egyptian queen, winning so easily
                              Politian ii 23

Eidolon
Where an Eidolon, named NIGHT
                    Dream-Land 3; 53

Eight
Instead of two sides, Job has nearly eight
                              Tempora 21

Eires
With gentle names—Eires and Charmion!
                              Politian ii 27

Eld
Vastness! and Age! and Memories of
    Eld!   Coliseum 10

Elderado
'T is—oh, 't is an Elderado!
                              Dream-Land 42
In search of Eldorado   Eldorado 6
That looked like Eldorado   Eldorado 12
This land of Eldorado!   Eldorado 18
If you seek for Eldorado!   Eldorado 24

Electric
And purified in their electric fire
                              Helen² 59

Element
To bathe in the pure element   Irene 50
Flounce like a fish in his new element
                              Tempora 50

Elf
Bring thee to meet his shadowy nameless
    elf   Silence 13
But if he won't he shall, the stupid elf
                              Tempora 90

Elfin
The Elfin from the green grass, and from
    me   To Science 13

Eliza
Eliza!—let thy generous heart   To F 50

Elizabeh
Elizabeth, it is in vain you say
                              Acrostic 1
Elizabeth, it surely is most fit
                              Elizabeth 1

Ellen
Is Ellen King, and were she mine
                              Divine Right 2

Eloquent
Into my heart of hearts! that eloquent
    voice   Politian iii 59
Three eloquent words, oft uttered in the
    hearing   Valentine (1849) 15

Else
Else how, when in the holy grove
Tamerlane 231
Elysian
And sanctified in their elysian fire
Helen² 60
Elysium
An image of Elysium lies   Serenade 6
Embassy
My embassy is given   Al Aaraaf i 115
Divulge the secrets of thy embassy
Al Aaraaf i 147
Ember
And each separate dying ember wrought
its ghost upon the floor   Raven 8
Emblem
Thou art an emblem of the glow
River 3
Emblems
Fit emblems of the model of her world
Al Aaraaf i 37
Embraced
Embrac'd two hamlets—those our own
Tamerlane (1827) 222
Eminence
Can struggle to its destin'd eminence
Al Aaraaf i 23
Of a mountain's eminence Fairy-Land 17
Empire
Ascend thy empire and so be
Al Aaraaf i 112
The magic empire of a flame
Tamerlane (1827) 104
The mystic empire and high power
Tamerlane (1827) 186
To gain an empire, and throw down
Tamerlane (1827) 243
Empires
Of empires—with the captive's prayer
Tamerlane 62
Striding o'er empires haughtily
Tamerlane 175
Employed
Employed in even the theses of the
school·   Elizabeth 13
Emptiness
Upon thy emptiness—a knell
Tamerlane 26
Empurpled
Amid empurpled vapors, far away
To³ 26
Empyrean
Empyrean splendor o'er th' unchained
soul·   Al Aaraaf i 21
Save when, between th' Empyrean and
that ring   Al Aaraaf ii 26
A thousand seraphs burst th' Empyrean
thro'   Al Aaraaf ii 157
Enamelled
High on a mountain of enamell'd head
Al Aaraaf ii 1
Henceforth I hold thy flower-enamelled
shore   Zante 12
Enamoured
The enamoured moon   Israfel 10

Encamp
Where the toad and the newt encamp
Dream-Land 28
Enchanted
Roses than grew in an enchanted garden
Helen² 9
That smiled and died in this parterre,
enchanted   Helen² 15
Ah, bear in mind this garden was
enchanted   Helen² 30
O'er the enchanted solitude
Nis (1836) 30
Desolate yet all undaunted, on this desert
land enchanted·   Raven 87
Of an enchanted life, which seems
Tamerlane (1827) 171
Like some enchanted far-off isle   To F 9
Encircles
Not all the wonder that encircles us
Coliseum 42
Enclosed
To the weak human eye enclosed
Dream-Land (1845) 46
Encumbered
Encumber'd with dew   Al Aaraaf ii 85
End
For the same end as before
Fairy-Land 36
Thou hast no end to gain—no heart to
break   Politian ii 72
At the end of our path a liquescent
Ulalume 33
And we passed to the end of the vista
Ulalume 75
Endeavor
And a resolute endeavor   Bells 48
Endeth
Thus endeth the history—and her maids
Politian ii 25
Endless
Shall be an endless theme of praise
To FSO 7
Endlessly
Lakes that endlessly outspread
Dream-Land 17
Endued
Endued with neither soul, nor sense, nor
art,   Elizabeth 11
Endure
That pleasure "to endure!"   To⁴ 38
Endure!—no—no—defy   To⁴ 40
Enduring
Which is enduring, so be deep!
Sleeper 38
Enduring joys and fleeting cares,
Stanzas² 6
Endymion
Endymion, recollect, when Luna tried
Arcostic 7
Endymion nodding from above
Serenade 9
Energetic
Giv'n by the energetic might
Tamerlane (1827) 187
Energy
From the wild energy of wantom haste
Al Aaraaf ii 52

With desp'rate energy 't hath beaten
down Stanzas[1] 31

Enforced
Zanthippe's talents had enforced so well
Acrostic 4

Engaged
This I sat engaged in guessing, but no
syllable expressing Raven 73

England
In merry England—never so plaintively
Politian iii 78

English
The song is English, and I oft have heard
it Politian iii 77

Enjewel
That enjewel its breast
Al Aaraaf ii 135

Enkindle
Their office is to illumine and enkindle
Helen[2] 57

Enormous
You know that most enormous flower
Fairy-Land (1831) 11

Enough
And, veritably, Sol is right enough
Enigma 9

Enshrined
Thine eyes, in Heaven of heart enshrined
To[1] 5

Entablatures
Whose entablatures intertwine
City (1831) 29
These vague entablatures—this crumbling
frieze Coliseum 28

Entered
As of one who entered madly into life
Politian i 59
Enthralling love, my Adeline
Serenade 17

Entity
A type of that twin entity which springs
Silence 3

Entombed
Of the old time entombed Palace 40
Inurned and entombed!—now, in a tone
Politian ii 68
How many thoughts of what entombed
hopes! Zante 6

Entombing
And thou, a ghost, amid the entombing
trees Helen[2] 50

Entrance
'T is some visitor entreating entrance
at my chamber door Raven 16
Some late visitor entreating entrance at
my chamber door; Raven 17

Entranced
Entranc'd, the spirit loves to lie
Irene 43
Seven Pleiades entranced in Heaven
Serenade 7
Gazing, entranced, adown the gorgeous
vista To[3] 23

Entreating
'T is some visitor entreating entrance at
my chamber door Raven 16

Some late visitor entreating entrance at
my chamber door Raven 17

Environs
In Heaven, and all its environs, the leaf
Al Aaraaf i 60
In the environs of Heaven
Al Aaraaf i 117

Envy
Virtues that challenge envy's praise
Stanzas 7
Might envy; her young heart the shrine
Tamerlane 89

Envying
Went envying her and me
Annabel Lee 22

Enwrapped
Upon this page, enwrapped from every
reader Valentine 4

Enwritten
What wild heart-histories seemed to lie
enwritten Helen[2] 42
Enwritten upon this page whereon are
peering Valentine 13

Ephemeral
Bubbles—ephemeral and so transparent
Enigma 11

Epiphanes
Who is king but Epiphanes?
Triumph 1, 3
There is none but Epiphanes
Triumph 5

Equipage
To thy dress and equipage—they are over
plain Politian i 24

Ere
And died, ere scarce exalted into birth
Al Aaraaf i 71
Pores for a moment, ere it go Irene 56
Pause ere too late!—oh, be not—be not
rash! Politian ii 111
To die ere I have lived Politian v 3
Ere, in a peasant's lowly guise
Tamerlane (1827) 360

Eros
And Sorrow shall be no more, and Eros
be all Politian iv 77

Err
Do err at times Politian v 57

Error
Sweet was that error—sweeter still that
death Al Aaraaf ii 162
Sweet was that error—ev'n with us the
breath Al Aaraaf ii 163
Which Error's glitter cannot blind.
Stanzas[3] 19

Erst
Inmate of Highest stars, where erst it
sham'd Al Aaraaf i 51

Escape
For at a ball what fair one can escape
Tempora 55

Essence
An essence—powerful to destroy
Happiest Day 23
The unembodied essence, and no more
Stanzas[1] 14

And I would feel its essence stealing
                    Tamelane (1829) 48

Estate
  From Hell unto a high estate within the
    utmost Heaven   Lenore 21
  Assailed the monarch's high estate
                    Palace 34

Eternal
  The eternal voice of God is passing by
                    Al Aaraaf i 131
  Have gone to their eternal rest   City 5
  Thro' an eternal day   Louisa 4
  Eternal dews come down in gems
                    Nis (1836) 48
  By what eternal streams   Paradise 26
  Think of eternal things   Politian ii 75
  Of late, eternal Condor years
                    Romance 11
  For in the eternal city thou shalt do me
                    Politian iii 34
  Beneath the eternal sky of Thought
                    Stanzas² 24
  It falls from an eternal shrine
                    Tamerlane (1827) 14
  Eternal dews come down in drops
                    Valley 25

Eternally
  But should it be—that dream eternally
                    Dreams 9

Eternity
  In Eternity—we feel   Al Aaraaf i 99
  Apart from Heaven's Eternity—and yet
    how far from Hell! Al Aaraaf ii 173
  Of an Eternity should bring the morrow
                    Dreams 3
  Are flashing thro' Eternity
                    Tamerlane 228

Ether
  Into the sunlit ether, caught the ray
                    Al Aaraaf ii 8
  She rolls through an ether of sighs
                    Ulalume 40

Ethereal
  In what ethereal dances   Paradise 25

Eulalie
  Till the fair and gentle Eulalie became
    my blushing bride   Eulalie 4
  Till the yellow-haired young Eulalie be-
    came my smiling bride   Eulalie 5
  Can vie with the modest Eulalie's most
    unregarded curl   Eulalie 12
  Can compare with the bright-eyed Eula-
    lie's most humble and careless curl
                    Eulalie 13
  While ever to her dear Eulalie upturns
    her matron eye   Eulalie 20
  While ever to her young Eulalie upturns
    her violet eye   Eulalie 21

Euphony
  What a gush of Euphony voluminously
    wells!   Bells 26

Evangelists
  The Holy Evangelists   Politian ii 31

Eve
  The single-mooned eve!—Earth we plight
                    Al Aaraaf i 152

Of sunken suns at eve—at noon of night
                    Al Aaraaf ii 9
She seemed not thus upon that autumn
  eve   Al Aaraaf ii 200
That eve—that eve—I should remember
  well   Al Aaraaf ii 202

Even
  All Nature speaks, and ev'n ideal things
                    Al Aaraaf i 128
  Than ev'n thy glowing bosom beats
    withal   Al Aaraaf ii 217
  Sweet was that error—ev'n with us the
    breath   Al Aaraaf ii 163
  Employed in even the theses of the
    school   Elizabeth 13
  Another brow may ev'n inherit
                    Happiest Day 10
  Ev'n then I felt—that brightest hour
                    Happiest Day 19
  While even in the meridian glare of day
                    Helen² 64
  With the rapid Pleiads, even   Israfel 13
  Whose wild'ring thought could even make
                    Lake (1827) 22
  Nothing, fair cousin, nothing—not even
    deep sorrow   Politian i 17
  There is an imp would follow me even
    there!   Politian iii 16
  There is an imp hath followed me even
    there!   Politian iii 17
  Oh! I am sick, sick, sick, even unto death
                    Politian iii 29
  Is even that Alessandra of whom he
    spoke   Politian iii 67
  Even for thy woes I love thee—even for
    thy woes   Politian iv 21
  Even unto death   Politian v 89
  And even the greybeard will o'erlook
                    Romance (1831) 65
  To mar the silence ev'n with lute
                    Serenade 4
  Which ev'n to my impassion'd mind
                    Tamerlane (1827) 92
  Which ev'n upon this perilous brink
                    Tamerlane (1827) 105
  Ev'n childhood knows the human heart
                    Tamerlane (1827) 126
  Ev'n such as from th' accursed time
                    Tamerlane (1827) 145
  Than even the seraph harper Israfel
                    To³ 14
  Not even one lonely rose   To F 4
  Uneasily, from morn till even
                    Valley 19

Evening
  Proud evening star   Star 15
  That soul will hate the ev'ning mist
                    Tamerlane 195
  Withering at the ev'ning hour
                    Tamerlane (1827) 391

Everlasting
  But there! that everlasting pall!
                    City (1831) 17

Everlastingly
  Rustling everlastingly   Nis 39

Evermore
Mountains toppling evermore
Dream-Land 13
And sparkling evermore   Palace 28
Nameless here for evermore   Raven 12
With its Phantom chased for evermore
Worm 19

Every
The mournful hope that every throb
Octavia 8
To ev'ry heart a barrier and a ban
Al Aaraaf i 149
And every sculptur'd cherub thereabout
Al Aaraaf ii 32
And they, and ev'ry mossy spring were
holy   Al Aaraaf ii 188
From ev'ry depth of good and ill
Alone 11
They have sever'd ev'ry vow   Ballad 2
For every sound that floats   Bells 76
Every moment of the night
Fairy-Land 7
Over every drowsy thing—
Fairy-Land 24
The mournful hope that every throb
Octavia 8
And every gentle air that dallied
Palace 13
In every tuneful thing around   Sarah 5
In every deed shall mingle, love
Serenade 25
Prophetic tones from every line
Stanzas² 3
On which my every hope and thought
Tamerlane 90
A snare in every human path
Tamerlane 230
And felt, with ev'ry flying hour
Tamerlane (1827) 301
Upon this page, enwrapped from every
reader   Valentine 4

Everything
Being everything which now thou art
To FSO 3

Evil
Lest an evil step be taken
Bridal Ballad 31
By you—by yours, the evil eyes,—by
yours, the slanderous tongue
Lenore 11
But evil things, in robes of sorrow
Palace 33
Wears it away like evil hours and wine
Politian i 18
From the evil taint of clouds?—and he
did say?   Politian v 27
"Prophet!" said I, "thing of evil!—
prophet still, if bird or devil
Raven 85, 91
No power hath he of evil in himself
Silence 11
Which left me in an evil hour
Tamerlane (1827) 174

Evinced
From matter and light, evinced in solid
and shade   Silence 4

Exactly
If I can tell exactly what about
Tempora 80

Exalted
And died, ere scarce exalted into birth
Al Aaraaf i 71

Example
Pure—as her young example taught
Tamerlane 93

Exceeding
Unto the Count—it is exceeding just
Politian v 36
Exceeding well!—thou darest not fight
with me?   Politian v (1835) 66

Exceeds
Lord! to be grave exceeds the power of
face   Tempora 64

Excellence
One of these fish, par excellence the beau
Tempora 59

Excellency
The roof of his Excellency—and perhaps
Politian iii 66

Except
I heard not any voice except thine own,
Politian iii 19
I could not love except where Death
Romance (1831) 31

Excessive
With what excessive fragrance the zephyr
comes   Politian v 15

Exhales
Exhales from out her golden rim
Sleeper 4

Existing
Of any feud existing, or any cause
Politian v 20

Expanding
Doth o'er us pass, when, as th' expanding
eye   Stanzas¹ 17

Expected
Politian is expected   Politian i 41
The presence is expected in the hall
Politian iii 89

Expiatory
Thus to the expiatory tomb
Politian v 59

Empire
For passion must, with youth, expire
Tamerlane 72

Expired
All—all expired save thee—save less than
thou   Helen² 36

Explore
Let me see, then, what thereat is, and
this mystery explore   Raven 34
Let my heart be still a moment and this
mystery explore   Raven 35

Exposed
Never its mysteries are exposed
Dream-Land 45

Expostulation
In a mad expostulation with the deaf
and frantic fire   Bells 45

Expressing
This I sat engaged in guessing, but no
syllable expressing   Raven 73

Expressive
Brightly expressive as the twins of Loeda
Valentine 2

Extinguished
When the light was extinguished
Annie 79

Extravagant
Which I think extravagant
Fairy-Land 38

Eye
(Thrown back from flowers) of Beauty's
eye Al Aaraaf i 2
Beneath thy burning eye
Al Aaraaf i 109
A shelter from the fervour of his eye
Al Aaraaf i 120
Beauty's eye is here the bluest
Al Aaraaf i (1831) 18
O Death! from eye of God upon that
star Al Aaraaf ii 161
What wonder? for each star is eye-like
there Al Aaraaf ii 186
Here state he with his love—his dark eye
bent Al Aaraaf ii 194
As glowing Beauty's bust beneath man's
eye Al Aaraaf ii 258
In each idol's diamond eye City 32
To the weak human eye unclosed
Dream-Land 46
To the delirious eye, more lovely things
Dreams 32
While ever to her dear Eulalie upturns
her matron eye Eulalie 20
While ever to her young Eulalie upturns
her violet eye Eulalie 21
With a dreaming eye! Imitation 10
The bright i-dea, or bright dear-eye
Impromptu 4
Lazily upon beauty's eye Irene 4
Like a banner o'er thy dreaming eye!
Irene 36
As long—as tears on Memory's eye
Irene 44
As for Locke, he is all in my eye
Lampoon 1
By you—by yours, the evil eye,—by
yours, the slanderous tongue
Lenore 11
See how her eye-balls glare! Louisa 6
Are where thy grey eye glances
Paradise 23
And a glittering beam from a maiden's
eye Parody 9
A child—with a most knowing eye
Romance 10
Forever with unopened eye Sleeper 43
And in thine eye a kindling light
Song 5
Doth o'er us pass, when, as th' expanding
eye Stanzas[1] 17
Appeared to my half-closing eye
Tamerlane 46
With loitering eye, till I have felt
Tamerlane 83
But turned on me her quiet eye!
Tamerlane 111

And homeward turn'd his soften'd eye
Tamerlane 190
The light'ning of his eagle eye
Tamerlane 239
And I have held to mem'ry's eye
Tamerlane (1827) 98
She'd look up in my wilder'd eye
Tamerlane (1827) 132
I pictur'd to my fancy's eye
Tamerlane (1827) 266
Sung life, and the fire o' the eye
Tamerlane (1827) 382
With a dreaming eye To[4] 12
In myriad types of the human eye
Valley 21

Eyed
Can compare with the bright-eyed Eula-
lie's most humble and careless curl
Eulalie 13
Trusting to the mild-eyed stars
Valley 4

Eyelid
Raising his heavy eyelid, starts and sees
Al Aaraaf ii 4

Eyelids
And on my eyelids—O the heavy light!
Al Aaraaf ii 206
Strange are thy eyelids—strange thy
dress Irene 27

Eyes
Breathe it less gently forth,—and veil
thine eyes Acrostic 6
But on the pillars Seraph eyes have seen
Al Aaraaf ii 28
With half closing eyes Al Aaraaf ii 73
Like—eyes of the maiden
Al Aaraaf ii 78
Thou hast bound many eyes
Al Aaraaf ii 116
Dim was its little disk, and angel eyes
Al Aaraaf ii 253
And the stars never rise but I see the
bright eyes Annabel Lee 36
Of the eyes of my Annie Annie 102
We liken our ladies' eyes to them
City (1831) 16
To him whose eyes are cast Dream 6
Than the eyes of the radiant girl!
Eulalie 8
I am star-stricken with thine eyes
Fairy-Land (1831) 5
Mine eyes shall see, have ever seen
Happiest Day 14
Save only the divine light in thine eyes
Helen[2] 37
Save but the soul in thine uplifted eyes
Helen[2] 38
Didst glide away. Only thine eyes re-
mained Helen[2] 51
Sancta Maria! turn thine eyes
Hymn (1835) 1
Stay! turn thine eyes afar!
Israfel (1831) 23
The life upon her yellow hair, but not
within her eyes Lenore 18
The life still there upon her hair, the
death upon her eyes Lenore 19

The soft head bows, the sweet eyes close
Physician 5
It speaks of sunken eyes, and wasted
cheeks Politian ii 65
Thine eyes are wild—tempt not the wrath
divine! Politian ii 110
And beautiful Lalage!—turn here thine
eyes! Politian iv 9
No mortal eyes have seen!—what said
the Count? Politian v 18
For thee, and in thine eyes—and thou
shalt be Politian iv 79
The eyes of the citizens Politian v 87
To the fowl whose fiery eyes now burned
into my bosom's core Raven 74
And his eyes have all the seeming of a
demon's that is dreaming Raven 105
Of her soul-searching eyes River 14
I saw no Heaven—but in her eyes
Tamerlane 101
The moment's converse; in her eyes
Tamerlane 148
My eyes are still on pomp and power
Tamerlane (1827) 355
In dusky grandeur to my eyes
Tamerlane (1827) 363
To weep, as he did, until his eyes were
sore Tempora 14
Then bright eyes on his Tom and Jerry
brim Tempora 66
Because to his cat's eyes I hold a glass
Tempora 87
Thine eyes, in Heaven of heart enshrined
To¹ 5
In the seraphic glancing of thine eyes
To MLS 12
Who alterest all things with thy peering
eyes To Science 2
To shine on us with her bright eyes
Ulalume 48
With love in her luminous eyes
Ulalume 50
For her these lines are penned, whose
luminous eyes Valentine 1
Such eager eyes, there lies, I say, perdu
Valentine 14

Eyraco
That stole upon the ear, in Eyraco
Al Aaraaf ii 42

Fabied
The fabled nectar that the heathen knew
Al Aaraaf i 53
Despair, the fabled vampire bat
Tamerlane (1831) 27

Fabric
Over fabric half so fair! Palace 8

Face
So impudently in my face
Fairy-Land (1831) 15
Thy hyacinth hair, thy classic face
Helen¹ 7
To look upon the face hidden by yon
lattice Politian iii 102
To gaze upon that veiled face, and hear
Politian iii 103
The more than beauty of a face
Tamerlane 78

Faced
That things should stare us in the face
Tempora 32
Lord! to be grave exceeds the power of
face Tempora 64
By the side of the pale-faced moon
Bells 50

Faces
With the breath from their pale faces
Fairy-Land 10
Upon the upturn'd faces of a thousand
Helen² 8
Fell on the upturn'd faces of these roses
Helen² 11, 14
Fell on the upturn'd faces of the roses
Helen² 19

Fact
But the fact is I was napping, and so
gently you came rapping Raven 21
One settled fact is better than ten pages
Tempora 78

Fading
And all the fires are fading away
Romance (1831) 49

Failed
Fail'd, as my pennon'd spirit leapt aloft
Al Aaraaf ii 232
Failed him at length Eldorado 14

Failing
And, failing in thy power to bless
Tamerlane 181
Whose failing sight will grow dim.
Tamerlane (1827) 316

Faint
On violet couches faint away
Al Aaraaf i (1831) 15
The hours are breathing faint and low
City 49
I am faint Politian v 1
Swung by angels whose faint foot-falls
tinkled on the tufted floor
Raven (1845) 80

Faintest
Owl-downy nonsense that the faintest
puff Enigma 7
Not hear it!—listen now! listen!—the
faintest sound Politian iii 52

Faintly
Where each star most faintly gloweth
Departed 3
And so faintly you came tapping, tapping
at my chamber door Raven 22

Fair
On the fair Capo Deucato, and sprang
Al Aaraaf i 44
Like guilty beauty, chasten'd, and more
fair Al Aaraaf i 65
Fair flowers, and fairy! to whose care is
given Al Aaraaf i 80
The terrible and fair Al Aaraaf i 84
While the moon danc'd with the fair
stranger light Al Aaraaf ii 10
Fair flowers, bright waterfalls, and angel
wings Al Aaraaf ii 65
Till the fair and gentle Eulalie became
my blushing bride Eulalie 4

To the beauty of fair Greece
Helen[1] (1831) 9
For her, the fair and debonair, that now
so lowly lies   Lenore 17
But thou did'st not die too fair
Paean 34
Of life—beloved, and fair
Paean (1836) 34
Over fabric half so fair   Palace 8
Once a fair and stately palace Palacc 3
Was the fair palace door   Palace 26
Nothing, fair cousin, nothing—not even
deep sorrow   Politian i 17
Cousin! fair cousin!—madam!
Politian i 34
Fair mirror and true! now tell me (for
thou canst)   Politian ii 62
Fair mirror and true! thou liest not!
Politian ii 71
Fair river! in thy bright, clear flow
River 1
Her own fair hand had rear'd around
Tamerlane (1827) 219
Full many a fair flow'r rais'd its head
Tamerlane (1827) 402
Fair maiden, let thy generous heart
To FSO (1839) 1
Toss back his fine curls from their fore-
head fair   Tempora 51
For at a ball what fair one can escape
Tempora 55
Fair isle, that from the fairest of all
flowers   Zante 1

Fairer
Never his fairy wing o'er fairer world!
Al Aaraaf ii 252
Laden from yonder bowers!—a fairer
day   Politian v 16

Fairest
What matters it, my fairest, and my best
Politian iv 42
Fair isle, that from the fairest of all
flowers   Zante 1
And blossom of the fairy plant, in grief
Al Aaraaf i 61

Fairy
Fair flowers, and fairy! to whose care is
given   Al Aaraaf i 80
The fairy light that kiss'd her golden
hair   Al Aaraaf ii 58
Never his fairy wing o'er fairer world!
Al Aaraaf ii 252
How fairy-like a melody there swells
Bells (1849) 4
Just now so fairy-like and well
Fairy-Land (1831) 3
And this ray is a fairy ray
Fairy-Land (1831) 24
All wreathed with fairy fruits and
flowers   Paradise 5
A fairy land of flowers, and fruit, and
sunshine   Politian iv 69
Which as it were, in fairy bound
Tamerlane (1827) 221

Faith
Our faith to one love—and one moon
adore   Al Aaraaf i 153

And, though my faith be broken
Bridal Ballad 22
Didst thou not speak of faith
Politian ii 92
Tho' not with Faith—with godliness—
whose throne   Stanzas[1] 30
I build no faith upon   To[4] 3
For the resurrection of deep-buried faith
To MLS 6

Faithful
The faithful heart yields to repose
Physician 6

Fall
Of molten stars their pavement, such as
fall   Al Aaraaf ii 16
My tinted shadows rise and fall
Irene 40
Like ghosts the shadows rise and fall!
Sleeper 29
Who otherwise would fall from life and
Heav'n   Stanzas[1] 27
Let life, then, as the day-flower, fall
Tamerlane 211
Then desolately fall   To[1] 6

Fallen
Unguided Love hath fallen—'mid " tears
of perfect moan." Al Aaraaf ii 181

Fallest
Which fall'st into the soul like rain
Tamerlane 179

Falling
Falling in wreaths thro' many a startled
star   Al Aaraaf i 32
Is the gently falling leaf
Al Aaraaf i (1831) 27
A pause—and then a sweeping, falling
strain   Al Aaraaf ii 50
Nor long the measure of my falling hours
Al Aaraaf ii 241
Falling—her veriest stepping-stone
Tamerlane 171

Falls
Here, where a hero fell, a column falls!
Coliseum 17
In easy drapery falls   Fairy-Land 19
Again!—again!—how solemnly it falls
Politian iii 56
Swung by seraphin whose foot-falls
tinkled on the tufted floor   Raven 80
It falls from an eternal shrine
Tamerlane (1827) 14
The pen falls powerless from my shiver-
ing hand   To[3] 17

False
False friends!ye loved her for her wealth
Lenore (1843) 20
Thou true—he false!—false!—false!
Politian ii 74

Falsehood
That Truth is Falsehood—or that Bliss
is Woe?   Al Aaraaf ii 167
When falsehood wore a ten-fold crime
Tamerlane (1827) 190
T'awake her, and a falsehood tell
Tamerlane (1827) 289

Falsest
In the falsest and untruest
                    Al Aaraaf i (1831) 19

Fame
Not all our power is gone—not all our
    fame   Coliseum 40
The former was well known to fame
                    Lampoon 7
In years, but grey in fame   Politian 47
Befit thee—Fame awaits thee—Glory
    calls   Politian iii 22
Thy withering portion with the fame
                    Tamerlane 16
She might recall in him, whom Fame
                    Tamerlane (1827) 271
The Zinghis' yet re-echoing fame
                    Tamerlane (1827) 337

Famed
All of the famed and the colossal left
                    Coliseum 31

Familiar
Hath been—a most familiar bird
                    Romance 6

Familiarly
Familiarly—whom Fortune's sun
                    Tamerlane (1827) 263

Family
Of her grand family funerals
                    Sleeper 53

Fan
With their own breath to fan his fire
                    Tamerlane 164

Fancied
Can it be fancied that Deity ever vindic-
    tively   Experiments 5
The " beau ideal " fancied for Adonis
                    Tempora 72

Fancies
Lying, it fancies   Annie 60
Shake off the idle fancies that beset thee
                    Politian iii 4
These fancies to the wind
                    Politian iii 96

Fancy
Might fancy me dead   Annie 16
That you fancy me dead   Annie 88, 92
Now be this Fancy, by Heaven, or be it
    Fate   Politian iii 110
Then this ebony bird beguiling my sad
    fancy into smiling   Raven 43
But the Raven still beguiling my sad
    fancy into smiling   Raven 67
Fancy unto fancy, thinking what this
    ominous bird of yore   Raven 70
I pictur'd to my fancy's eye
                    Tamerlane (1827) 266
For the flight on Earth to Fancy giv'n
                    Tamerlane (1827) 325

Fanes
Up fanes—up Babylon-like walls
                    City 18
There open fanes and gaping graves
                    City 30

Fangs
And seraphs sob at vermin fangs
                    Worm 31

Fantasies
To fantasies—with none
                    Tamerlane 85

Fantastic
Thrilled me—filled me with fantastic ter-
    rors never felt before   Raven 14

Fantastically
How fantastically it fell
                    Fairy-Land (1831) 26
Vast forms that move fantastically
                    Palace 43

Fantasy
By winged Fantasy   Al Aaraaf i 114
Yet it was not that Fantasy
                    Tamerlane 157

Far
Of rosy head, that towering far away
                    Al Aaraaf ii 7
Far down upon the wave that sparkled
    there   Al Aaraaf ii 14
Apart from Heaven's Eternity—and yet
    how far from Hell!   Al Aaraaf ii 173
How lovely 't is to look so far away!
                    Al Aaraaf ii 199
Far down within the crystal of the lake
                    Al Aaraaf ii (1829) 40
Of many far wiser than we
                    Annabel Lee 29
But our love it was stronger by far than
    the love   Annabel Lee 27
From a cavern not very far   Annie 43
Far down within the dim West   City 3
Gleams up the pinnacles far and free
                    City 16
Upon some far-off happier sea   City 39
Yet heavier far than your Petrarchan
    stuff   Enigma 6
And are far up in Heaven—the stars I
    kneel to   Helen² 62
The more lovely, the more far!
                    Israfel (1841) 29
From Hell unto a high estate far up
    within the Heaven   Lenore (1845) 25
Far away—far away   Nis 1, 6
Far away—as far at least   Nis 2
Over the hills and far away   Nis 46
By far Italian streams
                    Paradise (1834) 26
Far from it, love   Politian i 53
Here's far sterner story   Politian ii 21
Will there be found—" dew sweeter far
    than that   Politian ii 34
Far less a shadow which thou likenest to
    it   Politian iv 61
Far down within some shadowy lake
                    Romance 4
Sure thou art come o'er far-off seas
                    Sleeper 32
Far in the forest, dim and old
                    Sleeper 48
My wilder'd heart was far away
                    Tamerlane (1827) 356
The " good old times " were far the worst
    of any   Tempora 6
Richer, far wilder, far diviner visions
                    To³ 13

Amid empurpled vapors, far away
To³ 26
Like some enchanted far-off isle
To F 9
Some ocean throbbing far and free
To F 11

Fares
How fares good Ugo?—and when is it to be? Politian ii 44

Farewell
Farewell! for I have won the Earth
Tamerlane 186
A silent gaze was my farewell
Tamerlane (1827) 287

Farther
Can I do aught?—is there no farther aid
Politian ii 45
Is there no farther aid!
Politian ii 46
Shall then absolve thee of all farther duties Politian iii 37
Nothing farther then he uttered—not a feather then he fluttered Raven 57

Fashion
It is a fashion Politian i 8
A silly—a most silly fashion I have
Politian i 9
For thy lofty rank nad fashion—much depends Politian i 25

Fast
Followed fast and followed faster till his songs one burden bore— Raven 64

Faster
Followed fast and followed faster till his songs one burden bore— Raven 64

Fat
Why ask? who ever yet saw money made out of a fat old Experiments 9

Fatal
They never sever'd in one fatal hour
Ballad 7

Fate
By the corrosive Hours to Fate and me?
Coliseum 32
O! would she deign to rule my fate
Divine Right 9
Was is not Fate that, on this July midnight Helen² 21
Was is not Fate (whose name is also Sorrow) Helen² 22
Now, when storms of Fate o'ercast
Hymn 9
Yet now as Fate Politian iii 39
Now be this Fancy, by Heaven, or be it Fate Politian iii 110
But should some urgent fate (untimely lot!) Silence 12
To shun the fate, with which to cope
Tamerlane (1837) 4
To know the fate it will inherit
Tamerlane (1827) 192
To follow my high fate among
Tamerlane (1827) 237
But that you sorrow for my fate To² 7
Round his fate will hover To Hunter 13

Father
Father, this zeal is anything but well!
Politian ii 97
Think of my early days!—think of my father Politian ii 84
And the deed's register should tally, father! Politian ii 106
How, in thy father's halls, among the maidens Politian iv 24
Such, father, is not (now) my theme
Tamerlane 2
But, father, there liv'd one who, then
Tamerlane 69
The passion, father? You have not
Tamerlane 129
Father, I firmly do believe
Tamerlane 222
Say, holy father, breathes there yet
Tamerlane (1831) 177

Fathomless
How fathomless a capacity for love!
Helen² 47

Favored
And late to ours, the favor'd one of God
Al Aaraaf i 25

Fay
The elfin from the grass the dainty fay
To Science (1841) 13

Fear
Isabel, do you not fear
Fairy-Land (1831) 39
And much I fear me ill—it will not do
Politian v 2
Oh, lady dear, hast thou no fear?
Sleeper 30
Not Hell shall make me fear again
Tamerlane 20
I held no doubt—I knew no fear
Tamerlane (1827) 241

Feared
My heart half fear'd to be a crime
Romance (1831) 44

Fearful
Thou speakest a fearful riddle
Politian iii 38

Fearfully
For strangely—fearfully in this hall
Irene 39
So fitfully, so fearfully
Irene (1836) 35; Sleeper 25
Fearfully beautiful! the real
Tamerlane (1827) 169

Fearing
Deep into that darkness peering, long I stood there wondering, fearing
Raven 25

Fears
She fears to perfume, perfuming the night Al Aaraaf i 67
By all my wishes now—my fears hereafter Politian iv 37
No need to quiet any fears
Tamerlane 109
A play of hopes and fears Worm 6

Feast
O, feast my soul, revenge is sweet
Louisa 13

Feather
Nothing farther then he uttered—not a
feather then he fluttered   Raven 57
Fed
Ambition is chain'd down—nor fed
Tamerlane (1827) 252
Feeble
And, when she fell in feeble health, ye
blessed her—that she died
Lenore 9
Feebly
As if their tops had feebly given City 46
Feel
In Eternity—we feel   Al Aaraaf i 99
And the stars never rise but I feel the
bright eyes   Annabel Lee (1849) 36
But no matter!—I feel   Annie 11
Feel a glory in so rolling   Bells 84
I feel ye now—I feel ye in your strength
Coliseum 12
I feel hath flown   Happiest Day 4
I feel—have been   Happiest Day 16
Go up to God so solemnly the dead may
feel no wrong!   Lenore 14
Because I feel that, in the Heavens above
Mother 1
That the dead may feel no wrong
Paean 20
I feel thou lovest me truly
Politian iv 52
I feel thou art not góne—yet dare not
look   Politian iv 92
My heart would feel to be a crime
Romance 20
I feel it more than half a crime
Serenade 2
And I would feel its essence stealing
Tamerlane (1827) 48
Alas, I cannot feel; for 't is not feeling
To³ 20
Feeling
A feeling not the jewelled mine Lake 15
Wearing its own deep feeling as a crown
Stanzas¹ 32
With wisdom, virtue, feeling fraught
Stanzas² 22
A mingled feeling with my own
Tamerlane 150
My soul imbib'd unhallow'd feeling
Tamerlane (1827) 47
The only feeling which possest
Tamerlane (1827) 245
With thoughts such feeling can command
Tamerlane (1827) 256
A feeling not the jewell'd mine
Tamerlane (1831) 93
Alas, I cannot feel; for 't is not feeling
To³ 20
A feeling such as mine   To⁴ 34
Feels
The soul which feels its innate right
Tamerlane (1827) 185
Feet
Feet under ground   Annie 42
Feigned
Of a feign'd journey, were again
Tamerlane (1827) 290

Fell
And fell on gardens of the unforgiven
Al Aaraaf i 55
Fountains were gushing music as they fell
Al Aaraaf ii 62
That fell, refracted, thro' thy bounds,
afar   Al Aaraaf ii 160
But two: they fell: for Heaven no grace
imparts   Al Aaraaf ii 176
He was a goodly spirit—he who fell
Al Aaraaf ii 182
And fell—not swiftly as I rose before
Al Aaraaf ii 238
They fell: for Heaven to them no hope
imparts   Al Aaraaf ii 263
And then I fell gently   Annie 75
And the voice seemed his who fell
Bridal Ballad 10
For the words were his who fell
Bridal Ballad (1837) 10
Here, where a hero fell, a column falls!
Coliseum 17
Fell as he found   Eldorado 10
Here, dearest, where the moonbeam fell
Fairy-Land (1831) 2
How fantastically it fell
Fairy-Land (1831) 26
And as it flutter'd, fell
Happiest Day 22
There fell a silvery-silken veil of light
Helen² 6
Fell on the upturn'd faces of these roses
Helen² 11, 14
Fell on the upturn'd faces of the roses
Helen² 19
And, when she fell in feeble health, ye
blessed her—that she died
Lenore 9
Then grew paler as it fell   Nis 25
I fell in love with melancholy
Romance (1831) 28
So late from Heaven—that dew—it fell
Tamerlane 41
Like moonlight on my spirit fell
Tamerlane (1831) 101
Fellows
Thy riotous company, too—fellows low-
born   Politian i 20
We have been boys together—school-
fellows   Politian iii 32

Felt
I felt my bosom swell   Bridal Ballad 8
Ev'n then I felt—that brightest hour
Happiest Day 19
Thrilled me—filled me with fantastic
terrors never felt before   Raven 14
With loitering eye, till I have felt
Tamerlane 83
Which I felt not—its bodied forms
Tamerlane (1827) 164
All that I felt, or saw, or thought
Tamerlane (1827) 175
And deeply felt the silent tone
Tamerlane (1827) 180
And felt, with ev'ry flying hour
Tamerlane (1827) 301

Ferdinand
Thus speaketh one Ferdinand in the
words of the play Politian ii 17

Ferdinando
Like the knight Pinto (mendez Ferdinando) Valentine 18

Fervent
Of fervent prayer, and humble love
Hymn (1835) 3

Fervently
The truest—the most fervently devoted
To MLS 15

Ferver
As a burning and a ferver
Spirits (1827) 17
To a ferver by the moonbeam that hangs
o'er Stanzas¹ 10

Fervid
Whose fervid, flick'ring torch of life was
lit Stanzas¹ 4

Fervor
Of its own fervor—what had o'er it
power Stanzas¹ 8

Fervour
A shelter from the fervour of His eye;
Al Aaraaf i 120
With the fervour of thy lute
Israfel 38

Festive
And laughter crowns the festive hour
Octavia 2

Fettered
Was all on earth my fetter'd sight
Song (1829) 7

Feud
That knowing no cause of quarrel or of
fued Politian v 11
Of any fued existing, or any cause
Politian v 20

Fever
And the fever called "Living" Annie 5
Have ceased, with the fever Annie 27
With the fever called "Living"
Annie 29
As a burning and a fever Spirits 17
To a fever by the moonbeam that hangs
o'er Stanzas¹ 10
In the fever of a minute To M 4

Fevered
To what my fevered soul doth dream of
Heaven! Politian ii 12

Fevered
The fever'd diadem on my brow
Tamerlane 28

Few
From a spring but a very few Annie 41
How few! yet how they creep
Dream w. Dream 16
A few days more, thou knowest, my
Alessandra Politian i 3
Learned as few are learned
Politian i 56
When, a few fleeting years gone by
Tamerlane (1827) 268
Of all the cities, and I've seen no few
Tempora 41

Fickle
Trust to the fickle star within
Tamerlane (1827) 119

Fiction
The muses thro' their bowers of Truth
or Fiction Elizabeth 8

Field
To the field then—to the field
Politian iii 14
To the senate or the field
Politian iii 15

Fields
And greener fields than in yon world
above Al Aaraaf ii 229

Fiend
"Be that word our sign of parting, bird
or fiend!" I shrieked, upstarting
Raven 97

Fiends
"Avaunt!—avaunt! to friends from
fiends the indignant ghost is riven
Lenore 20

Fierce
Fierce deep grief is unavailing
Departed 22
Hath not the same fierce heirdom given
Tamerlane 30

Fiercer
Though its glow hath raised a fiercer
flame Song 11

Fiery
And roll'd, a flame, the fiery Heaven
athwart Al Aaraaf ii 236
O'er th' horizon's fiery wall Nis 42
To the fowl whose fiery eyes now burned
into my bosom's core Raven 72
Its fiery passion?—yet have not
Tamerlane (1827) 204

Fight
The Count Castiglione will not fight
Politian v 29
Avaunt—I will not fight thee—indeed I
dare not Politian v 63
Thou wilt not fight with me didst say,
Sir Count? Politian v 64
So fresh upon thy lips I will not fight
thee Politian v 68
For in the fight I will not raise a hand
Politian v 79
I will not fight thee Politian v 82
Dost hear? with cowardice—thou wilt
not fight me? Politian v 91
Exceeding well!—thou darest not fight
with me Politian v (1835) 66

Figure
Of yonder trees methought a figure past
Politian iv 54
A spectral figure, solemn, and slow, and
noiseless Politian iv 55

Fill
They fill my soul with Beauty (which is
Hope) Helen² 61
And fill my heart of hearts, where Death
installed you Mother 7

Filled
Thrilled me—filled me with fantastic
terrors never felt before Raven 14

Filling
Filling my heart of hearts, where God
installed you   Mother (1850) 7

Fills
Fills me with dread—thy ebony crucifix
Politian ii 82

Filmy
A void within the filmy Heaven   City 47
One more filmy than the rest
Fairy-Land 12

Find
"Seldom we find," says Solomon Don
Dunce   Enigma 1
Can find, among their burning terms of
love   Mother 3
Thy soul shall find itself alone Spirits 1
Find Pride the ruler of its will
Tamerlane (1827) 194
Shall find her own sweet name that,
nestling, lies   Valentine 3

Fine
Who knocked over a thousand so fine!
Latin Hymn 8
Toss back his fine curls from their fore-
head fair   Tempora 51

Finger
But Psyche, uplifting her finger
Ulalume 51

Fingers
Through my fingers to the deep
Dream w. Dream 17
Thro' my fingers to the deep!
Tamerlane (1831) 254

Fior
Isola d'oro!—Fior de Levante!
Al Aaraaf i 77; Zante (1837) 14

Fire
To be carriers of fire   Al Aaraaf i 94
The red fire of their heart
Al Aaraaf i 95
Apart—like fire-flies in Sicilian night
Al Aaraaf i 145
Gay fire-fly of the night we come and go
Al Aaraaf ii 248
It glows with the fire   Annie (1849) 99
In a clamorous appealing to the mercy of
the fire   Bells 44
In a mad expostulation with the deaf and
frantic fire   Bells 45
Surging, unto skies of fire
Dream-Land 16
And purified in their electric fire
Helen² 59
And sanctified in their elysian fire
Helen² 60
That Israfeli's fire   Israfel 18
Burned there a holier fire than burneth
now   Politian iv 19
His wit to love—his wine to fire
Romance (1831) 26
Thy distant fire   Star 22
You call it hope—that fire of fire!
Tamerlane 7
Then—in my boyhood—when their fire
Tamerlane 70
Trust to the fire within, for light?
Tamerlane 95

With their own breath to fan his fire
Tamerlane 164
On beds of fire that burn below
Tamerlane 220
Whom she had deem'd in his own fire
Tamerlane (1827) 275
Of young life, and the fire o' the eye
Tamerlane (1827) 382

Fires
And all the fires are fading away
Romance (1831) 49

Firm
Should shake the firm spirit thus
Politian iv 62

Firmament
With eagle gaze along the firmament
Al Aaraaf ii 195

Firmly
Father, I firmly do believe
Tamerlane 222

First
When first Al Aaraaf knew her course to
be   Al Aaraaf ii 255
But, when first he breathed his vow
Bridal Ballad 7
In thy own book that first thy name be
writ   Elizabeth 3
Always write first things uppermost in
the heart   Elizabeth 16
'T is his first visit   Politian i 43
Not mother, with her first-born on her
knee   Politian iv 16
And left the first fond kiss   Sarah 18
On mountain soil I first drew life
Tamerlane 35
Young love's first lesson is—the heart
Tamerlane 102
And bade it first to dream of crime
Tamerlane (1827) 149

Fish
Flounce like a fish in his own element
Tempora 50
One of these fish, par excellence the beau
Tempora 59

Fit
Fit emblems of the model of her world
Al Aaraaf i 37
Elizabeth, it surely is most fit
Elizabeth 1
Hast thou a crucifix fit for this thing?
Politian ii 98
A passionate light—such for his spirit
was fit   Stanzas¹ 6
Each fit to furnish forth four hours' de-
bate   Tempora 22

Fitfully
So fitfully—so fearfully   Sleeper 25
While the orchestra breathes fitfully
Worm 7

Fits
And, lest the guessing throw the fool in
fits   Tempora 91

Fitted
Seem'd fitted for a queenly throne
Tamerlane (1831) 164

Fitting
And in its gulf a fitting grave   Lake 19
There is a vow were fitting should be
    made   Politian ii 94
Methinks 't were fitting   Politian ii 104
It were most fitting   Politian v 77

Fixed
Hath fix'd my soul, tho' unforgiv'n
         Tamerlane (1827) 106

Flake
And never a flake   Eulalie 9

Flame
And roll'd, a flame, the fiery Heaven
    athwart   Al Aaraaf ii 236
Though its glow hath raised a fiercer
    flame   Song 11
The magic empire of a flame
         Tamerlane (1827) 104
With such as mine——that mystic flame
         Tamerlane (1827) 158

Flap
Flap shadowy sounds from visionary
    wings   Al Aaraaf i 129

Flapped
Some eager spirit flapp'd his dusky wing
         Al Aaraaf ii 27

Flapping
Flapping from out their Condor wings
         Worm 15

Flashing
Flashing from Parian marble that twin
    smile   Al Aaraaf ii 13
While the red flashing of the light
         Tamerlane 44
Are flashing thro' Eternity
         Tamerlane 228

Flattery
Of flattery round a sovereign's throne
         Tamerlane 64
Nor deal in flattery or aspersions foul
         Tempora 27

Fled
Repenting follies that full long have fled
         Al Aaraaf i 63
If my peace hath fled away   To⁴ 13

Fleecy
A fleecy cloud   Star 13

Fleeting
As in that fleeting, shadowy, misty strife
         Dreams 30
Enduring joys and fleeting cares
         Stanzas² 6
And fleeting vanities of dreams
         Tamerlane (1827) 168
When, a few fleeting years gone by
         Tamerlane (1827) 268

Flew
When the Hours flew brightly by
         Hymn 5
The sweet Lenore hath gone before, with
    Hope that flew beside   Lenore 15

Flickering
Whose fervid, flick'ring torch of life was
    lit   Stanzas¹ 4

Flickers
See!—it flickers up the sky through the
    night!   Ulalume 66

Since it flickers up to Heaven through the
    night"   Ulalume 71

Flies
Apart—like fire-flies in Sicilian night
         Al Aaraaf i 145
The motes, and dust, and flies
         Fairy-Land (1831) 35
Which, of light step, flies with the dew
         Tamerlane (1827) 200

Flight
It would weigh down your flight
         Al Aaraaf ii 95
Young dreams still hovering on their
    drowsy flight   Al Aaraaf ii 158
But waft the angel on her flight with a
    Paean of old days! "   Lenore 26
For the flight on Earth to Fancy giv'n
         Tamerlane (1827) 325

Flimsy
Through all the flimsy things we see at
    once   Enigma 3

Fling
That very blackness yet doth fling
         Romance (1831) 17
Its down upon my spirit fling
         Romance (1831) 41
Could fling, all lavishly and free
         Stanzas² 2

Flings
And I would rave, but that he flings
         Tamerlane (1831) 29

Flirt
Open here I flung the shutter, when, with
    many a flirt and flutter   Raven 37

Flit
Flit through thy chamber in and out
         Sleeper 23

Flitting
And the Raven, never flitting, still is sit-
    ting, still is sitting   Raven 103

Float
On the sweetest air doth float
         Al Aaraaf i (1831) 20
Should catch the note as it doth float up
    from the damned Earth!   Lenore 24
On its roof did float and flow
         Palace 10

Floating
Rich melodies are floating in the winds
         Politian iii 47
And my soul from out that shadow that
    lies floating on the floor   Raven 107
The gentle zephyr floating by   Sarah 13

Floats
And the Nelumbo bud that floats for ever
         Al Aaraaf i 78
What a liquid ditty floats   Bells 22
For every sound that floats   Bells 76
Let the bell toll!—a saintly soul floats on
    the Stygian river   Lenore 2

Flood
Hast thou not torn the Naiad from her
    flood   To Science 12

Floods
Bottomless vales and boundless floods
Dream-Land 9
Dim vales and shadowy floods
Fairy-Land 1

Floor
And each separate dying ember wrought
its ghost upon the floor   Raven 8
Swung by seraphim whose foot-falls
tinkled on the tufted floor   Raven 80
And the lamp-light o'er him streaming
throws his shadow on the floor
Raven 106
And my soul from out that shadow that
lies floating on the floor   Raven 107
That, o'er the floor and down the wall
Sleeper 28

Flounce
Flounce like a fish in his own element
Tempora 50

Flow
On the clear waters there that flow
Irene 57
Flow softly—gently—vital stream
Louisa 1
On its roof did float and flow   Palace 10
Of Heaven untrammelled flow—which air
to breathe   Politian iv 72
Fair River! in thy bright, clear flow
River 1
Thy lover's voice tonight shall flow
Serenade 19

Flower
And gemmy flower, of Trebizond mis-
nam'd   Al Aaraaf i 50
In Trebizond—and on a sunny flower
Al Aaraaf i 56
And that aspiring flower that sprang on
Earth   Al Aaraaf i 70
Which leaps down to the flower
Al Aaraaf ii 121
She, earth's bright and loveliest flower
Departed 17
You know that most enormous flower
Fairy-Land (1831) 11
Bore a bright golden flower, but not i'
this soil   Politian ii 7
Let life, then, as the day-flower, fall
Tamerlane 211
The trancient, passionate day-flow'r
Tamerlane (1827) 390
Full many a fair flow'r rais'd its head
Tamerlane (1827) 402
Henceforth I hold thy flower-enamelled
shore   Zante 12

Flowers
(Thrown back from flowers) of Beauty's
eye   Al Aaraaf i 2
Yet all the beauty—all the flowers
Al Aaraaf i 12
Of flowers: of lilies such as rear'd the
head   Al Aaraaf i 43
Fair flowers, and fairy! to whose care is
given   Al Aaraaf i 80
Up rose the maiden from her shrine of
flowers   Al Aaraaf i 156

Young flowers were whispering in melody
Al Aaraaf ii 60
To happy flowers that night—and tree to
tree   Al Aaraaf ii 61
Fair flowers, bright waterfalls, and angel
wings   Al Aaraaf ii 65
Where wild flowers, creeping
Al Aaraaf ii 136
On flowers, before, and mist, and love they
ran   Al Aaraaf ii 208
Of sculptured ivy and stone flowers
City 20
Like flowers by the low breath of June!
Fairy-Land (1831) 8
The happy flowers and the repining trees
Helen² 33
Those flowers that say (ah hear them
now!)   Irene 53
Our flowers are merely—flowers
Israfel 42
All wreathed with fairy fruits and flowers
Paradise 5
And all the flowers were mine
Paradise 6
A fairy land of flowers, and fruit, and sun-
shine   Politian iv 69
O craving heart, for the lost flowers
Tamerlane 21
As perfume of strange summer flow'rs
Tamerlane (1827) 139
Of flow'rs which we have known before
Tamerlane (1827) 140
To mind—not flow'rs alone—but more
Tamerlane (1827) 142
'T is not that the flowers of twenty
springs   To M 13
To keep watch above the flowers
Valley 6
Fair isle, that from the fairest of all
flowers   Zante 1

Floweth
Where the river ever floweth
Departed 1

Flowing
By that river, ever flowing
Departed 25
Through which came flowing, flowing,
flowing   Palace 27

Flown
And Valisnerian lotus thither flown
Al Aaraaf i 74
Yet if Hope has flown away
Dream w. Dream 6
I feel hath flown   Happiest Day 4
Ah, broken is the golden bowl!—the spirit
flown forever!   Lenore 1
Till I scarcely more than muttered, "Other
friends have flown before   Raven 58
On the morrow he will leave me, as my
Hopes have flown before   Raven 59
And all we seek to keep hath flown
Tamerlane 210
For all had flown who made it so
Tamerlane 214
If my peace hath flown away
Tamerlane (1831) 245

Flows
Of a water that flows   Annie 39
How the danger ebbs and flows   Bells 60

Flung
One half the garden of her globe was flung   Al Aaraaf ii 222
Open here I flung the shutter, when, with many a flirt and flutter   Raven 37
Some vault that oft hath flung its black   Sleeper 50

Flush
The flush on her bright cheek, to me   Tamerlane 151

Flushing
Her cheeks were flushing, and her lips apart   Al Aaraaf ii 53

Flutter
Open here I flung the shutter, when, with many a flirt and flutter   Raven 37

Fluttered
And as it flutter'd, fell   Happiest Day 22
Nothing farther then he uttered—not a feather then he fluttered   Raven 57

Fluttering
Flutt'ring triumphant o'er the palls   Irene 73
And wingéd pannels fluttering back   Sleeper 51

Fly
Leave tenantless thy crystal home, and fly   Al Aaraaf i 143
Gay fire-fly of the night we come and go   Al Aaraaf ii 248
There the gorgeous clouds do fly   Nis 38
No wind in Heaven, and clouds do fly   Nis (1836) 36
Fly to that Paradise—my Lalage, wilt thou   Politian iv 75
Fly thither with me   Politian iv 76, 86
Think not to fly me thus   Politian v 85
Where, tho' the garish lights that fly   Romance (1831) 13
Will fly thee—and vanish   Spirits (1827) 21
Who, in a dream of night, would fly   Tamerlane 199
No mote may shun—no tiniest fly   Tamerlane 238
Though I turn, I fly not   To Hunter 1
Ah, fly!—let us fly!—for we must   Ulalume 55
And hither and thither fly   Worm 11

Flying
Upon the flying footsteps of—deep pride   Al Aaraaf i 46
As it pass'd me flying by   Alone 18
And felt, with ev'ry flying hour   Tamerlane (1827) 301

Foam
No billow breaking into foam   Stanzas² 11

Fog
Wrapping the fog about its breast   Sleeper 11

Fold
There is a two-fold Silence—sea and shore   Silence 5
When falsehood were a ten-fold crime   Tamerlane (1827) 190

Folded
The folded scroll within thy hand   Helen¹ (1831) 13
With drowsy head and folded wing   Romance 2

Follies
Repenting follies that full long have fled   Al Aaraaf i 63
And in such follies had no part   Tamerlane (1827) 404

Follow
They follow me—they lead me through the years   Helen² 55
There is an imp would follow me even there   Politian iii 16
I'll follow thee   Politian v 87
Like an avenging spirit I'll follow thee   Politian v 88
To follow my high fate among   Tamerlane (1827) 237

Followed
There is an imp hath followed me even there   Politian iii 17
Followed fast and followed faster till his songs one burden bore   Raven 64

Folly
His folly—pride—and passion—for he died   Acrostic 9
Where all my love is folly, and the crowd   Al Aaraaf i 135
'T were folly still to hope for higher Heav'n   Dreams 12
And so, being young and dipt in folly   Romance (1831) 35
'T were folly now to veil a thought   Tamerlane (1827) 183

Fond
And left the first fond kiss   Sarah 18
With her own image, my fond breast   Tamerlane (1827) 246

Fondly
She fondly caressed   Annie 74
And fondly turn to thee   Octavia 5

Food
The mimes become its food   Worm 30

Fool
Read nothing, written less—in short's a fool   Elizabeth 10
I would not call thee fool, old man   Tamerlane 11
And lest the guessing throw the fool in fits   Tempora 91

Foolishly
Be foolishly said   Annie 46

Foot
And trample it under foot   Politian iv 41
Swung by seraphim whose foot-falls tinkled on the tufted floor   Raven 80
No foot of man, commend thyself to God!   Silence 15

Ah yes! his little foot and ankle trim
                              Tempora 81
He then, of course, must shake his foot
  instead   Tempora 84
At me in vengeance shall the foot be
  shaken   Tempora 85

Footstep
No footstep stirred: the hated world all
  slept   Helen² 25
And where thy footstep gleams
                              Paradise 24

Footsteps
Upon the flying footsteps of—deep pride
                              Al Aaraaf i 46

Forbid
So wills its King, who hath forbid
                              Dream-Land 47

Forbidden
To while away—forbidden things!
                              Romance 19

Force
She ne'er shall force an echo more
                              Sleeper 58

Forefathers
Which from my forefathers I did inherit
                              Politian iii 11

Forehead
Toss back his fine curls from their forehead fair   Tempora 51

Foreign
Two words—two foreign soft dissyllables
                              To³ 7

Forest
Far in the forest, dim and old
                              Sleeper 48
Roaming the forest and the wild
                              Tamerlane 97
Neath the forest tree   To Hunter 9
Of rock and forest, on the hills
                              Tamerlane 142

Forests
And crystal lakes, and over-arching
  forests   Politian iv 70

Foretells
What a world of merriment their melody
  foretells!   Bells 3
What a world of happiness their harmony
  foretells   Bells 17

Forever
Prophetic sounds and loud, arise forever
                              Coliseum 34
Do I wander on forever   Departed 11
Forever changing places   Fairy-Land 8
Ah, broken is the golden bowl!—the spirit
  flown forever   Lenore 1
A hideous throng rush out forever
                              Palace 47
Forever with unopened eye   Sleeper 43
Forever—and love a duty   To FSO 8

Forget
What she never can forget   Ballad 30
Called—I forget the heathenish Greek
  name   Elizabeth 14
In vain I struggle to forget Octavia 3
Thou dost forget thyself, remembering
  me!   Politian iv 23

Quaff, oh, quaff this kind nepenthe and
  forget this lost Lenore!   Raven 83
The words—the letters themselves. Do not
  forget   Valentine 8

Forgets
God nerve the soul that ne'er forgets
                              Physician 2

Forgetting
Forgetting, or never   Annie 55

Forgiven
With many a mutter'd "hope to be forgiven"   Al Aaraaf ii 5

Forgiveness
"Sir," said I, "or Madam, truly your forgiveness I implore   Raven 20

Forgot
Around, by lifting winds forgot   City 9
In such an hour, when are forgot
                              Sarah 19
Why really, sir, I almost had forgot
                              Tempora 30
That years of love have been forgot
                              To³ 3
It shall not be forgot   Worm 18

Forgotten
Up shadowy long-forgotten bowers
                              City 19
Over the old forgotten grave   Nis 32
That we go down unhonoured and forgot-
  ten   Politian iv 43
There Care shall be forgotten
                              Politian iv 76
And I have not forgotten it—thou'lt do
  me   Politian v 32
Over many a quaint and curious volume of
  forgotten lore   Raven 2

Form
A wreath that twined each starry form
  around   Al Aaraaf i 40
Is not its form—its voice—most palpable
  and loud?   Al Aaraaf ii 47
And the cloud that took the form
                              Alone 20
Take thy beak from out my heart, and
  take thy form from off my door
                              Raven 101
Form in the deep another seven
                              Serenade 8
Shall form the pedestal of a throne
                              Tamerlane 172
Its very form hath pass'd me by
                              Tamerlane (1827) 100
His form once seen becomes a part of
  sight   Tempora 70
Still form a synonym for truth. Cease
  trying!   Valentine 19
Mimes, in the form of God on high
                              Worm 9
And, over each quivering form   Worm 34

Former
The former was well known to fame
                              Lampoon 7

Formless
At bidding of vast formless things
                              Worm 13

Forms
With forms that no man can discover
        Dream-Land 11
Shrouded forms that start and sigh
        Dream-Land 35
White-robed forms of friends long given
        Dream-Land 37
Whose forms we can't discover
        Fairy-Land 3
Vast forms that move fantastically
        Palace 43
Which I felt not—its bodied forms
      Tamerlane (1827) 164

Forsaken
Lest the dead who is forsaken
       Bridal Ballad 32

Forth
Breathe it less gently forth,—and veil
 thine eyes   Acrostic 6
Let us go forth and taste the fragrant air
       Politian i 65
From the sun and stars, whence he had
 drawn forth   Stanzas¹ 5
Each fit to furnish forth four hours' de-
 bate   Tempora 22

Fortune
Familiarly—whom Fortune's sun
      Tamerlane (1827) 263
When Fortune mark'd me for her own
      Tamerlane (1827) 347

Foul
On bed of moss lies gloating the foul
 adder   Coliseum (1833) 25
Nor deal in flattery or aspersions foul
       Tempora 27
Who hath seduced thee to this foul revolt
      To Margaret 1

Found
The night had found (to him a night of
 wo)   Al Aaraaf ii 190
Fell as he found   Eldorado 10
They have found to be the best
       Fairy-Land 14
Will there be found—" dew sweeter far
 than that   Politian ii 34
With which all tongues are busy—a land
 new found   Politian iv 66
Miraculously found by one of Genoa
       Politian iv 67
I early found Anacrean rhymes
      Romance (1831) 21

Fount
Its fount is holier—more divine
      Tamerlane 10

Fountain
From the torrent, or the fountain
       Alone 13
From a fountain a very few
      Annie (1849) 41
A fountain and a shrine Paradise 4
There rose a fountain once, and there
      Tamerlane (1827) 401
The gentle Naiad from her fountain flood
     To Science (1829) 12

Fountains
Fountains were gushing music as they fell
      Al Aaraaf ii 62
Fountains toppling evermore
     Dream-Land (1845) 13

Founts
It is not that my founts of bliss
        To M 9

Four
Near four bright suns—a temporary rest
      Al Aaraaf i 18
Each fit to furnish forth four hours' de-
 bate   Tempora 22

Fowl
Much I marvelled this ungainly fowl to
 hear discourse so plainly Raven 49
To the fowl whose fiery eyes now burned
 into my bosom's core Raven 74

Fragrance
With what excessive fragrance the zephyr
 comes   Politian v 15
Fragrance as sweet as Hermia's dew
       Sarah 17

Fragrant
Let us go forth and taste the fragrant air
       Politian i 65
They wave:—from out their fragrant
 tops   Valley 24

Framing
Thou! thy framing is so holy
     Al Aaraaf (1831) i 78

Frantic
In a mad expostulation with the deaf and
 frantic fire   Bells 45

Fraught
I say that dream was fraught
       Imitation 5
But I will half believe that wild light
 fraught   Stanzas¹ 11
With wisdom, virtue, feeling fraught
       Stanzas² 22
With thine unearthly beauty fraught
      Tamerlane (1827) 177
With which this aching, breast is fraught
      Tamerlane (1827) 184
Of parting, were with madness fraught
      Tamerlane (1827) 296

Free
Gleams up the pinnacles far and free
       City 16
In setting my Virginia's spirit free
       Mother 8
A heaven so calm as this—so utterly free
      Politian v 26
Of young passion free Song (1827) 6
Could fling, all lavishly and free
       Stanzas² 2
Thy life's free course should ever roam
       Stanzas² 9
Some ocean throbbing far and free
       To F 11

Freedom
Is Happiness now, and will be Freedom
 hereafter   Politian iv 73

Freely
Freely would give the broad lands of my
 earldom   Politian iii 101

Fresh
So fresh upon thy lips I will not fight
thee Politian v 68

Friar
I have sent for thee, holy friar
Tamerlane (1827) 2
It boots me not, good friar, to tell
Tamerlane (1827) 349

Friend
Ha! here at least's a friend—too much a
friend Politian ii 60
In earlier days—a friend will not deceive
thee Politian ii 61
To give thee cause for grief, my honored
friend Politian iii 8
Unto thy friend Politian iii 38
Good-night, my friend, good-night
Politian iii 115
Thou art my friend, Baldazzar
Politian v 31
My lord!—my friend! Politian v 37
Ah growl, say you, my friend, and pray at
what Tempora 29
For I have travelled, friend, as well as
you Tempora 42
My friend, the beau, hath made a settled
matter Tempora 76

Friendly
And, when the friendly sunshine smil'd
Tamerlane 99

Friends
And my friends are all delighted
Bridal Ballad (1837) 21
White-robed forms of friends long given
Dream-Land 37
Where oft—in life—with friends—it went
Irene 49
Avaunt!—avaunt! to friends from fiends
the indignant ghost is riven
Lenore 20
False friends! ye loved her for her wealth
Lenore (1831) 20
When wit, and wine, and friends have met
Octavia 1
Her friends are gazing on her Paean 5
And now are friends—yet shall not be so
long Politian iii 33
Till I scarcely more than muttered,
" Other friends have flown before
Raven 58

Frieze
These vague entablatures—this crumbling
frieze Coliseum 28

Friezes
Friezes from Tadmore and Persepolis
Al Aaraaf ii 36
Whose wreathed friezes intertwine
City 22

Fright
Yet that terror was not fright
Lake 13; Tamerlane (1831) 91

Frightful
The frightful sounds of merriment below
Politian ii 78

Frigid
When saw you now, Baldazzar, in the
frigid Politian v 24

Fringed
The uplifting of the fringed lid
Dream-Land 48
Above the closed and fringed lid
Sleeper 26

Frisky
As this for a neat, frisky counter-hopper
Tempora 48

Fro
And million bright pines to and fro
Irene 18
That shift the scenery to and fro
Worm 14

Frog
Born and brought up with their snouts
deep down in the mud of the Frog-Pond
Experiments 8

Front
Straight I wheeled a cushioned seat in
front of bird and bust and door
Raven 68

Frown
The night, tho' clear, shall frown
Spirits 11

Fruit
A fairy land of flowers, and fruit, and
sunshine Politian iv 69

Fruits
All wreathed with fairy fruits and flowers
Paradise 5

Fulfilled
At the soft-murmured words that were
fulfilled To MLS 11

Full
Repenting follies that full long have fled
Al Aaraaf i 63
Full many a maid Al Aaraaf ii 139
As I lie at full length Annie 10
Then here's the White Eagle, full daring
is he Campaign 3
A full-orbed moon, that, like thine own
soul, soaring Helen² 4
With a visage full of meaning Nis 21
" She died full young "—one Bossola
answers him Politian ii 18
Full many a fair flow'r rais'd its head
Tamerlane (1827) 402

Fullness
The fullness of a cultured mind
Stanzas² 17

Fully
Yet the ear, it fully knows Bells 57

Funeral
Come, let the burial rite be read—the
funeral song be sung Lenore 5
The curtain, a funeral pall Worm 35

Funereal
O, God! on my funereal mind To¹ 7

Funerals
Of her grand family funerals
Sleeper 53

Furled
Save the airs with pinions furled
Nis (1836) 31

Furnish
Than all Syria can furnish of wine
Latin Hymn 12

Each fit to furnish forth four hours' debate   Tempora 22

Future
On the Future!—how it tells   Bells 29
Let my Future radiant shine   Hymn 11
A voice from out the Future cries   Paradise 10

Gaily
Not the gaily-jewelled dead   City 34
Gaily bedight   Eldorado 1

Gain
Thou hast no end to gain—no heart to break   Politian ii 72
To gain an empire, and throw down   Tamerlane (1827) 243

Gala
Lo!'t is a gala night   Worm 1

Gallant
A gallant knight   Eldorado 2

Gallons
Red gallons of gore   Latin Hymn 11

Gaping
There open fanes and gaping graves   City 30

Garden
Its way to Heaven, from garden of a king   Al Aaraaf i 73
A garden spot in desert of the blest   Al Aaraaf i (1829) 19
One half the garden of her globe was flung   Al Aaraaf ii 222
Roses that grew in an enchanted garden   Helen[2] 9
That bade me pause before that garden-gate   Helen[2] 23
Ah, bear in mind this garden enchanted   Helen[2] 30
Of the garden   Politian i 66
The sweet airs from the garden worry me   Politian ii 80
A wonder to these garden trees   Sleeper 33

Gardens
As in those gardens where the day   Al Aaraaf i 3
And fell on gardens of the unforgiven   Al Aaraaf i 55
In dreamy gardens, where do lie   Al Aaraaf i (1831) 12
Taught in the gardens of Gethsemane   Coliseum 14

Garish
Where, tho' the garish lights that fly   Romance (1831) 13

Garment
And cling around about us as a garment   Coliseum 45

Gate
That bade me pause before that garden-gate   Helen[2] 23
Hath left his iron gate ajar   Tamerlane 226
Threshold of the wide-open gate of dreams   To[3] 22

Gather
So like you gather in your breath   Tamerlane 205

Gaudy
And on her gaudy bier   Paean 6
The gay wall of this gaudy tower   Tamerlane (1827) 15

Gaunt
Gaunt vestibules! and phantom-peopled aisles   Coliseum (1833) 13
What this grim, ungainly, ghastly, gaunt, and ominous bird of yore   Raven 71

Gave
That gave out, in return for the love-light   Helen[2] 12
She has any more jewels—no—no—she gave me all   Politian ii 41
But the silence was unbroken, and the stillness gave no token   Raven 27

Gay
Gay fire-fly of the night we come and go   Al Aaraaf ii 24
Gay, volatile, and giddy—is he not   Politian i 52
The gay wall of this gaudy tower   Tamerlane (1827) 15
That bore me from my home, more gay   Tamerlane (1827) 302

Gaze
With eagle gaze along the firmament   Al Aaraaf ii 195
To gaze upon that veiled face and hear   Politian ii 103
A silent gaze was my farewell   Tamerlane (1827) 287
With its own living gaze upon   Tamerlane (1827) 317
To him, who still would gaze upon   Tamerlane (1827) 366

Gazed
I gazed a while   Star 9

Gazer
Of many a wild star gazer long ago   Al Aaraaf ii 43
A gazer on the lights that shine above   Al Aaraaf ii 184

Gazeth
Who, musing, gazeth on the distance dim   Al Aaraaf ii 45

Gazing
Her friends are gazing on her   Paean 5
Through gazing on the unquiet sky   Romance 15
Gazing, entranced, adown the gorgeous vista   To[3] 23

Gemmy
And gemmy flower, Trebizond misnam'd   Al Aaraaf i 50

Gems
Springs form the gems of Circassy   Al Aaraaf i 4
When from your gems of thought I turn   Impromptu 1
Perennial tears descend in gems   Valley 27

General
The general tuckermanities are arrant   Enigma 10
The blackness of the general Heaven   Romance (1831) 16

Generally
But take it generally upon the whole
                  Tempora 44
Generous
Eliza!—let thy generous heart
              To FSO (1835) 1
Genius
Of Genius, at its natal hour
        Tamerlane (1827) 188
Genoa
Miraculously found by one of Genoa
               Politian iv 67
Gentle
And zone that clung around her gentle
  waist   Al Aaraaf ii 54
Thou art now his gentle bride
                  Ballad 14
Till the fair and gentle Eulalie became my
  blushing bride   Eulalie 4
Some gentle wind hath thought it right
                  Irene 31
And every gentle air that dallied
               Palace 13
Sweet, gentle Lalage   Politian i 31
Lean over her and weep—two gentle
  maids   Politian ii 26
With gentle names—Eiros and Charmion
               Politian ii 27
A kind and gentle office, and a Power
               Politian iii 35
The gentle zephyr floating by   Sarah 13
A gentle guardian spirit given   Sarah 22
The gladness of a gentle heart
               Sanzas² 13
I'd lean upon her gentle breast
        Tamerlane (1831) 133
So with the world thy gentle ways
               To FOS 5
The gentle Naiad from her fountain flood
          To Science (1829) 12
Thy gentlest of all gentle names dost take
                 Zante 2
Gentler
But then a gentler, calmer spell
        Tamerlane (1831) 100
Gentlest
Thy gentlest of all gentle names dost take
                 Zante 2
Gently
Breathe it less gently forth,—and veil
  thine eyes   Acrostic 6
Is the gently falling leaf
       Al Aaraaf i (1831) 27
Sat gently on these columns as a crown
           Al Aaraaf ii 21
And then I fell gently   Annie 75
That gently, over a perfumed sea
               Helen¹ 3
When the Hours flew gently by
          Hymn (1835) 9
Flow softly—gently—vital stream
               Louisa 1
As of some one gently rapping, rapping,
  at my chamber door   Raven 4
But the fact is I was napping, and so
  gently you came rapping   Raven 21

Get
Get thee back into the tempest and the
  Night's Plutonian shore   Raven 98
Gethsemane
Taught in the gardens of Gethsemane
               Coliseum 14
Ghastly
And the ghastly wind went by
            Lake (1845) 9
While, like a ghastly rapid river
               Palace 45
Ghastly grim and ancient Raven wander-
  ing from the Nightly shore Raven 46
What this grim, ungainly, ghastly, gaunt,
  and ominous bird of yore   Raven 71
Ghost
And thou, a ghost, amid the entombing
  trees   Helen² 50
Avaunt!—avaunt! to friends from fiends
  the indignant ghost is riven
               Lenore 20
And each separate dying ember wrought
  its ghost upon the floor   Raven 8
Ghosts
Like ghosts the shadows rise and fall
               Sleeper 29
While the pale sheeted ghosts go by
               Sleeper 44
Ghoul
In the ghoul-haunted woodland of Weir
               Ulalume 9
Nor the ghoul-haunted woodland of Weir
              Ulalume 29
This ghoul-haunted woodland of Weir
              Ulalume 94
Ghouls
They are Ghouls   Bells 88
Where dwell the Ghouls
            Dream-Land 30
Have been that the woodlandish ghouls
              Ulalume 96
The pitiful, the merciful ghouls
              Ulalume 97
Giant
Of giant pasturage lying at his ease
           Al Aaraaf ii 3
With a despotic sway all giant minds
             Coliseum 38
I was mistaken—'t was but a giant bough
             Politian iv 57
Was giant like—so thou, my mind
        Tamerlane (1829) 57
Giantlike
Was giantlike—so thou, my mind
        Tamerlane (1829) 57
Giddy
And the giddy stars (so legends tell)
               Israfel 5
Gay, volatile, and giddy—is he not
             Politian i 52
Gift
But such is not a gift of thine
            Tamerlane 12
Were incense—then a goodly gift
            Tamerlane 91
Gigantically
Death looks gigantically down   City 29

Gilded
On th' Arabesque carving of a gilded hall
                            Al Aaraaf ii 204
Here, where the dames of Rome their
    gilded hair   Coliseum 20
Had gilded with a conqueror's name
                        Tamerlane (1827) 272
Gilead
For the wounded spirit in Gilead it is
    there   Politian ii 32
Is there—is there balm in Gilead?—tell
    me—tell me, I implore   Raven 89

Girl
Than the eyes of the radiant girl
                                Eulalie 8
Girlish
And laughing at her girlish wiles
                            Tamerlane 105
Girt
Upon the rock-girt shore of Time
                              Stanzas² 12
Give
Shall give his undivided time
                            City (1836) 56
Give up thy soul to pentence, and pray
                            Politian ii 76
Give way unto these humors
                            Politian iii 3
To give thee cause for grief, my honored
    friend   Politian iii 8
Give not thy soul to dreams: the camp—
    the court   Politian iii 21
Politian, give   Politian iii 95
Believe me, I would give
                           Politian iii 100
Freely would give the broad lands of my
    earldom   Politian iii 101
Give to live yet—yet a little while
                            Politian v 8
In the budding of my hopes—give me to
    live   Politian v (1835) 7
Bright with all hopes that Heaven can
    give   Stanzas² 28
Give a trickle and a tinkle and a knell
                          Valley (1845) 30
Given
Fair flowers, and fairy! to whose care is
    given   Al Aaraaf i 80
My embassy is given   Al Aaraaf i 115
Yet thine is my resplendency, so given
                           Al Aaraaf i 141
Be given our lady's bidding to discuss
                          Al Aaraaf ii 246
They have given her to another
                          Ballad 1, 3, 25
They have given thee to another
                             Ballad 13
As if their tops had feebly given
                               City 46
White-robed forms of friends long given
                          Dream-Land 37
In my young boyhood—should it thus be
    given   Dreams 11
He has given us more   Latin Hymn 10
And little given to thinking
                           Politian i 53

Would have given a real diamond to such
    as you   Politian ii 54
Having given thee no offence
                            Politian v 55
A gentle guardian spirit given   Sarah 22
With light like Hope to mortals given
                              Spirits 14
Of what in other worlds shall be—and
    given   Stanzas 25
Hath not the same fierce heirdom given
                           Tamerlane 30
O, human love! thou spirit given
                          Tamerlane 177
Given by the energetic might
                      Tamerlane (1827) 187
For the flight on Earth to Fancy given
                      Tamerlane (1827) 325
Gives
For her soul gives me sigh for sigh
                             Eulalie 16
Not within himself but gives
                      Tamerlane (1827) 308
Glade
Some have left the cool glade, and
                          Al Aaraaf ii 140
Gladness
The gladness of a gentle heart
                              Stanzas² 13
Glance
Till they glance thro' the shade, and
                           Al Aaraaf ii 76
The brightest glance of pride and power
                          Happiest Day 15
Glances
My quick glances now retreating
                            Departed 6
Where the Houri glances are
                              Israfel 26
Are where the grey eye glances
                             Paradise 23
Glancing
In the seraphic glancing of thine eyes
                              To MLS 12
Glare
While even in the meridian glare of day
                              Helen³ 64
See how her eye-balls glare   Louisa 6
Glared
Here, where the mimic eagle glared in
    gold   Coliseum 18
Glass
Along that wilderness of glass   City 37
Because to his cat's eyes I hold a glass
                             Tempora 87
Glasses
Beholds it but through darkened glasses
                          Dream-Land 50
Gleaming
Ah, we safely may trust to its gleaming
                             Ulalume 67
We surely may trust to a gleaming
                             Ulalume 69
Gleams
Gleams up the pinnacles far and free
                               City 16
And where thy footstep gleams
                             Paradise 24

Glide
Didst glide away. Only thine eyes re-
mained   Helen² 51
Glides
Glides, spectre-like, unto his marble home
Coliseum 23
Glides down the Stygian river
Lenore (1843) 4
Gliding
Gliding serenely to its goal
Stanzas² 23
Glistens
Which glistens then, and trembles
River 8
Glitter
Which Error's glitter cannot blind
Stanzas² 19
Glitering
Of other beauty glittering thro' the light
Al Aaraaf i 29
And a glittering beam from a maiden's
eye   Parody 9
Gloated
On the cushion's velvet lining that the
lamp-light gloated o'er   Raven 76
Gloating
On bed of moss lies gloating the foul
adder   Coliseum (1833) 25
But whose velvet-violet lining with the
lamp-light gloating o'er   Raven 77
Gloats
To the turtle-dove that listens, while she
gloats   Bells 23
Globe
One half the garden of her globe was flung
Al Aaraaf ii 222
Gloom
To heaven with that ungodly gloom
City (1831) 9
My very soul thy grandeur, gloom, and
glory   Coliseum 9
Spirits in the gloom   Departed 32
Is by (the very source of gloom)
Fairy-Land (1831) 34
Hist! hush! within the gloom
Politian iv 53
Throw over all things a gloom
Politian iv 64
Gone are the glory and the gloom
Romance (1831) 37
How now! why tremble, man of gloom
Tamerlane (1831) 179
And tempted her out of her gloom
Ulalume 73
And conquered her scruples and gloom
Ulalume 74
Gloomy
That my room it is gloomy   Annie 47
Glories
Succeeds the glories of the bowl
Romance (1831) 43
Glorious
But hug the glorious chains I wore
Divine Right 4
And strange thy glorious length of tress
Irene 28

Banners yellow, glorious, golden
Palace 9
Stranger thy glorious length of tress
Sleeper (1842) 35
Gloriously
Went gloriously away
Dream w. Dream (1829) 12;
Tamerlane (1831) 256;
To⁴ 24
Glory
But when its glory swelled upon the sky
Al Aaraaf ii 257
Of glory accurst   Annie (1849) 36
Feel a glory in so rolling   Bells 84
My very soul thy grandeur, gloom, and
glory   Coliseum 9
Clothing us in a robe of more than glory
Coliseum 46
To the glory that was Greece   Helen¹ 9
In state his glory well befitting
Palace 23
And round about his home the glory
Palace 37
Befit thee—Fame awaits thee—Glory calls
Politian iii 22
And with thy glory   Politian iv 30
Ha! glory!—now speak not of it
Politian iv 35
There is no deed I would more glory in
Politian iv 39
Than in thy cause to scoff at this same
glory   Politian iv 40
Gone are the glory and the gloom
Romance (1831) 37
In thy glory afar   Star 16
The searing glory which hath shone
Tamerlane 17
Of glory which the world hath known
Tamerlane 169
The glory of the summer sun
Tamerlane 194
With glory—such as might inspire
Tamerlane (1827) 273
Bowed down with its own glory grows
Tamerlane (1831) 222
Glow
The waves have now a redder glow
City 48
Thou art an emblem of the glow
River 3
Though its glow hath raised a fiercer
flame   Song 11
Burned with a still intenser glow
Tamerlane 71
Gloweth
Where each star most faintly gloweth
Departed 3
Glowing
Than even thy glowing bosom beats withal
Al Aaraaf ii 217
As glowing Beauty's bust beneath man's
eye   Al Aaraaf ii 258
With heaven's light upon her glowing
Departed 26
And all with pearl and ruby glowing
Palace 25

The fairy light that kisses her golden hair
                    Al Aaraaf ii 58
Light, brazen rays, this golden star unto
                    Al Aaraaf ii 240
Golden bells   Bells 16
Behold the golden token
                    Bridal Ballad 26
Here, where on golden throne the monarch
    lolled   Coliseum 22
Grains of the golden sand
                    Dream w. Dream 15
Ah, broken is the golden bowl!—the spirit
    flown forever   Lenore 1
From moan and groan to a golden throne
    beside the King of Heaven   Lenore 22
Down within the golden east   Nis 4
Banners yellow, glorious, golden
                    Palace 9
Bore a bright golden flower, but not i'
    this soil   Politian ii 7
The sands of Time are changed to golden
    grains   Politian iii 41
A thousand leagues within the golden west
                    Politian iv 68
Exhales from without her golden rim
                    Sleeper 4
This standing motionless upon the golden
                    To⁸ 21

Gomorrah
Of beautiful Gomorrah! O, the wave
                    Al Aaraaf ii 38

Gone
Have gone to their eternal rest   City 5
Not all our power is gone—not all our
    fame   Coliseum 40
Shadows of the gone   Departed 8
O'er my soul, is gone   Departed 20
Is it therefore the less gone
                    Dream w. Dream 9
They would not go—they never yet have
    gone   Helen² 52
And my worldly rest hath gone
                    Imitation 17
The sweet Lenore hath gone before, with
    Hope that flew beside   Lenore 15
Thou art not gone—thou art not gone,
    Politian   Politian iv 91
I feel thou art not gone—yet dare not
    look   Politian iv 92
To say thou art not gone,—one little
    sentence   Politian iv 96
Ha! ha! thou art not gone
                    Politian iv 98
Villain, thou art not gone—thou mockest
    me   Politian iv 101
He is gone, he is gone   Politian iv 102
Gone—gone   Politian iv 103
Gone are the glory and the gloom
                    Romance (1831) 37
The earth reel—and the vision gone
                    Tamerlane (1827) 97
Is it, therefore, the less gone
                    Tamerlane (1831) 248
When, a few fleeting years gone by
                    Tamerlane (1827) 268

Withered and blasted; who had gone
                    Tamerlane (1827) 276
They had gone unto the wars   Valley 3

Good
From every depth of good and ill
                    Alone 11
Where the good and the bad and the worst
    and the best   City 4
In joy and wo—in good and ill   Hymn 3
By good angels tenanted   Palace 2
Wilt thou, my good Jacinta, be so kind
                    Politian ii 29
How fares good Ugo?—and when is it to
    be   Politian ii 44
Good-night, Politian   Politian iii 114
Good-night, my friend, good-night
                    Politian iii 115
Thro' good and ill—thro' weal and woe I
    love thee   Politian iv 15
What answer was it you brought me, good
    Baldazzar   Politian v 14
The "good old times" were far the worst
    of any   Tempora 6
It boots me not, good friar, to tell
                    Tamerlane (1827) 349
The good, the bad, the ideal
                    Tamerlane (1831) 143

Goodly
He was a goodly spirit—he who fell
                    Al Aaraaf ii 182
Were incense—then a goodly gift
                    Tamerlane 91

Gordian
And yet there is in this no Gordian knot
                    Valentine 10

Gore
Red gallons of gore   Latin Hymn 11
In human gore imbued   Worm 32

Gorgeous
Of gorgeous columns on th' unburthened
    air   Al Aaraaf ii 12
I left her gorgeous halls—nor mourned to
    leave   Al Aaraaf ii 201
There the gorgeous clouds do fly   Nis 38
Gazing, entranced, adown the gorgeous
    vista   To⁸ 23

Governs
To check the power that governs here
                    Divine Right 8

Grace
But two: they fell: for Heaven no grace
    imparts   Al Aaraaf ii 176
Thy grace did guide to thine and thee
                    Hymn 8
Is grace to its heavenly bed of blue
                    Tamerlane (1827) 321
Thy grace, thy more than beauty
                    To FSO 6

Graces
Newly with grass overgrown; some solemn
    graces   Silence 7

Grains
Grains of the golden sand
                    Dream w. Dream 15
The sands of Time are changed to golden
    grains   Politian iii 41

We grew in age—and love—together
         Tamerlane 96
Then my heart it grew ashen and sober
         Ulalume 82

Grey
Witness the murmur of the grey twilight
         Al Aaraaf ii 41
But, Angelo, than thine grey Time un-
furled   Al Aaraaf ii 251
Lone amphitheatre! Grey Coliseum
         Coliseum (1833) 1
By the grey woods,—by the swamp
         Dream-Land 27
Grey towers are mouldering into rest
         Irene 11
Are where thy grey eye glances
         Paradise 23
In years, but grey in fame
         Politian i 47
The black hath mellowed into grey
         Romance (1831) 38

Greybeard
Why not an imp the greybeard hath
         Romance (1831) 63
And even the greybeard will o'erlook
         Romance (1831) 65

Greyish
The dimness of this world: that greyish
green   Al Aaraaf ii 29

Grief
And blossom of the fairy plant, in grief
         Al Aaraaf i 61
Disconsolate linger—grief that hangs her
head   Al Aaraaf i 62
Thou! thy truest type of grief
         Al Aaraaf i (1831) 26
Fierce deep grief is unavailing
         Departed 22
Thy grief, thy joy, thy hate, thy love
         Israfel 37
From grief and moan   Lenore (1843) 57
To give thee cause for grief, my honored
friend   Politian iii 8
While yet my vapid joy and grief
         Romance (1831) 61

Grieve
Lang and sairly shall I grieve thee
         Ballad 11, 23, 35
To grieve thee or to vex thee
         Politian ii 38
Politian, it doth grieve me
         Politian iii 6
Baldazzar, it doth grieve me
         Politian iii 7

Grieves
Thy presence grieves me—go!—thy
priestly raiment   Politian ii 81

Grievously
Am I not—am I not sorely—grievously
tempted   Politian v 83

Grim
Like the grim shadow Conscience, solemn
and noiseless   Politian iv 56
Ghastly grim and ancient Raven wandering from the Nightly shore
         Raven 46

What this grim, ungainly, ghastly, gaunt,
and ominous bird of yore   Raven 71

Grimace
But speak to him, he'll make you such a
grimace   Tempora 63

Grin
The page of life and grin at the dog-ears
         Tempora 17

Groan
Is a groan   Bells 78
From moan and groan to a golden throne
beside the King of Heaven   Lenore 22
That grown as they roll down Mount
Yaanek   Ulalume 18

Groaned
It was the dead who groaned within
         Sleeper 60

Groaning
The moaning and groaning   Annie 19
To the moaning and the groaning of the
bells   Bells 113

Ground
Feet under ground   Annie 42
Down under ground   Annie 44
No spot of ground   Eldorado 11
Thy memory no more! Accursed ground
         Zante 11

Grove
In many a star-lit grove, or moon-lit dell
         Al Aaraaf ii 63
Else how, when in the holy grove
         Tamerlane 231

Grow
The sands of Time grow dimmer as they
run   Al Aaraaf i 140
Whose failing sight will grow dim
         Tamerlane (1827) 316

Groweth
Where the green grass ever groweth
         Departed 2

Growing
From the growing of grass
         Al Aaraaf ii 125
That my voice is growing weak   Paean 15
The hour is growing late—the Duke
awaits us   Politian iii 88
On my grave is growing or grown
         To M 18
Till growing bold, he laughed and leapt
         Tamerlane 242

Growl
But, taking one by each hand, merely
growl   Tempora 28
Ah growl, say you, my friend, and pray
at what   Tempora 29

Grown
Where Love's a grown-up God
         Israfel 25
Love is a grown God   Israfel (1831) 23
On my grave is growing or grown
         To M 18

Grows
This weakness grows upon me
         Politian v 1
Grows dim around me—death is near
         Tamerlane (1827) 16
Drear path, alas! where grows   To F 3

Guard
These should be thine, to guard and shield
Stanzas² 25

Guardian
A gentle guardian spirit given   Sarah 22

Guessing
This I sat engaged in guessing, but no
syllable expressing   Raven 73
And, lest the guessing throw the fool in
fits   Tempora 91

Guide
Thy grace did guide to thine and thee
Hymn 8
To guide my wandering thoughts to
heaven   Sarah 23
Of Beauty, which did guide it through
Tamerlane (1827) 211
That cannot but guide us aright
Ulalume 70

Guiding
A lonely spirit guiding   Dream 12

Guileless
The grandeur of a guileless soul
Stanzas² 21

Guilt
Lest the stars totter in the guilt of man
Al Aaraaf i 150

Guilty
Like guilty beauty, chastened, and more
fair   Al Aaraaf i 65
What guilty spirit, in what shrubbery
dim   Al Aaraaf ii 174

Guise
But mystically—in such guise
Tamerlane 146
Ere, in a peasant's lowly guise
Tamerlane (1827) 360

Gulf
And in its gulf a fitting grave   Lake 19
Dim gulf! my spirit hovering lies
Paradise 12

Gulistan
With Persian Saadi in his Gulistan
Al Aaraaf ii 209

Gurgled
Gurgled within my ear the crush
Tamerlane 61

Gurgling
The silvery streamlet gurgling on
Sarah 7

Ha
Ha! glory!—now speak not of it
Politian iv 35
Ha! ha! thou art not gone
Politian iv 98
Ha!—am I right?   Politian v 55
Ha!—draw?—and villain? have at thee
then   Politian v 58
Ha!   Politian v 66

Hades
All Hades from a thousand thrones
City (1836) 52

Haggard
Thy looks are haggard—nothing so wears
away   Politian i 15
And the seraphs, all haggard and wan
Worm (1843) 37

Hail
Of all who hail thy presence as the morning   To MLS 1

Hair
Like woman's hair 'mid pearls until, afar
Al Aaraaf i 33
The fairy light that kiss'd her golden hair
Al Aaraaf ii 58
And looks so sweetly down on Beauty's
hair   Al Aaraaf ii 187
So softly that no single silken hair
Al Aaraaf ii 212
Here, where the dames of Rome their
gilded hair   Coliseum 20
Thy hair is lifted by the moon
Fairy-Land (1831) 7
Thy hyacinth hair, thy classic face
Helen¹ 7
The life upon her yellow hair, but not
within her eyes   Lenore 18
The life still there upon her hair, the
death upon her eyes   Lenore 19
Have nestled in my very hair
Tamerlane 40
In the tangles of Love's very hair?
Tamerlane 243

Haired
Till the yellow-haired young Eulalie became my smiling bride   Eulalie 5

Half
With half closing eyes
Al Aaraaf ii 73
One half the garden of her globe was
flung   Al Aaraaf ii 222
And half I wish'd to be again of men
Al Aaraaf ii 226
The angels, not half so happy in Heaven
Annabel Lee 21
Half an idea in the profoundest sonnet
Enigma 2
I saw thee half reclining; while the moon
Helen² 18
He would not sing one half as well
Israfel (1831) 44
One half as passionately
Israfel (1831) 46
Over fabric half so fair   Palace 8
My heart half fear'd to be a crime
Romance (1831) 44
I feel it more than half a crime
Serenade 2
But I will half believe that wild light
fraught   Stanzas¹ 11
Appeared to my half-closing eye
Tamerlane 46
Or half the world as all my own
Tamerlane 131
Laughing at her half silly wiles
Tamerlane (1827) 129

Halidom
Now by my halidom   Politian v 69

Hall
Within the centre of that hall to breathe
Al Aaraaf ii 56
On th' Arabesque carving of a gilded hall
Al Aaraaf ii 204

For strangely—fearfully in this hall
                     Irene 39
Thy presence is expected in the hall
                 Politian iii 89

Hallowed
And hallow'd all the beauty twice again
                 Al Aaraaf ii 25
Let no bell toll, then, lest her soul, amid
    its hallowed mirth   Lenore 23
To join the all-hallowed mirth
                 Paean (1836) 35
The hallow'd mem'ry of those years
            Tamerlane (1827) 136

Halls
And Nesace is in her halls again
                 Al Aaraaf ii 51
I left her gorgeous halls—nor mourn'd to
    leave   Al Aaraaf ii 201
Up domes—up spires—up kingly halls
                     City 17
Over hamlets, over halls
                 Fairy-Land 20
How, in thy father's halls, among the
    maidens   Politian iv 24

Halo
Halo, of Hell! and with a pain
                 Tamerlane 19

Hamadryad
And driven the Hamadryad from the wood
                 To Science 10

Hamlets
Over hamlets, over halls
                 Fairy-Land 20
Embrac'd two hamlets—those our own
           Tamerlane (1827) 222

Hand
The ring is on my hand   Bridal Ballad 1
Lo! the ring is on my hand
          Bridal Ballad (1837) 25
And I hold within my hand
          Dream w. Dream 14
The agate lamp within thy hand!
                 Helen[1] 13
Your hand from off my shoulder, if you
    please   Politian i 36
Stay—stay thy hand   Politian v 3
Hold off—thy sacred hand—avaunt I say!
                 Politian v 62
Hold off thy hand—with that beloved
    name   Politian v 67
For in the fight I will not raise a hand
                 Politian v 79
And crouches to a keeper's hand
                 Tamerlane 161
Above all cities? in her hand
                 Tamerlane 167
Her own fair hand had rear'd around
           Tamerlane (1827) 219
And I held within my hand
           Tamerlane (1831) 251
But, taking one by each hand, merely
    growl   Tempora 28
The pretty little hand that sold her tape
                 Tempora 56
The pen falls powerless from my shivering
    hand   To[3] 17

Hang
So eagerly around about to hang
                 Al Aaraaf i 45
But hang on the heart
           Al Aaraaf ii (1829) 99
Not all the memories that hang upon
                 Coliseum 44

Hangs
Disconsolate linger—grief that hangs her
    head   Al Aaraaf i 62
To the lone oak that nodding hangs
               Irene (1836) 14
Which hangs like chains of pearl on Her-
    mon hill   Politian ii 35
How it hangs upon the trees   Spirits 27
To a fever by the moonbeam that hangs
    o'er   Stanzas[1] 10
That hangs like chains of pearl on Her-
    mon hill   To[3] 10

Hapless
My passions, from that hapless hour
                 Tamerlane 65

Haply
Thus, haply, while in sleep she dream'd
           Tamerlane (1827) 293
As in a leader, haply—Power
           Tamerlane (1827) 44

Happier
Upon some far-off happier sea   City 39
Are happier, sweet, than I   To[2] 6
To seek a shelter in some happier star?
                 To Science 11

Happiest
Now happiest, loveliest in yon lovely
    Earth   Al Aaraaf i 30
The happiest day, the happiest hour
           Happiest Day 1, 13
Oh, I'm the happiest, happiest man in
    Rome!   Politian i 2

Happiness
What a world of happiness their harmony
    foretells!   Bells 17
Thy happiness!—what ails thee, cousin of
    mine?   Politian i 6
Is Happiness now, and will be Freedom
    hereafter   Politian iv 73
Though happiness around thee lay
                 Song 3, 15

Happy
To happy flowers that night—and tree to
    tree   Al Aaraaf ii 61
The angels, not half so happy in Heaven
                 Annabel Lee 21
In a happy Runic rhyme   Bells 107
And I am happy now   Bridal Ballad 5
And who is happy now
               Bridal Ballad 12
Oh, I am happy now   Bridal Ballad 19
That I am happy now!   Bridal Ballad 25
That proves me happy now!
               Bridal Ballad 27
If I am not happy now!
           Bridal Ballad (1837) 24
And I must be happy now!
           Bridal Ballad (1837) 30
May not be happy now
           Bridal Ballad (1837) 33

And hath been still, upon the lovely earth
                              Dreams 7
Than young Hope in his sunniest hour
    hath known   Dreams (1827) 34
My sear'd and blighted heart hath known
                           Happiest Day 2
I feel hath flown   Happiest Day 4
Which my spirit hath not seen
                              Imitation 8
And my wordly rest hath gone
                             Imitation 17
Some gentle wind hath thought it right
                                Irene 31
The sweet Lenore hath gone before, with
    Hope that flew beside   Lenore 15
Thereabout which Time hath said
                                 Nis 9
There is an imp hath followed me even
    there!   Politian iii 17
As hath been kindled within it
                         Politian iii 45
Who hath loved thee so long
                    Politian iii 72, 81, 91
Hath without doubt arisen: thou hast
    been urged   Politian v 49
" Wretch," I cried, " thy God hath lent
    thee—by these angels he hath sent thee
                                Raven 81
Leave no black plume as a token of that
    lie thy soul hath spoken   Raven 99
Hath been—a most familiar bird
                              Romance 6
But now my soul hath too much room
                         Romance (1831) 46
The black hath mellow'd into grey
                         Romance (1831) 48
My draught of passion hath been deep
                         Romance (1831) 50
Why not an imp the greybeard hath
                         Romance (1831) 63
No power hath he of evil in himself
                              Silence 11
That haunteth the lone regions where
    hath trod   Silence 14
Some vault that oft hath flung its black
                              Sleeper 50
Against whose portal she hath thrown
                              Sleeper 55
Though its glow hath raised a fierce flame
                                Song 11
Hath ever told—or is it of a thought
                            Stanzas¹ 13
That high tone of the spirit which hath
    striv'n   Stanzas¹ 29
With desp'rate energy 't hath beaten down
                            Stanzas¹ 31
Unearthly pride hath revell'd in
                             Tamerlane 5
The searing glory which hath shone
                            Tamerlane 17
Hath not the same fierce heirdom given
                            Tamerlane 30
And proud spirit which hath striven
                            Tamerlane 33
Of glory which the world hath known
                            Tamerlane 169

And all we seek to keep hath flown
                            Tamerlane 210
Hath left his iron gate ajar
                            Tamerlane 226
I do believe that Eblis hath
                            Tamerlane 229
Its very form hath passed me by
                         Tamerlane (1827) 100
Hath fix'd my soul, tho' unforgiv'n
                         Tamerlane (1827) 106
The passionate spirit which hath known
                         Tamerlane (1827) 179
When th' astonish'd earth hath seen
                         Tamerlane (1827) 334
Of our boyhood, his course hath run
                         Tamerlane (1827) 385
Hath long upon my bosom sat
                         Tamerlane (1831) 28
Hath nestled in my very hair
                         Tamerlane (1831) 44
If my peace hath flown away
                         Tamerlane (1831) 245
Hath—little of Earth in it   To² 2
My soul at least a solace hath   To F 5
Hath palsied many years   To M 12
Who hath seduced thee to this foul revolt
                           To Maragaret 1
Ah, what demon hath tempted me here
                              Ulalume 90

Hatred
That hatred portion, with the fame
                         Tamerlane (1827) 25
In the hatred of a minute   To² 4

Haughtily
Striding o'er empires haughtily
                            Tamerlane 175

Haunt
To haunt of the wide world a spot
                    Lake 2; Tamerlane (1831) 80

Haunted
To his love-haunted heart and melancholy
                            Al Aaraaf ii 189
Haunted by ill angels only
                         Dream-Land 2, 52
On this home by Horror haunted—tell me
    truly, I implore   Raven 88
In the ghoul-haunted woodland of Weir
                              Ulalume 9
Nor the ghoul-haunted woodland of Weir
                              Ulalume 29
This ghoul-haunted woodland of Weir
                              Ulalume 94

Haunteth
That haunteth the lone regions where hath
    trod   Silence 14

Have
Ha!—draw?—and villain? have at thee
    then   Politian v 58

Having
Having gone unto the wars   Nis 19
I cannot die, having within my heart
                          Politian iii 43
Having given thee no offence
                           Politian v 55
Thus I remember having dwelt
                           Tamerlane 81

Head
Of flowers: of lilies such as rear'd the
head   Al Aaraaf i 43
Disconsolate linger—grief that hangs her
head   Al Aaraaf i 62
High on a mountain of enamell'd head
  Al Aaraaf ii 1
Of rosy head, that towering far away
  Al Aaraaf ii 7
Radiant palace—reared its head
  Palace 4
The soft head bows, the sweet eyes close
  Physician 5
This and more I sat divining, with my
head at ease reclining   Raven 75
With drowsy head and folded wing
  Romance 2
Nightly their dews upon my head
  Tamerlane 37
The rain came down upon my head
  Tamerlane 55
Full many a fair flow'r rais'd its head
  Tamerlane (1827) 402
A wise philosopher would shake his head
  Tempora 83

Headlong
Headlong thitherward o'er the starry sea
  Al Aaraaf ii 256
And tumult of the headlong air
  Tamerlane 39

Health
And, when she fell in feeble health, ye
blessed her—that she died   Lenore 9
Of health, joy, peace, in store for thee
  Stanzas² 4

Hear
They slumber'd to hear
  Al Aaraaf ii 147
To those who hear not for their beating
hearts   Al Aaraaf ii 177
Who hear not for the beating of their
hearts   Al Aaraaf ii 264
Hear the sledges with the bells
  Bells 1
Hear the mellow wedding bells
  Bells 15
Hear the loud alarum bells   Bells 36
Hear the tolling of the bells   Bells 70
Hear the knells!   Bells (1849) 11
Those flowers that say (ah hear them
now!)   Irene 53
Did I dream, or did I hear
  Politian i 66
An her, the trumpet-tongued, thou wilt
not hear   Politian iii 23
Didst thou not hear it then?
  Politian iii 26
Indeed I hear not   Politian iii 51
Not hear it!—listen now! listen!—the
faintest sound   Politian iii 52
I myself hear it now   Politian iii 60
To gaze upon that veiled face, and hear
  Politian iii 103
And let me hear thy voice—one word—
one word   Politian iv 95
Dost hear? with cowardice—thou wilt not
fight me?   Politian v 91

Much I marvelled this ungainly fowl to
hear discourse so plainly   Raven 49
I think I hear thy voice's sound
  Sarah 4
Hear thou the secret of a spirit
  Tamerlane (1831) 13
Compose a sound delighting all to hear
  Valentine (1846) 18

Heard
Heard not the stirring summons of that
hymn?   Al Aaraaf ii 175
Maria! thou hast heard my hymn!
  Hymn 2
His blue-bell helmet, we have heard
  Parody 1
Heard I aright?   Politian i 32
I have heard much of this Politian
  Politian i 51
I heard it not   Politian iii 18
I heard not any voice except thine own
  Politian iii 19
I heard it not   Politian iii 26
And yet the sweetest that ear ever heard!
  Politian iii 53
Surely I never heard—yet it were well
  Politian iii 58
Had I but heard it with its thrilling
tones   Politian iii 59
The song is English, and I oft have heard
it   Politian iii 77
That I scarce was sure I heard you—here
I opened wide the door   Raven 23
Soon again I heard a tapping somewhat
louder than before   Raven 32
Your scorn, perhaps, when ye have heard
  Tamerlane (1827) 198

Heardst
Thou heardst it not!   Politian iii 27

Hearest
Thou hearest not now, Baldazzar?
  Politian iii 51

Hearing
A well-known name, oft uttered in the
hearing   Valentine 15

Hearkening
In hearkening to imaginary sounds
  Politian iii 24

Heart
Ah! if that language from thy heart arise
  Acrostic 5
Bursting its odorous heart in spirit to
wing   Al Aaraaf i 72
The red fire of their heart
  Al Aaraaf i 95
To ev'ry heart a barrier and a ban
  Al Aaraaf i 149
Had burst beneath the heaving of her
heart   Al Aaraaf ii 55
But lead on the heart   Al Aaraaf ii 99
To his love-haunted heart and melancholy
choly   Al Aaraaf ii 189
My heart to joy at the same tone
  Alone 7
At heart:—ah, that horrible   Annie 23
But my heart it is brighter   Annie 95
And my heart is lonely now   Ballad 4

And thy trusting heart beguil'd
      Ballad 18
And tho' my poor heart be broken
      Ballad 31
On the human heart a stone Bells 85
And, though my heart be broken
     Bridal Ballad 23
Yet are they my heart assailing
      Departed 23
Proud heart, never won! Departed 24
Its own core my wild heart eating
      Departed 35
For the heart whose woes are legion
     Dream-Land 39
Of waking life, to him whose heart must
be   Dreams 6
And loveliness,—have left my very heart
      Dreams 15
And o'er his heart a shadow
      Eldorado 9
Always write first things uppermost in
the heart   Elizabeth 16
My sear'd and blighted heart hath known
     Happiest Day 2
How my heart beats in coupling those
two words!   Helen² 27
What wild heart histories seemed to lie
enwritten   Helen² 42
To those pure orbs, your heart to learn
     Impromptu 2
Whose heart-strings are a lute
      Israfel 2
And I—to-night my heart is light:—no
dirge will I upraise Lenore 25
And fill my heart of hearts, where Death
installed you   Mother 7
Much about a broken heart Nis 13
Still does my heart confess thy power
      Octavia 4
My heart, of all that soothes its pain
      Octavia 7
The faithful heart yields to repose
      Physician 6
Thou hast no end to gain—no heart to
break   Politian ii 72
I cannot die, having within my heart
     Politian iii 43
Into my heart of hearts! that eloquent
voice   Politian iii 57
And is thy heart so strong
   Politian iii 70, 74, 83, 93
Thou lovest me, and in my heart of hearts
     Politian iv 51
So that now, to still the beating of my
heart, I stood repeating Raven 15
Let my heart be still a moment and this
mystery explore Raven 35
Take thy beak from out my heart, and
take thy form from off my door!
      Raven 101
Of beauty—the unhidden heart River 4
For in his heart, as in thy stream
      River 11
His heart which trembles at the beam
      River 13
My heart would feel to be a crime
     Romance 20

To thy withering heart shall seem
    Spirits (1827) 16
The gladness of a gentle heart
     Stanza² 13
Drawn by their heart's passion, and that
tone   Stanzas ¹ 28
For joy to my heart Star 18
O yearning heart! I did inherit
     Tamerlane 15
O craving heart, for the lost flowers
     Tamerlane 21
E'en then who knew this iron heart
     Tamerlane 73
Might envy; her young heart the shrine
     Tamerlane 89
Young Love's first lesson is—the heart
     Tamerlane 102
But leav'st the heart a wilderness!
     Tamerlane 182
There comes a sullenness of heart
     Tamerlane 192
An humbler heart—a deeper wo
     Tamerlane 221
Scorching my sear'd heart with a pain
   Tamerlane (1827) 27
O how would my wild heart rejoice
   Tamerlane (1827) 57
The proud heart burst in agony
   Tamerlane (1827) 200
Of her that heart's idolatry
   Tamerlane (1827) 202
To trust the weakness of my heart
   Tamerlane (1827) 291
I knew not woman's heart, alas!
   Tamerlane (1827) 297
My wilder'd heart was far away
   Tamerlane (1827) 356
My heart sunk with the sun's ray
   Tamerlane (1827) 365
Here he may revel to his heart's content
     Tempora 49
Thine eyes, in Heaven of heart enshrined
      To¹ 5
Thy heart—thy heart!—I wake and sigh
      To¹ 9
Have stirred from out the abysses of his
heart   To³ 11
Thou wouldst be loved?—then let thy
heart   To FSO 1
To release my heart To Hunter 4
Lie dead on my heart-strings To M 15
Why preyest thou thus upon the poet's
heart   To Science 3
These were days when my heart was
volcanic   Ulalume 13
Then my heart it grew ashen and sober
      Ulalume 82
That must be worn at heart. Search well
the measure   Valentine 7

Hearted
Or (music of the passion-hearted)
     Al Aaraaf i 7
Hath left me broken-hearted Dream 4

Hearts
To those who hear not for their beating
hearts   Al Aaraaf ii 177

Bright with all hopes that Heaven can
give   Stanzas² 28
Thou bearest in Heav'n at night   Star 20
So late from Heaven—that dew—it fell
                          Tamerlane 41
I saw no Heaven—but in her eyes
                          Tamerlane 101
On Earth, of all we hope in Heaven!
                          Tamerlane 178
Above with trellis'd rays from Heaven
                          Tamerlane 237
By what it lost for passion—Heav'n
                          Tamerlane (1827) 107
There are no words—unless of Heav'n
                          Tamerlane (1827) 236
This is a question which, Oh, Heaven,
withdraw   Tempora 19
Thine eyes, in Heaven of heart enshrined
                          To¹ 5
The blotting utterly from out high heaven
                          To MLS 3
Since it flickers up to Heaven through the
night   Ulalume 71
That rustle through the unquiet Heaven
                          Valley 18

Heavenly
Is grace to its heav'nly bed of blue
                          Tamerlane (1827) 321

Heavens
All the heavens, seem to twinkle   Bells 7
But the Heavens that angel trod
                          Israfel (1831) 21
Because I feel that, in the Heavens above
                          Mother 1
So shook the very Heavens on high
                          Romance (1831) 36
Herself in the Heavens   Star 7

Heavier
Yet heavier far than your Petrarchan
stuff   Enigma 6

Heaving
Heaving her white breast to the balmy
air   Al Aaraaf i 64
Had burst beneath the heaving of her
heart   Al Aaraaf ii 55

Heavings
No heavings hint that winds have been
                          City 40

Heavy
Raising his heavy eyelid, starts and sees
                          Al Aaraaf ii 4
And on my eyelids—O the heavy light!
                          Al Aaraaf ii 206
The heavy iron bells!   (Bells (1849) 9
Unshelter'd—and the heavy wind
                          Tamerlane 56

Hebrides
Around the misty Hebrides!   Valley 16

Heed
A tale—a pretty tale—and heed thou not
                          Politian ii 63
Sweet voice! I heed thee, and will surely
stay   Politian iii 109
I heed not that my earthly lot   To² 1
I heed not that the desolate   To M 5

Heedless
Now sounded to her heedless ear
                          Tamerlane (1827) 246

Height
Uprear'd upon such height arose a pile
                          Al Aaraaf ii 11
I clamber'd to the tottering height
                          Tamerlane (1827) 352

Heir
Yon heir, whose cheeks of pallid hue
                          Lenore (1843) 15
Ill suit the like with old Di Broglio's heir
                          Politian i 21
His son and heir   Politian iii 69

Heirdom
Hath not the same fierce heirdom given
                          Tamerlane 30
The heirdom of a kingly mind
                          Tamerlane (1827) 35

Heirs
By rivals loved, and mourned by heirs
                          Stanzas² 8

Held
And I held within my hand
                          Dream w. Dream (1831) 12
In secret, communing held—as he with it
                          Stanzas¹ 2
And I have held to mem'ry's eye
                          Tamerlane (1827) 98
I held no doubt—I knew no fear
                          Tamerlane (1827) 241
Awake, that I had held a thought
                          Tamerlane (1827) 295
And I held within my hand
                          Tamerlane (1831) 251
Philosophers have often held dispute
                          Tempora 73

Helen
Helen, thy beauty is to me   Helen¹ 1
Helen, like thy human eye   Nis 29
And Helen, like thy human eye
                          Nis (1836) 41
Helen, thy soul is riven   Paean (1836) 38

Hell
Apart from Heaven's Eternity—and yet
how far from Hell   Al Aaraaf ii 173
Hell, rising from a thousand thrones
                          City 52
From Hell unto a high estate within the
utmost Heaven   Lenore 21
Now's Death and Hell!   Politian v 82
Halo of Hell! and with a pain
                          Tamerlane 19
Not Hell shall make me fear again
                          Tamerlane 20
Upon me with the touch of Hell
                          Tamerlane 43
O, I defy thee, Hell, to show
                          Tamerlane 219
From the Hell of the planetary souls?
                          Ulalume 104

Helm
She throws aside the sceptre—leaves the
helm   Al Aaraaf i 27

Helmet
His blue-bell helmet, we have heard
                          Parody 1

Hills
It lit on hills Achaian, and there dwelt
                                    Al Aaraaf i 34
Over the hills and far away   Nis 46
Of rock and forest, on the hills
                                    Tamerlane 142
That dwindled hills! begirt with bowers
                                    Tamerlane 143

Hindering
Each hindering thing   Al Aaraaf ii 93

Hindrance
Here is no let or hindrance to thy weapon
                                    Politian v 81

Hint
No heavings hint that winds have been
                                    City (1831) 37

Hinted
As the star-dials hinted of morn
                                    Ulalume 32

Hist
Hist! hist! thou canst not say
                                    Politian iii 50
Hist! hist! it comes again!
                                    Politian iii 79
Hist! hush! within the gloom
                                    Politian iv 53

Histories
What wild heart-histories seemed to lie
enwritten   Helen² 42

History
Thus endeth the history—and her maids
                                    Politian ii 25

Hither
Now prythee, leave me—hither doth come
a person   Politian v 41
And hither and thither fly   Worm 11

Hold
But hold!—these dark, these perishing
arcades   Coliseum (1842) 31
And hold this maxim all life long
                                    Divine Right 11
And I hold within my hand
                                    Dream w. Dream 14
By all I hold most sacred and most
solemn   Politian iv 36
Hold him a villain?—thus much, I pry-
thee, say   Politian v 35
Hold off—thy sacred hand—avaunt I say
                                    Politian v 62
Hold off thy hand—with that beloved
name   Politian v 67
Because to his cat's eyes I hold a glass
                                    Tempora 87
Search narrowly these words which hold
a treasure   Valentine (1846) 5
Henceforth I hold thy flower-enamelled
shore   Zante 12

Holds
A midnight vigil holds the swarthy bat!
                                    Coliseum 19
Such language holds the solemn sea
                                    Paradise 17
Search narrowly this rhyme, which holds
a treasure   Valentine 5

Holier
A holier odor   Annie 61
And with a holier lustre the quiet moon
                                    Politian iii 49
Burned there a holier fire than burneth
now   Politian iv 19
Its fount is holier—more divine
                                    Tamerlane 10

Holily
Thrillingly, holily   Experiments 3

Hollow
Of the hollow and high-sounding vanities
                                    Politian iii 30

Holy
With Indian Cupid down the holy river
                                    Al Aaraaf i 79
Thou! thy framing is so holy
                                    Al Aaraaf i (1831) 28
And they, and ev'ry mossy spring were
holy   Al Aaraaf ii 188
No rays from the holy heaven come down
                                    City 12
That holy dream—that holy dream
                                    Dream 9
Are Holy Land!   Helen¹ 15
From thy holy throne above
                                    Hymn (1835) 4
For the holy Jesus' sake   Irene 38
The Holy Evangelists   Politian ii 31
I tell thee, holy man   Politian ii 101
In the Vatican—within the holy walls
                                    Politian v (1835) 47
This chamber changed for one more holy
                                    Sleeper 40
Else now, when in the holy grove
                                    Tamerlane 231
I have sent for thee, holy friar
                                    Tamerlane (1827) 1
Say, holy father, breathes there yet
                                    Tamerlane (1831) 177

Home
Leave tenantless thy crystal home, and fly
                                    Al Aaraaf i 143
Glides, spectre-like, unto his marble home
                                    Coliseum 23
I have wandered home but newly
                                    Dream-Land 55
I have reached my home but newly
                                    Dream-Land (1844) 21
I have journeyed home but newly
                                    Dream-Land (1844) 50
From mine own home, with beings that
have been   Dreams 17
Thy Naiad airs have brought me home
                                    Helen¹ 8
Lighting my lonely pathway home that
night   Helen² 53
And round about his home the glory
                                    Palace 27
And mother in Heaven! think of our
quiet home   Politian ii 85
Strike thou home   Politian v 80
Strike home   Politian v 82
On this home by Horror haunted—tell me
truly, I implore   Raven 88
I reach'd my home—my home no more
                                    Tamerlane 213

That bore me from my home, more gay
        Tamerlane (1827) 302
My home—my hope—my early love
        Tamerlane (1831) 220

Homeward
And homeward turn'd his soften'd eye
        Tamerlane 190

Honied
All other loveliness: its honied dew
        Al Aaraaf i 52

Honored
To give thee cause for grief, my honored
  friend   Politian iii 8

Honors
With the ancestral honors of thy house
        Politian iv 29

Honourable
Such squalid wit to honourable rhyme
        To Margaret 4

Hop
And hop o'er counters with a Vestris air
        Tempora 52

Hope
With many a mutter'd "hope to be for-
  given   Al Aaraaf ii 5
They fell: for Heaven to them no hope
  imparts   Al Aaraaf ii 263
Yet if Hope has flown away
        Dream w. Dream 6
'T were folly still to hope for higher
  Heav'n   Dreams 12
Than young Hope in his sunniest hour
  hath known   Dreams (1827) 34
Do tell! when may we hope to make men
  of sense out of the Pundits
        Experiments 7
The highest hope of pride and power
        Happiest Day 3
But were that hope of pride and power
        Happiest Day 17
How dark a wo! yet how sublime a hope
        Helen² 44
They fill my soul with Beauty (which is
  Hope)   Helen² 51
For that bright hope at last
        Imitation 15
The sweet Lenore hath gone before, with
  Hope that flew beside Lenore 15
The mournful hope that every throb
        Octavia 8
Ah, starry Hope! that didst arise
        Paradise 8
Oh Joy departed—Hope, the Seraph Hope
        Politian ii 67
By all I scorn on earth and hope in heaven
        Politian iv 38
Shall wait upon thee, and the angel Hope
        Politian iv 81
In the budding of my Paradisal Hope
        Politian v 7
Till the dirges of his Hope that melan-
  choly burden bore   Raven 65
Followed fast and followed faster so, when
  Hope he would adjure
        Raven (1845) 64

Stern Despair returned, instead of the
  sweet Hope he dared adjure
        Raven (1845) 65
With light like Hope to mortals given
        Spirits 14
You call it hope—that fire of fire!
        Tamerlane 7
If I can hope—oh, God! I can
        Tamerlane 9
On which my every hope and thought
        Tamerlane 90
On Earth, of all we hope in Heaven!
        Tamerlane 178
When Hope, the eagle that tower'd, could
  see   Tamerlane 187
But 't was not with the drunken hope
        Tamerlane (1827) 2
But hope is not a gift of thine
        Tamerlane (1827) 12
For short the time my high hope lent
        Tamerlane (1827) 269
My home—my hope—my early love
        Tamerlane (1831) 220
Could hope to utter. And I! my spells
  are broken   To³ 16
Hourly for hope—for life—ah! above all
        To MLS 5
With Hope and in Beauty to-night
        Ulalume 65

Hopeless
Yes! tho' that long dream were of hopeless sorrow   Dreams 4

Hopelessness
A sullen hopelessness of heart
        Tamerlane (1827) 369

Hopes
My early hopes?—No—they
      Dream w. Dream (1829) 11,
    Tamerlane (1831) 255, To⁴ 23
They have not left me (as my hopes
  have) since   Helen² 54
With sweet hopes of thee and thine!
        Hymn 12
In the budding of my hopes—give me to
  live   Politian v (1835) 7
Bright with all hopes that Heaven can
  give   Stanzas² 28
On the morrow he will leave me, as my
  Hopes have flown before   Raven 59
And my proud hopes had reach'd a throne
        Tamerlane (1827) 348
And my hopes are dying   To Hunter 5
A play of hopes and fears   Worm 6
How many thoughts of what entombed
  hopes!   Zante 6

Hopper
As this for a neat, frisky counter-hopper
        Tempora 48

Horizon
O'er th' horizon's fiery wall
        Nis (1836) 40

Horn
Arose with a duplicate horn
        Ulalume 36
Distinct with its duplicate horn
        Ulalume 38

Horned
Lit by the wan light of the hornéd moon
                              Coliseum 24

Horrible
With that horrible throbbing   Annie 22
At heart;—ah, that horrible   Annie 23
Horrible throbbing!   Annie 24
How horrible a monody there floats
                              Bells (1849) 12

Horrified
Too much horrified to speak   Bells 41

Horror
What a horror they outpour   Bells 55
Thou Horror with blood-chilling cries
                              Louisa 11
With horror and awe!   Politian ii 83
On this home by Horror haunted—tell me
      truly, I implore   Raven 88
And Horror the soul of the plot
                              Worm 24

Hour
So like its own above, that, to this hour
                              Al Aaraaf i 57
And years I left behind me in an hour
                              Al Aaraaf ii 220
From childhood's hour I have not been
                              Alone 1
They have sever'd in one fatal hour.
                              Ballad 17
'T was once—and only once—and the wild
      hour   Dreams 19
Than young Hope in his sunniest hour
      hath known   Dreams (1827) 34
The happiest day, the happiest hour
                              Happiest Day 1
Ev'n then I felt—that brightest hour
                              Happiest Day 19
Curs'd was the hour that saw us meet
                              Louisa 15
The hour when we were born   Louisa 16
And laughter crowns the festive hour
                              Octavia 2
The hour is growing late—the Duke
      awaits us   Politian iii 88
And when an hour with calmer wings
                              Romance 16
That little hour with lyre and rhyme
                              Romance (1831) 42
Recalls the hour of bliss   Sarah 15
In such an hour, when are forgot
                              Sarah 19
So sweet the hour, so calm the time
                              Serenade 1
Into thine hour of secrecy   Spirits 4
And yet that spirit knew not—in the hour
                              Stanzas¹ 7
Each hour before us—but then only, bid
                              Stanzas¹ 22
Kind solace in a dying hour
                              Tamerlane 1
My passions from that hapless hour
                              Tamerlane 65
The minute—the hour—the day—oppress
                              Tamerlane 137
I had not thought, until this hour
                              Tamerlane (1827) 17

The infant monarch of the hour
                              Tamerlane (1827) 45
Which left me in an evil hour
                              Tamerlane (1827) 174
Oh Genius, at its natal hour
                              Tamerlane (1827) 188
My Ada. In that peaceful hour
                              Tamerlane (1827) 286
There—in that hour—a thought came o'er
                              Tamerlane (1827) 234
And felt, with ev'ry flying hour
                              Tamerlane (1827) 301
Withering at the ev'ning hour
                              Tamerlane (1827) 391
As if 't were not the dying hour
                              Tamerlane (1827) 342

Houri
Where the Houri glances are
                              Israfel 26

Hourly
Hourly in Rome—Politian, Earl of Lei-
      cester!   Politian i 42
Hourly for hope—for life—ah! above all
                              To MLS 5

Hours
As sprang that yellow star from downy
      hours   Al Aaraaf i 155
These star-litten hours
                              Al Aaraaf ii 83
Nor long the measure of my falling
      hours   Al Aaraaf ii 241
The hours are breathing faint and low
                              City 49
By the corrosive Hours to Fate and me?
                              Coliseum 32
I saw but them—saw only them for hours
                              Helen² 40
When the hours flew brightly by
                              Hymn 5
And all my hours are trances
                              Paradise (1834) 21
Late hours and wine, Castiglione,—these
                              Politian i 13
The constitution as late hours and wine
                              Politian i 16
Wears it away like evil hours and wine
                              Politian i 18
Approaches, and the Hours are breathing
      low   Politian iii 40
And sunshine of my summer hours!
                              Tamerlane 22
Comes o'er me in these lonely hours
                              Tamerlane (1827) 137
Each fit to furnish forth four hours' de-
      bate   Tempora 22
How many memories of what radiant
      hours   Zante 3

House
With the ancestral honors of thy house
                              Politian iv 29

Hover
Round his fate will hover
                              To Hunter 13

Hovered
Flashing from cloud that hover'd o'er
                              Tamerlane (1827) 50

Hovering
Young dreams still hovering on their
    drowsy flight   Al Aaraaf ii 158
(Dim gulf!) my spirit hovering lies
                    Paradise 12
However
Too coldly—or the stars—howe'er it was
                    Dreams 25
Its atomies, however   Fairy-Land 39
Hue
Yon heir, whose cheeks of pallid hue
                Lenore (1843) 15
Of the pale cloud therein, whose hue
                Tamerlane (1827) 320
Hues
His cloak, of a thousand mingled hues
                    Parody 5
Hug
But hug the glorious chains I wore
                Divine Right 4
Huge
Huge moons there wax and wane
                Fairy-Land 5
Hum
The hum of suitors—and the tone
                Tamerlane 63
Human
On the human heart a stone   Bells 85
They are neither brute nor human
                    Bells 87
To the weak human eye unclosed
                Dream-Land 46
For we cannot help agreeing that no living
    human being   Raven 51
Some human memories and tearful lore
                    Silence 8
Triumphantly with human kind
                Tamerlane 34
Of human battle, where my voice
                Tamerlane 50
O, human love! thou spirit given
                Tamerlane 177
A snare in every human path
                Tamerlane 230
Ev'n childhood knows the human heart
                Tamerlane (1827) 126
Nothing have I with human hearts
                Tamerlane (1827) 346
A thought arose within the human brain
                    To³ 4
Beyond the utterance of the human tongue
                    To³ 5
To write is human—not to write divine
                To Margaret 7
In myriad types of the human eye
                    Valley 21
In human gore imbued   Worm 32
Humanity
In Truth, in Virtue, in Humanity
                    To MLS 7
Humble
I kneel, an altered and an humble man
                Coliseum 7
Can compare with the bright-eyed Eula-
    lie's most humble and careless curl
                    Eulalie 13

Of fervent prayer, and humble love
                Hymn (1835) 3
Sit down!—for I am humble, most humble
                Politian ii 4
Humbler
An humbler heart—a deeper wo
                Tamerlane 221
Humblily
Virginal Lillian, rigidly, humblily dutiful
                Experiments 1
Humiliation
That in this deep humiliation I perish
                Politian v 78
Humming
Was plumed with the down of the hum-
    ming-bird   Parody 2
Humors
Give way unto these humors
                Politian iii 3
Hums
Thus hums the moon within her ear
                    Irene 25
Hung
What time upon her airy bounds I hung
                Al Aaraaf ii 221
That rose—that what d' ye call it—that
    hung   Fairy-Land (1831) 12
From clouds that hung, like banners, o'er
                Tamerlane 45
Hunter
A mountain hunter, I had known
                Tamerlane (1827) 397
Hurled
I left so late was into chaos hurl'd
                Al Aaraaf ii 234
Hurried
And hurried madly on my way
                Tamerlane (1827) 300
Hurriedly
All hurriedly she knelt upon a bed
                Al Aaraaf i 42
Came hurriedly upon me, telling
                Tamerlane 49
Husband
And Alessandra's husband
                Politian i 22
Hush
Hist! hush! within the gloom
                Politian iv 53
Hushed
'T is hushed and all is still
                Politian iii 86
Hyacinth
Thy hyacinth hair, thy classic face
                    Helen¹ 7
Hyacinthine
O hyacinthine isle! O purple Zante!
                    Zante 13
Hymen
Or hymen, Time, and Destiny
                Romance (1831) 33
Hymn
Heard not the stirring summons of the
    hymn?   Al Aaraaf ii 175
Maria! thou hast heard my hymn!
                    Hymn 2

Hymns
And, amid incense and high spiritual
   hymns   Al Aaraaf i 28
Ceasing their hymns, attend the spell
                    Israfel 6

Ianthe
Ianthe, dearest, see! how dim that ray!
              Al Aaraaf ii 198
Ianthe, beauty crowded on me then
              Al Aaraaf ii 225
But, list, Ianthe! when the air so soft
              Al Aaraaf ii 231

Icy
In the icy air of night!   Bells 5
No icy worms about her creep   Irene 62

Idea
Whence sprang the "Idea of Beauty"
   into birth   Al Aaraaf i 31
Whose harshest idea   Al Aaraaf i 102
Half an idea in the profoundest sonnet
                  Enigma 2
The bright i-dea, or bright dear-eye
               Impromptu 4
Idea! which bindest life around
               Tamerlane 183

Ideal
All Nature speaks, and ev'n ideal things
              Al Aaraaf i 128
The unsatisfactory and ideal thing
              Politian iv 32
That was new pleasure—the ideal
             Tamerlane 120
Which, ideal, still may be
         Tamerlane (1827) 304
The "beau ideal" fancied for Adonis
               Tempora 72

Idle
Shake off the idle fancies that beset thee
             Politian iii 4
I have no time for idle cares
             Romance 14
For, being an idle boy lang syne
         Romance (1831) 19
An idle longing night and day
         Romance (1831) 54
In childhood, many an idle stone
             Sleeper 56
The idle words, which, as a dream
         Tamerlane (1827) 239

Idleness
In vacant idleness of woe
         Tamerlane (1827) 395

Idol
In each idol's diamond eye   City 33
I wandered of the Idol, Love
             Tamerlane 232

Idolatry
Of her that heart's idolatry
         Tamerlane (1827) 202

Ignorant
Being ignorant of one important rule
              Elizabeth 12

Ill
From ev'ry depth of good and ill
               Alone 11
Haunted by ill angels only
         Dream-Land 2, 52

In joy and wo—in good and ill Hymn 3
Ill suit the like with old Di Broglio's heir
              Politian i 21
Thro' good and ill—thro' weal and woe I
   love thee   Politian iv 15
And much I fear me ill—it will not do
              Politian v 2
Of some ill demand, with a power
         Tamerlane (1827) 173
The worst ill of mortality
         Tamerlane (1827) 305

Illness
And the lingering illness   Annie 3

Illumine
Their office is to illumine and enkindle
                Helen² 57

Image
Thy image may be   Al Aaraaf ii 113
Its image on my spirit—or the moon
               Dreams 23
Made in his image a mannikin merely to
   madden it   Experiments 6
Her image deeply lies   River 12
An image of Elysium lies Serenade 6
Thine image and—a name—a name!
               Tamerlane 126
With her own image, my fond breast
         Tamerlane (1827) 246

Imaginary
In hearkening to imaginary sounds
             Politian iii 24

Imagining
In climes of mine imagining, apart
               Dreams 16
To his lone imagining   Lake 21
Solace to my imagining
         Tamerlane (1831) 97

Imbibe
Which with my mother's milk I did imbibe   Politian iii 12

Imbib'd
My soul imbib'd unhallow'd feeling
         Tamerlane (1827) 47

Imbued
Imbued with all the beauty Israfel 27
In human gore imbued   Worm 32

Imitating
Who would be men by imitating apes
              Tempora 34

Immemorial
Of my most immemorial year
             Ulalume 5

Immortal
Stable, opaque, immortal—all by dint
             Enigma 13

Immortality
Beyond that death no immortality
          Al Aaraaf ii 170

Imp
There is an imp would follow me even
   there!   Politian iii 17
There is an imp hath followed me even
   there!   Politian iii 17
Why not an imp the greybeard hath
          Romance (1831) 63

Imparts
But two: they fell: for Heaven no grace
  imparts   Al Aaraaf ii 176
They fell: for Heaven to them no hope
  imparts   Al Aaraaf ii 263
Its venom secretly imparts
        Tamerlane (1827) 345

Impassion'd
Which ev'n to my impassion'd mind
        Tamerlane (1827) 92

Impeding
Seen but in beauty—not impeding sight
        Al Aaraaf i 38

Impels
Of the rapture that impels   Bells 30

Imperative
A sacred vow, imperative, and urgent
        Politian ii 95

Imperial
To the imperial city   Politian i 44

Implore
"Sir," said I, "or Madam, truly your
  forgiveness I implore   Raven 20
On this home by Horror haunted—tell me
  truly, I implore   Raven 88
Is there—is there balm in Gilead?—tell
  me—tell me, I implore   Raven 89

Important
Being ignorant of one important rule
        Elizabeth 12

Impotent
We are not impotent—we pallid stones
        Coliseum 39

Impudently
So impudently in my face
        Fairy-Land (1831) 15

Incense
And, amid incense and high spiritual
  hymns   Al Aaraaf i 21
To breathe the incense of those slumbering
  roses?   Helen² 24
Were incense—then a goodly gift
        Tamerlane 91
With incense of burnt offerings
        Tamerlane 234

Incorporate
There are some qualities—some incorporate things   Silence 1

Incumbent
Incumbent on night   Al Aaraaf ii 108

Indeed
I crave thy pardon—indeed I am not well
        Politian i 35
Indeed she is very troublesome
        Politian ii 36
Jacinta,—now indeed, Jacinta
        Politian ii 49
Thou must not—nay indeed, indeed, thou
  shalt not   Politian iii 2
Indeed I hear not   Politian iii 51
This mockery is most cruel—most cruel
  indeed!   Politian iv 4
Avaunt—I will not fight thee—indeed I
  dare not   Politian v 63
I do—indeed I pity thee   Politian v 74
Now this indeed is just!   Politian v 92

Indian
With Indian Cupid down the holy river
        Al Aaraaf i 79

Indignant
Indignant from the tomb doth take
        Irene 47
Avaunt!—avaunt! to friends from fiends
  the indignant ghost is riven
        Lenore 20

Indulge
Indulge me with this pleasing dream
        Louisa 3

Indulged
Thou hast indulged   Politian i 11

Infancy
Love—as in infancy was mine
        Tamerlane 87
In infancy, which seen, recall
        Tamerlane (1827) 141
And raise his infancy's delight
        Tamerlane (1827) 281

Infant
My infant spirit would awake
        Lake (1827) 11
The infant monarch of the hour
        Tamerlane (1827) 45
My infant spirit would awake
        Tamerlane (1831) 89

Infelicity
I think not so—her infelicity
        Politian ii 19

Infernal
Rise—rise—infernal spirits, rise
        Louisa 9

Infinite
E'en then who knew that as infinite
        Tamerlane (1831) 77

Infinity
She look'd into Infinity—and knelt
        Al Aaraaf i 35
Have dream'd for thy Infinity
        Al Aaraaf i 104
By that infinity with which my wife
        Mother 13

Influence
An influence dewy, drowsy, dim
        Irene 9
But left its influence with me still
        Tamerlane (1827) 101

Ingratitude
Be all ingratitude requited
        Fairy-Land (1831) 19

Inherit
Another brow may ev'n inherit
        Happiest Day 10
Let none of earth inherit
        Imitation 11
Which from my forefathers I did inherit
        Politian iii 11
O yearning heart!—I did inherit
        Tamerlane 15
To know the fate it will inherit
        Tamerlane (1827) 192

Inmate
Inmate of highest stars, where erst it
  sham'd   Al Aaraaf i 51

Innate
Besides my innate love of contradiction
                              Elizabeth 6
My innate nature—be it so
                              Tamerlane 68
The soul which feels its innate right
                        Tamerlane (1827) 185

Innocence
That did to death the innocence that died,
   and died so young   Lenore 12

Inspire
With glory—such as might inspire
                        Tamerlane (1827) 273

Installed
And fill my heart of hearts, where Death
   installed you   Mother 7

Instant
And in an instant all things disappeared
                                 Helen² 29
Not the least obeisance made he; not an
   instant stopped or stayed he
                             Raven (1845) 39

Instead
Stern Despair returned, instead of the
   sweet Hope he dared adjure
                             Raven (1845) 65
Instead of two sides, Job has nearly eight
                              Tempora 21
He then, of course, must shake his foot
   instead   Tempora 84

Insult
For public insult in the streets—before
                             Politian v 86

Intellectuality
In the mad pride of intellectuality
                                  To³ 2

Intenser
Thrills with intenser love than I for thee
                             Politian iv 17
Burn'd with a still intenser glow
                              Tamerlane 71

Intent
To its most desperate intent
                        Tamerlane (1827) 270

Interefere
No subject vice dare interfere
                            Divine Right 7

Interminable
Of interminable pride   Imitation 2
With its interminable chime
                              Tamerlane 24

Intermits
The pulse beats ten and intermits
                             Physician 1

Interpreted
Shall not be interpreted   Nis 10

Intertwine
Whose wreathed friezes interwine
                                 City 22

Intimate
Two separate—yet most intimate things
                             Tamerlane 127

Intrude
Upon thy slumber shall intrude
                             Serenade 23
A crawling shape intrude!   Worm 26

Inurned
Inurned and entombed!—now, in a tone
                             Politian ii 68

Invisible
Invisible Wo!   Worm 16

Irene
Irene, with her Destinies!   Sleeper 17

Iron
Iron bells!   Bells 71
E'en then who knew this iron heart
                              Tamerlane 73
Hath left his iron gate ajar
                             Tamerlane 226

Irrevocable
An irrevocable vow
                        Bridal Ballad (1837) 20

Isabel
Sit down beside me, Isabel
                        Fairy-Land (1831) 1
Did you not say so, Isabel?
                        Fairy-Land (1831) 25
Isabel, do you not fear
                        Fairy-Land (1831) 39

Island
Just o'er that one bright island smile
                                  To F 14

Isle
Stole o'er my senses in that lovely isle
                             Al Aaraaf ii 211
A green isle in the sea, love   Paradise 3
Like some enchanted far-off isle   To F 9
Fair isle, that from the fairest of all
   flowers   Zante 1
O Hyacinthine isle! O purple Zante!
                                 Zante 13

Isles
At the many star-isles Al Aaraaf ii 134

Isola
Isola d'oro!—Fior di Levante!
                     Al Aaraaf i 77; Zante (1827) 14

Israfel
As the angel Israfel   Israfel 4
Where Israfel   Israfel 46
Than even the seraph harper, Israfel
                                  To³ 14

Israfeli
That Israfeli's fire   Israfel 18
Israfeli, who despisest   Israfel 30

Italian
By far Italian streams
                        Paradise (1834) 26
Italian tones made only to be murmured
                                  To³ 8

Italy
Or one more worthy Italy, methinks
                             Politian v 17

Ivory
Here, where on ivory couch the Caesar
   sate   Coliseum (1833) 24
Her bosom is an ivory throne
                            Divine Right 5

Ivy
Of sculptured ivy and stone flowers
                                 City 20
But stay!—these walls—these ivy-clad
   arcades   Coliseum 26

But, just like any other dream
                Tamerlane 133
Just o'er that one bright island smile
                To F 14

Keen
Seraphs in all but " Knowledge," the keen
  light   Al Aaraaf ii 159
So keen a relish for the beautiful
                Politian iii 44
So that the blade be keen—the blow be
  sure   Politian iv 104

Keep
To keep watch with delight
                Al Aaraaf ii 110
Which thy vigilance keep
                Al Aaraaf ii 119
To keep me from harm   Annie 82
Heaven have her in its sacred keep!
                Sleeper 39
And all we seek to keep hath flown
                Tamerlane 210
And always keep from laughing when I
  can   Tempora 62
To keep watch above the flowers
                Valley 6

Keeper
And crouches to a keeper's hand
                Tamerlane 161

Keeping
Keeping time, time, time
          Bells 9, 96, 100, 105

Keeps
That keeps from the dreamer
              Al Aaraaf ii 70

Killing
And killing my Annabel Lee
             Annabel Lee 26

Kind
A kind which, upon trial Fairy-Land 13
Wilt thou, my good Jacinta, be so kind
                Politian ii 29
A kind and gentle office, and a Power
                Politian iii 35
Quaff, oh, quaff this kind nepenthe and
  forget this lost Lenore   Raven 83
Kind solace in a dying hour!
                Tamerlane 2
Triumphantly with human kind
                Tamerlane 34
No need to quiet her kind fears
            Tamerlane (1827) 134

Kindled
As hath been kindled within it
                Politian iii 45

Kindling
And in thine eye a kindling light Song 5
That kindling thought—did not the beam
            Tamerlane (1827) 210

King
Its way to Heaven, from garden of a king
              Al Aaraaf i 73
And their king it is who tolls Bells 89
O spells more sure than e'er Judaean king
                Coliseum 13
The only king by right divine
              Divine Right 1

Is Ellen King, and were she mine
              Divine Right 2
The King—my King—can do no wrong
             Divine Right 12
So wills its King, who hath forbid
             Dream-Land 47
From moan and groan to a golden throne
  beside the King of Heaven Lenore 22
Long life to our king   Latin Hymn 7
The wit and wisdom of their king
                Palace 32
The king Napoleon   To⁴ 4
Who is king but Epiphanes
              Triumph 1, 3

Kingdom
In a kingdom by the sea
             Annabel Lee 2
In this kingdom by the sea
       Annabel Lee 8, 14, 20, 24
A kingdom for a broken—heart
        Tamerlane (1827) 406

Kingly
Up domes—up spires—up kingly halls
                City 17
I'd worship Kings and kingly state
            Divine Right 10
The heritage of a kingly mind
              Tamerlane 32

Kings
I'd worship Kings and kingly state
            Divine Right 10

Kinsman
So that her high born kinsman came
         Annabel Lee (1850) 17

Kinsmen
So that her high born kinsmen came
             Annabel Lee 17

Kiss
Take this kiss upon the brow
          Dream w. Dream 1
Kiss her, Castiglione! kiss her
              Politian i 39
And left the first fond kiss   Sarah 18
Or that the thrill of a single kiss
                To M 11

Kissed
The fairy light that kiss'd her golden
  hair   Al Aaraaf ii 58
She tenderly kissed me   Annie 73
And he kissed my pallid brow
             Bridal Ballad 14
Thus I pacified Psyche and kissed her
              Ulalume 72

Kisses
The breath of those kisses
             Al Aaraaf ii 86
Those kisses of true love
             Al Aaraaf ii 90

Knee
Thus on my bended knee I answer thee
              Politian iv 13
Not mother, with her first-born on her
  knee   Politian iv 16
Thus on my bended knee
              Politian v 77
Why do the people bow the knee
        Tamerlane (1831) 181

Kneel
I kneel, an altered and an humble man
                  Coliseum 7
And are far up in Heaven—the stars I
   kneel to   Helen² 62
Attend thee ever; and I will kneel to thee
                Politian iv 82

Knees
Uprear'd its purple stem around her
   knees   Al Aaraaf i 49

Knell
For the words rang as a knell
            Bridal Ballad 9
Upon my emptiness—a knell
            Tamerlane 26
Give a trickle and a tinkle and a knell
           Valley (1845) 30

Knells
As he knells, knells, knells   Bells 106

Knelt
She look'd into Infinity—and knelt
           Al Aaraaf i 35
All hurriedly she knelt upon a bed
           Al Aaraaf i 42

Knew
The fabled nectar that the heathen knew
           Al Aaraaf i 53
Awoke that slept—or knew that he was
   there   Al Aaraaf ii 213
When first Al Aaraaf knew her course to
   be   Al Aaraaf ii 255
For she knew I loved her child
           Ballad 20
A soul that knew it well
        Happiest Day 24
And thus are dearer than the mother I
   knew   Mother 12
I knew thou wouldst not, couldst not,
   durst not go   Politian iv 100
O speak to me! I knew thou wouldst not
   go!   Politian iv 99
And yet that spirit knew not—in the hour
           Stanzas¹ 7
E'en then who knew this iron heart
          Tamerlane 73
I held no doubt—I knew no fear
      Tamerlane (1827) 241
I knew not woman's heart, alas!
      Tamerlane (1827) 297
In childhood but he knew me not
      Tamerlane (1827) 398
For we knew not the month was October
         Ulalume 23

Knight
A gallant knight   Eldorado 2
This knight so bold   Eldorado 8
Like the knight Pinto (Mendez Ferdi-
   nando)   Valentine 18

Knocked
Who knocked over a thousand so fine!
         Latin Hymn 8

Knot
Jew, or downright upright nutmegs out of
   a pine-knot   Experiments 10
And yet there is in this no Gordian knot
         Valentine 10

Know
Who livest—that we know
        Al Aaraaf i 98
For what (to them) availeth it to know
       Al Aaraaf ii 166
That a maiden there lived whom you may
   know   Annabel Lee 3
Yes! that was the reason (as all men
   know   Annabel Lee 23
Sadly, I know   Annie 7
But I know with gold they won thee
           Ballad 17
But I know that she hath spoken
           Ballad 29
For I dream I know not how
       Bridal Ballad 29
You know that most enormous flower
      Fairy-Land (1831) 11
So like a thing alive you know
      Fairy-Land (1831) 16
I scarce know which to prize most high
        Impromptu 3
And know him well—nor learned nor
   mirthful he   Politian i 62
I did not know, Jacinta, you were in
   waiting   Politian ii 2
I know—I know it all   Politian iv 7
Knowing what I know, and seeing what I
   have seen   Politian iv 11
Know thou the secret of a spirit
         Tamerlane 13
For all we live to know is known
        Tamerlane 209
To know the fate it will inherit
      Tamerlane (1827) 192
Yes! I was proud—and ye who know
      Tamerlane (1827) 195
I know—for Death who comes for me
       Tamerlane 223
God help me, it has been my lot to know
        Tempora 60
Say—do you know?   Triumph 2
Well I know, now, this dim lake of Auber
         Ulalume 91
Well I know, now, this dank tarn of
   Auber   Ulalume 93

Knowest
A few days more, thou knowest, my
   Alessandra   Politian i 3
Knowest thou the land Politian iv 65

Knowing
Knowing her love   Annie 87
Knowing what I know, and seeing what I
   have seen   Politian iv 11
That knowing no cause of quarrel or of
   feud   Politian v 11
A child—with a most knowing eye
        Romance 10

Knowledge
Till secrecy shall knowledge be
        Al Aaraaf i 116
Seraphs in all but "Knowledge" the keen
   light   Al Aaraaf ii 159

Known
Thy messenger, hath known
        Al Aaraaf i 103

Was Love, the blind, near sober Duty
known?   Al Aaraaf ii 180
Than young Hope in his sunniest hour
hath known   Dreams 34
My sear'd and blighted heart hath known
Happiest Day 2
He never was known to lie   Lampoon 3
The former was well known to fame
Lampoon 7
But the latter's well known " to report."
Lampoon 8
I have known men have seen
Politian i 57
In youth have I known one with whom
the Earth   Stanzas¹ 1
I was ambitious—have you known
Tamerlane 128
Of flowr's which we have known before
Tamerlane (1827) 140
Of glory which the world hath known
Tamerlane 169
To the sound of the coming darkness
(known   Tamerlane 197
For all we live to know is known
Tamerlane 209
Of one whom I had earlier known
Tamerlane 218
The passionate spirit which hath known
Tamerlane (1827) 179
My mind, it had not known before
Tamerlane (1827) 235
Who, that had known the secret thought
Tamerlane (1827) 247
A well-known name, oft uttered in the
hearing   Valentine 15

Knows
Yet the ear, it fully knows   Bells 57
Ev'n childhood knows the human heart
Tamerlane (1827) 126
Which knows (believe me at this time
Tamerlane (1827) 189
The soul, which knows such power, will
still   Tamerlane (1827) 193
A tale the world but knows too well
Tamerlane (1827) 250
In dreams of thee, and therein knows
To F 6

L. E. L.
In vain those words from thee or L. E. L.
Acrostic 3

Labor
The trivialest point, or you may lose your
labor   Valentine 9

Labyrinth
In a labyrinth of light   Fairy-Land 26
Of labyrinth-like water   River (1829) 2

Laden
Laden from yonder bowers!—a fairer day
Politian v 16
Tell this soul with sorrow laden if, within
the distant Aidenn   Raven 93

Ladies
We liken our ladies' eyes to them
City (1831) 16

And having cheated ladies, dance with
them   Tempora 54
The hearts of all the ladies are with him
Tempora 65

Lady
Trash of all trash!—how can a lady don it
Enigma 6
Be given our làdy's bidding to discuss
Al Aaraaf ii 246
O lady sweet! how camest thou here
Irene 26
Lady, awake! lady awake   Irene 37
The lady sleeps: the dead all sleep
Irene 41
Lady, awake! awake! awake
Irene (1836) 39
Seemed to have years too many "—Ah,
luckless lady   Politian ii 20
A lady's voice!—and sorrow in the tone
Politian iii 54
But with mien of lord or lady, perched
above my chamber door   Raven 40
Oh, lady bright! can it be right
Sleeper 18
Oh, lady dear, hast thou no fear
Sleeper 30
The lady sleeps! oh, may her sleep
Sleeper 37
Lady! I would that verse of mine
Stanzas² 1
I cannot be, lady, alone   To M 20

Laid
Weary—I laid me on a couch to rest
Poetry 2

Lair
And nursled the young mountain in its
lair   Al Aaraaf ii 15
Come up through the lair of Lion
Ulalume 49

Lake
To lone lake that smiles
Al Aaraaf ii 132
Far down within the crystal of the lake
Al Aaraaf ii (1829) 40
Its way to some remember'd lake
Irene 48
Of a wild lake, with black rock bound
Lake 5
To the terror of the lone lake   Lake 12
An Eden of that dim lake   Lake 23
Far down within some shadowy lake
Romance 4
Looking like Lethe, see! the lake
Sleeper 13
Of a wild lake with black rock bound
Tamerlane (1831) 83
To the terror of that lone lake
Tamerlane (1831) 90
An Eden of that dim lake
Tamerlane (1831) 99
Some lake beset as lake can be   To F 11
It was hard by the dim lake of Auber
Ulalume 6
We noted not the dim lake of Auber
Ulalume 26
Well I know, now, this dim lake of Auber
Ulalume 91

Will start, which lately slept in apathy
                                    Stanzas[1] 19
Had lately been but had pass'd by
                          Tamerlane (1827) 383

Latter
But the latter's well known " to report."
                                    Lampoon 8
For that the power of thought attend the
  latter   Tempora 75
Within the lonesome latter years
                                       Worm 2

Lattice
Proceeds from yonder lattice—which you
  may see   Politian iii 62
To look upon the face hidden by yon lat-
  tice   Politian iii 102
Very plainly through the window—that
  lattice belongs
                         Politian iii (1835) 63
" Surely," said I, " surely that is some-
  thing at my window lattice   Raven 33
Laughingly through the lattice drop
                                    Sleeper 21
This lattice open to the night
                             Sleeper (1842) 20

Laugh
And laugh—but smile no more
                                     Palace 48
Or rather laugh with him, that queer
  Philosopher   Tempora 15
I'll neither laugh with one or cry with
  t'other   Tempora 26
I laugh to think how poor   To[4] 37

Laughed
Till growing bold, he laughed and leapt
                                 Tamerlane 242

Laughing
And laughing at her girlish wiles
                                 Tamerlane 105
And always keep from laughing when I
  can   Tempora 62

Laughingly
Laughingly through the lattice drop
                                    Sleeper 21

Laughter
And the light laughter chokes the sigh
                                     Irene 46
And laughter crowns the festive hour
                                    Octavia 2

Laurels
To thee the laurels belong   Israfel 32
Laurels upon me: and the rush
                                 Tamerlane 59

Lavas
As the lavas that restlessly roll
                                   Ulalume 15

Laves
Laves in quadruple light her angel limbs
                                 Al Aaraaf i 29

Lavishly
Could fling, all lavishly and free
                                    Stanzas[2] 2

Law
To a lute's well-tuned law   Palace 20

Lay
Her world lay lolling on the golden air
                                 Al Aaraaf i 17

Lay bare, thro' vistas thunder-riven
                             Romance (1831) 15
Though happiness around thee lay
                                    Song 3, 15
Where in a deep, still slumber lay
                          Tamerlane (1827) 285
What shall be done? I'll lay it on the
  table   Tempora 23
The red sun-light lazily lay   Valley 8

Lazily
Lazily upon beauty's eye   Irene 4
The red sun-light lazily lay   Valley 8

Lea
On moorland and lea
                                 Al Aaraaf ii 143

Lead
But lead on the heart
                                 Al Aaraaf ii 99
They follow me—they lead me through
  the years   Helen[2] 55
Lead on thy hideous train   Louisa 12
And be sure it will lead us aright
                                   Ulalume 68

Leader
As in a leader, haply—Power
                          Tamerlane (1827) 344

Leaf
In Heaven, and all its environs, the leaf
                                 Al Aaraaf i 60
Is the gently falling leaf
                           Al Aaraaf i (1831) 27
Are tintless of the yellow leaf
                             Romance (1831) 62
The leaf where now are peering
                             Valentine (1849) 13

Leagues
A thousand leagues within the golden
  west   Politian iv 68

Lean
Lean over her and weep—two gentle
  maids   Politian ii 26
I'd lean upon her gentle breast
                          Tamerlane (1831) 133

Leaning
O'er the unguarded flowers were leaning
                                     Nis 22

Leap
And leap within me at the cry
                                 Tamerlane 53

Leaping
Leaping higher, higher, higher   Bells 46

Leaps
Which leaps down to the flower
                                 Al Aaraaf ii 121

Leapt
Fail'd, as my pennon'd spirit leapt aloft
                                 Al Aaraaf ii 232
Till growing bold, he laughed and leapt
                                 Tamerlane 242

Learn
To those pure orbs, your heart to learn
                                  Impromptu 2

Learned
Learned as few are learned
                                  Politian i 56
And know him well—nor learned nor
  mirththful he   Politian i 62

Least
At least as long as Love doth weep
                              Irene 42
Far away—as far at least   Nis 2
Ha! here at least's a friend—too much a
    friend   Politian ii 60
Not the least obeisance made he; not a
    minute stopped or stayed he
                              Raven 39
For men have none at all, or bad at least
                              Tempora 4
At least by sight, for I'm a timid man
                              Tempora 61
My soul at least a solace hath   To F 5

Leave
Leave tenantless thy crystal home, and
    fly   Al Aaraaf i 143
I left her gorgeous halls—nor mourn'd to
    leave   Al Aaraaf ii 201
O! leave them apart   Al Aaraaf ii 97
Oh! was it weal to leave me
                        Ballad 9, 21, 33
As for to leave me thus
              Politian iii 71, 75, 80, 84
Now prythee, leave me—hither doth come
    a person   Politian v 41
On the morrow he will leave me, as my
    Hopes have flown before   Raven 59
Leave no black plume as a token of that
    lie thy soul hath spoken   Raven 99
Leave my loneliness unbroken!—quit the
    bust above my door   Raven 100
But 't will leave thee, as each star
                        Spirits (1827) 19
Why did I leave it, and, adrift
                        Tamerlane 94
To leave her while we both were young
                 Tamerlane (1827) 236
Who wouldst not leave him in his wan-
    dering   To Science 6
And now I leave these riddles to their
    seer   Valentine (1846) 21

Leaves
She throws aside the sceptre—leaves the
    helm   Al Aaraaf i 27
Among the green leaves as they shake
                              Romance 3
Leaves not its memory behind
                 Tamerlane (1827) 93
The leaves they were crispéd and sere
                              Ulalume 2
The leaves they were withering and sere
                              Ulalume 3
As the leaves that were crispéd and sere
                              Ulalume 83
As the leaves that were withering and
    sere   Ulalume 84

Leavest
But leav'st he heart a wilderness
                         Tamerlane 182

Leaving
Leaving thee wild for the dear child that
    should have been thy bride
                              Lenore 16

Led
But one, who phantasy had led
                 Tamerlane (1827) 250

Lee
By the name of Annabel Lee
                        Annabel Lee 4
I and my Annabel Lee
                        Annabel Lee 10
Chilling my Annabel Lee
                        Annabel Lee 16
And killing my Annabel Lee
                        Annabel Lee 26
Of the beautiful Annabel Lee
                 Annabel Lee 33, 35, 37

Left
Her way—but left not yet her Thera-
    saean reign   Al Aaraaf i 158
Some have left the cool glade, and
                       Al Aaraaf ii 140
I left her gorgeous halls—nor mourn'd to
    leave   Al Aaraaf ii 201
And years I left behind me in an hour
                       Al Aaraaf ii 220
I left so late was into chaos hurl'd
                       Al Aaraaf ii 234
Of lofty contemplation left to Time
                              Coliseum 2
All of the famed and colossal left
                              Coliseum 31
Hath left me broken-hearted
                              Dream 4
And loveliness,—have left my very heart
                              Dreams 15
Came o'er me in the night, and left
    behind   Dreams 22
And, thro' the opening left, as soon
                     Fairy-Land (1831) 21
They have not left me (as my hopes have)
    since   Helen² 54
Till thoughts and locks are left, alas
                              Irene 7
Ungenial Britain which we left so lately
                         Politian v 25
And left the first fond kiss   Sarah 18
Hath left his iron gate ajar
                         Tamerlane 226
But left its influence with me still
                 Tamerlane (1827) 101
Which left me in an evil hour
                 Tamerlane (1827) 174
What was there left me now? despair
                 Tamerlane (1827) 405
Upon the left, and all the way along
                              To³ 25

Legended
By the door of a legended tomb
                              Ulalume 77
On the door of this legended tomb
                              Ulalume 79

Legends
And the giddy stars (so legends tell)
                              Israfel 5

Legion
For the heart whose woes are legion
                         Dream-Land 39

Leicester
Hourly in Rome—Politian, Earl of Lei-
    cester   Politian i 42
Of Britain, Earl of Leicester
                         Politian i 45

Now, Earl of Leicester
                Politian iv 50
Unto this man, that I, the Earl of Lei-
  cester   Politian v 34
The Earl of Leicester here
                Politian v 45
I am the Earl of Leicester, and thou
  seest   Politian v 46
Against thee, Earl of Leicester
                Politian v 80

Lemnos
The sun-ray dropp'd, in Lemnos, with a
  spell   Al Aaraaf ii 203

Length
As I lie at full length   Annie 10
I am better at length   Annie 12
At length—at length—after so many days
                Coliseum 4
Failed him at length   Eldorado 14
But now, at length, dear Dian sank from
  sight   Helen² 48
A thousand hearts—losing at length her
  own   Politian ii 24
Strange, above all, thy length of tress
                Sleeper 35
Thine should be length of happy days
                Stanzas² 5

Lenore
See! on yon drear and rigid bier low lies
  thy love, Lenore   Lenore 4
The sweet Lenore hath gone before, with
  Hope that flew beside   Lenore 15
From my books surcease of sorrow—sor-
  row for the lost Lenore   Raven 10
For the rare and radiant maiden whom
  the angels name Lenore   Raven 11
And the only word there spoken was the
  whispered word, " Lenore?"
                Raven 28
This I whispered, and an echo murmured
  back the word "Lenore!" Raven 29
Respite—respite and nepenthe from thy
  memories of Lenore   Raven 82
Quaff, oh, quaff this kind nepenthe and
  forget this lost Lenore   Raven 83
It shall clasp a sainted maiden whom the
  angels name Lenore   Raven 94
Clasp a rare and radiant maiden whom
  the angels name Lenore   Raven 95

Lent
" Wretch," I cried, " thy God hath lent
  thee—by these angels he hath sent thee
                Raven 81
Ambition lent it a new tone
             Tamerlane 115
For short the time my high hope lent
         Tamerlane (1827) 269

Less
Breathe it less gently forth,—and veil
  thine eyes   Acrostic 6
On seas less hideously serene City 41
Is it therefore the less gone
            Dream w. Dream 9
Read nothing, written less—in short's a
  fool   Elizabeth 10
Ah, less—less bright   Eulalie 6

All—all expired save thee—save less than
  thou   Helen² 36
The which I could not love the less
                Lake 3
Far less a shadow which thou likenest
  to it   Politian iv 61
The which I could not love the less
            Tamerlane (1831) 81
Is it, therefore, the less gone
          Tamerlane (1831) 248

Lesson
Young Love's first lesson is—the heart
             Tamerlane 102

Lest
Lest the stars totter in the guilt of man
            Al Aaraaf i 150
Lest an evil step be taken
           Bridal Ballad 31
Lest the dead who is forsaken
           Bridal Ballad 32
My soul, lest it should truant be
             Hymn 7
Let no bell toll, then, lest her soul, amid
  its hallowed mirth   Lenore 23
Lest I behold thee not; thou couldst not
  go   Politian iv 93
And, lest the guessing throw the fool in
  fits   Tempora 91

Let
A dome, by linked light from Heaven let
  down   Al Aaraaf ii 20
And ah! let it never   Annie 45
Thus much let me avow
          Dream w. Dream 3
That dream was as the night-wind—let it
  pass   Dreams 26
But let them pass   Happiest Day 8
Let my future radiant shine Hymn 11
Had I let them pass me by Imitation 9
Let none of earth inherit Imitation 11
Soho!—let us sing   Latin Hymn 6
Soho!—let us roar   Latin Hymn 9
Let the bell toll!—a saintly soul floats on
  the Stygian river   Lenore 2
Come, let the burial rite be read—the
  funeral song be sung   Lenore 5
Peccavimus; yet rave not thus! but let a
  Sabbath song   Lenore 13
Let no bell toll, then, lest her soul, amid
  its hallowed mirth   Lenore 23
Ah, let us mourn!—for never morrow
              Palace 35
Let us go forth and taste the fragrant air
            Politian i 65
Sit down!—let not my presence trouble
  you   Politian ii 3
Let us go down   Politian iii 87
Let us descend!—'t is time
            Politian iii 95
Let us descend   Politian iii 100
Let me beg you, sir Politian iii 104
Let us go down, I pray you
            Politian iii 106
And let me hear thy voice—one word—
  one word   Politian iv 95
O pity me! let me not perish now
            Politian v 6

'Tis there the seat of reason lies in him
　　　　　　　　　　Tempora 82
From the secret that lies in these wolds
　　　　　　　　　　Ulalume 99
From the thing that lies hidden in these
　wolds　　　　　　　Ulalume 100
Shall find her own sweet name that, nest-
　ling, lies　　　　　　Valentine 3
Such eager eyes, there lies, I say, perdu
　　　　　　　　　　Valentine 14

Liest
Fair mirror and true! thou liest not
　　　　　　　　　　Politian ii 71
Thou liest! thou shalt　Politian v 92

Lieth
From a wild weird clime that lieth, sub-
　lime　　　　　　　Dream-Land 7

Life
With the last ecstasy of satiate life
　　　　　　　　　　Al Aaraaf ii 169
Of a most stormy life—was drawn
　　　　　　　　　　Alone 10
Of my darling, my darling, my life and
　my bride　　　　Annabel Lee 39
And hold this maxim all life long
　　　　　　　　　　Divine Right 11
But a wakening dream of life and light
　　　　　　　　　　Dream 3
Of wakening life, to him whose heart must
　be　　　　　　　　Dream 6
Oh! that my young life were a lasting
　dream　　　　　　　Dreams 1
Dreams! in their vivid coloring of life
　　　　　　　　　　Dreams 29
Should my early life seem　Imitation 4
Where oft—in life—with friends—it went
　　　　　　　　　　Irene 49
Long life to our king　Latin Hymn 7
The life upon her yellow hair, but not
　within her eyes　　　Lenore 18
The life still there upon her hair, the
　death upon her eyes　Lenore 19
Ye crimson life-drops, stay　Louisa 2
Was dearer to my soul than its soul-life
　　　　　　　　　Mother (1849) 14
Thou dieds't in thy life's June　Paean 33
Thy life and love are riven　Paean 38
Of life—beloved, and fair
　　　　　　　　　Paean (1836) 34
The light of Life is o'er　Paradise 15
As of one who entered madly into life
　　　　　　　　　　Politian i 59
And life shall then be mine, for I will live
　　　　　　　　　　Politian iv 78
'T is I who pray for life—I who so late
　　　　　　　　　　Politian v 9
To dream my very life away
　　　　　　　　　Romance (1831) 45
That have a double life, which thus if
　made　　　　　　　Silence 2
In life before thee are again　Spirits 8
Whose fervid, flick'ring torch of life was
　lit　　　　　　　　Stanzas¹ 4
From us in life—but common—which doth
　lie　　　　　　　　Stanzas¹ 21
Who otherwise would fall from life and
　Heav'n　　　　　　Stanzas¹ 27

Thy life's free course should ever roam
　　　　　　　　　Stanzas² 8
And this the life thy spirit live
　　　　　　　　　Stanzas² 26
On mountain soil I first drew life
　　　　　　　　　Tamerlane 35
Idea! which bindest life around
　　　　　　　　　Tamerlane 183
Let life, then, as the day-flower, fall
　　　　　　　　　Tamerlane 211
Of one whom in life I made
　　　　　　　　Tamerlane (1827) 20
In spring of life have ye ne'er dwelt
　　　　　　　　Tamerlane (1824) 94
Our earthly life, and love—and all
　　　　　　　　Tamerlane (1827) 143
Nothings of mid-day waking life
　　　　　　　　Tamerlane (1827) 170
Of an enchanted life, which seems
　　　　　　　　Tamerlane (1827) 171
That they shall stoop in life to one
　　　　　　　　Tamerlane (1827) 261
Of young life, and the fire o' the eye
　　　　　　　　Tamerlane (1827) 382
The page of life and grin at the dog-ears
　　　　　　　　　Tempora 17
Should my early life seem　　To⁴ 1
Hourly for hope—for life—ah! above all
　　　　　　　　　To MLS 5

Lifted
Thy hair is lifted by the moon
　　　　　　　Fairy-Land (1831) 7
Shall be lifted—nevermore　Raven 108

Lifting
Around, by lifting winds forgot　City 9

Ligeia
Ligeia! Ligeia!　　Al Aaraaf ii 100
Ligeia! wherever　　Al Aaraaf ii 112

Light
Laves in quadruple light her angel limbs
　　　　　　　　　Al Aaraaf i 29
Of other beauty glittering thro' the light
　　　　　　　　　Al Aaraaf i 39
Nyctanthes, too, as sacred as the light
　　　　　　　　　Al Aaraaf i 66
And wing to other worlds another light
　　　　　　　　　Al Aaraaf i 146
Bathe me in light
　　　　　　　Al Aaraaf i (1831) 8
While the moon danc'd with the fair
　strange light　Al Aaraaf ii 10
A dome, by linked light from Heaven let
　down　　　　　Al Aaraaf ii 20
The fairy light that kiss'd her golden
　hair　　　　　　Al Aaraaf ii 58
They are light on the tresses
　　　　　　　　　Al Aaraaf ii 98
Seraphs in all but "Knowledge," the keen
　light　　　　　　Al Aaraaf ii 159
And on my eyelids—O the heavy light
　　　　　　　　　Al Aaraaf ii 206
But O that light!—I slumber'd —Death,
　the while　　　　Al Aaraaf ii 210
Light, brazen rays, this golden star unto
　　　　　　　　　Al Aaraaf ii 240
When the light was extinguished
　　　　　　　　　Annie 79

Glides, spectre-like, unto his marble home
  Coliseum 25
Like lightning from the sky
  Dream w. Dream (1829) 13;
  Tamerlane (1831) 257;
  To⁴ 25
That looked like Eldorado   Eldorado 12
Like—almost anything   Fairy-Land 33
Just now so fairy-like and well
  Fairy-Land (1831) 3
Like flowers by the low breath of June
  Fairy-Land (1831) 8
Up like a dog-star in this bower
  Fairy-Land (1831) 13
So like a thing alive you know
  Fairy-Land (1831) 16
With a tinkling like a bell
  Fairy-Land (1831) 29
Like joy upon sorrow
  Fairy-Land (1831) 37
Like those Nicean barks of yore
  Helen¹ 2
How statue-like I see thee stand
  Helen¹ 12
A full-orbed moon, that, like thine own
  soul, soaring   Helen² 4
Like a banner o'er thy dreaming eye
  Irene 36
Like music of another sphere
  Irene (1836) 27
And vamp-wing-like pannels back
  Irene (1836) 72
And the sultan-like pines that towered
  around   Lake (1831) 6
In a dirge-like melody
  Lake (1845) 10
Helen, like thy human eye   Nis 29
Rolling like a waterfall   Nis 41
Rolling, like a waterfall   Nis (1836) 39
And Helen, like thy human eye
  Nis (1836) 41
All banner-like above a grave
  Nis (1836) 44
While, like a ghastly rapid river
  Palace 45
Wears it away like evil hours and wine
  Politian i 18
Ill suit the like with old Di Broglio's
  heir   Politian i 21
Oh, beautiful!—most beautiful!—how
  like   Politian ii 11
But like—oh, very like in its despair
  Politian ii 22
Baldazzar, it oppresses me like a spell
  Politian iii 55
Behold the cross wherewith a vow like
  mine   Politian ii 107
Like the grim shadow Conscience, solemn
  and noiseless   Politian iv 56
Of labyrinth-like water
  River (1829) 2
Then roll'd like tropic storms along
  Romance (1831) 12
Looking like Lethe, see! the lake
  Sleeper 13
Like ghosts the shadows rise and fall
  Sleeper 29

With light like Hope to mortal given
  Spirits 14
From clouds that hung, like banners, o'er
  Tamerlane 45
But, just like any other dream
  Tamerlane 133
Which fall'st into the soul like rain
  Tamerlane 179
So like you gather in your breath
  Tamerlane 205
And the sultan-like pines that tower'd
  around   Tamerlane (1831) 84
Lonely, like me, the desert rose
  Tamerlane (1831) 221
I like your Yankee words and Yankee
  ways   Tempora 10
As Members say they like their logic
  taken   Tempora 45
Those won't turn on anything like men
  Tempora 68
Like starlight on a pall   To¹ 8
That hangs like chains of pearl on Her-
  mon hill   To³ 10
Unthought-like thoughts that are the souls
  of thought   To³ 12
Like some enchanted far-off isle   To F 9
Like that bird the lover   To Hunter 12
And he smiles—like me   To Hunter 15
That palpitate like the chill seas
  Valley 15
Like the knight Pinto (Mendez Ferdi-
  nando)   Valentine 18

Liken
We liken our ladies' eyes to them
  City (1831) 16
Likeness
A likeness taken when the breath
  Tamerlane (1827) 381
I think he'll take this likeness to himself
  Tempora 89
Likenest
Far less a shadow which thou likenest to
  it   Politian iv 61
Lilies
Of flowers: of lilies such as rear'd the
  head   Al Aaraaf i 43
Abash'd, amid the lilies there, to seek
  Al Aaraaf i 119
Over the lilies there that wave
  Valley 22
Lillian
Virginal Lillian, rigidly, humblily dutiful
  Experiments 1
Lily
With the snows of the lolling lily
  Dream-Land 20, 24
The lily lolls upon the wave
  Sleeper 10
From the depth of each pallid lily-bell
  Valley (1845) 29
Limbo
From the limbo of lunary souls
  Ulalume 102
Limbs
Laves in quadruple light her angel limbs
  Al Aaraaf i 29

Line
Beyond the line of blue   Al Aaraaf i 86
Pure and reproachless, of thy princely
    line   Politian iv 25
Prophetic tones fom every line
                        Stanzas² 3
Lineaments
Whose lineaments, upon my mind
                        Tamerlane 79
Lines
Not long ago, the writer of these lines
                        To³ 1
And think that these weak lines are
    written by him   To MLS 16
For her these lines are penned, whose
    luminous eyes   Valentine 1
Search narowly the lines!—they hold a
    treasure   Valentine (1840) 5
Linger
Disconsolate linger—grief that hangs her
    head   Al Aaraaf i 62
Ah, hasten!—ah, let us not linger
                        Ulalume 54
Lingering
And the lingering illness   Annie 3
No lingering winters there, no snow, nor
    shower   Politian ii 8
Lining
On the cushion's velvet lining that the
    lamp-light gloated o'er   Raven 76
But whose velvet-violet lining with the
    lamp-light gloating o'er   Raven 77
Linked
Link'd to a little system and one sun
                        Al Aaraaf i 134
A dome, by linked light from Heaven let
    down   Al Aaraaf ii 20
Linking
Then, upon the velvet sinking, I betook
    myself to linking   Raven 69
Lion
Lion ambition is chain'd down
                        Tamerlane 160
And has come past the stars of the Lion
                        Ulalume 44
Come up, in despite of the Lion
                        Ulalume 47
Come up through the lair of the Lion
                        Ulalume 49
Lip
Of lip-begotten words   To¹ 4
Lips
Her cheeks were flushing, and her lips
    apart   Al Aaraaf ii 53
And speak a purpose unholy—thy lips
    are livid   Politian ii 109
With those words upon my lips—O, speak
    to me   Politian iv 94
So fresh upon thy lips I will not fight
    thee   Politian v 68
When from thy balmy lips I drew
                        Sarah 16
Are lips—and all thy melody   To¹ 3
Liquescent
At the end of our path a liquescent
                        Ulalume 33

Liquid
What a liquid ditty floats   Bells 22
Lisp
To lisp my very earliest word
                        Romance 8
So often lovely, and will lisp
                        Tamerlane (1827) 371
List
That list our Love, and deck our bowers
                        Al Aaraaf i 13
But, list, Ianthe! when the air so soft
                        Al Aaraaf ii 231
But list, O list,—so soft and low
                        Serenade 18
So often lovely, and will list
                        Tamerlane 196
Listen
While, to listen, the red levin Israfel 12
Not hear it!—listen now! listen—the
    faintest sound   Politian iii 52
And beautiful Lalage!—and listen to me
                        Politian iv (1835) 9
Listening
And the other listening things
                        Israfel 17
Listens
To the turtle-dove that listens, while she
    gloats   Bells 23
Lit
It lit on hills Achaian, and thére dwelt
                        Al Aaraaf i 34
In many a star-lit grove, or moon-lit dell
                        Al Aaraaf ii 63
Lit by the wan light of the horned moon
                        Coliseum 24
Where the moon-lit blossoms quiver
                        Departed 10
Whose fervid, flick'ring torch of life was
    lit   Stanzas 4
Litten
These star-litten hours
                        Al Aaraaf ii 83
Through the red-litten windows see
                        Palace 42
Little
Link'd to a little system and one sun
                        Al Aaraaf i 134
Little—oh! little dwells in thee
                        Al Aaraaf i (1831) 16
Dim was its little disk, and angel eyes
                        Al Aaraaf ii 253
The little silver bells   Bells (1849) 3
Has studied very little of his part
                        Elizabeth 9
Lo! that little window-niche
                        Helen² (1831) 11
And little given to thinking
                        Politian i 53
Think of my little sisters!—think of them
                        Politian ii 87
To say thou art not gone,—one little
    sentence   Politian iv 96
Give me to live yet—yet a little while
                        Politian v 8
Though its answer little meaning—little
    relevancy bore   Raven 50

That little time with lyre and rhyme
                         Romance 18
When, from our little cares apart
                         Tamerlane 104
Its joy—its little lot of pain
                         Tamerlane 119
Yet still I think these worse than them a
  little   Tempora 8
But pray be patient: yet a little while
                         Tempora 38
The pretty little hand that sold her tape
                         Tempora 56
Ah yes! his little foot and ancle trim
                         Tempora 81
Hath—little of Earth in it   To² 2

Live
I would not live again
                         Happiest Day 20
Merrily live, and long   Israfel 34
And live, for now thou diest
                         Politian iii 5
Surely I live   Politian iii 6
And life shall then be mine, for I will live
                         Politian iv 78
Give me to live yet—yet a little while
                         Politian v 8
In the budding of my hopes—give me to
  live   Politian v (1835) 7
And this the life thy spirit live
                         Stanzas² 26
For all we live to know is known
                         Tamerlane 209

Lived
That a maiden there lived whom you may
  know   Annabel Lee 3
And this maiden she lived with no other
  thought   Annabel Lee 5
To die ere I have lived   Politian v 3
But, father, there liv'd one who, then
                         Tamerlane 69

Livelong
The livelong summer day, oppress
                         Tamerlane (1827) 212

Lives
Castiglione lives   Politian iv 87
Too real, to his breast who lives
                         Tamerlane (1827) 307

Livest
Who livest—that we know
                         Al Aaraaf i 98

Livid
And speak a purpose unholy—thy lips are
  livid   Politian ii 109

Living
And the fever called "Living"   Annie 5
With the fever called "Living"
                         Annie 29
I' the summer sky, in dreams of living
  light   Dreams 14
The trembling living wire   Israfel 21
For we cannot help agreeing that no living
  human being   Raven 51
With ray of the all living light
                         Tamerlane (1827) 155
With its own living gaze upon
                         Tamerlane (1827) 317

Lizard
The swift and silent lizard of the stones
                         Coliseum 25

Lo
Lo! the ring is on my hand
                         Bridal Ballad (1837) 25
Lo! Death has reared himself a throne
                         City 1
But lo, a stir is in the air   City 42
Lo! one is coming down
                         Fairy-Land (1831) 41
Lo! in yon brilliant window-niche
                         Helen¹ 11
No wind in Heaven, and lo! the trees
                         Nis (1836) 33
All Beauty sleeps!—and lo! where lies
                         Sleeper 16
Lo! 'tis a gala night   Worm 1

Loath
The monkey made me swear, though something loath   Tempora 36

Loathe
I hate—I loathe the name; I do abhor
                         Politian iv 31

Locke
As for Locke, he is all in my eye
                         Lampoon 1
John Locke was a notable name
                         Lampoon 5
Joe Locke is a greater: in short
                         Lampon 6

Locks
Till thoughts and locks are left, alas
                         Irene 7

Locust
Was once the locust's coat of gold
                         Parody 4

Loeda
Brightly expressive as the twins of Loeda
                         Valentine 2

Loftier
And a loftier note than this would swell
                         Israfel (1836) 45

Lofty
Of lofty contemplation left to Time
                         Coliseum 2
Shone on my slumbers in her lofty noon
                         Dreams 24
For thy lofty rank and fashion—much
  depends   Politian i 25

Logic
Logic and common usage so commanding
                         Elizabeth 2
As Members say they like their logic
  taken   Tempora 45

Loitering
With loitering eye, till I have felt
                         Tamerlane 83

Lolled
Here, where on golden throne the monarch
  lolled   Coliseum 22

Lolling
Her world lay lolling on the golden air
                         Al Aaraaf i 17

How lovely 'tis to look so far away
                          Al Aaraaf ii 199
That you shudder to look at me
                          Annie 93
To look upon the face hidden by yon lat-
tice   Politian iii 102
Look at me, brightest   Politian iv 8
I feel thou art not gone—yet dare not
look   Politian iv 92
And the stars shall look not down
                          Spirits 12
She'd look up in my wilder'd eye
                     Tamerlane (1827) 132
Look around thee now on Samarcand
                          Tamerlane 165
To him who still would look upon
                          Tamerlane 193
Now, as I look back, the strife
                     Tamerlane (1827) 172
In short his shirt-collar, his look, his
tone is   Tempora 71
I look not up afar   To⁴ 5

Looked
She look'd into Infinity—and knelt
                          Al Aaraaf i 35
Look'd out above into the purple air
                          Al Aaraaf ii 23
That looked like Eldorado   Eldorado 12
Save only thee and me. I paused—I
looked   Helen 28
Of a high mountain which look'd down
                          Tamerlane 140

Looking
And cloudy-looking woods
                          Fairy-Land 2
Looking like Lethe, see! the lake
                          Sleeper 13
Dim! tho' looking on all bright
                     Tamerlane (1827) 322

Looks
And looks so sweetly down on Beauty's
hair   Al Aaraaf ii 187
Deth looks gigantically down   City 29
Thy looks are haggard—nothing so wears
away   Politian i 15
But when within thy wave she looks
                          River 7

Loom
O! no—O! no—ours never loom
                          City (1831) 8

Lord
And my lord he loves me well
                          Bridal Ballad 6
No more, my lord, than I have told you,
sir   Politian v 28
My lord!—my friend   Politian v 37
My lord, some strange   Politian v 47
Alas, my lord   Politian v 71
But, with mien of lord or lady, perched
above my chamber door   Raven 40
Lord! to be grave exceeds the power of
face   Tempora 64

Lordly
Tell me what thy lordly name is on the
Night's Plutonian shore   Raven 47

Lordship
Your lordship's pleasure
                          Politian iii 113
Of quarrel between your lordship and
himself   Politian v 21

Lore
Thirst for the springs of lore that in thee
lie   Coliseum 6
Over many a quaint and curious volume
of forgotten lore   Raven 2
Some human memories and tearful lore
                          Silence 8
With more of sov'reignty than ancient
lore   Stanzas¹ 12
Some page of early lore upon
                          Tamerlane 82

Lose
The trivialest point, or you may lose your
labor   Valentine 9

Losing
A thousand hearts—losing at length her
own   Politian ii 24

Lost
Lost, lost Rosabel   Ballad 12, 24, 36
From my books surcease of sorrow—sor-
row for the lost Lenore   Raven 10
Quaff, oh, quaff this kind nepenthe and
forget this lost Lenore   Raven 83
O craving heart, for the lost flowers
                          Tamerlane 21
By what it lost for passion—Heav'n
                     Tamerlane (1827) 107
'Tis the vault of my lost Ulalume
                          Ulalume 81

Lot
In spring of youth it was my lot
                          Lake 1
The world, its cares, and my own lot
                          Sarah 20
But should some urgent fate (untimely
lot!)   Silence 12
For in those days it was my lot
                     Tamerlane (1831) 79
Its joy—its little lot of pain
                          Tamerlane 119
And murmur'd at such lowly lot
                          Tamerlane 132
God help me, it hath been my lot to know
                          Tempora 60
I heed not that my earthly lot   To² 1
In the terror of my lot   To⁴ 36

Lotus
And Valisnerian lotus thither flown
                          Al Aaraaf i 74

Loud
Is not its form—its voice—most palpable
and loud   Al Aaraaf ii 47
Hear the loud alarum bells   Bells 36
Wakening the broad welkin with his loud
battle cry   Campaign 2
Prophetic sounds and loud, arise forever
                          Coliseum 34
Thus on the coffin loud and long
                          Paean 29

Louder
Soon again I heard a tapping somewhat
louder than before   Raven 32

They seem to whisper thoughts of love
Sarah 10
Sees in the sea a second love
Serenade 10
Enthralling love, my Adeline
Serenade 17
In every deed shall mingle, love
Serenade 25
My love, she sleeps! Oh, may her sleep
Sleeper 45
The world all love before thee
Song 4, 16
O, she was worthy of all love
Tamerlane 86
Love—as in infancy was mine
Tamerlane 87
We grew in age—and love—together
Tamerlane 96
Young Love's first lesson is—the heart
Tamerlane 102
Yet more than worthy of the love
Tamerlane 112
O, human love! thou spirit given
Tamerlane 177
I wandered of the idol, Love
Tamerlane 232
In the tangles of Love's very hair
Tamerlane 243
Our earthly life, and love—and all
Tamerlane (1827) 143
For passionate love is still divine
Tamerlane (1827) 153
The love he plighted then—again
Tamerlane (1827) 280
Tho' lov'd, and loving—let it pass
Tamerlane (1827) 298
The which I could not love the less
Tamerlane (1831) 81
Nor love, Ada! tho' it were mine
Tamerlane (1831) 95
My home—my hope—my early love
Tamerlane (1831) 220
That years of love have been forgot
To² 3
And love— a simple duty
To FSO (1835) 8
How should he love thee? or how deem
thee wise
To Science 5
With love in her luminous eyes
Ulalume 50

Loved
Of her who lov'd a mortal—and so died
Al Aaraaf i 47
And all I lov'd—I lov'd alone
Alone 8
Than to love and be loved by me
Annabel Lee 6
But we loved with a love that was more
than love
Annabel Lee 9
Had I lov'd thee as a brother
Ballad 15
For she knew I lov'd her child
Ballad 20
He has loved me long and well
Bridal Ballad (1837) 7
Wretches! ye loved her for her wealth,
and ye hated her for her pride
Lenore 8

Are mother to the one I loved so dearly
Mother 11
Castiglione lied who said he loved
Politian ii 73
Who hath loved thee so long
Politian iii 72, 81, 91
By rivals loved, and mourned by heirs
Stanzas 8
To the lov'd object—so the tear to the lid
Stanzas 18
I lov'd—and O, how tenderly
Tamerlane (1827) 108
I lov'd her as an angel might
Tamerlane (1827) 154
Tho' lov'd, and loving—let it pass
Tamerlane (1827) 298
Thou wouldst be loved?—then let thy
heart
To FSO 1

Loveliest
Now happiest, loveliest in yon lovely
Earth
Al Aaraaf i 30
She, earth's bright and loveliest flower
Departed 17
The requiem for the loveliest dead
Paean 3

Loveliness
All other loveliness: its honied dew
Al Aaraaf i 52
And woman's loveliness—and passionate
love
Al Aaraaf ii 230
And loveliness,—have left my very heart
Dreams 15
A rarer loveliness bedecks the earth
Politian iii 48
Of Loveliness could see
Song 8
The loveliness of loving well
Tamerlane 76
My mind with double loveliness
Tamerlane 138
Her overpow'ring loveliness
Tamerlane (1827) 314
That loveliness around: the sun
Tamerlane (1827) 318

Lovely
Now happiest, loveliest in yon lovely
Earth
Al Aaraaf i 30
And thy most lovely purple perfume,
Zante
Al Aaraaf i 76
How lovely 't is to look so far away
Al Aaraaf ii 199
Stole o'er my senses in that lovely isle
Al Aaraaf ii 211
Lonely, by that lovely river
Departed 9
Hath cheered me as a lovely beam
Dream 11
And hath been still, upon the lovely earth
Dreams 7
To the delirious eye, more lovely things
Dreams 32
The more lovely, the more far
Israfel (1831) 29
So lovely was the loneliness
Lake 4
A dirge for the most lovely dead
Lenore (1843) 7
All things lovely—are not they
Nis 5
So often lovely, and will list
Tamerlane 196

Maddened

That maddened my brain   Annie 28

Maddening

Was mad'ning—for 't man that shed
Tamerlane (1827) 63

Made

Made in his image a mannikin merely to
madden it   Experiments 6

Why ask? who ever yet saw money made
out of a fat old   Experiments 9

There is a vow were fitting should be made
Politian ii 94

Not the least obeisance made he; not a
minute stopped or stayed he
Raven 39

That have a double life, which thus is
made   Silence 2

For all have flown who made it so
Tamerlane 214

Of one whom in life I made
Tamerlane (1827) 20

The monkey made me swear, though something loath   Tempora 36

My friend, the beau, hath made a settled
matter   Tempora 76

Italian tones made only to be murmured
To³ 8

Madly

As of one who entered madly into life
Politian i 59

I will not madly deem that power
Tamerlane 3

And hurried madly on my way
Tamerlane (1827) 300

Madness

With madness, and unwonted reverie
Al Aaraaf i 50

Thy words are madness, daughter
Politian ii 108

Of parting, were with madness fraught
Tamerlane (1827) 296

And much of Madness, and more of Sin
Worm 23

Magic

No Magic shall sever
Al Aaraaf ii 114

Not all the magic of our high renown
Coliseum 41

The magic empire of a flame
Tamerlane (1827) 104

The magic of that meaning word
Tamerlane (1827) 196

Over the magic solitude   Valley 13

Magical

No more! alas, that magical sad sound
Zante 9

Maid

Full many a maid   Al Aaraaf ii 139

The servant maid!—but courage!—'tis
but a viper   Politian ii 58

For ruined maid   Politian ii 71

Maiden

Up rose the maiden in the yellow night
Al Aaraaf i 151

Up rose the maiden form her shrine of
flowers   Al Aaraaf i 156

Dreamy maidens all the day
Al Aaraaf i (1831) 13

Bore burthen to the charm the maiden
sang   Al Aaraaf ii 67

Like—eyes of the maiden
Al Aaraaf ii 78

Arouse them, my maiden
Al Aaraaf ii 142

A maiden-angel and her seraph-lover
Al Aaraaf ii 178

That a maiden there lived whom you may
know   Annabel Lee 3

And this maiden she lived with no other
thought   Annabel Lee 5

And a glittering beam from a maiden's
eye   Parody 9

She died!—the maiden died
Politian ii 13

O still more happy maiden who couldst
die   Politian ii 14

For the rare and radiant maiden whom
the angels name Lenore   Raven 11

It shall clasp a sainted maiden whom the
angels name Lenore   Raven 94

Clasp a rare a radiant maiden whom the
angels name Lenore   Raven 95

That blush, perhaps, was maiden shame
Song 89

Fair maiden let thy generous heart
To FSO (1839) 1

How many visions of a maiden that is
Zante 7

Maidens

How, in thy father's halls, among the
maidens   Politian iv 24

Maids

Thus endeth the history—and her maids
Politian ii 25

Lean over her and weep—two gentle
maids   Politian ii 26

Maintained

Maintained "the power of words"—
denied that ever   To³ 3

Make

That the vapor can make   Eulalie 10

Do tell! when may we hope to make new
of sense out of the pundits
Experiments 7

Whose solitary soul could make
Lake 22

Will make it break for thee
Octavia 9

Will make thee mine   Politian i 4

You dog! and make it up, I say, this
minute   Politian i 40

Baldazzar, make   Politian iii 111

Not Hell shall make me fear again
Tamerlane 20

My solitary soul—how make
Tamerlane (1831) 98

But speak to him, he'll make you such
grimace   Tempora 63

Man

Lest the stars totter in the guilt of man
Al Aaraaf i 150

As glowing Beauty's bust beneath man's
eye   Al Aaraaf ii 258

For man never slept   Annie 49

They are neither man nor woman
Bells 86

Marvelled
Much I marvelled this ungainly fowl to
hear discourse so plainly　　Raven 49

Marvellous
Up many and many a marvellous shrine
City 21

Mary
Mary, amid the cares—the woes
To F (1835) 1

Mask
The mask—the viol—and the vine
City (1831) 30

Mass
A ne'er-to-be untangled mass　　Irene 8

Master
Caught from some unhappy master whom
unmerciful Disaster　　Raven 63

Mastered
So deep abstruse he has not mastered it
Politian i 55

Material
Yet silence came upon material things
Al Aaraaf ii 64

Matron
While ever to her dear Eulalie upturns
her matron eye　　Eulalie 20

Matted
I pass'd from out the matted bow'r
Tamerlane (1827) 284
I went from out the matted bow'r
Tamerlane (1827) 299
In mine own Ada's matted bow'r
Tamerlane (1827) 358

Matter
But no matter!—I feel　　Annie 11
My son, I've news for thee!—hey? what's
the matter　　Politian i 38
From matter and light, evinced in solid
and shade　　Silence 4
And take the matter up when I'm more
able　　Tempora 24
My friend, the beau, hath made a settled
matter　　Tempora 76

Matters
What matters it　　Politian iv 41
What matters it, my fairest, and my best
Politian iv 42
And hold this maxim all life long
Divine Right 11

May
Nor that the grass—O! may it thrive
To M 17

Maziness
The playful maziness of art　　River 5

Me
To me, Politian, of thy camps and courts
Politian iii 28

Mean
Yet should I swear I mean alone
Romance (1831) 58
I mean the reign of manners hath long
ceased　　Tempora 3

Meandering
The mossy banks and the meandering
paths　　Helen² 32

Meaning
Called anything, its meaning is the same
Elizabeth 15
With a visage full of meaning　　Nis 21
Though its answer little meaning—little
relevance bore　　Raven 50
The letters—with their meaning—melt
Tamerlane 84
The magic of that meaning word
Tamerlane (1827) 196

Means
Means the "valley of unrest."　　Nis 16

Meant
That's meant for me　　Politian ii 47
Meant in croaking "Nevermore."
Raven 72

Meantime
Meantime from afar
Al Aaraaf i (1831) 7
And in the meantime, to prevent all
bother　　Tempora 25

Meanwhile
With storms—but where meanwhile
To F 12

Measure
Nor long the measure of my falling hours
Al Aaraaf ii 241
That must be worn at heart. Search well
the measure　　Valentine 7
With thy burning measures suit
Israfel 36

Measures
I'll mend my manners and my measures
too　　Tempora 40

Meddle
But that you meddle with my fate
To M 7

Meet
Curs'd was the hour that saw us meet
Louisa 15
I go—to-morrow we meet
Politian v 43
If that we met at all, it were as well
Politian v (1835) 45
That I should meet him in the Vatican
Politian v (1835) 46
Bring thee to met his shadow (nameless
elf　　Silence 13
Science! meet daughter of Old Time thou
art　　To Science (1829) 1

Meeting
And, with bold advance, now meeting
Departed 7
Were it not for that dim meeting
Departed 33

Meets
There the traveller meets, aghast
Dream-Land 33

Melancholy
Sorrow is not melancholy
Al Aaraaf i (1831) 29
To his love-haunted heart and melancholy
Al Aaraaf ii 189
At the melancholy menace of their tone
Bells 75
From the melancholy throats
Bells (1849) 16

But, taking one by each hand, merely
    growl   Tempora 28
If one could merely understand the plot
                                Valentine 12

Merest
    " Silence "—which is the merest word of
    all   Al Aaraaf i 127

Meridian
    While even in the meridian glare of day
                                Helen² 64

Merrily
    Merrily live, and long   Israfel 34

Merriment
    What a world of merriment their melody
    foretells   Bells 3
    The frightful sounds of merriment below
                                Politian ii 78

Merry
    And his merry bosom swells   Bells 93
    The merry wedding bells
                            Bells (1849) 2
    In merry England—never so plaintively
                                Politian iii 78

Message
    I know what thou wouldst say—not send
    the message   Politian v 39

Messenger
    Thy messenger hath known
                            Al Aaraaf i 103

Met
    He met a pilgrim shadow   Eldorado 15
    When wit, and wine, and friends have met
                                Octavia 1
    There met me on its threshold stone
                        Tamerlane (1827) 396

Meteor
    And rays from God shot down that
    meteor chain   Al Aaraaf ii 24

Methinks
    Methinks thou hast a singular way of
    showing   Politian i 5
    Methinks 't were fitting   Politian ii 104
    Methinks the air   Politian iii 45
    Or one more worthy Italy, methinks
                                Politian v 17

Methought
    Methought, my sweet one, then I ceased
    to soar   Al Aaraaf ii 237
    Of yonder trees methought a figure past
                                Politian iv 54
    Then, methought, the air grew denser,
    perfumed from an unseen censer
                                Raven 79

'Mid
    Away—away—'mid seas of rays that roll
                            Al Aaraaf i 20
    Like woman's hair 'mid pearls, until, afar
                            Al Aaraaf i 33
    Unguided Love hath fallen—'mid " tears
    of perfect moan."
                            Al Aaraaf ii 181
    'Mid dark thoughts of the gray tomb-
    stone   Spirits 2
    And mid-time of night   Star 2
    'Mid planets her slaves   Star 6
    'Mid dreams of an unholy night
                            Tamerlane 42

For 'mid that sunshine and those smiles
                            Tamerlane 103
Nothings of mid-day waking life
                        Tamerlane (1827) 170
I was standing 'mid the roar
                        Tamerlane (1831) 249
For 'mid the earnest cares and woes
                            To F (1842) 1
In the misty mid region of Weir
                                Ulalume 7
This misty mid region of Weir
                                Ulalume 92

Midnight
    A midnight vigil holds the swarthy bat
                                Coliseum 19
    It was a July midnight: and from out
                                Helen² 3
    Was is not Fate that, on this July mid-
    night   Helen² 21
    Once upon a midnight dreary, while I
    pondered, weak and weary   Raven 1
    At midnight, in the month of June
                                Sleeper 1

Midst
    In the midst of which all day   Valley 7

Mien
    But, with mien of lord or lady, perched
    above my chamber door   Raven 40

Might
    Giv'n by the energetic might
                        Tamerlane (1827) 187
    How by what hidden deeds of might
                        Tamerlane (1827) 351

Mightiest
    We rule the hearts of mightiest men—we
    rule   Coliseum 37

Mild
    Trusting to the mild-eyed stars
                                Valley 4

Milk
    Which with my mother's milk I did imbibe
                                Politian iii 12

Million
    And million bright pines to and fro
                                Irene 18

Mimes
    Mimes, in the form of God on high
                                Worm 9
    The mimes become its food   Worm 30

Mimic
    Here, where the mimic eagle glared in
    gold   Coliseum 18
    But see, amid the mimic rout   Worm 25

Mind
    And my mind is much benighted
                        Bridal Ballad (1837) 23
    Ah, bear in mind this garden was en-
    chanted   Helen² 30
    Springing from a darken'd mind
                            Lake (1827) 16
    Perhaps it may that my mind is wrought
                                Stanzas¹ 9
    The fullness of a cultured mind
                                Stanzas² 17
    The heritage of a kingly mind
                                Tamerlane 32

Moaning
The moaning and groaning   Annie 19
To the moaning and the groaning of the
bells   Bells 113

Moans
And when, amid no earthly moans
                                   City 50

Mock
The mock-bird chirping on the thorn
                                   Sarah 3

Mockery
It would be mockery to call
                                   City (1831) 18
This mockery is most cruel—most cruel
indeed   Politian iv 4
And now, as if in mockery of that boast
                                   To¹ 6

Mockest
Thou mockest me, sir   Politian i 30
Villain, thou art not gone—thou mockest
me   Politian iv 101

Model
Fit emblems of the model of her world
                                   Al Aaraaf i 37
A model of their own   Al Aaraaf i 105

Modelled
But are modell'd, alas
                                   Al Aaraaf ii 127

Modest
Can vie with the modest Eulalie's most
unregarded curl   Eulalie 12

Molten
Of molten stars their pavement, such as
fall   Al Aaraaf ii 16
From the molten-golden notes
                                   Bells 20

Moment
Every moment of the night
                                   Fairy-Land 7
Pores for a moment, ere it go   Irene 56
Let my heart be still a moment and this
mystery explore   Raven 35
The moment's converse; in her eyes
                                   Tamerlane 148
Not the least obeisance made he; not a
moment stopped or stayed he
                                   Raven (1846) 39

Monarch
Here, where on golden throne the monarch
lolled   Coliseum 22
In the morarch Thought's dominion
                                   Palace 5
Assailed the monarch's high estate
                                   Palace 34
The pageantry of monarchy
                                   Tamerlane 47
The infant monarch of the hour
                                   Tamerlane (1827) 45

Money
Why ask? who ever yet saw money made
out of a fat old   Experiments 9

Monkey
The monkey made me swear, though something loath   Tempora 36

Monody
What a world of solemn thought their
monody compels   Bells 72

Monotone
In that muffled monotone   Bells 83
To break upon Time's monotone
                                   Romance (1831) 60

Month
At midnight, in the month of June
                                   Sleeper 1
For we knew not the month was October
                                   Ulalume 23

Moon
Our faith to one love—and one moon
adore   Al Aaraaf i 153
What time the moon is quadrated in
Heaven   Al Aaraaf ii 6
While the moon danc'd with the fair
stranger light   Al Aaraaf ii 10
In many a star-lit grove, or moon-lit dell
                                   Al Aaraaf ii 63
Beneath the moon ray
                                   Al Aaraaf ii 131
Beneath the cold moon
                                   Al Aaraaf ii 151
For the moon never beams without bring-
ing me dreams   Annabel Lee 34
On the moon   Bells 24
By the side of the pale-faced moon
                                   Bells 50
Lit by the wan light of the horned moon
                                   Coliseum 24
Where the moon-lit blossoms quiver
                                   Departed 10
When the weary moon descendeth
                                   Departed 13
Its image on my spirit—or the moon
                                   Dreams 23
Of the moon   Eldorado 20
With the moon-tints of purple and pearl
                                   Eulalie 11
About twelve by the moon-dial
                                   Fairy-Land 11
They use the moon no more
                                   Fairy-Land 35
Thy hair is lifted by the moon
                                   Fairy-Land (1831) 7
As she threw off her cloak, you moon
                                   Fairy-Land (1831) 22
We can discover a moon ray
                                   Fairy-Land (1831) 31
A full-orbed moon, that, like thine own
soul, soaring   Helen² 4
I saw thee half reclining; while the moon
                                   Helen² 18
The pearly lustre of the moon went out
                                   Helen² 31
Saw only them until the moon went down
                                   Helen² 41
Thus hums the moon within her ear
                                   Irene 25
The enamoured moon   Israfel 10
There the moon doth shine by night
                                   Nis 43
And with a holier lustre the quiet moon
                                   Politian iii 49
I stand beneath the mystic moon
                                   Sleeper 2
Of the brighter, cold moon   Star 5
What tho' the moon—the white moon
                                   Tamerlane 201

Moonbeam
The moonbeam away   Al Aaraaf ii 71
A dreamer in the moonbeam by his love
Al Aaraaf ii 185
Here, dearest, where the moonbeam fell
Fairy-Land (1831) 2
To a fever by the moonbeam that hangs
o'er   Stanzas¹ 10
Mooned
The single-mooned eve!—on Earth we
plight   Al Aaraaf i 152
Moonlight
Like moonlight on my spirit fell
Tamerlane (1831) 101
Moonlit
By angels dreaming in the moonlit "dew"
To³ 9
Moons
Huge moons there wax and wane
Fairy-Land 5
Moony
With all thy train, athwart the moony
sky   Al Aaraaf i 144
And their moony covering   Fairy-land 30
Moorland
On moorland and lea   Al Aaraaf ii 143
More
Like guilty beauty, chasten'd, and more
fair   Al Aaraaf i 65
The birth-place of young Beauty had no
more   Al Aaraaf i 154
More beauty clung around her column'd
wall   Al Aaraaf ii 216
But we loved with a love that was more
than love   Annabel Lee 9
And Death to some more happy clime
City (1836) 55
O spells more sure than e'er Judaean king
Coliseum 13
O charms more potent than the rapt
Chaldee   Coliseum 15
Clothing us in a robe of more than glory
Coliseum 46
I'd strive for liberty no more
Divine Right 3
What could there be more purely
Dream 15
Of mine own thought—what more could
I have seen   Dreams 18
To the delirious eye, more lovely things
Dreams 32
One more filmy than the rest
Fairy-Land 12
They use the moon no more
Fairy-Land 35
Were seen no more: the very roses' adore
Helen² 34
The more lovely, the more fair
Israfel (1841) 29
He has given us more
Latin Hymn 10
And, Guy De Vere, hast thou no tear?—
Weep now or never more   Lenore 3
You who are more than mother unto me
Mother 6
Are thus more precious than the one I
knew   Mother (1850) 12

From more than fiends on earth
Paean 37
Of more than thrones in heaven
Paean 40
An laugh—but smile no more   Palace 48
No more—no more—no more
Paradise 16
A few days more, thou knowest, my Ales-
sandra   Politian i 3
Attend thou also more   Politian i 23
Then see to it!—pay more attention, sir
Politian i 27
O still more happy maiden who couldst
die   Politian ii 14
She has any more jewels—no—no—she
gave me all   Politian ii 41
And be no more Politian, but some other
Politian iii 13
Baldazzar speak no more
Politian iii 27
Once more that silent tongue
Politian iii 104
What need we more   Politian iv 35
There is no deed I would more glory in
Politian iv 39
And Sorrow shall be no more, and Eros
be all   Politian iv 77
No more a mourner—but the radiant Joys
Politian iv 80
Or one more worthy Italy, methinks
Politian v 17
No more, my lord, than I have told you,
sir   Politian v 28
Draw, villain, and prate no more
Politian v 57
Only this and nothing more   Raven 6
This is it and nothing more   Raven 18
Darkness there and nothing more
Raven 24
Merely this and nothing more
Raven 30
'Tis the wind and nothing more
Raven 36
Perched, and sat, and nothing more
Raven 42
Till I scarcely more than muttered,
" Other friends have flown before
Raven 58
This and more I sat divining, with my
head at ease reclining   Raven 75
I feel it more than half a crime
Serenade 2
Render him terrorless: his name's " No
more   Silence 9
This chamber changed for one more holy
Sleeper 40
This bed for one more melancholy
Sleeper 41
She ne'er shall force an echo more
Sleeper 58
No more—like dew-drop from the grass
Spirits 22
With more of sov'reignty than ancient
lore   Stanzas¹ 12
The unembodied essence, and no more
Stanzas¹ 14
And more I admire   Star 21

Its fount is holier—more divine
        Tamerlane 10
The more than beauty of a face
        Tamerlane 78
Yet more than worthy of the love
        Tamerlane 112
Shadows—and a more shadowy light
        Tamerlane 123
I reache'd my home—my home no more
        Tamerlane 213
Is more than crime may dare to dream
        Tamerlane (1827) 5
To mind—not flow'rs alone—but more
        Tamerlane (1827) 142
A more than agony to him
        Tamerlane (1827) 315
Redoubling age! and more, I ween
        Tamerlane (1827) 336
That bore me from my home, more gay
        Tamerlane (1827) 502
Thy grace, thy more than beauty
        To FSO 6
To write? to scribble? nonsense and no
more   To Maragaret 5
And much of Madness, and more of Sin
        Worm 23
No more—no more upon thy verdant
slopes   Zante 8
No more! alas, that magical sad sound
        Zante 9
Transforming all! Thy charms shall
please no more   Zante 10
Thy memory no more! Accursed ground
        Zante 11

Morn
And star-dials pointed to morn
        Ulalume 31
With the morn-tints of purple and pearl
        Eulalie (1845) 11
At morn—at noon—at twilight dim
        Hymn 1
As the star-dials hinted of morn
        Ulalume 32
Uneasily, from morn till even
        Valley 19

Morning
In the morning they arise
        Fairy-land 29
In the morning light afar
        Spirits (1827) 20
Of all who hail thy presence as the
morning   To MLS 1

Morrow
Of an Eternity should bring the morrow
        Dreams 3
O, when will come the morrow
        Fairy-Land (1831) 38
Ah, let us mourn!—for never morrow
        Palace 35
Eagerly I wished the morrow;—vainly I
had sought to borrow   Raven 9
On the morrow he will leave me, as my
Hopes have flown before   Raven 59

Mortal
Of her who lov'd a mortal—and so died
        Al Aaraaf i 47

Spirit, cooped in mortal bower
        Departed 18
A mortal melody   Israfel 49
No mortal eyes have seen!—what said
the count   Politian v 18
Doubting, dreaming dreams no mortal
ever dared to dream before Raven 26
It writhes!—it writhes!—with mortal
pangs   Worm 29

Mortality
The worst ill of mortality
        Tamerlane (1827) 305

Mortals
Doubting, dreaming dreams no mortals
ever dared to dream before
        Raven (1850) 26
With light like Hope to mortals give
        Spirits 14

Moss
A wanderer by moss-y-mantled well
        Al Aaraaf ii 183
On bed of moss lies gloating the foul
adder   Coliseum (1833) 24
I sit on some moss-covered stone
        Sarah 2

Mossy
And they, and ev'ry mossy spring were
holy   Al Aaraaf ii 188
The mossy banks and the meandering
paths   Helen² 32
I pass'd from out its mossy door
        Tamerlane 215

Most
And thy most lovely purple perfume,
Zante   Al Aaraaf i 76
The most sad and solemn note
        Al Aaraaf i (1831) 21
Is not its form—its voice—most palp--
able and loud   Al Aaraaf ii 47
Of a most stormy life—was drawn
        Alone 10
Where each star most faintly gloweth
        Departed 3
By each spot the most unholy
        Dream-Land 31
In each nook most melancholy
        Dream-Land 32
Elizabeth, it surely is most fit
        Elizabeth 1
Can vie with the modest Eulalie's most
unregarded curl   Eulalie 12
Can compare with the bright-eyed Eula-
lie's most humble and careless curl
        Eulalie 13
You know that most enormous flow
        Fairy-Land (1831) 11
I scarce know which to prize most high
        Impromptu 3
A dirge for the most lovely dead
        Lenore (1843) 7
For her most wrong'd of all the dead
        Lenore (1843) 26
With a most unsteady light   Nis 44
A silly—a most silly fashion I have
        Politian i 9
This air is most oppressive
        Politian i 37

Mourner
No more a mourner—but the radiant Joys
                Politian iv 80

Mournful
Around the mournful waters lie
                City (1845) 25
The mournful hope that every throb
                Octavia 8

Mournfully
Go up to God so mournfully that she may
    feel no wrong   Lenore (1843) 31
So mournfully—so mournfully   Paean 19

Move
And no muscle I move   Annie 9
Vast forms that move fantastically
                Palace 43

Moved
My Lalage—my love! why art thou moved
                Politian iv 59

Movement
The wave—there is movement there
                City 43

Moving
The eternal voice of God is moving by
         Al Aaraaf i (1829) 131
Spirits moving musically   Palace 19

Much
Too much horrified to speak   Bells 41
And my mind is much benighted
        Bridal Ballad (1837) 23
Thus much let me avow
        Dream w. Dream 3
Much about a broken heart   Nis 13
Too much of late, and I am vexed to see it
              Politian i 12
For thy lofty rank and fashion—much
    depends   Politian i 25
To a becoming carriage—much thou want-
    est   Politian i 28
Much, much, oh much I want
              Politian i 29
I have heard much of this
              Politian i 51
Ha! here at least's a friend—too much a
    friend   Politian ii 60
Your bearing lately savored much of
    rudeness   Politian iii 97
And much I fear me ill—it will not do
              Politian v 2
Hold him a villain?—thus much, I pry-
    thee, say   Politian v 35
Much I marvelled this ungainly fowl to
    hear discourse so plainly   Raven 49
But now my soul hath too much room
          Romance (1831) 46
And much of madness, and more of Sin
              Worm 23

Mud
Born and brought up with their snouts
    deep in the mud of the Frog Pond
           Experiments 8

Muffled
In that muffled monotone   Bells 83

Mumble
Mutter and mumble low   Worm 10

Murmur
Like the murmur in the shell
      Al Aaraaf (1831) i 25
That, like the murmur in the shell
          Al Aaraaf i 9
Witness the murmur of grey twilight
          Al Aaraaf ii 41
The murmur that springs
         Al Aaraaf ii 124
I strike—the murmur sent   Paean 30
And the black wind murmur'd by
         Lake (1829) 9

Murmured
This I whispered, and an echo murmured
    back the word, " Lenore "   Raven 29
And murmur'd at such lowly lot
          Tamerlane 132
And the black wind murmur'd by
      Tamerlane (1831) 87
Italian tones made only to be murmured
              To³ 8
At thy soft-murmured words, " Let there
    be light! "   To MLS 10
At the soft-murmured words that were
    fulfilled   To MLS 11

Murmuring
No murmuring ripples curl, alas
          City (1845) 28
Murmuring lowly, murmuring ever
          Dream-Land 26
Murmuring in melody   Lake 10
Beside a murm'ring stream   Sarah 3

Muscle
And no muscle I move   Annie 9

Muses
The muses thro' their bowers of Truth and
    Fiction   Elizabeth 8

Music
Or (music of the passion-hearted)
          Al Aaraaf i 7
The dreamy poets name " the music of the
    sphere."   Al Aaraaf i 125
A music with it—'t is the rush of wings
          Al Aaraaf ii 49
Fountains were gushing music as they fell
          Al Aaraaf ii 62
Thy music from thee   Al Aaraaf ii 115
Are music of things   Al Aaraaf ii 126
Like music of another sphere
        Irene (1836) 127
My words the music of a dream
          Serenade 21
With music of so strange a sound
         Tamerlane 184
The music of the spheres   Worm 8

Musical
The musical number   Al Aaraaf ii 146
His very voice is musical delight
          Tempora 69
A musical name, oft uttered in the hear-
    ing   Valentine (1846) 15

Musically
To the tintinnabulation that so musically
    wells   Bells 11
Spirits moving musically   Palace 19
Steals drowsily and musically
          Sleeper 7

Musing
Who, musing, gazeth on the distance dim
                              Al Aaraaf ii 45
Musing on the past   Departed 12
Must
Thou wilt—thou must   Politian i 23
Ah, fly!—let us fly!—for we must
                              Ulalume 55
Mute
While the mute earth sheds her blessing
                              Departed 30
Of his voice, all mute   Israfel 7
Well may the stars be mute   Israfel 39
Mute, motionless, aghast   Paradise 13
When Nature sleeps and stars are mute
                              Serenade 3
Mutter
Mutter and mumble low   Worm 10
With many a mutter'd "hope to be for-
given,"   Al Aaraaf ii 5
Muttered
"'T is some visitor," I muttered, "tap-
ping at my chamber door   Raven 5
Till I scarcely more than muttered,
"Other friends have flown before
                              Raven 58
Myriad
In myriad types of the human eye
                              Valley 21
Myrtles
Of myrtles and roses   Annie 58
Mysteries
Not all the mysteries that in us lie
                              Coliseum 43
Never its mysteries are exposed
                              Dream-Land 45
A mystery of mysteries   Spirits 28
Mysterious
Mysterious star   Al Aaraaf i (1831) 1
And the sly, mysterious stars   Nis 20
Mystery
The mystery which binds me still
                              Alone 12
A mystery, and a dream   Imitation 3
Let me see, then what thereat is, and this
mystery explore   Raven 34
A mystery of mysteries   Spirits 28
All mystery but a simple name
                              Tamerlane (1827) 21
My soul in mystery to sleep
                              Tamerlane (1827) 74
Mystic
And the mystic wind went by   Lake 9
I stand beneath the mystic moon
                              Sleeper 2
With such as mine—that mystic flame
                              Tamerlane (1827) 158
The mystic empire and high power
                              Tamerlane (1827) 186
A mystic throng, bewinged, bedight
                              Worm (1843) 3
Mystically
But mystically—in such guise
                              Tamerlane 146
Naiad
Thy Naiad airs have brought me home
                              Helen¹ 8

Hast thou not torn the Naiad from her
blood   To Science 12
Nais
The gentle Nais from the fountain flood
                              To Science (1830) 12
Naivete
His naivete to wild desire
                              Romance (1831) 25
Name
Which dreamy poets name "the music of
the spheres   Al Aaraaf i 125
By the name of Annabel Lee
                              Annabel Lee 4
In thy own book that first thy name be
writ   Elizabeth 3
Called—I forget the heathenish Greek
name   Elizabeth 14
Was it not Fate (whose name is also sor-
row   Helen² 22
John Locke was a notable name
                              Lampoon 5
Therefore by that dear name I long have
called you   Mother 5
My seared and blighted name, how would
it tally   Politian iv 29
I hate—I loathe the name; I do abhor
                              Politian iv 31
In the name of Lalage   Politian v 61
Hold off thy—with that beloved name
                              Politian v 67
The rare and radiant maiden whom the
angels name   Raven 11
Tell me what thy lordly name is on the
Night's Plutonian shore   Raven 47
With such name as "Nevermore."
                              Raven 54
It shall clasp a sainted maiden whom the
angels name Lenore   Raven 94
Clasp a rare and radiant maiden whom
the angels name Lenore   Raven 95
Render him terrorless: his name's "No
More."   Silence 9
Thine image and—a name—a name
                              Tamerlane 126
All mystery but a simple name
                              Tamerlane (1827) 21
'Tis not to thee that I should name.
                              Tamerlane (1827) 102
It is not surely sin to name
                              Tamerlane (1827) 157
Had gilded with a conqueror's name
                              Tamerlane (1827) 272
And now what has he? what! a name
                              Tamerlane (1827) 338
I close the portrait with the name of Pitts
                              Tempora 92
With thy dear name as text, though bid-
den by thee   To³ 18
At the paltriness of name   To⁴ 32
Shall find her own sweet name that, nest-
ling, lies   Valentine 3
A well-known name, oft uttered in the
hearing   Valentine 15
Of poets, by poets; as the name is a
poet's too   Valentine 16

Named
Where an Eidolon, named Night
Dream-Land 3, 53
For the rare and radiant maiden whom
the angels named Lenore
Raven (1846) 11

Nameless
Nameless here for evermore   Raven 12
Bring thee to meet his shadow nameless
elf   Silence 13
And weep above a nameless grave
Valley 23

Names
Of the dear names that lie concealed
within't   Enigma (1848) 14
With gentle names—Eiros and Charmoin
Politian ii 27
Thy gentlest of all gentle names dost take
Zante 2

Naphthaline
For the napthaline river   Annie 35

Naples
As easily as through a Naples bonnet
Enigma 4

Napoleon
The king Napoleon   To⁴ 4

Napping
While I nodded, nearly napping, suddenly
there came a tapping   Raven 3
But the fact is I was napping, and so
gently you came rapping   Raven 21

Narrow
And narrow my bed   Annie 48

Narrowly
Search narrowly this rhyme, which holds
a treasure   Valentine 5

Natal
Of Genius, at its natal hour
Tamerlane (1827) 188

Nations
The strife of nations, and redeem
Tamerlane (1827) 238

Native
To his own native shore   Helen¹ 5

Natural
Afar from its proud natural towers
Tamerlane 141

Naturally
Its letters, although naturally lying
Valentine 17

Nature
All Nature speaks, even ideal things
Al Aaraaf i 128
That Nature loves the best for Beauty's
grave   Al Aaraaf ii 30
At thy behest I will shake off that nature
Politian iii 10
With whom affairs of a most private
nature   Politian v 42
When Nature sleeps and stars are mute
Serenade 3
My innate nature—be it so
Tamerlane 68
The child of Nature, without care
Tamerlane (1827) 76
With Nature, in her wild paths; tell
Tamerlane (1827) 312

Nausea
The sickness—the nausea   Annie 25

Nay
Thou must not—nay indeed, indeed, thou
shalt not   Politian iii 2
Say nay—say nay
Politian iii 76, 85, 94, 106

Near
Near four bright suns—a temporary rest
Al Aaraaf i 18
Was Love, the blind, near sober Duty
known   Al Aaraaf ii 180
Sound loves to revel near a summer night
Al Aaraaf ii (1829) 40
By the mountains—near the river
Dream-Land 25
The cause—but none are near to pry
Spirits (1827) 8
Grows dim around me—death is near
Tamerlane (1827) 16
Of human battle, near me swelling
Tamerlane (1829) 50

Nearer
And, nearer Heaven, some lilies wave
Nis (1836) 43

Nearest
For nearest of all stars was thine to ours
Al Aaraaf ii 242
Nearest resembles worship—oh, remember
To MLS 14

Nearly
While I nodded, nearly napping, suddenly
there came a tapping   Raven 3
Instead of two sides, Job has nearly eight
Tempora 21

Neat
As this for a neat, frisky counter-hopper
Tempora 48

'Neath
'Neath blue-bell or streamer
Al Aaraaf ii 68
'Neath which thy slumb'ring soul lies hid
Sleeper 27
Neath the forest tree   To Hunter 9

Nebulous
And nebulous lustre was born
Ulalume 34

Nectar
The fabled nectar that the heathen knew
Al Aaraaf i 53

Need
I'm sure, Madam, you need not
Politian ii 47
What need we more   Politian iv 35
And yet it need not be—that object—hid
Stanzas¹ 20
There was no need to speak the rest
Tamerlane 108
No need to quiet any fears
Tamerlane 109

Needest
Thou needest, Jacinta   Politian ii 46

Needeth
It needeth not be—thus—O let me die
Politian v 76

Apart—like fire-flies in Sicilian night
          Al Aaraaf i 145
Up rose the maiden in the yellow night
          Al Aaraaf i 151
All a long summer night
          Al Aaraaf i (1831) 3
Of sunken suns at eve—at noon of night
          Al Aaraaf ii 9
Sound loves to revel in a summer night
          Al Aaraaf ii 40
To happy flowers that night—and tree to
  tree   Al Aaraaf ii 61
The dew of the night   Al Aaraaf ii 94
Incumbent on night   Al Aaraaf ii 108
The night had found (to him a night of
  wo)   Al Aaraaf ii 190
How drowsily it weighed them into night
          Al Aaraaf ii 207
Dread star! that came, amid a night of
  mirth   Al Aaraaf ii 243
Gay fire-fly of the night we come and go
          Al Aaraaf ii 248
The night that waned and waned and
  brought no day   Al Aaraaf ii 262
A wind blew out of a cloud by night
          Annabel Lee 15
And so, all the night-tide, I lie down by
  the side   Annabel Lee 38
That the wind came out of the cloud by
  night   Annabel Lee (1849) 25
In the icy air of night   Bells 5
Through the balmy air of night Bells 18
In the startled ear of night   Bells 39
In the silence of the night   Bells 73
On the long night-time of that town
          City 13
Silence and Desolation! and dim night
          Coliseum 11
In visions of the dark night   Dream 1
What through the light, thro' storm and
  night   Dream 13
Where an Eidolon, named Night
          Dream-Land 3, 53
In a night, or in a day
          Dream w. Dream 7
Came o'er me in the night, and left
  behind   Dreams 22
That dream was as that night-wind—let
  it pass   Dreams 26
The stars of the night   Eulalie 7
Every moment of the night
          Fairy-Land 7
The night and the wonders here
          Fairy-Land (1831) 40
Lighting my lonely pathway home that
  night   Helen² 53
In the sad, silent watches of my night
          Helen² 63
To the night-winds as they pass Irene 54
But when the night had thrown her pall
          Lake 7
There the moon doth shine by night
          Nis 43
Therefore, to thee this night   Paean 41
In calm or storm, by night or day
          Physician 3

Last night with many cares and toils
  oppress'd   Poetry 1
Drew in the night-time of my bitter
  trouble   Politian ii 33
Good-night   Politian iii 114
Good-night, my friend, good-night
          Politian iii 115
But the night wind   Politian iv 62
Tell what thy lordly name is on the
  Night's Plutonian shore   Raven 47
Get thee back into the tempest and the
  Night's Plutonian shore   Raven 98
An idle longing night and day
          Romance (1831) 54
This window open to the night
          Sleeper 19
The night, tho' clear, shall frown
          Spirits 11
As dew of the night-time, o'er the summer
  grass   Stanzas¹ 16
And mid-time of night   Star 2
Thou bearest in Heaven at night
          Star 20
'Mid dreams of an unholy night
          Tamerlane 42
Dim, vanities of dreams by night
          Tamerlane 121
Who, in a dream of night, would fly
          Tamerlane 199
The sound of revelry by night
          Tamerlane (1827) 339
But when the night had thrown her pall
          Tamerlane (1831) 85
In a night—or in a day
          Tamerlane (1831) 246
Complete at night what he began A. M.
          Tempora 53
Of all to whom thine absence is the night
          To MLS 2
It was night, in the lonesome October
          Ulalume 4
And we marked not the night of the year
          Ulalume 24
Ah, night of all nights in the year
          Ulalume 25
And now, as the night was senescent
          Ulalume 30
See!—it flickers up the sky through the
  night   Ulalume 66
Since it flickers up to Heaven through the
  night   Ulalume 71
On this very night of last year
          Ulalume 86
On this night of all nights in the year
          Ulalume 89
Lo! 't is a gala night   Worm 1

Nightly
Where the nightly blossoms shiver
          Departed 39
And all my nightly dreams
          Paradise 22
Ghastly grim and ancient Raven wander-
  ing from the Nightly shore Raven 46
Nightly their dews upon my head
          Tamerlane 37
Nightly, from their azure towers
          Valley 5

Be nothing which thou art not
                                    To FSO 4
I replied: "This is nothing but dream-
    ing"   Ulalume 61
Nothing there is motionless   Valley 11
Nothing save the airs that brood
                                   Valley 12

Notwithstanding
Zeno and other sages notwithstanding
                                 Elizabeth 4

Nought
That she might deem it nought beside
                               Tamerlane 147

Number
The musical number   Al Aaraaf ii 146
The rhythmical number
                        Al Aaraaf ii 154

Nuptial
As nuptial dowry—a queen's crown
                       Tamerlane (1827) 244

Nursled
And nursled the young mountain in its
    lair   Al Aaraaf ii 15

Nutmegs
Jew, or downright upright nutmegs out of
    a pine knot   Experiments 10

Nyctanthes
Nyctanthes, too, as sacred as the light
                         Al Aaraaf i 66

Oak
To the lone oak that reels with bliss
                                   Irene 20

Oasis
An oasis in the desert of the blest
                         Al Aaraaf i 19

Oath
Swear not the oath—, oh, swear it not
                             Politian ii 112
I beg your pardon, reader, for an oath
                               Tempora 35

Obeisance
Not the least obeisance made he; not a
    minute stopped or stayed he   Raven 39

Object
To the lov'd object—so the tear to the lid
                               Stanzas¹ 18
And yet it need not be—that object—hid
                               Stanzas¹ 20
Some object of delight upon
                       Tamerlane (1827) 95
One object—and but one—until
                       Tamerlane (1827) 99

Obscure
By a route obscure and lonely
                          Dream-Land 1, 51

Obscured
And not a cloud obscured the sky
                                   Hymn 6

Obtained
And dove-tailed coat, obtained at cost;
    while then   Tempora 67

Ocean
The storm, the earthquake, and the ocean
    wrath   Al Aaraaf i 137
But ocean ever to refresh mankind
                            Politian ii 9

At rest an ocean's brilliant dyes
                               Serenade 5
Some ocean throbbing far and free
                                   To F 11
On oceans not so sad-serene
                            City (1845) 33

Octavia
But Octavia do not strive to rob
                               Octavia 6

October
It was night, in the lonesome October
                                 Ulalume 4
For we knew not the month was October
                                Ulalume 23
And I cried: "It was surely October
                                Ulalume 85

Odor
A holier odor   Annie 61
A rosemary odor   Annie 63
A winged odor went away   Palace 16

Odorous
Bursting its odorous heart in spirit to
    wing   Al Aaraaf i 72
Their odorous souls in an ecstatic death
                                 Helen² 13

Odors
The bear the goddess' song, in odors, up to
    Heaven   Al Aaraaf i 81
Were seen no more: the very roses' odors
                                 Helen² 34

O'er
Empyrean splendor o'er th' unchained
    soul   Al Aaraaf i 21
But o'er the sheeny mountain and dim
    plain   Al Aaraaf i 157
Stole o'er my senses in that lovely isle
                       Al Aaraaf i 211
Never his fairy wing o'er fairer world
                       Al Aaraaf ii 252
Headlong thitherward o'er the starry sea
                       Al Aaraaf ii 256
While a reverie came o'er me
                           Bridal Ballad 15
As he sails on his pinions o'er valley and
    sea   Campaign 4
O'er my soul, is gone   Departed 20
Came o'er me in the night, and left behind
                               Dreams 22
And o'er his heart a shadow   Eldorado 9
O'er the strange woods—o'er the sea
                             Fairy-Land 22
That gently, o'er a perfumed sea
                                 Helen¹ 3
Like a banner o'er thy dreaming eye
                                  Irene 36
O'er the unguarded flowers were leaning
                                   Nis 22
O'er th' horizon's fiery wall   Nis 42
O'er the enchanted solitude
                             Nis (1836) 30
That slumber o'er that valley-world
                             Nis (1836) 32
"On! on!"—but o'er the Past
                             Paradise 11
O'er th' horizon's fiery world
                             Nis (1836) 40
The light of Life is o'er   Paradise 15

They bore thee o'er the billow
Paradise (1836) 28
On the cushion's velvet lining that the lamp-light gloated o'er   Raven 76
But whose velvet-violet lining with the lamp-light gloated o'er   Raven 77
And the lamp-light o'er him streaming throws his shadow on the floor
Raven 106
That, o'er the floor and down the wall
Sleeper 28
Sure thou art come o'er far-off seas
Sleeper 32
Triumphant, o'er the crested palls
Sleeper 52
When a burning blush came o'er thee
Song 2
When that deep blush would come o'er thee   Song 14
Of its own fervor—what had o'er it power
Stanzas¹ 8
To a fever by the moonbeam that hangs o'er   Stanzas¹ 10
That with a quick'ning spell doth o'er us pass   Stanzas¹ 15
As dew of the night-time, o'er the summer grass   Stanzas¹ 16
Doth o'er us pass, when, as th' expanding eye   Stanzas¹ 17
From clouds that hung, like banners, o'er
Tamerlane 45
Striding o'er the empires hautily
Tamerlane 175
Pass'd quickly o'er me—but my mind
Tamerlane (1827) 62
Then—in that hour—a thought came o'er
Tamerlane (1827) 234
Comes o'er me in these lonely hours
Tamerlane (1827) 137
And hop o'er counters with a Vestris air
Tempora 52
Just o'er that one bright island smile
To F (1835) 14

O'ercast
Now, when storms of Fate o'ercast
Hymn 9

O'ergrown
Newly with grass o'ergrown; some solemn graces   Silence 7

O'erlook
And even the greybeard will o'erlook
Romance (1831) 65

O'ershadow
Shall then o'ershadow thee: be still
Spirits (1827) 10

Offence
Having given thee no offence
Politian v 55

Offended
Descend with me—the Duke may be offended   Politian iii 105

Offer'd
Now offer'd, with the pain
Happiest Day 18

Offerings
With incense of burnt offerings
Tamerlane 234

Office
Their office is to illume and enkindle
Helen² 57
A kind and gentle office, and a Power
Politian iii 35

Oft
Where oft—in life—with friends—it went
Irene 49
The song is English, and I oft have heard it   Politian iii 77
Some vault that oft hath flung its black
Sleeper 50
So oft perverted, will bestow
Tamerlane (1827) 197
For he does think although I'm oft in doubt   Tempora 79
A well-known name, oft uttered in the hearing   Valentine 15

Often
So often lonely, and will list
Tamerlane 196
Philosophers have often held dispute
Tempora 73

Old
And when old Time my wing did disenthral   Al Aaraaf ii 218
Its old agitations   Annie 57
As in old days from Memnon to the Sun
Coliseum (1833) 40
But he grew old   Eldorado 7
Why ask? who ever yet saw money made out of a fat old   Experiments 9
And the grandeur of old Rome
Helen (1831) 10
In a panoply of old romance   Irene 6
Of her old family funerals   Irene 74
But waft the angel on her flight with a Paean of old days   Lenore 26
Over the old forgotten grave   Nis 32
Of the old time entombed   Palace 40
Ill suit the like with old Di Broglio's heir
Politian i 21
In old Alberto's daughter   River 6
Far in the forest, dim and old
Sleeper 48
I would not call thee fool, old man
Tamerlane 11
Something he spoke of the old cot
Tamerlane (1827) 399
The " good old times " were far the worst of any   Tempora 6
Science! true daughter of Old Time thou art   To Science 1

Olden
This—all this—was in the olden
Palace 11

Older
Of those who were older than we
Annabel Lee 28

Ominous
Fancy unto fancy, thinking what this ominous bird of yore   Raven 70
What this grim, ungainly, ghastly, gaunt, and ominous bird of yore   Raven 71

Once
At once—and so will I
Dream w. Dream (1829) 14

'T was once—and only once—and the wild
hour   Dreams 19
Through all the flimsy things we see at
once   Enigma 3
I saw thee once—once only—years ago
                                  Helen² 1
Once a fair and stately palace   Palace 3
Was once the locust's coat of gold
                                  Parody 4
Once more that silent tongue
                                  Politian iii 104
At once   Politian v 58
Once upon a midnight dreary, while I
pondered, weak and weary   Raven 1
There rose a fountain once, and there
                                  Tamerlane (1827) 401
His form once seen becomes a part of
sight   Tempora 70
At once—and so will I   To¹ 26
Here once, through an alley Titanic
                                  Ulalume 10
Though once we had journeyed down here
                                  Ulalume 27
Once it smiled a silent dell   Valley 1
At sight of thee and thine at once awake
                                  Zante 4

One
And late to ours, and favor'd one of God
                                  Al Aaraaf i 25
Link'd to a little system and one sun
                                  Al Aaraaf i 134
Our faith to one love—and one moon
adore   Al Aaraaf i 153
A window of one circular diamond, there
                                  Al Aaraaf ii 22
My beautiful one   Al Aaraaf ii 101
One half the garden of her globe was flung
                                  Al Aaraaf ii 222
Methought, my sweet one, then I ceased to
soar   Al Aaraaf ii 237
It trembled to one constant star again
                                  Al Aaraaf ii (1829) 197
They have sever'd in one fatal hour
                                  Ballad 7
One from the pitiless wave
                                  Dream w. Dream 22
Being ignorant of one important rule
                                  Elizabeth 12
One more filmy than the rest
                                  Fairy-Land 12
He would not sing one half as well
                                  Israfel (1831) 45
One half as passionately
                                  Israfel (1831) 46
We, with one warrior, have slain
                                  Latin Hymn 3
The angels, whispering to one another
                                  Mother 2
Are mother to the one I loved so dearly
                                  Mother 11
Are thus more precious than the one I
knew   Mother (1850) 12
One by one from the tree top   Nis 33
One and all, too far away Nis (1836) 6
Ah, one by one, from off their stems
                                  Nis (1836) 41

And one by one, from out their tops
                                  Nis (1836) 45
As of one who entered madly into life
                                  Politian i 59
Thus speaketh one Ferdinand in the
words of the play   Politian ii 17
" She died full young "—one Bossola
answers him   Politian ii 18
Miraculously found by one of Genoa
                                  Politian iv 67
And let me hear thy voice—one word—
one word   Politian iv 95
To say thou art not gone,—one little
sentence   Politian iv 96
Or one more worthy Italy, methinks
                                  Politian v 17
As of someone gently rapping, rapping at
my chamber door   Raven 4
That one word, as if his soul in that one
word he did outpour   Raven 56
Followed fast and followed faster till his
songs one burden bore   Raven 64
Body and soul. One dwells in lonely
places   Silence 6
This chamber changed for one more holy
                                  Sleeper 41
Not one, of all the crowd, to pry
                                  Spirits 3
In youth have I known one with whom the
earth   Stanzas¹ 1
But, father, there liv'd one who, then
                                  Tamerlane 69
To those whose spirits harken as one
                                  Tamerlane 198
Whose waning is the dreariest one
                                  Tamerlane 206
Of one whom I had earlier known
                                  Tamerlane 218
Of one whom in life I made
                                  Tamerlane (1827) 20
One object—and but one—until
                                  Tamerlane (1827) 99
At one upbraiding word or token
                                  Tamerlane (1827) 201
But one, whom phantasy had led
                                  Tamerlane (1827) 250
That they shall stoop in life to one
                                  Tamerlane (1827) 261
Perforce, a passing thought of one
                                  Tamerlane (1827) 274
One noon of a bright summer's day
                                  Tamerlane (1827) 283
Of one, in whom they did rejoice
                                  Tamerlane (1827) 343
As the portrait of one after death
                                  Tamerlane (1827) 380
'Mid dreams of one unholy night
                                  Tamerlane (1829) 42
I'll neither laugh with one or cry with
t'other   Tempora 26
But, taking one by each hand, merely
growl   Tempora 28
I don't remember one, upon my soul
                                  Tempora 43
For at a ball what fair one can escape
                                  Tempora 55

Other

All other loveliness: its honied dew
              Al Aaraaf i 52
And wing to other worlds another light
            Al Aaraaf i 146
Of other beauty glittering thro' the light
            Al Aaraaf ii 39
And this maiden she lived with no other
   thought   Annabel Lee 5
Zeno and other sages notwithstanding
              Elizabeth 4
And I have other reasons for so doing
              Elizabeth 5
And other listening things   Israfel 17
And be no more Politian, but some other
             Politian iii 13
Of what in other worlds shall be—and
   giv'n   Stanzas¹ 25
But, just like any other dream
             Tamerlane 133
I had no other solace—then
        Tamerlane (1827) 288

Others

As others were— I have not seen
                Alone 2
As others saw—I could not bring
                Alone 3
Which has in others' joys apart
            Stanzas² 15
While in its own all others share
            Stanzas² 16

Otherwise

Who otherwise would fall from life and
   Heav'n   Stanzas¹ 27

Ours

Oh, nothing of the dross of ours
            Al Aaraaf i 11

Outlaw

A diadem'd outlaw   Tamerlane 176

Outpour

What a horror they outpour   Bells 55
That one word, as if his soul in that one
   word he did outpour   Raven 56

Outspread

Lakes that endlessly outspread
            Dream-Land 17
By the lakes that thus outspread
            Dream-Land 21

Over

O! where (and ye may seek the wide skies
   over)   Al Aaraaf ii 179
Is over at last   Annie 4
For the tears that drip all over
   Dream-Land 12; Fairy-Land 4
Over hamlets, over halls
            Fairy-Land 20
Over spirits on the wing
            Fairy-Land 23
Over every drowsy thing
            Fairy-Land 24
And over the wet grass rippled away
        Fairy-Land (1831) 28
Over ruin'd walls
        Fairy-Land (1831) 60
Over waterfalls   Fairy-Land (1831) 61
Alas! over the sea
        Fairy-Land (1831) 64

Over the Mountains   Eldorado 19
Sing a thousand over again
              Latin Hymn 5
Who knocked over a thousand so fine
              Latin Hymn 8
Over the old forgotten grave   Nis 32
Over the hills and far away   Nis 46
Over fabric half so fair   Palace 8
To thy dress and equipage—they are over
   plain   Politian i 24
Lean over her and weep—two gentle
   maids   Politian ii 216
Throw over all things a gloom
            Politian iv 64
And crystal lakes, and over-arching
   forests   Politian iv 70
Over many a quaint and curious volume of
   forgotten lore   Raven 2
Had thrown her mantle over me
             Tamerlane 158
Democritus of Thrace, who used to toss
   over   Tempora 16
Till the blow is over   To Hunter 14
Over the magic solitude   Valley 13
Over the violets there that lie
              Valley 20
Over the lilies there that wave
              Valley 22
And, over each quivering form Worm 34

Overcast

But to be overcast   Paradise 9

Overgone

Of the barrier overgone
            Al Aaraaf i 90

Overhead

Thro' the tulips overhead   Nis 24

Overpowering

Her overpow'ring loveliness
        Tamerlane (1827) 314

Overshadow

Shall overshadow thee: be still
             Spirits 10

Oversprinkle

While the stars that oversprinkle
             Bells 6

Owe

Of all who owe thee most—whose gratitude   To MLS 13

Owing

Is owing to that lyre   Israfel 19

Owl

Owl downy nonsense that the faintest puff
              Enigma 7

Own

What tho' in worlds which own a single
   sun   Al Aaraaf i 139

Pacified

Thus I pacified Psyche and kissed her
             Ulalume 72

Paean

A paean from the bells   Bells 92
With the paean of the bells   Bells 94
To the paean of the bells   Bells 98
But waft the angel on her flight with a
   Paean of old days   Lenore 26

Par
One of these fish, par excellence the beau
                    Tempora 59

Paradisal
In the budding of my Paradisal Hope
                    Politian v 7

Paradise
Of Paradise and Love—and all our own
                    Dreams 33
Now thou art dress'd for paradise
                    Fairy-Land (1831) 4
Fly to that Paradise—my Lalage, wilt
thou   Politian iv 75

Parian
Flashing from Parian marble that twin
smile   Al Aaraaf ii 13

Pardon
I crave thy pardon—indeed I am not well
                    Politian i 35
I beg your pardon, reader, for the oath
                    Tempora 35

Paroquet
To me a painted paroquet   Romance 5

Part
And with pain that shall not part
                    Al Aaraaf i 97
He studied very little of his part
                    Elizabeth 9
Which has in others joys a part
                    Stanzas² 15
Is the proud part   Star 19
In woman's weakness had a part
                    Tamerlane 74
'T was sunset: when the sun will part
                    Tamerlane 191
To her soft thrilling voice: To part
                    Tamerlane (1827) 292
And in such folies had no part
                    Tamerlane (1827) 404
His form once seen becomes a part of
sight   Tempora 70
From its present pathway part not
                    To FSO 2

Parted
Parted upon their misty wings
                    Tamerlane 124

Parterre
That smiled and died in this parterre,
enchanted   Helen² 15

Parthenon
Was a proud temple called the Parthenon
                    Al Aaraaf ii 215

Particles
Some particles of sand
                    Dream w. Dream (1831) 15;
                    Tamerlane (1831) 252;
                    To⁴ 20

Parting
And, in parting from you now
                    Dream within a Dream 2
Of parting, were with madness fraught
                    Tamerlane (1827) 296
They remembered not our parting
                    Ballad 5
" Be that word our sign of parting, bird
or fiend! " I shrieked, upstarting
                    Raven 97

Partner
A partner of thy throne
                    Al Aaraaf i 113

Pass
As they pass the wanderer by
                    Dream-Land 36
From my remembrance shall not pass—
some pow'r   Dreams 20
That dream was as that night-wind—let
it pass   Dreams 26
But let them pass   Happiest Day 8
Had I let them pass me by   Imitation 9
To the night-winds as they pass
                    Irene 54
And the wind would pass me by
                    Lake (1827) 9
As such it well may pass   Song 10
From thy spirit shall they pass
                    Spirits 21
That with a quickening spell doth o'er us
pass   Stanzas¹ 15
Doth o'er us pass, when, as th' expanding
eye   Stanzas¹ 17
Tho' lov'd, and loving—let it pass
                    Tamerlane (1827) 298
O God! when the thoughts that may not
pass   Tamerlane (1827) 323
Had I let them pass me by   To⁴ 11

Passed
As it pass'd me flying by   Alone 18
With a sight as it pass'd on
                    Imitation 18
There pass'd, as a shroud   Star 12
I pass'd from out its mossy door
                    Tamerlane 215
Pass'd quickly o'er me—but my mind
                    Tamerlane (1827) 62
And as it pass'd me by, there broke
                    Tamerlane (1827) 72
Its very form hath pass'd me by
                    Tamerlane (1827) 100
But it had pass'd me as a dream
                    Tamerlane (1827) 208
I pass'd from out the matted bower
                    Tamerlane (1827) 284
Had lately been but had pass'd by
                    Tamerlane (1827) 383
And we pass'd to the end of the vista
                    Ulalume 75

Passer
Who am a passer by   To² 8

Passes
And thus the sad Soul that here passes
                    Dream-Land 49

Passing
The eternal voice of God is passing by
                    Al Aaraaf i 131
When passing from the earth, that ear
                    Tamerlane (1827) 18
Or thought, save of the passing scene
                    Tamerlane (1827) 77
Perforce, a passing thought of one
                    Tamerlane (1827) 274

Passion
His folly—pride—and passion—for he
died   Acrostic 9

Peaceful
Tis a peaceful, soothing region
Dream-Land 40
In that peaceful hour
Tamerlane (1827) 286

Peacefully
Joy's voice so peacefully departed
Al Aaraaf i 8
Joy so peacefully departs
Al Aaraaf (1831) i 23
Peacefully happy—yet alone
Tamerlane (1827) 223

Peak
When, on the mountain peak, alone
Tamerlane 114

Pearl
With the moon-tints of purple and pearl
Eulalie 11
And all with pearl and ruby glowing
Palace 25
Which hangs like chains of pearl on Hermon hill
Politian ii 35
That hangs like chains of pearl on Hermon hill
To² 10

Pearls
Like woman's hair 'mid pearls, until, afar
Al Aaraaf i 33

Pearly
The pearly lustre of the moon went out
Helen² 31

Peasant
Of a young peasant's bosom then
Tamerlane (1827) 248
Ere, in a peasant's lowly guise
Tamerlane (1827) 360

Peccavimus
Peccavimus; yet rave not thus! but let a Sabbath song
Lenore 13

Pedestal
Shall form the pedestal of a throne
Tamerlane 172

Peered
That from this marble dwelling peered out
Al Aaraaf ii 33

Peering
Deep into that darkness peering, long I stood there wondering, fearing
Raven 25
Who alterest all things with thy peering eyes
To Science 2
Enwritten upon this page whereon are peering
Valentine 13

Pen
The pen falls powerless from my shivering hand
To³ 17

Pendulous
That all seem pendulous in air
City 27

Penitence
Give up thy soul to penitence, and pray
Politian ii 76
And penitence
Politian ii 92

Penned
For her these lives are penned, whose luminous eyes
Valentine 1

Pennoned
Failed, as my pennoned spirit leapt aloft
Al Aaraaf ii 232

Pens
By him who, as he pens them, thrills to think
To MLS 17

Pensive
In chorus to my pensive sigh
Sarah 14

People
And the people—ah, the people
Bells 79
Whom the astonished people saw
Tamerlane 174
Why do the people bow the knee
Tamerlane (1831) 181
Where the people did not dwell
Valley 2

Peopled
Gaunt vestibules! and phantom-peopled aisles
Coliseum (1833) 13

Perchance
Descend together—and then—and then perchance
Politian iv 45
And then perchance
Politian iv 46

Perched
But, with mien of lord or lady, perched above my chamber door
Raven 40
Perched upon a bust of Pallas just above my chamber door
Raven 41
Perched, and sat, and nothing more
Raven 42

Perdu
Such eager eyes, there lies, I say, perdu
Valentine 14

Perdus
Eyes scintillating soul, there lie perdus
Valentine (1849) 14

Perennial
Perennial tears descend in gems
Valley 27

Perfect
And the shadow of thy perfect bliss
Israfel 43
Unguided Love hath fallen—'mid "tears of perfect moan"
Al Aaraaf ii 181

Perforce
Perforce, a passing thought of one
Tamerlane (1827) 274

Perfume
She fears to perfume, perfuming the night
Al Aaraaf i 67
And thy most lovely perfume, Zanthe
Al Aaraaf i 76
As perfume of strange-summer flow'rs
Tamerlane (1827) 139

Perfumed
That gently, over a perfumed sea
Helen¹ 3
All perfumed there
Paean 26
Then, methought, the air grew denser, perfumed from an unseen censer
Raven 79

Perfuming
She fears to perfume, perfuming the night
Al Aaraaf i 67

Perhaps
Perhaps my brain grew dizzy—but the world
Al Aaraaf ii 233
Oh! perhaps, perhaps she may
Ballad 28
Oh! perhaps not
Politian ii 50

Pious
A crucifix whereon to register a pious vow
                              Politian ii (1845) 99
Pitiful
The pitiful, the merciful ghouls
                              Ulalume 97
Pitiless
The pitiless pain   Annie 26
One from the pitiless wave
                      Dream w. Dream 22
Pitts
I close the portrait with the name of
Pitts   Tempora 92
Pity
Of Darkness and the Tomb, O pity me
                              Politian v 5
O pity me! let me not perish now
                              Politian v 6
O pity me   Politian v 73
I do—indeed I pity thee
                              Politian v 74
Place
The birth-place of young Beauty had no
more   Al Aaraaf i 154
A brighter dwelling-place is here for thee
                      Al Aaraaf ii 228
I tore it from its pride of place
                      Fairy-Land (1831) 17
Places
Forever changing places   Fairy-Land 8
One dwells in lonely places   Silence 6
Placid
But the Raven, sitting lonely on the
placid bust, spoke only   Raven 55
Plain
And bent over sheeny mountain and dim
plain   Al Aaraaf i 157
To thy dress and equipage—they are over
plain   Politian i 24
Upon the Siroc-withered plain
                              Tamerlane 180
Plainly
Very plainly through the window—it
belongs   Politian iii 63
Much I marvelled this ungainly fowl to
hear discourse so plainly   Raven 49
Plaintively
In merry England—never so plaintively
                              Politian iii 78
Planet
Have drawn up the spectre of a planet
                              Ulalume 101
This sunfully scintillant planet
                              Ulalume 103
Planetary
From the Hell of the planetary souls
                              Ulalume 104
Planets
Mid planets her slaves   Star 6
Plant
And blossom of the fairy plant, in grief
                      Al Aaraaf i 61
Play
Thus speaketh one Ferdinand in the
words of the play   Politian ii 17

A play of hopes and fears   Worm 6
That the play is the tragedy, "Man"
                              Worm 39
Playful
The playful maziness of art   River 5
Pleasant
Oh! what a pleasant dream   Sarah 6
Whose pleasant bowers are yet so riven
                      Tamerlane 236
Please
Your hand from off my shoulder, if you
please   Politian i 36
Transforming all! Thy charms shall
please no more   Zante 10
Pleased
Gurgled in my pleas'd ear the crash
                      Tamerlane (1827) 66
Pleasing
Indulge me with this pleasing dream
                              Louisa 3
Pleasure
Drinking the cup of pleasure to the dregs
                              Politian i 60
Your lordship's pleasure
                              Politian iii 113
That was new pleasure—the ideal
                              Tamerlane 120
Of pleasure or of pain
                      Tamerlane (1831) 142
That pleasure "to endure"   To⁴ 38
Pleasures
His pleasure always turned to pain
                      Romance (1831) 24
Pleiades
Seven Pleiades entranced in Heaven
                              Serenade 7
Pleiads
With the rapid Pleiads, even   Israfel 13
Plight
The single-mooned eve!—on Earth we
plight   Al Aaraaf i 152
Her own Alexis, who should plight
                      Tamerlane (1827) 279
Plighted
And this the plighted vow
                              Bridal Ballad 21
And thus they said I plighted
                      Bridal Ballad (1837) 19
So plighted in his early youth
                      Tamerlane (1827) 278
The love he plighted then—again
                      Tamerlane (1827) 280
Plinths
These mouldering plinths—these sad and
blackened shafts   Coliseum 27
Plot
If one could merely understand the plot
                              Valentine 12
And Horror the soul of the plot
                              Worm 24
Plume
Leave no black plume as a token of that
lie thy soul hath spoken   Raven 99
Plumed
Along the ramparts plumed and pallid
                              Palace 15

Was plumed with the down of the hum-
ming-bird   Parody 2
Plumes
Plumes till they trailed in the dust
                                 Ulalume 59
Plutonian
Tell me what thy lordly name is on the
Night's Plutonian shore   Raven 47
Get thee back into the tempest and the
Night's Plutonian shore   Raven 98
Poet
Each poet—if a poet—in pursuing
                                 Elizabeth 7
Why preyest thou thus upon the poet's
heart   To Science 3
Of poets, by poets; as the name is a
poet's, too   Valentine 16
Poets
Which dreamy poet's name " the music of
the sphere "   Al Aaraaf i 125
Of poets, by poets; as the name is a
poet's, too   Valentine 16
Poetry
By thee, and by the poetry of thy presence
                                 Helen² 16
Point
To point us the path to the skies
                                 Ulalume 45
The trivialest point, or you may lose your
labor   Valentine 9
Pointed
And star-dials pointed to morn
                                 Ulalume 31
Poisoned
Death was in that poison'd wave
                             Lake (1827) 18
Poisonous
Death was in that poisonous wave
                                 Lake 18
Pole
In the ultimate climes of the Pole
                                 Ulalume 17
In the realms of the Boreal Pole
                                 Ulalume 19
Politian
Politian is expected   Politian i 41
Hourly in Rome—Politian, Earl of Lei-
cester   Politian i 42
Politian   Politian i 44; iv 58, 64, 90
I have heard much of this Politian
                                 Politian i 51
I have known men have seen Politian
                                 Politian i 57
Now I have seen Politian
                                 Politian i 61
Politian was a melancholy man
                                 Politian i 67
Arouse thee now, Politian
                                 Politian iii 1
Politian, it doth grieve me
                                 Politian iii 6
And be no more Politian, but some other
                                 Politian iii 13
To me, Politian, of thy camps and courts
                                 Politian iii 28
What ails thee, Earl Politian
                                 Politian iii 90

Politian give
                                 Politian iii 95
Good-night, Politian
                                 Politian iii 114
To me, Politian?—dost thou speak of love
                                 Politian iv 2
Art thou not Lalage and I Politian
                                 Politian iv 33
Why dost thou pause, Politian
                                 Politian iv 48, 49
Thou art not gone—thou art not gone,
Politian   Politian iv 91
Between the Earl Politian and himself
                                 Politian v 12
Politicians
Will change me, and as politicians do
                                 Tempora 39
Pomp
By buried centuries of pomp and power
                                 Coliseum 3
My eyes were still on pomp and power
                             Tamerlane (1827) 355
Pond
Born and brought up with their snouts
deep down in the mud of the Frog-
Pond   Experiments 8
Ponder
Bright beings! that ponder
                             Al Aaraaf ii 72
Pondered
Once upon a midnight dreary, while I
pondered, weak and weary   Raven 1
Pondereth
But sleep that pondereth and is not " to
be "   Al Aaraaf ii 171
Pondering
And Clytia pondering between many a
sun   Al Aaraaf i 68
Pools
By the dismal tarns and pools
                             Dream-Land 29
Poor
And tho' my poor heart be broken
                                 Ballad 31
Poor Lalage!—and is it come to this
                                 Politian ii 57
Thrilling to think, poor child of sin
                                 Sleeper 59
I laugh to think how poor   To⁴ 37
Populous
Of the populous Earth! Bear with me yet
awhile   Politian iii 31
Pores
Pores for a moment, ere it go.   Irene 56
Porphyrogene
Porphyrogene   Palace 22
Portal
Against whose portal she hath thrown
                                 Sleeper 55
Portion
Thy withering portion with the fame
                                 Tamerlane 16
A portion of his willing soul
                             Tamerlane (1827) 309

Portrait
A portrait taken after death
                              Tamerlane 206
I close the portrait with the name of Pitts
                              Tempora 92

Possest
The only feeling which possest
                    Tamerlane (1827) 245

Possessing
Happy in that dim possessing
                              Departed 31

Potent
O charms more potent than the rapt
  Chaldee   Coliseum 15

Pour
And pour my spirit out in tears
                              Tamerlane 107

Poured
The venom thou hast pour'd on me
                            Happiest Day 11

Pouts
I' the pouts   Politian i 39

Power
By buried centuries of pomp and power
                              Coliseum 3
Not all our power is gone—not all our
  fame   Coliseum 40
She, whose voice alone had power
                              Departed 19
To check the power that governs here
                            Divine Rights 8
From my remembrance shall not pass—
  some power   Dreams 20
The brightest hope of pride and power
                            Happiest Day 3
Of power! said I? yes! such I ween
                            Happiest Day 5
The brightest glance of pride and power
                           Happiest Day 15
But were that hope of pride and power
                           Happiest Day 17
Still does my heart confess thy power
                              Octavia 4
A kind and gentle office, and a Power
                            Politian iii 35
A Power, august, benignant and supreme
                            Politian iii 36
No power hath he of evil in himself
                              Silence 11
Of its own fervor—what had o'er it power
                              Stanzas¹ 8
I will not madly deem that power
                              Tamerlane 3
Have deemed, since I have reach'd to
  power   Tamerlane 67
I spoke to her of power and pride
                             Tamerlane 145
And, failing in thy power to bless
                             Tamerlane 181
And slumber, in my pride of power
                       Tamerlane (1827) 44
Of some ill demon, with a power
                      Tamerlane (1827) 173
The mystic empire and high power
                      Tamerlane (1827) 186
There is a power in the high spirit
                      Tamerlane (1827) 191

The soul, which knows such power, will
  still   Tamerlane (1827) 193
As in a leader, haply—Power
                      Tamerlane (1827) 344
My eyes were still on pomp and power
                      Tamerlane (1827) 355
Lord! to be grave exceeds the power of
  face   Tempora 64
For that the power of thought attend the
  latter   Tempora 75
Maintained "the power of words"—
  denied that ever   To 3³

Powerful
An essence—powerful to destroy
                           Happiest Day 23

Powerless
The pen falls powerless from my shivering hand   To³ 17

Powers
Are thus more precious than the one I
  knew   Mother (1850) 12
Prince of the Powers   Politian v 4

Praise
Virtues that challenge envy's praise
                              Stanzas² 7
Shall be an endless theme of praise
                              To FSO 7

Prate
Draw, villain, and prate no more
                             Politian v 57

Pray
Give up thy soul to penitence, and pray
                             Politian ii 76
I cannot pray   Politian ii 77, 79
Remember, pray   Politian iii 96
Let us go down, I pray you
                            Politian iii 106
'T is I who pray for life—I who so late
                              Politian v 9
I pray to God that she may lie
                              Sleeper 42
Ah growl, say you, my friend, and pray at
  what   Tempora 29
But pray be patient: yet a little while
                              Tempora 38

Prayed
And she prayed to the angels   Annie 81

Prayer
Of fervent prayer, and humble love
                            Hymn (1835) 3
Yet stay! yet stay!—what was it thou
  saidst of prayer   Politian ii 91
Pure as the wishes breathed in prayer
                              Stanzas² 14
Of empires—with the captive's prayer
                             Tamerlane 62

Precious
Think of thy precious soul
                             Politian ii 83

Precipitant
Sought a precipitant pathway up through
  heaven   Helen (1848) 5

Precipitate
Sought a precipitate pathway up through
  heaven   Helen² 5

Pre-eminent
Pre-eminent in arts and arms, and wealth
Politian i 49
Prefer
So banished from true wisdom to prefer
To Margaret 3
Prepare
Do thou prepare Politian v 85
Presence
By thee, and by the poetry of thy presence
Helen² 16
Sit down—let not my presence trouble you
Politian ii 3
Thy presence grieves me—go—they
priestly raiment Politian ii 81
Thy presence is expected in the hall
Politian iii 89
Of all who hail thy presence as the morn-
ing To MLS 1
Present
Darkly my present and my Past
Hymn 10
From its present pathway part not
To FSO 2
Presently
Presently my soul grew stronger; hesitat-
ing then no longer Raven 19
Press
She shall press, ah, nevermore Raven 78
Prettiest
Why, then, the prettiest of brooks
River 9
Pretty
A tale—a pretty tale—and heed thou not
Politian ii 63
The pretty little hand that sold her tape
Tempora 56
Prevent
And in the meantime, to prevent all
bother Tempora 25
Preyest
Why preyest thou thus upon the poet's
heart To Science 3
Pride
His folly—pride—and passion for he died
Acrostic 9
Upon the flying footsteps of—deep pride
Al Aaraaf i 46
From their pride and from their throne
Al Aaraaf i 92
I tore it from its pride of place
Fairy-Land (1831) 77
The highest hope of pride and power
Happiest Day 3
And, pride, what have I now with thee
Happiest Day 9
The brightest glance of pride and power
Happiest Day 15
But were that hope of pride and power
Happiest Day 17
How silently serene a sea of pride
Helen² 45
Of interminable pride Imitation 2
Wretches! ye loved her for her wealth,
and ye hated her for her pride
Lenore 8
Unearthly pride hath revelled in
Tamerlane 5

Bow'd from its wild pride into shame
Tamerlane 14
I spoke to her of power and pride
Tamerlane 145
Is she not queen of Earth? her pride
Tamerlane 166
And slumber, in my pride of power
Tamerlane (1827) 44
Find pride the ruler of its will
Tamerlane (1827) 194
In the mad pride of intellectuality To³ 2
Pries
Which thro' some tattered curtain pries
Fairy-Land (1831) 32
Priestly
Thy presence grieves me—go!—thy
priestly raiment Politian ii 81
Prince
Prince of the Powers Politian v 4
Princely
Pure and reproachless, of thy princely line
Politian iv 25
Private
With whom affairs of a most private
nature Politian v 42
Prize
I scarce know which to prize most high
Impromptu 3
Proceeds
Proceeds from yonder lattice—which you
may see Politian iii 62
Proclaim
Proclaim her deep despair Louisa 8
Prodigy
But Rumor speaks of him as of a prodigy
Politian i 48
Profoundest
Half an idea in the profoundest sonnet
Enigma 2
Proof
Another proof of thought, I'm not mis-
taken Tempora 86
Proper
In proper dignity Politian i 30
So pat, agreeable, and vastly proper
Tempora 47
And let him see himself a proper ass
Tempora 88
Prophet
"Prophet!" said I, "thing of evil!—
prophet still, if bird or devil!"
Raven 85
"Prophet!" said I, "Thing of evil!—
prophet still, if bird or devil!"
Raven 91
Prophetic
Prophetic sounds and loud, arise forever
Coliseum 34
Prophetic tones from every line
Stanzas² 3
Prospect
To where the prospect terminates—thee
only To³ 27
Proud
To the proud orbs that twinkle—and so be
Al Aaraaf ii 148

Was a proud temple called the Parthenon
                    Al Aaraaf ii 215
While from a proud tower in the town
                    City 28
All of the proud and the colossal left
                  Coliseum (1842) 31
Proud heart, never won   Departed 24
Alas, proud Earl   Politian iv 22
Proud Earl   Politian v 59
Proud Evening Star   Star 15
Is the proud part   Star 19
And a proud spirit which hath striven
                   Tamerlane 33
Afar from its proud natural towers
                  Tamerlane 141
Yes! I was proud—and ye who know
           Tamerlane (1827) 195
That the proud spirit had been broken
           Tamerlane (1827) 199
The proud heart burst in agony
           Tamerlane (1827) 200
And my proud hopes had reached a throne
           Tamerlane (1827) 348
But they tell thee I am proud   To⁴ 29

Proudly
Was⹁ the lance which he proudly wav'd
   on high   Parody 10
Stands she not proudly and alone
           Tamerlane (1827) 332

Proves
That proves me happy now
           Bridal Ballad 27

Pry
Not one, of all the crowd, to pry
                  Spirits 3

Prythee
Hold him a villain?—thus much, I prythee, say   Politian v 35
Now prythee, leave me—hither doth come
   a person   Politian v 41

Pshaw
Pshaw   Politian ii 31

Psyche
Ah, Psyche, from the regions which
                   Helen¹ 14
Of cypress, with Psyche, my soul
                Ulalume 12
But Psyche, uplifting her finger
                Ulalume 51
Thus I pacified Psyche and kissed her
                Ulalume 72

Public
For public insult in the streets—before
           Politian v 86

Puff
Owl-downy nonsense that the faintest puff
                  Enigma 7

Pulse
The pulse beats ten and intermits
              Physician 1

Pulses
My thick pulses hastily beating
             Departed 5

Pundits
Do tell! when may we hope to make men
   of sense out of the Pundits
             Experiments 7

Puppets
Mere puppets they, who come and go
                 Worm 12

Pure
To those pure orbs, your heart to learn
           Impromptu 2
To bathe in the pure element   Irene 50
Pure and reproachless, of thy princely
   line   Politian iv 25
Pure as the wishes breathed in prayer
           Stanzas² 14
Pure—as her young example taught
            Tamerlane 93
From the pure well of Beauty undefiled
           To Margaret 2

Purely
What could there be more purely bright
                 Dream 15

Purer
We still were young; no purer thought
           Tamerlane (1827) 151

Purified
And purified in their electric fire
                   Helen² 59

Puritan
Puritian pansies   Annie 66

Purple
Upreared its purple stem around her
   knees   Al Aaraaf i 49
And thy most lovely purple perfume,
   Zante   Al Aaraaf i 76
Looked out above into the purple air
           Al Aaraaf ii 23
With the moon-tints of purple and pearl
                Eulalie 11
And the silken, sad, uncertain rustling of
   each purple curtain   Raven 13
O hyacinthine isle! O purple Zante
                 Zante 13

Purpose
And speak a purpose unholy—thy lips are
   livid   Politian ii 109

Pursuing
Each poet—if a poet—in pursuing
              Elizabeth 7

Put
And they put out the star light
              Fairy-Land 9
And put out the sun   Triumph 8

Quadrated
What time the moon is quadrated in
   Heaven   Al Aaraaf ii 6

Quadruple
Laves in quadruple light her angel limbs
           Al Aaraaf i 29

Quaff
Quaff, oh quaff this kind nepenthe and
   forgot this lost Lenore   Raven 83

Quaint
Over many a quaint and curious volume
   of forgotten lore   Raven 2

Quake
Thy swollen pillars tremble—and so quake
           Al Aaraaf iii (1829) 41

Qualities
There are some qualities—some incorporate things   Silence 1

Quarrel
That knowing no cause of quarrel or of
feud   Politian v 11
Of quarrel between your lordship and
himself   Politian v 21
Having no cause for quarrel
                                  Politian v 30
He should have cause for Quarrel
                                  Politian v 37

Queen
To the queen of the angels   Annie 83
Of that Egyptian queen, winning so easily
                                  Politian ii 23
Is she not queen of Earth? her pride
                                  Tamerlane 166
As nuptial dowry—a queen's crown
                                  Tamerlane (1827) 244
The bride and queen of Tamerlane
                                  Tamerlane (1827) 282

Queenliest
An anthem for the queenliest dead that
ever died so young   Lenore 6

Queenly
Seemed to become a queenly throne
                                  Tamerlane 152

Queer
Or rather laugh with him, that queer
Philosopher   Tempora 15

Quenches
That quenches all thirst   Annie 38

Query
The luckless query from a Member's claw
                                  Tempora 20

Question
This is a question which, oh Heaven, withdraw   Tempora 19

Quick
Quick they registered the vow
                                  Bridal Ballad (1841) 21
My quick glances now retreating
                                  Departed 6

Quickening
That with a quickening spell doth over us
pass   Stanza¹ 15

Quickly
Pass'd quickly over me—but my mind
                                  Tamerlane (1827) 62

Quiet
Ours is a world of words: Quiet we call
                                  Al Aaraaf i 126
Ever drew down from out the quiet stars
                                  Coliseum 16
On the quiet Asphodel   Nis 26
And mother in Heaven! think of our quiet
home   Politian ii 85
And with a holier lustre the quiet moon
                                  Politian iii 49
The starry and quiet dwellings of the
blest   Politian iv 48
And quiet all away in jest
                                  Romance (1831) 30
Upon the quiet mountain top   Sleeper 6
No need to quiet any fears
                                  Tamerlane 109
But turned on me her quiet eye
                                  Tamerlane 111

Quieted
Are quieted now   Annie 21

Quietly
For now, while so quietly   Annie 59

Quietude
With quietude, and sultriness, and slumber
                                  Helen² 7

Quite
A man quite young   Politian i 46
And buries them up quite Fairy-Land 25

Quit
Leave my loneliness unbroken!—quit the
bust above my door   Raven 100

Quiver
Where the moon-lit blossoms quiver
                                  Departed 10

Quivering
Upon their quivering wings
                                  Fairy-Land 46
And, over each quivering form   Worm 34

Quoth
Quoth the Raven, "Nevermore"
                                  Raven 48, 84, 90, 96, 102

Rabble
But that, among the rabble—men
                                  Tamerlane 159

Radiant
Than the eyes of the radiant girl!
                                  Eulalie 8
Let my Future radiant shine   Hymn 11
Then, for thine own all radiant sake
                                  Irene (1836) 39
Radiant palace—reared its head
                                  Palace 4
No more a mourner—but the radiant Joys
                                  Politian iv 80
For the rare and radiant maiden whom
the angels name Lenore   Raven 11
Clasp a rare and radiant maiden whom
the angels name Lenore   Raven 95
How many memories of what radiant
hours   Zante 3

Raiment
Thy presence grieves me—go!—thy
priestly raiment   Politian ii 81

Raiments
Thy raiments and thy ebony cross affright
me!   Politian ii 102

Rain
The sound of the rain Al Aaraaf ii 120
The rain came down upon my head
                                  Tamerlane 55
Which fallest into the soul like rain
                                  Tamerlane 179

Rainbow
Rainbow and Dove!—Jacinta!
                                  Politian ii 28

Raise
I will no requiem raise   Paean 42
For in the fight I will not raise a hand
                                  Politian v 79
And raise his infancy's delight
                                  Tamerlane (1827) 281

Raised
Though its glow hath raised a fiercer
flame   Song 11
Full many a fair flower rais'd its head
                                  Tamerlane (1827) 402

Raising
Raising his heavy eyelid, starts and sees
                     Al Aaraaf ii 4

Ramparts
Along the ramparts plumed and pallid
                     Palace 15

Ran
On flowers, before, and mist, and love
they ran   Al Aaraaf ii 208
The winds ran off with it delighted
               Fairy-Land (1831) 20
And the rivulet that ran before the door!
                   Politian ii 86

Rang
For the words rang as a knell
                 Bridal Ballad 9

Rank
For thy lofty rank and fashion—much
depends   Politian i 25

Rapid
With the rapid Pleiads, even   Israfel 13
While, like a ghastly rapid river
                   Palace 45

Rapping
As of some one gently rapping, rapping at
my chamber door   Raven 4
But the fact is I was napping, and so
gently you came rapping   Raven 21

Rapt
O charms more potent than the rapt
Chaldee   Coliseum 15

Rapture
Of the rapture that impels   Bells 30

Rare
For the rare and radiant maiden whom
the angels name Lenore   Raven 11
Clasp a rare and radiant maiden whom
the angels name Lenore   Raven 11

Rarer
A rarer loveliness bedecks the earth
                Politian iii 48

Rash
Pause ere too late!—oh, be not—be not
rash!   Politian ii 111

Rather
Or rather laugh with him, that queer
Philosopher   Tempora 15

Rave
Peccavimus: yet rave not thus! but let a
Sabbath song   Lenore 13
And I would rave, but that he flings
            Tamerlane (1831) 29

Raven
In there stepped a stately Raven of the
saintly days of yore   Raven 38
Ghastly grim and ancient Raven wan-
dering from the Nightly shore
                   Raven 46
Quoth the Raven, " Nevermore "
         Raven 48, 84, 90, 96, 102
But the Raven, sitting lonely on the placid
bust, spoke only   Raven 55
But the Raven, still beguiling my sad
fancy into smiling   Raven 67
And the Raven, never flitting, still is sit-
ting, still is sitting   Raven 103

Ray
O! Nothing earthly save the ray
                   Al Aaraaf i 1
Into the sunlit ether, caught the ray
                   Al Aaraaf ii 8
Beneath the moon-ray
                 Al Aaraaf ii 131
Ianthe, dearest, see! how dim that ray!
                 Al Aaraaf ii 198
The sun-ray dropped, in Lemnos, with a
spell   Al Aaraaf ii 203
On things around him with a ray
                   Dream 7
Has sent a ray down with a tune
               Fairy-Land (1831) 23
And this ray is a fairy ray
               Fairy-Land (1831) 24
We can discover a moon ray
               Fairy-Land (1831) 31
Or the sun ray dripped all red   Nis 23
With ray of the all living light
              Tamerlane (1827) 155
My heart sunk with the sun's ray
              Tamerlane (1827) 365

Rays
Away—away—'mid seas of rays that roll
                   Al Aaraaf i 20
And rays from God shot down that meteor
chain   Al Aaraaf ii 24
Light, brazen rays, this golden star unto!
                 Al Aaraaf ii 240
No rays from the holy heaven come down
                   City 12
And rays of truth you cannot see
                 Tamerlane 227
Above with trellised rays from Heaven
                 Tamerlane 237

Reached
I have reached these lands but newly
                 Dream-Land 5
Have deemed, since I have reached to
power   Tamerlane 67
I reached my home—my home no more
                 Tamerlane 213
And my proud hopes had reached a
throne   Tamerlane (1827) 348

Read
Read nothing, written less—in short's a
fool   Elizabeth 10
Come, let the burial rite be read—the
funeral song be sung   Lenore 5
How shall the ritual, then, be read—the
requiem how be sung   Lenore 10
I read, perhaps too carelessly
                 Tamerlane 149
Who read Anacreon, and drank wine
               Romance (1831) 20
You will not read the riddle though you
do the best you can do   Valentine 20

Reader
I beg your pardon, reader, for the oath
                 Tempora 35
Upon this page, enwrapped from every
reader   Valentine 4

Real
Would have given a real diamond to such
as you   Politian ii 54

And dimmer nothings which were real
Tamerlane 122
Too real, to his breast who lives
Tamerlane (1827) 307

Realities
Vulture, whose wings are dull realities?
To Science 4

Reality
'T were better than the cold reality
Dreams 5
Of semblance with reality which brings
Dream 31
'T is bliss, in its own reality
Tamerlane (1827) 306

Really
Why really, sir, I almost had forgot
Tempora 30

Realm
But, now, the ruler of an anchored realm
Al Aaraaf i 26
The ruler of the realm was seen
Palace 24

Realms
But ah! not so when, thus, in realms on
high
Al Aaraaf i 130
In the realms of the Boreal Pole
Ulalume 19

Rear
Of flowers: of lilies such as rear the head
Al Aaraaf i (1829) 43

Reared
Of flowers: of lilies such as rear'd the
head
Al Aaraaf i 43
Her own fair hand had reared around
Tamerlane (1827) 219
But she who reared them was long dead
Tamerlane (1827) 403
Lo! Death has reared himself a throne
City 1
Radiant palace—reared its head
Palace 4

Reason
Nor ask a reason save the angel-nod
Al Aaraaf ii 249
And this was the reason that, long ago
Annabel Lee 13
Yes! that was the reason as all men know
Annabel Lee 23
Of her—who asked no reason why
Tamerlane 110
Astray from reason—Among men
Tamerlane (1827) 251
'Tis there the seat of reason lies in him
Tempora 82

Reasons
And I have other reasons for so doing
Elizabeth 5

Reassure
But he spoke to re-assure me
Bridal Ballad 13

Rebel
A rebel or a Bajazet?
Tamerlane (1831) 178

Recall
In infancy, which seen, recall
Tamerlane (1827) 141

She might recall in him whom Fame
Tamerlane (1827) 271

Recalls
Recalls the hour of bliss
Sarah 15

Reclining
I saw thee half reclining; while the moon
Helen² 18
This and more I sat divining, with my
head at ease reclining
Raven 75

Recollect
Endymion, recollect, when Luna tried
Acrostic 7

Red
The red fire of their heart
Al Aaraaf i 95
And the red winds are withering in the
sky!
Al Aaraaf 132
A red Daedalion on the timid Earth
Al Aaraaf ii 244
From the red cliff of the mountain
Alone 14
While, to listen, the red levin
Israfel 12
Red gallons of gore
Latin Hymn 11
Through the red-litten windows see
Palace 42
But their red orbs, without beam
Spirits 15
While the red flashing of the light
Tamerlane 44
The red sun-light lazily lay
Valley 8
A blood-red thing that writhes from out
Worm 27

Redder
The waves have now a redder glow
City 48

Redeem
The strife of nations, and redeem
Tamerlane (1827) 238

Redolent
Are redolent of sleep, as I
Serenade 15
Am redolent of thee and thine
Serenade 16

Redoubling
Redoubling age! and more, I ween
Tamerlane (1827) 336

Re-echoing
The Zinghis' yet re-echoing fame
Tamerlane (1827) 337

Reed
Waved to the wind, now wave the reed
and thistle
Coliseum 21

Reedy
There the reedy grass doth wave
Nis 31

Reel
There the sun doth reel by day
Nis 45
The earth reel—and the vision gone?
Tamerlane (1827) 97

Reels
To the lone oak that reels with bliss
Irene 20

Refracted
That fell, refracted, thro' thy bounds, afar
Al Aaraaf ii 160

Refresh
But Ocean ever to refresh mankind
                        Politian ii 9

Refuge
Refuge thou hast   Politian ii 74

Refuse
Or who so cold, so callous to refuse
                        Tempora 57

Region
Far off in a region unblest
                    City (1845) 3
'T is a peaceful, soothing region
                   Dream-Land 40
In the misty mid region of Weir
                       Ulalume 7
She revels in a region of sighs
                     Ulalume 41
This misty mid region of Weir
                     Ulalume 92

Regions
Ah, Psyche, from the regions which
                     Helen¹ 14
That haunteth the lone regions where hath
  trod   Silence 14
From regions of the blest afar
                   Tamerlane 224

Register
A crucifix whereon to register
                  Politian ii 99
And the deed's register should tally,
  father!   Politian ii 106

Registered
Quick they registered the vow
          Bridal Ballad (1841) 21

Regretting
Regretting its roses   Annie 56

Reign
Her way—but left not yet her Therasaean reign   Al Aaraaf i 158
I mean the reign of manners hath long
  ceased   Tempora 3

Reigns
Where tyrant virtue reigns alone
                Divine Right 6
On a black throne reigns upright
         Dream-Land 4, 54

Rejoice
O! how my spirit would rejoice
                 Tamerlane 52
Of one, in whom they did rejoice
        Tamerlane (1827) 343

Release
To release my heart   To Hunter 4

Relevancy
Though its answer little meaning—little
  relevancy bore   Raven 50

Reliquary
Type of the antique Rome! Rich reliquary
                  Coliseum 1

Relish
So keen a relish for the beautiful
                  Politian iii 44

Relying
While, on dreams relying
                 To Hunter 6

Remained
Didst glide away. Only thine eyes remained   Helen² 51

Remaineth
It still remaineth, torturing the bee
               Al Aaraaf i 51

Remember
That eve—that eve—I should remember
  well   Al Aaraaf ii 202
Remember, pray   Politian iii 96
Arouse thee! and remember!
                 Politian iii 98
Remember? I do. Lead on! I do remem-
  ber   Politian iii 99
Ah, distinctly I remember it was in the
  bleak December   Raven 7
Thus I remember having dwelt
                 Tamerlane 81
I don't remember one, upon my soul
                 Tempora 43
Nearest resembles worship—oh, remember
                 To MLS 14

Remembered
They remembered not our parting
                 Ballad 5
They remembered not our tears Ballad 6
Its way to some remembered lake
                 Irene 48
Is but a dim-remembered story
                 Palace 39
We remembered not the dank tarn of
  Auber   Ulalume 28

Remembering
Thou dost forget thyself, remembering
  me!   Politian iv 23

Remembers
And Beauty long deceased—remembers
  me   Politian ii 66

Remembrance
From my remembrance shall not pass—
  some power   Dreams 20

Remind
Remind me, love, of thee   Sarah 9

Remote
Some sepulchre, remote, alone
                 Sleeper 54

Render
Render him terrorless: his name's "No
  More"   Silence 9

Rendered
Rendered me mad and deaf and blind
                 Tamerlane 57

Renown
Not all the magic of our high renown
                 Coliseum 41

Repeating
So that now, to still the beating of my
  heart, I stood repeating   Raven 15

Repenting
Repenting follies that full long have
  fled   Al Aaraaf i 63

Repining
The happy flowers and the repining trees
                 Helen² 33

Replied
The shade replied   Eldorado 23

I replied: "This is nothing but dreaming: "
Ulalume 61
She replied: " Ulalume—Ulalume! "
Ulalume 80

Reply
Startled at the stillness broken by reply
so aptly spoken
Raven 61

Report
But the latter's well known " to report "
Lampoon 8

Repose
The faithful heart yields to repose
Physician 6
An Eden of bland repose
To F 7

Reposes
Here blandly reposes
Annie 54

Reproachless
Pure and reproachless, of thy princely line
Politian iv 25

Requiem
How shall the ritual, then, be read—the
requiem how be sung
Lenore 10
The requiem for the loveliest dead
Paean 3
I will no requiem raise
Paean 42

Requited
That his love I have requited
Bridal Ballad (1837) 22
Be all ingratitude requited
Fairy-Land (1831) 19

Resemble
Resemble nothing that is ours
City 8

Resembles
Her worshipper resembles
River 10
Nearest resembles worship—oh, remember
To MLS 14

Resignedly
Resignedly beneath the sky
City 10, 24

Resolute
And a resolute endeavor
Bells 48

Respectful
Trustworthy and respectful
Politian ii 40

Respite
Respite—respite and nepenthe from thy
memories of Lenore
Raven 82

Resplendency
Yet thine is my resplendency, so given
Al Aaraaf i 141

Rest
Near four bright suns—a temporary rest
Al Aaraaf i 18
And longed to rest, yet could but sparkle
there!
Al Aaraaf ii 59
That lulled ye to rest!
Al Aaraaf ii 91
In its dream of deep rest
Al Aaraaf ii 133
Which lulled him to rest?
Al Aaraaf ii 155
When the rest of Heaven was blue
Alone 21
And I rest so composedly
Annie 13
And I rest so contentedly
Annie 89
Have gone to their eternal rest
City 5

One more filmy than the rest
Fairy-Land 12
And my worldly rest hath gone
Imitation 17
Weary—l laid me on a couch to rest
Poetry 2
And used to throw my earthly rest
Romance (1831) 29
At rest on ocean's brilliant dyes
Serenade 5
The ruin moulders into rest
Sleeper 12
There was no need to speak the rest—
Tamerlane 108

Restlessly
Seas that restlessly aspire
Dream-Land 15
As the lavas that restlessly roll
Ulalume 15

Restlessness
The sad valley's restlessness
Valley 10

Resurrection
For the resurrection of deep-buried faith
To MLS 6

Retreating
My quick glances now retreating
Departed 6

Return
That gave out, in return for the love-light
Helen² 12

Returned
Stern Despair returned, instead of the
sweet Hope he dared adjure
Raven (1845)¹ 65

Returneth
Through a circle that ever returneth in
Worm 21

Reveal
What spirit shall reveal?
Al Aaraaf i 101

Reveille
In bed at a reveille roll-call
Lampoon 4

Revel
Sound loves to revel in a summer night
Al Aaraaf ii 40
Here may he revel to his heart's content
Tempora 49

Revelled
For I have revelled, when the sun was
bright
Dreams 13
I revelled, and I now would sleep
Romance (1830) 51
Unearthly pride hath revelled in
Tamerlane 5

Revelry
The sound of revelry by night
Tamerlane (1827) 339

Revels
Unseen, amid the revels there
Tamerlane 241
She revels in a region of sighs
Ulalume 41

Revenge
O, feast my soul, revenge is sweet
Louisa 13

Reverence
Shall do it reverence
City 53

Reverie
With madness, and unwonted reverie
Al Aaraaf i 59
While a reverie came over me
Bridal Ballad 15

Revolt
Who hath seduced thee to this foul revolt   To Margaret 1

Rhone
From struggling with the waters of the Rhone   Al Aaraaf i 75

Rhyme
In a sort of Runic rhyme
Bells 10, 98, 101
In a happy Runic rhyme   Bells 107
That little time with lyre and rhyme
Romance 18
Such squalid wit to honourable rhyme
To Margaret 4
Search narrowly this rhyme, which holds a treasure   Valentine 5
For her this rhyme is penned, whose luminous eyes   Valentine (1849) 1

Rhymes
I early found Anacreon rhymes
Romance (1831) 21

Rhyming
To the rhyming and the chiming of the bells!   Bells 35

Rhythm
In the rhythm of the shower
Al Aaraaf ii 123

Rhythmical
The rhythmical number
Al Aaraaf ii 154

Ribbon
The youth who cut the ribbon for her shoes   Tempora 58

Rich
Rich clouds, for canopies, about her curled   Al Aaraaf i 36
Achaian statues in a world so rich!
Al Aaraaf ii 35
Type of the antique Rome! Rich reliquary   Coliseum 1
Over hamlets and rich halls
Fairy-Land (1829) 20
Rich melodies are floating in the winds
Politian iii 47

Richer
Richer, far wilder, far diviner visions
To³ 13

Ridden
The star hath ridden high
Al Aaraaf i 107

Riches
But not the riches there that lie City 32

Riddle
Thou speakest a fearful riddle
Politian iii 38
You will not read the riddle though you do the best you can do   Valentine 20

Riddles
And now I leave these riddles to their seer   Valentine (1846) 21

Ride
Ride, boldly ride   Eldorado 22

Ridiculous
Ridiculous   Politian i 61

Rife
Sweet was their death—with them to die was rife   Al Aaraaf ii 168
Though it be rife with woe
Politian ii 64

Right
The only king by right divine
Divine Right 1
And, veritably, Sol is right enough
Enigma 9
May the d—l right soon for his soul call
Lampoon 2
Ha!—am I right?   Politian v 55
Oh, lady bright! can it be right
Sleeper 18
The soul which feels its innate right
Tamerlane (1827) 185
And thrilling as I see upon the right
To³ 24

Righteous
Most righteous, and most just, avenging Heaven!   Politian v 93

Rigid
See! on yon drear and rigid bier low lies thy love, Lenore   Lenore 4

Rigidly
Virginal Lillian, rigidly, humblily dutiful
Experiments 1

Rill
Of melody in woodland rill
Al Aaraaf i 6

Rills
And shouting with a thousand rills
Tamerlane 144

Rim
Exhales from out her golden rim
Sleeper 4

Ring
Save when, between the Empyrean and that ring   Al Aaraaf ii 26
How they ring out their delight!
Bells 19
The ring is on my hand
Bridal Ballad 1
Here is a ring as token Bridal Ballad 24
There's Ugo says the ring is only paste
Politian ii 52

Ringing
To the swinging and the ringing
Bells 31

Rings
Rings, in the spirit of a spell
Tamerlane 25

Riotous
Thy riotous company, too—fellows lowborn   Politian i 20

Ripple
The wave—there is a ripple there
City (1831) 44

Rippled
And over the wet grass rippled away
Fairy-Land (1831) 28

Ripples
For no ripples curl, alas!   City 36

Rise
And the stars never rise but I see the
bright eyes   Annabel Lee 36
My tinted shadows rise and fall
Irene 40
Rise—rise—infernal spirits, rise
Louisa 9
And the stars of Hope did rise
Paradise (1835) 8
Like ghosts the shadows rise and fall!
Sleeper 29
By sunset did its mountains rise
Tamerlane (1827) 362

Rising
Hell, rising from a thousand thrones
City 52

Rite
Come, let the burial rite be read—the
funeral song be sung!   Lenore 5

Ritual
How shall the ritual, then, be read—the
requiem how be sung   Lenore 10

Rivals
By rivals loved, and mourned by heirs
Stanzas² 8

Riven
Avaunt!—avaunt! to friends from fiends
the indignant ghost is riven
Lenore 20
Lay bare, thro' vistas thunder-riven
Romance (1831) 15
Whose pleasant bowers are yet so riven
Tamerlane 236

River
With Indian Cupid down the holy river
Al Aaraaf i 79
For the naphthaline river   Annie 35
Where the river ever floweth Departed 1
Lonely, by that lovely river   Departed 9
By that river, ever flowing   Departed 25
Now along that lonely river   Departed 37
By the mountains—near the river
Dream-Land 25
Let the bell toll!—a saintly soul floats on
the Stygian river   Lenore 2
While, like a ghastly rapid river
Palace 45
Fair river! in thy bright, clear flow
River 1

Rivers
As the scoriac rivers that roll
Ulalume 14

Rivulet
And the rivulet that ran before the door!
Politian ii 86

Roam
On desperate seas long wont to roam
Helen¹ 6
Arise together, Lalage, and roam
Politian iv 47
Thy life's course should ever roam
Stanzas² 9

Roamed
Of cypress, I roamed with my Soul
Ulalume 11

Roaming
Roaming the forest and the wild
Tamerlane 97

Roar
How they clang, and clash, and roar!
Bells 54
I stand amid the roar
Dream w. Dream 12
Soho!—let us roar   Latin Hymn 9
And the deep trumet-thunder's roar
Tamerlane 48
I was standing 'mid the roar
Tamerlane (1831) 249

Rob
But Octavia do not strive to rob
Octavia 6

Robe
Clothing us in a robe of more than glory
Coliseum 46

Robed
White-robed forms of friends long given
Dream-Land 37

Robes
But evil things, in robes of sorrow
Palace 33

Rock
Of a wild lake, with black rock bound
Lake 5
Upon the rock-girt shore of Time
Stanzas² 12
Of rock and forest, on the hills
Tamerlane 142
Of a wild lake with black rock bound
Tamerlane (1831) 83

Rocking
Are rocking lullabies as they go
Irene 19

Rode
To distant spheres, from time to time, she
rode   Al Aaraaf i 24
Thro' many a tempest, but she rode
Al Aaraaf i 108

Roll
Away—away—'mid seas of rays that
roll   Al Aaraaf i 20
In bed at a reveille roll-call   Lampoon 4
Do roll like seas in northern breeze
Nis 36
As the scoriac rivers that roll
Ulalume 14
As the lavas that restlessly roll
Ulalume 15
That groan as they roll down Mount
Yaanek   Ulalume 18

Rolled
And rolled, a flame, the fiery Heaven
athwart   Al Aaraaf 236
From the sun that round me rolled
Alone 15
Then rolled like tropic storms along
Romance (1831) 12

Rolling
Feel a glory in so rolling	Bells 84
To the rolling of the bells	Bells 108
Rolling like a waterfall	Nis 41

Rolls
Rolls	Bells 71
And he rolls, rolls, rolls	Bells 90
She rolls through an ether of sighs	Ulalume 40

Romance
In panoply of old romance	Irene 6
Romance, who loves to nod and sing	Romance 1

Rome
Type of the antique Rome! Rich re-liquary	Coliseum 1
Here, where the dames of Rome their gilded hair	Coliseum 20
And the grandeur that was Rome	Helen¹ 10
Oh, I'm the happiest, happiest man in Rome!	Politian i 2
Hourly in Rome—Politian, Earl of Leicester!	Politian i 42
Before all Rome, I'll taunt thee, villain — I'll taunt thee	Politian v 90
Rome to the Caesar—this to me?	Tamerlane 31

Rood
And many a rood of land	Bridal Ballad (1837) 4

Roof
On its roof did float and flow	Palace 10
The roof of his Excellency—and perhaps	Politian iii 66

Room
That my room it is gloomy	Annie 47
Into the darkness of a room	Fairy-Land (1831) 33
But now my soul hath too much room	Romance (1831) 36
This room for one more melancholy	Sleeper (1842) 41

Rosabel
Lost, lost Rosabel!	Ballad 12, 24, 36

Rose
Up rose the maiden in the yellow night	Al Aaraaf i 151
Up rose the maiden from her shrine of flowers	Al Aaraaf i 156
And fell—not swiftly as I rose before	Al Aaraaf ii 238
That rose—that what d' ye call it—that hung	Fairy-Land (1831) 12
There rose a fountain once, and there	Tamerlane (1827) 401
Lonely, like me, the desert rose	Tamerlane (1831) 215
Not even one lonely rose	To F 4
Which have withered as they rose	To M 14

Rosemary
A rosemary odor	Annie 63
The rosemary nods upon the grave	Sleeper 9

Roses
Regretting, its roses	Annie 56
Of myrtles and roses	Annie 58
Roses that grew in an enchanted garden	Helen² 9
Fell on the upturned faces of these roses	Helen² 11, 14
Fell on the upturned faces of the roses	Helen² 19
To breathe the incense of those slumbering roses?	Helen² 24
Were seen no more: the very roses' odors	Helen² 34

Rosy
Of rosy head, that towering far away	Al Aaraaf ii 7

Round
Lurked in each cornice, round each architrave	Al Aaraaf ii 31
From the sun that round me rolled	Alone 15
Round about a throne where, sitting	Palace 21
And round about his home the glory	Palace 37
All wreathed round with wild flowers	Paradise (1834) 5
Of flattery round a sovereign's throne	Tamerlane 64
Look round thee now on Samarcand!	Tamerlane 165
Round his fate will hover	To Hunter 13

Rout
The bodiless airs, a wizard rout	Sleeper 22
But see, amid the mimic rout	Worm 25

Route
By a route obscure and lonely	Dream-Land 1, 51

Ruby
And all with pearl and ruby glowing	Palace 25

Rude
Thus, while no single sound too rude	Serenade 22

Rudeness
Your bearing lately savored much of rudeness	Politian iii 97

Rue
With rue and the beautiful	Annie 65

Ruin
These shattered cornices—this wreck—this ruin	Coliseum 29
From us, and from all Ruin, unto the wise	Coliseum 35
Will ruin thee! thou art already altered	Politian i 14
And confidence—his vows—my ruin—think—think	Politian ii 89
The ruin moulders into rest	Sleeper 12

Ruined
Over ruined walls	Fairy-Land (1831) 60
For ruined maid	Politian ii 71

Rule
O! would she deign to rule my fate	Divine Right 9

Sainted
It shall clasp a sainted maiden whom the angels name Lenore   Raven 94

Saintlily
Saintlily, lowlily   Experiments 2

Saintly
Let the bell toll!—a saintly soul floats on the Stygian river   Lenore 2
In there stepped a stately Raven of the saintly days of yore   Raven 38

Sairly
Lang and sairly shall I grieve thee
Ballad 11, 23, 35

Sake
For the holy Jesus' sake   Irene 38
Then, for thine own all radiant sake
Irene (1836) 38

Samarcand
Look round thee now on Samarcand
Tamerlane 165
I dwelt not long in Samarcand
Tamerlane (1827) 354

Same
From the same source I have not taken
Alone 5
My heart to joy at the same tone
Alone 7
Called anything, its meaning is the same
Elizabeth 15
For the same end as before
Fairy-Land 36
The same, my love   Politian i 45
Than in thy cause to scoff at this same glory   Politian iv 40
To the self-same spot   Worm 22

Sancta
Sancta Maria! turn thine eyes
Hymn (1835) 1

Sanctified
And sanctified in their elysian fire
Helen² 60

Sand
Grains of the golden sand
Dream w. Dream 15
Some particles of sand
Dream w. Dream (1831) 15;
Tamerlane (1831) 252;
To⁴ 20

Sands
The sands of Time grow dimmer as they run   Al Aaraaf i 140
To the sands upon the shore   Paradise 18
The sands of Time are changed to golden grains   Politian iii 41

Sang
Bore burthen to the charm the maiden sang   Al Aaraaf ii 67

Sank
But now, at length, dear Dian sank from sight   Helen² 48

Sarcasm
Unchecked by sarcasm, and scorn
Tamerlane (1827) 257

Sat
Sat gently on these columns as a crown
Al Aaraaf ii 21

Perched, and sat, and nothing more
Raven 42
This I sat engaged in guessing, but no syllable expressing   Raven 73
This and more I sat divining, with my head at ease reclining   Raven 75
Hath long upon my bosom sat
Tamerlane (1831) 28

Satan
Something about Satan's dart   Nis 11

Sate
Here sate he with his love—his dark eye bent   Al Aaraaf ii 184
Wherein I sate, and on the draperied wall
Al Aaraaf ii 205
Here, where on ivory couch the Caesar sate   Coliseum (1833) 24

Satiate
With the last ecstasy of satiate life
Al Aaraaf ii 169

Satins
Satins and jewels grand
Bridal Ballad 3

Save
O! Nothing earthly save the ray
Al Aaraaf i 1
O! Nothing earthly save the thrill
Al Aaraaf i 5
Save when, between th' Empyrean and that ring   Al Aaraaf ii 26
Is now upon thee—but too late to save
Al Aaraaf ii 39
Nor ask a reason save the angel-nod
Al Aaraaf ii 249
O God! can I not save
Dream w. Dream 21
Save only thee and me. (O Heaven!—oh, God!   Helen² 26
Save only thee and me). I paused—I looked   Helen² 28
All—all expired save thee—save less than thou   Helen² 36
Save only the divine light in thine eyes
Helen² 37
Save but the soul in thine uplifted eyes
Helen² 38
Save the airs with pinions furled
Nis (1836) 31
Or thought, save of the passing scene
Tamerlane (1827) 77
Nothing save the airs that brood
Valley 12

Saved
My duty, to be saved by their bright light
Helen² 58

Savored
Your bearing lately savored much of rudeness   Politian iii 87

Saw
As others saw—I could not bring
Alone 3
Why ask? who ever yet saw money made out of a fat old   Experiments 9
I saw thee once—once only—years ago
Helen² 1
I saw thee half reclining; while the moon
Helen² 18

Bird or beast upon the sculptured bust
  above his chamber door   Raven 53

Sea

Headlong thitherward over the starry
  sea   Al Aaraaf ii 256
In a kingdom by the sea Annabel Lee 2
In this kingdom by the sea
                Annabel Lee 8, 14, 20, 24
Nor the demons down under the sea
                Annabel Lee 31
In her sepulchre there by the sea
                Annabel Lee 40
In her tomb by the side of the sea
                Annabel Lee 41
As he sails on his pinions over valley and
  sea   Campaign 4
But light from out the lurid sea   City 14
Upon some far-off happier sea   City 39
Over the strange woods—over the sea
                Fairy-Land 22
Alas! over the sea!
                Fairy-Land (1831) 64
That gently, over a perfumed sea
                Helen¹ 3
How silently serene a sea of pride
                Helen² 45
A green isle in the sea, love   Paradise 3
Such language holds the solemn sea
                Paradise 17
Of the small sea Sidrophel   Parody 8
Told of a beauteous dame beyond the sea
                Politian ii 16
Sees in the sea a second love
                Serenade 10
And earth, and stars, and sea, and sky
                Serenade 14
There is a two-fold Silence—sea and
  shore   Silence 5
In the earth—the air—the sea
                Tamerlane 118
In some tumultuous sea   To F 10

Search

In search of Eldorado   Eldorado 6
Search narrowly this rhyme, which holds
  a treasure   Valentine 5
That must be worn at heart. Search well
  the measure   Valentine 7

Searching

Of her soul-searching eyes   River 14

Seared

My seared and blighted heart hath known
                Happiest Day 2
My seared and blighted name, how would
  it tally   Politian iv 28
Scorching my seared heart with a pain
                Tamerlane (1827) 28

Searing

The searing glory which hath shone
                Tamerlane 17

Seas

Away—away—'mid seas of rays that roll
                Al Aaraaf i 20
On seas less hideously serene   City 41
Into seas without a shore
                Dream-Land 14

Seas that restlessly aspire
                Dream-Land 15
On desperate seas long wont to roam
                Helen¹ 6
Sure thou art come over far-off seas
                Sleeper 32
That palpitate like the chill seas
                Valley 15

Seat

Straight I wheeled a cushioned seat in
  front of bird and bust and door
                Raven 68
'T is there the seat of reason lies in him
                Tempora 82
As to the seat of thought in man and
  brute   Tempora 74

Second

Sees in the sea a second love
                Serenade 10

Secrecy

Till secrecy shall knowledge be
                Al Aaraaf i 116
Into thine hour of secrecy   Spirits 4
Secrecy in thee   Spirits (1827) 28

Secret

In secret, communing held—as he with it
                Stanzas 2
Know thou the secret of a spirit
                Tamerlane 13
Who, that had known the secret thought
                Tamerlane (1827) 247
From the secret that lies in these
                Ulalume 99

Secretly

Its venom secretly imparts
                Tamerlane (1827) 345

Secrets

To bear my secrets thro' the upper
  Heaven   Al Aaraaf i 142
Divulge the secrets of thy embassy
                Al Aaraaf i 147

Seduced

Who hath seduced thee to this foul revolt
                To Margaret 1

See

Like unto what on earth we see
                Al Aaraaf i (1831) 17
Ianthe, dearest, see! how dim that ray
                Al Aaraaf ii 198
Alone could see the phantom in the skies
                Al Aaraaf ii 254
And the stars never rise but I see the
  bright eyes   Annabel Lee 36
I might see thee by his side   Ballad 16
See the White Eagle soaring aloft to the
  sky   Campaign 1
All that we see or seem
                Dream w. Dream 10
Is all that we see or seem
                Dream w. Dream 23
Through all the flimsy things we see at
  once   Enigma 3
Huge moons see! wax and wane
                Fairy-Land (1831) 45
Mine eyes shall see, have ever seen
                Happiest Day 14

I see them still—two sweetly scintillant
                              Helen² 65
I see thee half reclining; while the moon
                              Helen (1848) 18
See! on yon drear and rigid bier low lies
    thy love, Lenore   Lenore 4
See—see—my soul, her agony   Louisa 5
See how her eye-balls glare   Louisa 6
Through the red-litten windows see
                              Palace 42
Too much of late, and I am vexed to see
    it   Politian i 12
I'll see to it   Politian i 26
Then see to it!—pay more attention, sir
                              Politian i 27
To see thee thus   Politian iii 7
Proceeds from yonder lattice—which you
    may see   Politian iii 62
Let me see, then, what thereat is, and this
    mystery explore   Raven 34
Looking like Lethe, see! the lake
                              Sleeper 14
Of Loveliness could see   Song 8
When Hope, the eagle that towered, could
    see   Tamerlane 187
And rays of truth you cannot see
                              Tamerlane 227
Whom daily they are wont to see
                         Tamerlane (1827) 262
And let him see himself a proper ass
                              Tempora 88
The bowers whereat, in dreams, I see
                              To¹ 1
And thrilling as I see upon the right
                              To³ 24
To come down and see   To Hunter 11
See!—it flickers up the sky through the
    night   Ulalume 66
Sit in a theatre, to see   Worm 5
But see, amid the mimic rout   Worm 25

Seeing
Knowing what I know, and seeing what I
    have seen   Politian iv 11
Ever yet was blessed with seeing bird
    above his chamber door   Raven 52

Seek
Abashed, amid the lilies there, to seek
                              Al Aaraaf i 119
O! where (and ye may seek the wide skies
    over)   Al Aaraaf ii 179
If you seek for Eldorado   Eldorado 24
Of Earth, who seek the skies
                              Fairy-Land 42
And all we seek to keep hath flown
                              Tamerlane 210
To seek for treasure in the jewelled skies
                              To Science 7
To seek a shelter in some happier star
                              To Science 11

Seem
All the heavens, seem to twinkle Bells 7
That all seem pendulous in air   City 27
All that we see or seem
                              Dream w. Dream 10
Is all that we see or seem
                              Dream w. Dream 23

Should my early life seem
                              Imitation 4
They seem to whisper thoughts of love
                              Sarah 10
To thy weariness shall seem   Spirits 16
In that time of dreariness, will seem
                              Tamerlane 204
Would seem to my half closing eye
                         Tamerlane (1827) 51
Should my early life seem   To⁴ 1

Seemed
Seemed earthly in the shadow of his niche
                              Al Aaraaf ii 34
She seemed not thus upon that autumn
    eve   Al Aaraaf ii 200
And the voice seemed his who fell
                              Bridal Ballad 10
What wild heart-histories seemed to lie
    enwritten   Helen² 42
Seemed to have years too many
                              Politian ii 20
Seemed to become a queenly throne
                              Tamerlane 152
Seemed then to my half-closing eye
                         Tamerlane (1829) 42

Seemest
Thou seemest then to be   Sarah 21

Seeming
And his eyes have all the seeming of a
    demon's that is dreaming   Raven 105

Seems
A conscious slumber seems to take
                              Sleeper 14
Of an enchanted life, which seems
                         Tamerlane (1827) 171

Seen
Seen but in beauty—not impeding sight
                              Al Aaraaf i 38
But on the pillars Seraph eyes have seen
                              Al Aaraaf ii 28
As others were—I have not seen
                              Alone 2
Of mine own thought—what more could I
    have seen   Dreams 18
Were seen no more: the very roses' odors
                              Helen² 34
Mine eyes shall see, have ever seen
                              Happiest Day 14
Which my spirit hath not seen
                              Imitation 8
The ruler of the realm was seen
                              Palace 24
I have not seen him   Politian i 47
I have known men have seen Politian
                              Politian i 57
Now I have seen Politian   Politian i 61
Knowing what I know, and seeing what I
    have seen   Politian iv 11
No mortal eyes have seen!—what said the
    Count   Politian v 18
In infancy, which seen, recall
                         Tamerlane (1827) 141
Whom the astonished earth hath seen
                         Tamerlane (1827) 334
It had seen better days, he said
                         Tamerlane (1827) 400

Of all the cities, and I've seen no few
                Tempora 41
His form once seen becomes a part of sight
                Tempora 70
Whom my spirit had not seen   To⁴ 10
Thou hast not seen my brow   To⁴ 28
She has seen that the tears are not dry on
                Ulalume 4

Seer
And now I leave these riddles to their seer
                Valentine (1846) 21

Sees
Raising his heavy eyelid, starts and sees
                Al Aaraaf ii 4
And sees the darkness coming as a cloud
                Al Aaraaf ii 46
Sees only, through   Lenore (1843) 17
Sees in the sea a second love
                Serenade 10

Seest
I am the Earl of Leicester, and thou seest
                Politian v 46

Seize
With chamois, I would seize his den
                Tamerlane (1827) 43
By a crowd that seize it not   Worm 20

Seldom
" Seldom we find," says Solomon Don
   Dunce   Enigma 1

Self
Not Conscience' self   Politian iv 60
Of its own self supremacy
                Tamerlane (1827) 181
To the self-same spot   Worm 22

Semblance
Of semblance with reality which brings
                Dreams 31

Senate
To the senate or the field
                Politian iii 15

Send
I know what thou wouldst say—not send
   the message   Politian v 39
I will not send it   Politian v 40

Sendeth
Then my soul strong memories sendeth
                Departed 15

Senescent
And now, as the night was senescent
                Ulalume 30

Sense
Endued with neither soul, nor sense, nor
   art   Elizabeth 11
Do tell! when may we hope to make men
of sense out of the Pundits
                Experiments 7

Senses
Stole over my senses in that lovely isle
                Al Aaraaf ii 211
Disturb my senses—go   Politian ii 79

Sent
Has sent a ray down with a tune
                Fairy-Land (1831) 23
I strike——the murmur sent   Paean 30
" Wretch," I cried, " thy God hath lent
thee—by these angels he hath sent thee
                Raven 81

Whether Tempter sent, or whether tempest tossed thee here ashore   Raven 86
I have sent for thee, holy friar
                Tamerlane (1827) 1

Sentence
To say thou art not gone—one little
   sentence   Politian iv 96

Separate
And each separate dying ember wrought
   its ghost upon the floor   Raven 8
Two separate—yet most intimate things
                Tamerlane 127

Sephalica
The Sephalica, budding with young bees
                Al Aaraaf i 48

Sepulchre
To shut her up in a sepulchre
                Annabel Lee 19
In her sepulchre there by the sea
                Annabel Lee 40
Untimely sepulchre, I do devote thee
                Politian v 60
Some sepulchre, remote, alone
                Sleeper 54

Sequence
In common sequence set, the letters lying
                Valentine 17

Serangs
Above yon cataract of Serangs
                Irene (1863) 21

Seraph
But on the pillars seraph eyes have seen
                Al Aaraaf ii 28
A maiden-angel and her seraph-lover
                Al Aaraaf ii 178
Never seraph spread a pinion   Palace 7
Hope, the Seraph Hope   Politian ii 67
Dwell in a seraph's breast than thine
                Tamerlane (1827) 152
Than even the seraph harper, Israfel
                To³ 14
Seraph thy memory is to me
                To F (1842) 8

Seraphic
In the seraphic glancing of thine eyes
                To MLS 12

Seraphim
Swung by seraphim whose foot-falls
   tinkled on the tufted floor   Raven 80

Seraphs
A thousand seraphs burst th' Empyrean
   thro'   Al Aaraaf ii 157
Seraphs in all but " Knowledge," the keen
   light   Al Aaraaf ii 159
With a love that the wingéd seraphs of
   Heaven   Annabel Lee 11
And seraphs sob at vermin fangs
                Worm 31
And the seraphs, all haggard and wan
                Worm (1843) 37

Sere
The leaves were crispéd and sere
                Ulalume 2
The leaves they were withering and sere
                Ulalume 3
But our thoughts they were palsied and
   sere   Ulalume 21

Our memories were treacherous and sere
Ulalume 22
As the leaves that were crispéd and sere
Ulalume 83
As the leaves that were withering and sere
Ulalume 84
Serene
On seas less hideously serene   City 41
On oceans not so sad-serene
City (1845) 33
How silently serene a sea of pride
Helen² 45
Serenely
Gliding serenely to its goal   Stanzas² 23
Serenest
Serenest skies continually   To F 13
Serious
Our talk had been serious and sober
Ulalume 20
Seriously
To take things seriously or all in jest
Tempora 12
Servant
Thy servant maid!—but courage!—'tis
but a viper   Politian ii 58
Served
For thou hast served me long and ever
been   Politian ii 39
Service
A piece of service; wilt thou go back and
say   Politian v 33
Setting
In setting my Virginia's spirit free
Mother 8
Settle
Down, down that town shall settle hence
City 51
Settled
My friend, the beau, hath made a settled
matter   Tempora 76
One settled fact is better than ten sages
Tempora 78
Seven
Which were seven   Israfel 14
Seven Pleiades entranced in Heaven
Serenade 7
Form in the deep another seven
Serenade 8
Sever
No magic shall sever   Al Aaraaf ii 114
Severed
They have severed in one fatal hour
Ballad 7
Shade
Till they glance thro' the shade, and
Al Aaraaf ii 76
Have mingled their shade
Al Aaraaf ii 137
The shade replied   Eldorado 23
From matter and light, evinced in solid
and shade   Silence 4
Of any, were it not the shade
Tamerlane (1827) 19
What! shade of Zeno   To⁴ 39
Shadow
But the shadow of whose brow
Al Aaraaf i 100

Seemed earthly in the shadow of his niche
Al Aaraaf ii 34
For the spirit that walks in shadow
Dream-Land 41
In sunshine and in shadow   Eldorado 3
And over his heart a shadow
Eldorado 9
He met a pilgrim shadow   Eldorado 15
" Shadow," said he   Eldorado 16
Down the Valley of the Shadow
Eldorado 21
And the shadow of thy perfect bliss
Israfel 43
Like the grim shadow Conscience, solemn
and noiseless   Politian iv 56
Far less a shadow which thou likenest to
it   Politian iv 61
And the lamp-light over him streaming
throws his shadow on the floor
Raven 106
And my soul from out that shadow that
lies floating on the floor   Raven 107
Will shake his shadow in my path
Romance (1831) 64
Bring thee to meet his shadow (nameless
elf)   Silence 13
Shadows
So blend the turrets and shadows there
City 26
Amid thy shadows, and so drink within
Coliseum 8
Shadows of the gone   Departed 8
My tinted shadows rise and fall   Irene 40
Like ghosts the shadows rise and fall
Sleeper 29
Are—shadows on th' unstable wind
Tamerlane 80
Shadows—and a more shadowy light
Tamerlane 123
Shadowy
Flap shadowy sounds from visionary
wings   Al Aaraaf i 129
Up shadowy long-forgotten bowers
City 19
As in that fleeting, shadowy, misty strife
Dreams 30
Dim vales—shadowy floods
Fairy-Land 1
Lo! that shadowy window-niche
Helen¹ (1845) 11
Th' uncertain, shadowy heaven below
Irene 59
Far down within some shadowy lake
Romance 4
Shadowy—shadowy—yet unbroken
Spirits 25
Shadows—and a more shadowy light
Tamerlane 123
At bidding of vast shadowy things
Worm (1843) 13
Shafts
These mouldering plinths—these sad and
blackened shafts   Coliseum 27
Shake
And shake from your tresses
Al Aaraaf ii 84

Up!—shake from your wing
             Al Aaraaf ii 92
Shake off the idle fancies that beset thee
             Politian iii 4
At thy behest I will shake off that nature
             Politian iii 10
Should shake the firm spirit thus
             Politian iv 62
Among the green leaves as they shake
             Romance 3
So shake the very Heaven on high
             Romance 12
Will shake his shadow in my path
             Romance (1831) 64
A wise philosopher would shake his head
             Tempora 83
He then, of course, must shake his foot
instead   Tempora 84

Shaken
And my soul is sorely shaken
             Bridal Ballad 30
Because divided it may chance be shaken
             Tempora 46
At me in vengeance shall that foot be
shaken   Tempora 85

Shalt ,
Thou must not—nay indeed, indeed, thou
shalt not   Politian iii 2
For in the eternal city thou shalt do me
             Politian iii 34
For thee, and in thine eyes—and thou
shalt be   Politian iv 79
Thou liest! thou shalt   Politian v 92
Now are thoughts thou shalt not banish
             Spirits 19

Shame
That blush, perhaps, was maiden shame
             Song 9
Bowed from its wild pride into shame
             Tamerlane 14
Shame said'st thou
             Tamerlane (1827) 24
My bosom beats with shame   To[4] 31

Shamed
Inmate of highest stars, where erst it
shamed   Al Aaraaf i 51

Shape
A crawling shape intrude   Worm 26

Share
While in its own all others share
             Stanzas[2] 16
The world—its joy—its share of pain
             Tamerlane (1827) 163

Shattered
These shattered cornices—this wreck—
this ruin   Coliseum 29

Shaven
Though thy crest be shorn and shaven,
thou, I said, art sure no craven
             Raven 45

Shed
The mists of the Taglay have shed
             Tamerlane 36
It was but man, I thought, who shed
             Tamerlane 58
Shed all the splendor of her noon
             Tamerlane 202

Sheds
While the mute earth sheds her blessing
             Departed 30

Sheeny
And bent over sheeny mountain and dim
plain   Al Aaraaf i 157

Sheeted
Sheeted Memories of the Past
             Dream-Land 34
While the pale sheeted ghosts go by
             Sleeper 44

Shell
That, like the murmur in the shell
             Al Aaraaf i 9
His target was the crescent shell
             Parody 7

Shelter
A shelter from the fervour of His eye
             Al Aaraaf 120
To seek a shelter in some happier star
             To Science 11

Sheltered
But barely sheltered—and the wind
             Tamerlane (1827) 61

Shepherd
Such as the drowsy shepherd on his bed
             Al Aaraaf ii 2

Shield
To shield me from harm   Annie 84
These should be thine, to guard and shield
             Stanzas[2] 25
My breast her shield in wintry weather
             Tamerlane 98

Shift
That shift the scenery to and fro
             Worm 14

Shine
A gazer on the lights that shine above
             Al Aaraaf ii 184
Let my Future radiant shine   Hymn 11
There the moon doth shine by night
             Nis 43
Shine on his path, in her high noon
             Tamerlane (1827) 377
To shine on us with her bright eyes
             Ulalume 48

Shines
Shines, bright and strong   Eulalie 18

Shirt
In short, his shirt-collar, his look, his tone
is   Tempora 71

Shiver
How we shiver with affright   Bells 74
Where the nightly blossoms shiver
             Departed 39

Shivering
The pen falls powerless from my shivering
hand   To[3] 17

Shoes
The youth who cut the ribbon for her
shoes   Tempora 58

Shone
So dimly shone from afar
             Dream (1827) 18
Shone on my slumbers in her lofty noon
             Dreams 24
Shone pale, thro' the light   Star 4

The searing glory which hath shone
Tamerlane 17
Hath ne'er shone dazzlingly upon
Tamerlane (1827) 264
Shook
And shook it into pieces—so
Fairy-Land (1831) 18
So shook the very Heavens on high
Romance (1831) 36
Shore
Into seas without a shore
Dream-Land 14
Of a surf-tormented shore
Dream w. Dream 13
To his own native shore   Helen¹ 5
To the sands upon the shore
Paradise 18
Ghastly grim and ancient Raven wander-
ing from the Nightly shore   Raven 46
Tell me what thy lordly name is on the
Night's Plutonian shore   Raven 47
Get thee back into the tempest and the
Night's Plutonian shore   Raven 98
There is a two-fold Silence—sea and shore
Silence 5
Upon the rock-girt shore of Time
Stanzas² 12
Of a wind-beaten shore
Tamerlane (1831) 250
Henceforth I hold thy flower-enamelled
shore   Zante 12
Shorn
I am shorn of my strength   Annie 8
"Though thy crest be shorn and shaven,
thou," I said, "art sure no craven."
Raven 45
Short
Read nothing, written less—in short's a
fool   Elizabeth 10
Joe Locke is a greater: in short .
Lampoon 6
For short the time my high hope lent
Tamerlane (1827) 269
In short, his shirt-collar, his look, his
tone is   Tempora 71
Shot
And rays from God shot down that
meteor chain   Al Aaraaf ii 24
Shoulder
Your hand from off my shoulder, if you
please   Politian i 36
Shouting
And shouting with a thousand rills
Tamerlane 144
Shoutingly
Gush'd shoutingly a thousand rills
Tamerlane (1827) 220
Show
O, I defy thee, Hell, to show
Tamerlane 219
Shower
In the rhythm of the shower
Al Aaraaf ii 123
Into a shower dissever   Fairy-Land 40
No lingering winters there, nor snow, nor
shower   Politian ii 8

Showing
Sometimes comes she to me, showing
Departed 27
Methinks thou hast a singular way of
showing   Politian i 5
Shown
The worldly glory, which has shown
Tamerlane (1827) 26
Shriek
They can only shriek, shriek   Bells 42
Shrieked
"Be that word our sign of parting, bird
or fiend!" I shrieked, upstarting
Raven 97
Shrieks
Those shrieks, delightful harmony
Louisa 7
Shrill
Breathes the shrill spirit of the western
wind   Politian ii 10
Shrilly
By notes so very shrilly blown
Romance (1831) 49
Shrine
Up rose the maiden from her shrine of
flowers   Al Aaraaf i 156
Up many and many a marvellous shrine
City 21
A fountain and a shrine   Paradise 4
Might envy; her young heart the shrine
Tamerlane 89
It fall from an eternal shrine
Tamerlane (1827) 14
Which blazes upon Edis' shrine
Tamerlane (1827) 156
Shrines
There shrines and palaces and towers
City 6
Shrive
Of Earth may shrive me of the sin
Tamerlane 4
Shroud
There passed, as a shroud   Star 12
Shrouded
Shrouded forms that start and sigh
Dream-Land 35
Shrubbery
What guilty spirit, in what shrubbery
dim   Al Aaraaf ii 174
The summer dream beneath the shrubbery
To Science (1829) 14
Shudder
That you shudder to look at me
Annie 93
How I shudder at the notes
Bells (1849) 15
Shun
Thy mother, too, did shun me   Ballad 19
No mote may shun—no tiniest fly
Tamerlane 238
To shun the fate, with which to cope
Tamerlane (1827) 14
Shut
To shut her up in a sepulchre
Annabel Lee 19
He is a dreamer and a man shut out
Politian i 63

Shutter
Open here I flung the shutter, when, with
   many a flirt and flutter   Raven 37

Sibyllic
Its Sibyllic splendor is beaming
                              Ulalume 64

Sicilian
Apart—like fire-flies in Sicilian night
                        Al Aaraaf i 145

Sick
Oh! I am sick, sick, sick, even unto
   death   Politian iii 29

Sickness
The sickness—the nausea   Annie 25

Side
And so, all the night-tide, I lie down by
   the side   Annabel Lee 38
In her tomb by the side of the sea
                        Annabel Lee 41
I might see thee by his side   Ballad 16
By the side of the pale-faced moon
                              Bells 50
With young hope at her side   Lenore 34
With young Hope at her side   Paean 22

Sides
Instead of two sides, Job has nearly
   eight   Tempora 21

Sidrophel
Of the small sea Sidrophel   Parody 8

Sigh
Shrouded forms that start and sigh
                        Dream-Land 35
For her soul gives me sigh for sigh
                              Eulalie 16
And the light laughter chokes the sigh
                              Irene 46
Why didst thou sigh so deeply?
                        Politian i 7
Did I sigh?   Politian i 7, 10
In chorus to my pensive sigh   Sarah 14
Thy heart—thy heart!—I wake and sigh
                              To¹ 9

Sighed
And I sighed to him before me
                        Bridal Ballad 17

Sighing
The sighing and sobbing   Annie 20

Sighs
My soul is lolling on thy sighs
                        Fairy-Land (1831) 6
She rolls through an ether of sighs
                              Ulalume 40
She revels in a region of sighs
                              Ulalume 41

Sight
Seen but in beauty—not impeding sight
                        Al Aaraaf i 38
But now, at length, dear Dian sank from
   sight   Helen² 48
With a sight as it pass'd on
                        Imitation 18
Was all on Earth my aching sight
                              Song 7
Whose failing sight will grow dim
                        Tamerlane (1827) 316
At least by sight, for I'm a timid man
                        Tempora 61

His form once seen becomes a part of sight
                              Tempora 70
At sight of thee and thine at once awake
                              Zante 4

Sightless
What tho' in worlds which sightless
   cycles run   Al Aaraaf i 133

Sign
" Be that word our sign of parting, bird
   or fiend! " I shrieked, upstarting
                              Raven 97

Silence
A sound of silence on the startled ear
                        Al Aaraaf i 124
" Silence "—which is the merest word of
   all   Al Aaraaf i 127
Silence is the voice of God
                 Al Aaraaf i (Yankee) 125
Yet silence came upon material things
                        Al Aaraaf ii 64
In the silence of the night   Bells 73
Silence! and Desolation! and dim Night
                              Coliseum 11
But the silence was unbroken, and the
   stillness gave no token   Raven 27
To mar the silence ev'n with lute
                              Serenade 4
There is a two-fold Silence—sea and shore
                              Silence 5
He is the corporate Silence: dread him
   not   Silence 10

Silent
The swift and silent lizard of the stones
                              Coliseum 25
Silent waterfalls
                        Fairy-Land (1831) 62
In the sad, silent watches of my night
                              Helen² 63
Once more that silent tongue
                        Politian iii 104
Be silent in that solitude   Spirits 5
And deeply felt the silent tone
                        Tamerlane (1827) 180
Her silent, deep astonishment
                        Tamerlane (1827) 267
A silent gaze was my farewell
                        Tamerlane (1827) 287
Once it smiled a silent dell   Valley 1

Silently
Streams up the turrets silently   City 15
How silently serene a sea of pride
                              Helen² 45

Silentness
And this all solemn silentness
                              Sleeper 36

Silken
So softly that no single silken hair
                        Al Aaraaf ii 212
There fell a silvery silken veil of light
                              Helen² 6
And the silken, sad, uncertain rustling of
   each purple curtain   Raven 13

Silly
A silly—a most silly fashion I have
                        Politian i 9

Silver
My own voice, silly child! was swelling
Tamerlane 51
Laughing at her half silly wiles
Tamerlane (1827) 129

Silver
While the silver winds of Circassy
Al Aaraaf i (1831) 14
Silver bells Bells 2
From the silver tinkling cells
Bells (1849) 5
Where weeps the silver willow
Paradise (1835) 32
Light on the lightning's silver wing
Romance (1831) 18

Silvery
There fell a silvery-silken veil of light
Helen² 6
The silvery streamlet gurgling on
Sarah 7
What though the moon—the silvery moon
Tamerlane (1827) 376

Similar
Again!—a similar tale
Politian ii 15

Simoon
To them 't were the Simoon, and would
destroy Al Aaraaf ii 165
As if my words were the Simoon
Tamerlane (1831) 180

Simple
All mystery but a simple name
Tamerlane (1827) 21
And love—a simple duty
To FSO (1825) 8

Sin
The luridness of beauty—and of sin
Al Aaraaf ii (1829) 43
Thrilling to think, poor child of sin
Sleeper 59
Of Earth may shrive me of the sin
Tamerlane 4
For they were childish, without sin
Tamerlane (1827) 116
It is not surely sin to name
Tamerlane (1827) 157
And much of Madness, and more of Sin
Worm 23

Since
They have not left me (as my hopes
have) since Helen² 54
Have deem'd, since I have reach'd to
power Tamerlane 67
Since it flickers up to Heaven through
the night Ulalume 71

Sinfully
This sinfully scintillant planet
Ulalume 103

Sing
None sing so wildly well Israfel 3
He might not sing so wildly well
Israfel 48
Sing a thousand over again
Latin Hymn 5
Soho!—let us sing Latin Hymn 6
That I should not sing at all Paean 16

Was but to sing Palace 30
Romance, who loves to nod and sing
Romance 1

Singer
The singer is undoubtedly beneath
Politian iii 65

Singing
Singing a song Eldorado 5
Devoutly singing unto one another
Mother (1850) 2
The wantonest singing birds To¹ 2

Single
What tho' in worlds which own a single
sun Al Aaraaf i 139
The single-mooned eve!—on Earth we
plight Al Aaraaf i 152
So softly that no single silken hair
Al Aaraaf ii 212
Thus, while no single sound too rude
Serenade 22
Or that the thrill of a single kiss
To M 11

Sings
'Tis now (so sings the soaring moon)
Irene 1
By which he sits and sings Israfel 20

Singular
Methinks thou hast a singular way of
showing Politian i 5
Some singular mistake—misunderstand-
ing Politian v 48

Sink
In terror she spoke, letting sink her
Ulalume 56
In agony sobbed, letting sink her
Ulalume 58

Sinking
By the sinking or the swelling in the
anger of the bells Bells 65
In slightly sinking, the dull tide City 45
Then, upon the velvet sinking, I betook
myself to linking Raven 69

Sinks
How the danger sinks and swells
Bells 64
Then sinks within (weigh'd down by wo)
Irene 58

Sinner
Upon the sinner's sacrifice
Hymn (1835) 2

Sir
Then see to it!—pay more attention, sir
Politian i 27
Thou mockest me, Sir Politian i 30
Sir Count! what art thou dreaming? he's
not well! Politian i 33
What ails thee, sir Politian i 34
Command me, sir! what wouldst thou
have me do Politian iii 9
Command me, sir Politian iii 14
Let me beg you, sir Politian iii 104
When saw you, sir Politian v 23
No more, my lord, than I have told you,
sir Politian v 28
Thou wilt not fight with me didst say, Sir
Count Politian v 64

But mark me, sir   Politian v 84
"Sir," said I, "or Madam, truly your
  forgiveness I implore   Raven 20
Why really, sir, I almost had forgot
                       Tempora 30
But damn it, sir, I deem it a disgrace
                       Tempora 32

Siroc
Upon the Siroc-wither'd plain
                     Tamerlane 180

Sister
And I said: "What is written, sweet
  sister   Ulalume 78

Sisters
Think of my little sisters!—think of them
                    Politian ii 87

Sit
Now—now to sit, or never   Bells 49
Sit down beside me, Isabel
            Fairy-Land (1831) 1
Sit down, sit down—how came we here
            Fairy-Land (1831) 9
Sit down!—let not my presence trouble
  you   Politian ii 3
Sit down!—for I am humble, most humble
               Politian ii 4
I sit on some moss-covered stone
                    Sarah 2
Sit in a theatre, to see   Worm 2

Sits
By which he sits and sings   Israfel 20

Sitteth
Sitteth in heaven   Politian iii 50

Sitting
Round about a throne where, sitting, Porphyrogene   Palace 21
But the Raven, sitting lonely on the
  placid bust, spoke only   Raven 55
And the Raven, never flitting, still is sitting, still is sitting   Raven 103

Skies
Hath drawn from the skies
                Al Aaraaf ii 75
O! where (and ye may seek the wide skies
  over)   Al Aaraaf ii 179
Alone could see the phantom in the skies
               Al Aaraaf ii 254
Surging, unto skies of fire
                Dream-Land 16
Is soaring in the skies   Fairy-Land 31
Of Earth, who seek the skies
                 Fairy-Land 42
With casement open to the skies
                    Irene 23
But the skies that angel trod Israfel 23
Her casement open to the skies
            Sleeper (1843) 17
And she would mark the opening skies
               Tamerlane 100
Serenest skies continually   To F 13
To seek for treasure in the jewelled skies
               To Science 7
The skies they were ashen and sober
                  Ulalume 1

To point us the path to the skies
                  Ulalume 45
To the Lethean peace of the skies
                  Ulalume 46

Sky
In the deep sky   Al Aaraaf i 85
And the red winds are withering in the
  sky   Al Aaraaf i 132
With all thy train, athwart the moony
  sky   Al Aaraaf i 144
Adorning then the dwellings of the sky
                Al Aaraaf ii 19
Beetling it bends athwart the solemn sky
               Al Aaraaf ii 192
But when its glory swell'd upon the sky
               Al Aaraaf ii 257
From the lightning in the sky
                  Alone 17
Stars in the sky   Annie 97
See the White Eagle soaring aloft to the
  sky   Campaign 1
Resignedly beneath the sky
                 City 10, 24
Like lightning from the sky
      Dream w. Dream (1829) 13;
           Tamerlane (1831) 257;
                     To⁴ 25
I' the summer sky, in dreams of living
  light   Dreams 14
Astarte within the sky   Eulalie 19
And not a cloud obscured the sky
                   Hymn 6
From my lyre within the sky
                   Israfel 51
Through the terror-stricken sky Nis 40
Through gazing on the unquiet sky
                 Romance 15
Dying along the troubled sky
            Romance (1831) 14
And earth, and stars, and sea, and sky
                 Serenade 14
Beneath the eternal sky of Thought
                Stanzas² 24
No cliff beyond him in the sky
               Tamerlane 188
The blue sky—the misty light
          Tamerlane (1827) 319
See!—it flickers up the sky through the
  night   Ulalume 66

Slain
We, with one warrior, have slain
               Latin Hymn 3

Slanderous
By you—by yours, the evil eye,—by yours,
  the slanderous tongue   Lenore 11

Slave
They are my ministers—yet I their slave
                  Helen² 56

Slaves
'Mid planets her slaves   Star 6

Sledges
Hear the sledges with the bells Bells 1

Sleep
In a dreamy sleep Al Aaraaf ii 117
Whose sleep hath been taken
              Al Aaraaf ii 150

Snouts
Born and brought up with their snouts
  deep down in the mud of the Frog-Pond
              Experiments 8

Snow
Snow-white palace—reared its head
              Palace (1839) 4
No lingering winters there, nor snow, nor
  shower   Politian ii 8

Snows
With the snows of the lolling lily
          Dream-Land 20, 24
With the weight of an age of snows
              To M 16

Snowy
Who daily scents his snowy wings
              Tamerlane 233

Soar
Methought, my sweet one, then I ceased
  to soar   Al Aaraaf ii 237
Or the stricken eagle soar   Paradise 20
Albeit he soar with an undaunted wing
          To Science (1829) 8

Soared
Albeit he soared with an undaunted wing
              To Science 8

Soaring
See the White Eagle soaring aloft to the
  sky   Campaign 1
Is soaring in the skies   Fairy-Land 31
A full-orbed moon, that, like thine own
  soul, soaring   Helen² 4
'Tis now (so sings the soaring moon)
              Irene 1
I stand beneath the soaring moon
          Irene (1836) 1

Sob
Weep not! oh, sob not thus!—thy bitter
  tears   Politian iv 5
And seraphs sob at vermin fangs
              Worm 31

Sobbed
In agony sobbed, letting sink her
              Ulalume 58

Sobbing
The sighing and sobbing   Annie 20
To the sobbing of the bells   Bells 104

Sober
Was Love, the blind, near sober Duty
  known   Al Aaraaf ii 180
The skies they were ashen and sober
              Ulalume 1
Our talk had been serious and sober
              Ulalume 20
Then my heart it grew ashen and sober
              Ulalume 82

Soft
But, list, Ianthe! when the air so soft
          Al Aaraaf ii 231
The soft head bows, the sweet eyes close
              Physician 5
But list, O list,—so soft and low
              Serenade 18
Soft may the worms about her creep
              Sleeper 47
And, tho' my tread was soft and low
              Tamerlane 216

To her soft thrilling voice: To part
          Tamerlane (1827) 292
Two words—two foreign soft dissyllables
              To³ 7
At thy soft-murmured words, " Let there
  be light! "   To MLS 10
At the soft-murmured words that were
  fulfilled   To MLS 11

Softened
And homeward turn'd his soften'd eye
              Tamerlane 190

Softly
All softly in ear   Al Aaraaf ii 145
So softly that no single silken hair
          Al Aaraaf ii 212
Flow softly—gently—vital stream
              Louisa 1
And softly dripping, drop by drop
              Sleeper 5

Soho
Soho!—let us sing   Latin Hymn 6
Soho!—let us roar   Latin Hymn 9

Soil
Bore a bright golden flower, but not i' this
  soil   Politian ii 7
On mountain soil I first drew life
              Tamerlane 35

Sol
And, veritable, Sol is right enough
              Enigma 9

Solace
For him who thence could solace bring
              Lake 20
Kind solace in a dying hour
              Tamerlane 1
I had no other solace—then
          Tamerlane (1827) 288
Solace to my imagining
          Tamerlane (1831) 97
My soul at least a solace hath   To F 5

Sold
The pretty little hand that sold her tape
              Tempora 56

Sole
A troop of Echoes, whose sole duty
          Palace (1839) 29

Solemn
The most sad and solemn note
          Al Aaraaf i (1831) 21
Beetling it bends athwart the solemn sky
          Al Aaraaf ii 192
What a world of solemn thought their
  monody compels   Bells 72
And let the solemn song
          Lenore (1843) 30
The solemn song be sung   Paean 2
Tun'd to such solemn song   Paean 8
Such language holds the solemn sea
              Paradise 17
Low, sad, and solemn, but most audible
              Politian ii 69
A solemn vow   Politian ii 96
By all I hold most sacred and most solemn
              Politian iv 36
A spectral figure, solemn, and slow, and
  noiseless   Politian iv 55

Eagerly I wished the morrow;—vainly I
had sought to borrow   Raven 9
I sought my long-abandon'd land
                    Tamerlane (1827) 361

Soul
Empyrean splendor o'er th' unchained
soul   Al Aaraaf i 21
The soul that scarce (the billows are so
dense)   Al Aaraaf i 22
Can ever dissever my soul from the soul
                    Annabel Lee 32
And my soul is sorely shaken
                    Bridal Ballad 30
My very soul thy grandeur, gloom, and
glory   Coliseum 9
Then my soul strong memories sentdeth
                    Departed 15
O'er my soul, is gone   Departed 20
Where wand'rest thou my soul
                    Dream (1827) 14
And thus the sad Soul that here passes
                    Dream-Land 49
Endued with neither soul, nor sense, nor
art   Elizabeth 11
And my soul was a stagnant tide
                    Eulalie 3
For her soul gives me sigh for sigh
                    Eulalie 16
My soul is lolling on thy sighs
                    Fairy-Land (1831) 6
A soul that knew it well
                    Happiest Day 24
A full-orbed moon, that, like thine own
soul, soaring   Helen² 4
Save but the soul in thine uplifted eyes
                    Helen² 38
They fill my soul with Beauty (which is
Hope)   Helen² 61
My soul, lest it should truant be
                    Hymn 7
As a spell upon his soul   Imitation 14
Whose solitary soul could make Lake 22
May the d—l right soon for his soul call
                    Lampoon 2
Let the bell toll!—a saintly soul floats on
the Stygian river   Lenore 2
Let no bell toll, then, lest her soul, amid
its hallowed mirth   Lenore 23
See—see—my soul, her agony Louisa 5
O, feast my soul, revenge is sweet
                    Louisa 13
Was dearer to my soul than its soul-life
                    Mother 14
Helen, thy soul is riven
                    Paean (1836) 38
For which my soul did pine
                    Paradise 2
God nerve the soul that ne'er forgets
                    Physician 2
To what my fevered soul doth dream of
Heaven   Politian ii 12
Whom thou hast cherished to sting thee to
the soul   Politian ii 59
Give up thy soul to penitence, and pray
                    Politian ii 76
My soul is at war with God
                    Politian ii 77

Think of thy precious soul
                    Politian ii 83
Give not thy soul to dreams: the camp—
the court   Politian iii 21
Presently my soul grew stronger; hesi-
tating then no longer   Raven 19
Back into the chamber turning, all my
soul within me burning   Raven 31
That one word, as if his soul in that one
word he did outpour   Raven 56
Tell this soul with sorrow laden if, within
the distant Aidenn   Raven 93
Leave no black plume as token of that lie
thy soul hath spoken   Raven 99
And my soul from out that shadow that
lies floating on the floor   Raven 107
But the Raven still beguiling all my sad
soul into smiling   Raven (1845) 67
Of her soul-searching eyes   River 14
But now my soul hath too much room
                    Romance (1831) 46
And after-drunkenness of soul
                    Romance (1831) 52
That, scarce awake, thy soul shall deem
                    Serenade 20
Body and soul. One dwells in lonely places
                    Silence 6
'Neath which thy slumb'ring soul lies hid
                    Sleeper 27
Thy soul shall find itself alone
                    Spirits 1
The grandeur of a guileless soul
                    Stanzas² 21
Which fall'st into the soul like rain
                    Tamerlane 179
That soul will hate the ev'ning mist
                    Tamerlane 195
My soul imbib'd unhallow'd feeling
                    Tamerlane (1827) 47
My soul in mystery to sleep
                    Tamerlane (1827) 74
Hath fixed my soul, tho' unforgiv'n
                    Tamerlane (1827) 106
The soul which feels its innate right
                    Tamerlane (1827) 185
The soul, which knows such power, will
still   Tamerlane (1827) 193
A portion of his willing soul
                    Tamerlane (1827) 309
My soul—so was the weakness in it
                    Tamerlane (1831) 78
My solitary soul—how make
                    Tamerlane (1831) 98
I don't remember one, upon my soul
                    Tempora 43
My soul at least a solace hath   To F 5
Of cypress, I roamed with my Soul
                    Ulalume 11
Of cypress, with Psyche, my Soul
                    Ulalume 12
Eyes scintillating soul, there lies perdus
                    Valentine (1849) 14
And Horror the soul of the plot
                    Worm 24

Souls
Their odorous souls in an ecstatic death
                    Helen² 13

Our thoughts, our souls—O God above
                    Serenade 24
Unthought-like thoughts that are the
    souls of thought   To³ 12
From the limbo of lunary souls
                    Ulalume 102
From the Hell of the planetary souls
                    Ulalume 104

Sound
A sound of silence on the startled ear
                    Al Aaraaf 124
Sound loves to revel in a summer night
                    Al Aaraaf ii 40
And sound alone, that from the spirit
    sprang   Al Aaraaf ii 66
The sound of the rain   Al Aaraaf ii 120
With a lullaby sound   Annie 40
For every sound that floats   Bells 76
Not hear it!—listen now! listen!—the
    faintest sound   Politian iii 52
I think I hear thy voice's sound
                    Sarah 4
Thus while no single sound too rude
                    Serenade 22
With a strange sound, as of a harp-string
    broken   Stanzas¹ 23
With music of so strange a sound
                    Tamerlane 184
To the sound of the coming darkness
                    Tamerlane 197
The sound of revelry by night
                    Tamerlane (1827) 339
Of which sound doctrine I believe each
    tittle   Tempora 7
Compose a sound delighting all to hear
                    Valentine (1846) 18
No more! alas, that magical sad sound
                    Zante 9

Sounded
Now sounded to her heedless ear
                    Tamerlane (1827) 240

Sounding
In her tomb by the sounding sea
                    Annabel Lee (1849) 41
Oh, from out the sounding cells
                    Bells 25
Against whose sounding door she hath
    thrown   Irene 69
Of the hollow and high-sounding vanities
                    Politian iii 30
Some tomb from out whose sounding door
                    Sleeper 57

Sounds
Flap shadowy sounds from visionary
    wings   Al Aaraaf i 129
Prophetic sounds and loud, arise forever
                    Coliseum 34
And hark the sounds so low yet clear
                    Irene (1836) 26
The frightful sounds of merriment below
                    Politian ii 78
In hearkening to imaginary sounds
                    Politian iii 24

Source
From the same source I have not taken
                    Alone 5
Is by (the very source of gloom)
                    Fairy-Land (1831) 34

Sours
Is a world of sweets and sours
                    Israfel 41

Sovereign
The sovereign of the realm was seen
                    Palace (1839) 24
And who her sovereign? Timour—he
                    Tamerlane 173
Of flattery round a sovereign's throne
                    Tamerlane 64
Of flattery round a sovereign-throne
                    Tamerlane (1839) 64

Sovereignty
With more of sov'reignty than ancient
    lore   Stanzas¹ 12

Space
Out of Space—out of Time
                    Dream-Land 8

Sparkle
And long'd to rest, yet could but sparkle
    there   Al Aaraaf ii 59

Sparkled
Far down upon the wave that sparkled
    there   Al Aaraaf ii 14

Sparkles
For it sparkles with Annie   Annie 98

Sparkling
And sparkling evermore   Palace 28

Speak
Too much horrified to speak   Bells 41
They tell me (while they speak Paean 13
I speak to him—he speaks of Lalage
                    Politian i 32
They speak of him   Politian i 58
Didst thou not speak of faith
                    Politian ii 92
And speak a purpose unholy—thy lips are
    livid   Politian ii 109
Baldazzar speak no more
                    Politian iii 27
And dost thou speak of love
                    Politian iv 1
To me, Politian?—dost thou speak of love
                    Politian iv 10
Speak not to me of glory
                    Politian iv 30
Ha! glory!—now speak not of it
                    Politian iv 35
O, speak to me   Politian iv 94
O speak to me   Politian iv 99
There was no need to speak the rest
                    Tamerlane 108
I speak thus openly to thee
                    Tamerlane (1827) 182
But speak to him, he'll make you such
    grimace   Tempora 63
I cannot write—I cannot speak or think
                    To³ 19

Speaketh
Thus speaketh one Ferdinand in the
    words of the play   Politian ii 17

Speakest
Thou speakest a fearful riddle
                    Politian iii 38
Thou speakest to me of love
                    Politian iv 65

Speaks
All Nature speaks, and ev'n ideal things
                              Al Aaraaf i 128
I speak to him—he speaks of Lalage
                              Politian i 32
But Rumor speaks of him as of a prodigy
                              Politian i 48
It speaks of sunken eyes, and wasted
cheeks   Politian ii 65

Specimen
Have brought a specimen
                              Fairy-Land 45

Spectral
A spectral figure, solemn, and slow, and
noiseless   Politian iv 55
And on the spectral mountain's crown
                              Serenade 12

Spectre
Glides, spectre-like, unto his marble home
                              Coliseum 23
Have drawn up the spectre of a planet
                              Ulalume 101

Speed
With speed that may not tire
                              Al Aaraaf i 96

Spell
As the spell which no slumber
                              Al Aaraaf ii 152
The sun-ray dropp'd, in Lemnos, with a
spell   Al Aaraaf ii 202
Or spell had bound me—'t was the chilly
wind   Dreams 21
As a spell upon his soul   Imitation 14
Ceasing their hymns, attend the spell
                              Israfel 6
Baldazzar, it oppresses me like a spell
                              Politian iii 55
That with a quick'ning spell doth o'er us
pass   Stanzas¹ 15
Rings, in the spirit of a spell
                              Tamerlane 25
But then a gentler, calmer spell
                              Tamerlane (1831) 100

Spelled
I am spelled by art   To Hunter 7

Spells
O spells more sure than e'er Judaean
king   Coliseum 13
Could hope to utter. And I! my spells are
broken   To³ 16

Sphere
Which dreamy poets name " the music of
the sphere."   Al Aaraaf i 125
Like music of another sphere
                              Irene (1836) 27
In their own sphere—will not believe
                              Tamerlane (1827) 260

Spheres
To distant spheres, from time to time, she
rode   Al Aaraaf i 24
Upon those crystalline, celestial spheres
                              Helen² 43
The music of the spheres   Worm 8

Spiral
With a spiral twist and a swell
                              Fairy-Land (1831) 27

Spires
Up domes—up spires—up kingly halls
                              City 17

Spirit
Bursting its odorous heart in spirit to
wing   Al Aaraaf i 72
Spirit! that dwellest where
                              Al Aaraaf i 82
What spirit shall reveal
                              Al Aaraaf i 101
Some eager spirit flapp'd his dusky wing
                              Al Aaraaf ii 27
And sound alone, that from the spirit
sprang   Al Aaraaf ii 66
And there—oh! may my weary spirit
dwell   Al Aaraaf ii 172
What guilty spirit, in what shrubbery dim
                              Al Aaraaf ii 174
He was a goodly spirit—he who fell
                              Al Aaraaf ii 182
Fail'd, as my pennon'd spirit leapt aloft
                              Al Aaraaf ii 232
My tantalized spirit   Annie 53
Spirit, cooped in mortal bower
                              Departed 18
A lonely spirit guiding   Dream 12
My spirit spurn'd control
                              Dream (1827) 2
For the spirit that walks in shadow
                              Dream-Land 41
My spirit not awak'ning till the beam
                              Dreams 2
Its image on my spirit—or the moon
                              Dreams 23
Be still, my spirit   Happiest Day 12
Which my spirit hath not seen
                              Imitation 8
That vision on my spirit   Imitation12
Entranc'd, the spirit loves to lie
                              Irene 43
In Heaven a spirit doth dwell
                              Israfel 1
My infant spirit would awake
                              Lake (1827) 11
Ah, broken is the golden bowl!—the
spirit flown forever   Lenore 1
In setting my Virginia's spirit free
                              Mother 8
(Dim gulf!) my spirit hovering lies
                              Paradise 12
Breathes the shrill spirit of the western
wind   Politian ii 10
For the wounded spirit in Gilead it is
there   Politian ii 32
Within my spirit for thee
                              Politian iv 20
Should shake the firm spirit thus
                              Politian iv 62
Like an avenging spirit I'll follow thee
                              Politian v 88
Its down upon my spirit flings
                              Romance 17
A gentle guardian spirit given
                              Sarah 22
From thy spirit shall they pass
                              Spirits 21
A passionate light—such for his spirit
was fit   Stanzas¹ 6

And yet that spirit knew not—in the
  hour   Stanzas[1] 7
That high tone of the spirit which hath
  striv'n   Stanzas[1] 29
And this the life thy spirit live
                    Stanzas[2] 26
Know thou the secret of a spirit
                  Tamerlane 13
Rings, in the spirit of a spell
                  Tamerlane 25
And a proud spirit which hath striven
                  Tamerlane 33
O! how my spirit would rejoice
                  Tamerlane 52
And pour my spirit out in tears
                 Tamerlane 107
My spirit struggled with, and strove
                 Tamerlane 113
O, human love! thou spirit given
                 Tamerlane 177
In spirit cradled me to sleep
              Tamerlane (1827) 71
The passionate spirit which hath known
             Tamerlane (1827) 179
There is a power in the high spirit
             Tamerlane (1827) 191
That the proud spirit had been broken
             Tamerlane (1827) 199
To him, whose loving spirit will dwell
             Tamerlane (1827) 311
My spirit what it e'er had been
             Tamerlane (1827) 354
Like moonlight on my spirit fell
             Tamerlane (1831) 10
My infant spirit would awake
             Tamerlane (1831) 89
Whom my spirit had not seen   To[4] 10
His spirit is communing with an angel's
                 To MLS 18

Spirits
Spirits in wing, and angels to the view
             Al Aaraaf ii 156
Spirits in the gloom   Departed 32
Over spirits on the wing   Fairy-Land 23
Rise—rise—infernal spirits, rise
                   Louisa 9
Spirits moving musically   Palace 19
The spirits of the dead who stood
                   Spirits 7
Tho those whose spirits harken) as one
               Tamerlane 198
The bodiless spirits of the storms
             Tamerlane (1827) 166

Spiritual
And, amid incense and high spiritual
  hymns   Al Aaraaf i 28

Spite
And spite all dogmas current in all ages
                 Tempora 77

Splendor
Empyrean splendor o'er th' unchained
  soul   Al Aaraaf i 21
Shed all the splendor of her noon
                 Tamerlane 202
Its Sibyllic splendor is beaming
                 Ulalume 64

Spoilt
Hast thou not spoilt a story in each star
            To Science (1841) 11

Spoke
But he spoke to re-assure me
              Bridal Ballad 13
Is even that Alessandra of whom he spoke
                Politian iii 67
Who spoke the words
                Politian iv 89
But the Raven, sitting lonely on the
  placid bust, spoke only   Raven 55
Startled at the stillnes broken by reply so
  aptly spoken   Raven 61
I spoke to her of power and pride
                Tamerlane 145
Something he spoke of the old cot
            Tamerlane (1827) 399
In terror she spoke, letting sink her
                 Ulalume 56

Spoken
And thus the words were spoken
             Bridal Ballad 20
But I know that she hath spoken
                Ballad 29
Thou hast not spoken lately of thy wed-
  ding   Politian ii 43
And the only word there spoken was the
  whispered word " Lenore "   Raven 28
Leave no black plume as a token of that
  life thy soul hath spoken
                   Raven 99

Spot
A garden-spot in desert of the blest
           Al Aaraaf i (1829) 19
The last spot of Earth's orb I trod upon
             Al Aaraaf ii 214
By each spot the most unholy
             Dream-Land 31
No spot of ground   Eldorado 11
To haunt of the wide world a spot
                   Lake 2
Upon that spot, as upon all   Lake 8
To haunt of the wide world a spot
             Tamerlane (1831) 80
Upon that spot as upon all
             Tamerlane (1831) 86
To the self-same spot   Worm 22

Sprang
Whence sprang the " Idea of Beauty " into
  birth   Al Aaraaf i 31
On the fair Capo Deucato, and sprang
              Al Aaraaf i 44
And that aspiring flower that sprang on
  Earth   Al Aaraaf i 70
As sprang that yellow star from downy
  hours   Al Aaraaf i 155
And sound alone, that from the spirit
  sprang   Al Aaraaf ii 66
Thence sprang I—as the eagle from his
  tower   Al Aaraaf ii 219
Sprang from her station, on the winds
  apart   Al Aaraaf ii 235

Spray
Or tufted wild spray   Al Aaraaf ii 69

Spread
Never seraph spread a pinion   Palace 7

Spring
And they, and ev'ry mossy spring were
　holy　　　　　　　Al Aaraaf ii 188
My passions from a common spring
　　　　　　　　　　　　Alone 4
From a spring but a very few
　　　　　　　　　　　　Annie 41
In spring of youth it was my lot
　　　　　　　　　　　　Lake 1
In spring of life have ye ne'er dwelt
　　　　　　　　Tamerlane (1827) 94

Springing
Springing from a darken'd mind
　　　　　　　　　　Lake (1827) 16

Springs
Springs from the gems of Circassy
　　　　　　　　　　Al Aaraaf i 4
The murmur that springs
　　　　　　　　　　Al Aaraaf ii 124
To springs that lie clearest
　　　　　　　　　　Al Aaraaf ii 130
Thirst for the springs of lore that in thee
　lie　　　　　　　　　Coliseum 6
A type of that twin entity which springs
　　　　　　　　　　　　Silence 3
'Tis not that the flowers of twenty springs
　　　　　　　　　　　　To M 13

Sprite
The witch, the sprite, the goblin—where
　are they　　　To Science (1841) 14

Spurned
My spirit spurn'd control
　　　　　　　　　　Dream (1827) 2

Squalid
Such squalid wit to honourable rhyme
　　　　　　　　　　To Margaret 4

Stable
Stable, opaque, immortal—all by dint
　　　　　　　　　　　　Enigma 13

Stagnant
And my soul was a stagnant tide
　　　　　　　　　　　　Eulalie 3

Stalking
Were stalking between her and me
　　　　　　　　　Romance (1831) 34

Stand
I stand amid the roar
　　　　　　　　Dream w. Dream 12
How statue-like I see thee stand
　　　　　　　　　　　Helen¹ 12
I stand beneath the soaring moon
　　　　　　　　　Irene (1836) 1
Stand back　　　　　Politian ii 103
I stand beneath the mystic moon
　　　　　　　　　　　Sleeper 2

Standing
I am standing amid the roar
　　　　　　Dream w. Dream (1829) 10
I was standing 'mid the roar
　　　　　　　Tamerlane (1831) 249
This standing motionless upon the golden
　　　　　　　　　　　　To³ 21
I am standing 'mid the roar　　　To⁴ 17

Stands
Stands she not nobly and alone
　　　　　　　　　Tamerlane 170

Star
The wandering star　　　Al Aaraaf i 15

Falling in wreaths thro' many a startled
　star　　　　　　Al Aaraaf i 32
The boundary of the star
　　　　　　　　　Al Aaraaf i 87
The star hath ridden high
　　　　　　　　　Al Aaraaf i 107
As sprang that yellow star from downy
　hours　　　　　　Al Aaraaf i 155
Mysterious star!
　　　　　　　Al Aaraaf i (1831) 1
Of many a wild star gazer long ago
　　　　　　　　　Al Aaraaf ii 43
In many a star-lit grove, or mon-lit dell
　　　　　　　　　Al Aaraaf ii 63
These star-litten hours
　　　　　　　　　Al Aaraaf ii 83
At the many star-isles
　　　　　　　　　Al Aaraaf ii 134
O Death! from eye of God upon that star
　　　　　　　　　Al Aaraaf ii 161
What wonder? for each star is eye-like
　there　　　　　　Al Aaraaf ii 186
Light, brazen rays, this golden star unto
　　　　　　　　　Al Aaraaf ii 240
Dread star! that came, amid a night of
　mirth　　　　　　Al Aaraaf ii 243
And thy star trembled—as doth Beauty
　then　　　　　　Al Aaraaf ii 260
It trembled to one constant star again
　　　　　　　Al Aaraaf ii (1829) 197
Where each star most faintly gloweth
　　　　　　　　　　Departed 3
When each pale star earthward bendeth
　　　　　　　　　　Departed 14
In Truth's day-star　　　　Dream 16
And they put out the star-light
　　　　　　　　　　Fairy-Land 9
I am star-stricken with thine eyes
　　　　　　　　Fairy-Land (1831) 5
Up like a dog-star in this bower
　　　　　　　Fairy-Land (1831) 13
Which we worship in a star　　Israfel 28
And the star of Hope did rise
　　　　　　　　Paradise (1835) 8
But 't will leave thee, as each star
　　　　　　　　Spirits (1827) 19
Proud Evening Star　　　　Star 15
Trust to the fickle star within
　　　　　　　Tamerlane (1827) 119
For my destiny in a star　　　To⁴ 6
To seek a shelter in some happier star
　　　　　　　　To Science 11
And star-dials pointed to morn
　　　　　　　　　　Ulalume 31
As the star-dials hinted of morn
　　　　　　　　　　Ulalume 32
Said: "Sadly this star I mistrust
　　　　　　　　　　Ulalume 52

Stare
That things should stare us boldly in the
　face　　　　　　　Tempora 32

Starlight
Like starlight on a pall　　　To¹ 8

Starry
A wreath that twined each starry form
　around　　　　　　Al Aaraaf i 40
And scowls on starry worlds that down
　beneath it lie　　　Al Aaraaf ii 193

Stems

They weep:—from off their delicate stems
Valley 26

Step

Lest an evil step be taken
Bridal Ballad 31
Which, of light step, flies with the dew
Tamerlane (1827) 209

Stepped

In there stepped a stately Raven of the saintly days of yore
Raven 38

Stepping

Falling—her veriest stepping-stone
Tamerlane 171

Stern

By the grave and stern decorum of the countenance it wore
Raven 44
Stern Despair returned, instead of the sweet Hope he dared adjure
Raven (1845)[1] 65

Sterner

Here's a far sterner story
Politian ii 21

Still

It still remaineth, torturing the bee
Al Aaraaf i 58
Still think my terrors but the thunder cloud
Al Aaraaf i 136
That its echo still doth dwell
Al Aaraaf i (1831) 24
Or, capriciously still   Al Aaraaf ii 106
But the strains still arise
Al Aaraaf ii 118
Young dreams still hovering on their drowsy flight   Al Aaraaf ii 158
Sweet was that error—sweeter still that death   Al Aaraaf ii 162
The mystery which binds me still
Alone 12
Their still waters, still and chilly
Dream-Land 19
And hath been still, upon the lovely earth
Dreams 7
'T were folly still to hope for higher Heav'n   Dreams 12
Comes down—still down—and down
Fairy-Land 15
I see them still—two sweetly scintillant
Helen[2] 65
Mother of God, be with me still
Hymn 4
Be still, my spirit   Happiest Day 12
The life still there upon her hair, the death upon her eyes   Lenore 19
The life still there   Lenore 39
Still does my heart confess thy power
Octavia 4
O still more happy maiden who couldst die   Politian ii 14
Be still!—the voice, if I mistake not greatly   Politian iii 61
Be still!—it comes again
Politian iii 69
'T is hushed and all is still. All is not still   Politian iii 86
Still will I not descend
Politian iii 111

And still I speak of love
Politian iv 8
And still   Politian iv 49
And still together—together
Politian iv 50
So that now, to still the beating of my heart, I stood repeating   Raven 15
Let my heart be still a moment and this mystery explore   Raven 35
But the Raven still beguiling my sad fancy into smiling   Raven 67
"Prophet!" said I, "thing of evil!— prophet still, if bird or devil
Raven 85, 91
And the Raven, never flitting, still is sitting, still is sitting   Raven 103
Shall overshadow thee: be still
Spirits 10
The breeze—the breath of God—is still
Spirits 23
Burn'd with a still intenser glow
Tamerlane 71
To him who would look upon
Tamerlane 193
But left its influence with me still
Tamerlane (1827) 101
We still were young: no purer thought
Tamerlane (1827) 151
For passionate love is still divine
Tamerlane (1827) 153
The soul, which knows such power, will still   Tamerlane (1827) 193
Where in a deep, still slumber lay
Tamerlane (1827) 285
Which, ideal, still may be
Tamerlane (1827) 304
I still was young; and well I ween
Tamerlane (1827) 353
My eyes were still on pomp and power
Tamerlane (1827) 355
Yet still I think these worse than them a little   Tempora 8
Still form a synonym for truth. Cease trying   Valentine 19

Stillness

But the silence was unbroken, and the stillness gave no token   Raven 27
Startled at the stillness broken by reply so aptly spoken   Raven 61

Stilly

From Balbec, and the stilly, clear abyss
Al Aaraaf ii 37
In its stilly melody   Lake (1827) 10

Sting

Whom thou hast cherished to sting thee to the soul   Politian ii 59

Stir

But lo, a stir is in the air   City 42
Where no wind dared to stir, unless on tiptoe   Helen[2] 10

Stirred

She stirr'd not—breath'd not—for a voice was there   Al Aaraaf i 122
No footstep stirred: the hated world all slept   Helen[2] 25
Stirred by the autumn wind
Politian iv 58

Strangely
For strangely—fearfully in this hall
                              Irene 39
Her pallor I strangely mistrust
                              Ulalume 53
Stranger
While the moon danc'd with the fair
    stranger light   Al Aaraaf ii 10
Stray
If they should stray from thee
                              Sarah 24
Stranger
Stranger thy glorious length of tress
                          Sleeper (1842) 35
Stream
By this clear stream
                      Al Aaraaf i (1831) 5
Flow softly—gently—vital stream
                              Louisa 1
For in his heart, as in thy stream
                              River 11
Beside a murm'ring stream   Sarah 3
Streamer
'Neath blue-bell or streamer
                          Al Aaraaf ii 68
Streaming
With tears are streaming wet
                          Lenore (1843) 16
And the lamp-light o'er him streaming
    throws his shadow on the floor
                              Raven 106
Streamlet
The silvery streamlet gurgling on
                              Sarah 7
Streams
Streams up the turrets silently   City 15
By what eternal streams   Paradise 26
Street
And daily strut the street with bows and
    scrapes   Tempora 33
Streets
For public insult in the streets—before
                          Politian v 86
Strength
I am shorn of my strength   Annie 8
I feel ye now—I feel ye in your strength
                          Coliseum 12
And, as his strength   Eldorado 13
Stricken
I am star-stricken with thine eyes
                      Fairy-Land (1831) 5
Through the terror-stricken sky   Nis 40
Or the stricken eagle soar   Paradise 20
Striding
Striding o'er empires haughtily
                          Tamerlane 175
Strife
As in that fleeting, shadowy, misty strife
                              Dreams 30
And, I believe, the winged strife
                          Tamerlane 38
Now as I look back, the strife
                      Tamerlane (1827) 172
The strife of nations and redeem
                      Tamerlane (1827) 238
Strike
I strike—the murmur sent   Paean 30

Strike thou home   Politian v 80
Strike home   Politian v 82
String
Unless it trembled with the string
                          Romance (1831) 45
With a strange sound, as of a harp-string
    broken   Stanzas[1] 23
Strings
Whose heart-strings are a lute   Israfel 2
Of those unusual strings   Israfel 22
Unless it trembled with the strings
                          Romance 21
Lie dead on my heart-strings   To M 15
Strive
I'd strive for liberty no more
                          Divine Right 3
But Octavia do not strive to rob
                              Octavia 6
Striven
That high tone of the spirit which hath
    striv'n   Stanzas[1] 29
And a proud spirit which hath striven
                          Tamerlane 33
Strong
Then my soul strong memories sendeth
                          Departed 15
Shines, bright and strong   Eulalie 18
And is thy heart so strong
                    Politian iii 70, 74, 83, 93
Is it so strong   Politian iii 79
Stronger
But our love it was stronger by far than
    the love   Annabel Lee 27
Presently my soul grew stronger; hesi-
    tating then no longer   Raven 19
Strove
My spirit struggled with, and strove
                          Tamerlane 113
Struggle
Can struggle to its destin'd eminence
                          Al Aaraaf i 23
In vain I struggle to forget   Octavia 3
My spirit struggled with, and strove
                          Tamerlane 113
Struggling
From struggling with the waters of the
    Rhone   Al Aaraaf i 75
Strut
And daily strut the street with bows and
    scrapes   Tempora 33
Studied
Has studied very little of his part
                          Elizabeth 9
Stuff
Yet heavier far than your Petrarchan
    stuff   Enigma 6
Stupid
But if he won't he shall, the stupid elf
                          Tempora 90
Stygian
Let the bell toll '—a saintly soul floats
    on the Stygian river   Lenore 2
Style
I'm apt to be discursive in my style
                          Tempora 37

Subject
No subject vice dare interfere
      Divine Right 7
Sublime
From a wild weird clime that lieth, sublime
      Dream-Land 7
How dark a wo! yet how sublime a hope
      Helen² 44
Sublunary
For we cannot help agreeing that no sublunary being Raven (A. W. R.) 51

Succeeding
Succeeding years, too wild for song
      Romance (1831) 11
Succeeds
Succeeds the glories of the bowl
      Romance (1831) 53
Such
Of flowers: of lilies such as rear'd the head Al Aaraaf i 43
Such as the drowsy shepherd on his bed
      Al Aaraaf ii 2
Uprear'd upon such height arose a pile
      Al Aaraaf ii 11
Of molten stars their pavement, such as fall   Al Aaraaf ii 16
In just such a bed   Annie 52
Such dreariness a heaven at all
      City (1831) 19
Of power! said I? yes! such I ween
      Happiest Day 5
Tun'd to such solemn song Paean 18
Such language holds the solemn sea
      Paradise 17
Would have given a real diamond to such as you Politian ii 54
In such a cause Politian v 72
With such name as " Nevermore."
      Raven 54
In such an hour, when are forgot
      Sarah 19
As such it well may pass Song 10
A passionate light—such for his spirit was fit   Stanzas¹ 6
Such father, is not (now) my theme
      Tamerlane 2
But such is not a gift of thine
      Tamerlane 12
'T was such as angel minds above
      Tamerlane 88
And murmur'd at such lowly lot
      Tamerlane 132
But mystically—in such guise
      Tamerlane 146
Such as in infancy was mine
      Tamerlane (1827) 110
Ev'n such as from th' accursed time
      Tamerlane (1827) 145
With such as mine—that mystic flame
      Tamerlane (1827) 158
The soul, which knows such power, will still Tamerlane (1827) 193
With thoughts such feeling can command
      Tamerlane (1827) 256
With glory—such as might inspire
      Tamerlane (1827) 273

And in such follies had no part
      Tamerlane (1827) 404
But speak to him, he'll make you such grimace   Tempora 63
A feeling such as mine To⁴ 34
Such squalid wit to honourable rhyme
      To Margaret 4
Such eager eyes, there lies, I say, perdu
      Valentine 14
Suddenly
While I nodded, nearly napping, suddenly there came a tapping Raven 3
Lying down to die, have suddenly arisen
      To MLS 9
Suit
With thy burning measures suit
      Israfel 36
Ill suit the like with old Di Broglio's heir
      Politian i 21
Suitors
The hum of suitors—and the tone
      Tamerlane 63
Sullen
A sullen hopelessness of heart
      Tamerlane (1827) 369
Sullenness
There comes a sullenness of heart
      Tamerlane 192
Sulphurous
Their sulphurous currents down Yaanek
      Ulalume 16
Sultan
And the sultan-like pines that towered around   Lake (1831) 6
And the sultan-like pines that tower'd around Tamerlane (1831) 84
Sultriness
With quietude, and sultriness, and slumber   Helen² 7
Summer
All a long summer night
      Al Aaraaf (1831) 3
Sound loves to revel in a summer night
      Al Aaraaf ii 40
I' the summer sky, in dreams of living light   Dreams 14
By that summer breeze unbrok'n
      Spirits (1827) 25
As dew of the night-time, o'er the summer grass   Stanzas¹ 16
'T was noontide of summer Star 1
And the sunshine of my summer hours
      Tamerlane 22
The glory of the summer sun
      Tamerlane 194
And boyhood is a summer sun
      Tamerlane 207
As perfume of strange summer flow'rs
      Tamerlane (1827) 139
The livelong summer day, oppress
      Tamerlane (1827) 212
One noon of a bright summer's day
      Tamerlane (1827) 283
The summer dream beneath the tamarind tree   To Science 14
The summer's dream beneath the tamarind tree To Science (1830) 14

Summits

And mountains, around whose towering
summits the winds
Politian iv 71

Summons

Heard not the stirring summons of that
hymn　Al Aaraaf ii 175

Sun

And Clytia pondering between many a
sun　Al Aaraaf i 68

Link'd to a little system and one sun
Al Aaraaf i 134

What tho' in worlds which own a single
sun　Al Aaraaf i 139

The sun-ray dropp'd, in Lemnos, with a
spell　Al Aaraaf ii 203

From the sun that round me roll'd
Alone 15

As melody from Memnon to the Sun
Coliseum 36

For I have revell'd, when the sun was
bright　Dreams 13

Venuses, unextinguished by the sun
Helen² 66

There the sun doth reel by day　Nis 45

From the sun and stars, whence he had
drawn forth　Stanzas¹ 5

'T was sunset: when the sun will part
Tamerlane 191

The glory of the summer sun
Tamerlane 194

And boyhood is a summer sun
Tamerlane 207

Familiarly—whom Fortune's sun
Tamerlane (1827) 263

That loveliness around: the sun
Tamerlane (1827) 318

My heart sunk with the sun's ray
Tamerlane (1827) 365

The sacred sun—of all who, weeping,
bless thee　To MLS 4

And put out the sun　Triumph 8

The red sun-light lazily lay　Valley 8

Sung

Come, let the burial rite be read—the
funeral song be sung　Lenore 5

How shall the ritual, then, be read—the
requiem how be sung　Lenore 10

Sunk

My heart sunk with the sun's ray
Tamerlane (1827) 365

Sunken

Of sunken runs at eve—at noon of night
Al Aaraaf ii 9

It speaks of sunken eyes, and wasted
cheeks　Politian ii 65

Sunlit

Into the sunlit ether, caught the ray
Al Aaraaf ii 8

Sunniest

Than young Hope in his sunniest hour
hath known　Dreams 34

Sunny

In Trebizond—and on a sunny flower
Al Aaraaf i 56

Suns

Near four bright suns—a temporary rest
Al Aaraaf i 18

Of sunken suns at eve—at noon of night
Al Aaraaf ii 9

Sunset

'T was sunset: when the sun will part
Tamerlane 191

By sunset did its mountains rise
Tamerlane (1827) 362

Sunshine

In sunshine and in shadow
Eldorado 3

Is the sunshine of ours　Israfel 44

A fairy land of flowers, and fruit, and
sunshine　Politian iv 69

And sunshine of my summer hours
Tamerlane 22

And, when the friendly sunshine smil'd
Tamerlane 99

For 'mid that sunshine and those smiles
Tamerlane 103

The sunshine, and the calm—the ideal
Tamerlane (1827) 167

Supremacy

Of its own self supremacy
Tamerlane (1827) 181

Supreme

A Power august, benignant and supreme
Politian iii 36

Surcease

From my books surcease from sorrow—
sorrow for the lost—Lenore　Raven 10

Sure

O spells more sure than e'er Judaean king
Coliseum 13

I'm sure, Madam, you need not
Politian ii 47

For he's sure the Count Castiglione never
Politian ii 53

So that the blade be keen—the blow be
sure　Politian iv 104

That I scarce was sure I heard you "—
here I opened wide the door　Raven 23

" Though thy crest be shorn and shaven,
thou," I said, " art sure no craven
Raven 45

Sure thou art come o'er far-off seas
Sleeper 32

And be sure it will lead us aright
Ulalume 68

That motley drama—oh, be sure
Worm 17

Surely

Elizabeth, it surely is most fit
Elizabeth 1

Surely I live　Politian iii 6

Surely I never heard—yet it were well
Politian iii 58

I heed thee, and will surely stay
Politian iii 109

" Surely," said I, " surely that is something at my window lattice　Raven 33

It is not surely sin to name
Tamerlane (1827) 157

Swellings
No swellings tell that winds may be
City 38

Swells
How it swells   Bells 27
How the danger sinks and swells Bells 64
And his merry bosom swells   Bells 93
How fairy-like a melody there swells
Bells (1849) 4

Swift
The swift and silent lizard of the stone
Coliseum 25
Swift dart across her brain   Louisa 10

Swiftly
And fell—not swiftly as I rose before
Al Aaraaf ii 236

Swinging
To the swinging and the ringing   Bells 31

Swollen
Thy swollen pillars tremble—and so
quake   Al Aaraaf ii (1829) 41

Sworn
But then I might have sworn it
Politian ii 51
But I might have sworn it
Politian ii 56
'T is sworn   Politian ii 113

Swung
To-day (the wind blew, and) it swung
Fairy-Land (1831) 14
Swung by seraphim whose foot-falls
tinkled on the tufted floor   Raven 80

Syllable
This I sat engaged in guessing, but no
syllable expressing   Raven 73

Syllables
The words—the syllables
Valentine (1849) 8

Symbol
The deed—the vow—the symbol of the
deed   Politian ii 105
Is a symbol and a token   Spirits 26
T'awake us—'T is a symbol and a token
Stanzas[1] 24

Syne
For being an idle boy lang syne
Romance (1831) 19

Synonym
Still form a synonym for truth. Cease
trying   Valentine 19

Syria
Than all Syria can furnish of wine
Latin Hymn 12

Syriac
And a Syriac tale there is   Nis 8

System
Link'd to a little system and one sun
Al Aaraaf i 134

Table
What shall be done? I'll lay it on the
table   Tempora 23

Tadmor
Friezes from Tadmor and Perseopolis
Al Aaraaf ii 36

Taglay
The mists of the Taglay have shed
Tamerlane 36
In vallies of the wild Taglay
Tamerlane (1827) 357

Tailed
And dove-tailed coat, obtained at cost;
while then   Tempora 67

Taint
From the evil taint of clouds?—and he
did say   Politian v 27

Tainted
Thy wife, and with a tainted memory
Politian iv 27

Take
Take this kiss upon the brow
Dream w. Dream 1
Indignant from the tomb doth take
Irene 47
Louisa, take thy scorn   Louisa 14
To take thee at thy word
Politian v 84
Take thy beak from out my heart, and
take thy form from off my door
Raven 101
A conscious slumber seems to take
Sleeper 14
To take things seriously or all in jest
Tempora 12
And take the matter up when I'm more
able   Tempora 24
But take it generally upon the whole
Tempora 44
I think he'll take this likeness to himself
Tempora 89
Thy gentlest of all names dost take
Zante 2

Taken
Whose sleep hath been taken
Al Aaraaf ii 150
From the same source I have not taken
Alone 5
Lest an evil step be taken
Bridal Ballad 31
A portrait taken after death
Tamerlane 206
As Members say they like their logic
taken   Tempora 45

Taking
But, taking one by each hand, merely
growl   Tempora 28

Tale
What a tale of terror, now, their turbu-
lency tells   Bells 38
What a tale their terror tells   Bells 52
And a Syriac tale there is   Nis 8
Again!—a similar tale   Politian ii 15
A tale—a pretty tale—and heed thou not
Politian ii 63
A tale the world but knows too well
Tamerlane (1827) 350

Talents
Zanthippe's talents had enforced so well
Acrostic 4

Talisman
Divine—a talisman—an amulet
Valentine 6

Talk
Our talk has been serious and sober
Ulalume 20

Tall
And the tall pines that towered around
Lake 6
Thro' tall tulips overhead Nis (1836) 24
For her may some tall vault unfold
Sleeper 49

Tally
And the deed's register should tally,
father   Politian ii 106
My seared and blighted name, how would
it tally   Politian iv 28

Tamarind
The summer dream beneath the tamarind
tree   To Science 14

Tamerlane
The bride and queen of Tamerlane
Tamerlane (1827) 282
To the young Tamerlane—to me
Tamerlane (1831) 182

Tangles
In the tangles of Love's very hair
Tamerlane 243

Tantalized
My tantalized spirit   Annie 53

Tape
The pretty little hand that sold her tape
Tempora 56

Tapping
While I nodded, nearly napping, suddenly
there came a tapping   Raven 3
" 'T is some visitor," I muttered, " tapping at my chamber door   Raven 5
And so faintly you came tapping, tapping
at my chamber door   Raven 22
Soon again I heard a tapping somewhat
louder than before   Raven 32

Target
His target was the crescent shell
Parody 8

Tarn
It was down by the dank tarn of Auber
Ulalume 8
We remembered not the dank tarn of
Auber   Ulalume 28
Well I know, now, this dank tarn of
Auber   Ulalume 93

Tarns
By the dismal tarns and pools
Dream-Land 29

Taste
Let us go forth and taste the fragrant
air   Politian i 65

Tattered
Which thro' some tatter'd curtain pries
Fairy-Land (1831) 32

Taught
Taught in the gardens of Gethsemane
Coliseum 14
Taught me my alphabet to say
Romance 7

Pure—as her young example taught
Tamerlane 93
My phrenzy to her bosom taught
Tamerlane (1827) 150

Taunt
Before all Rome, I'li taunt thee, villain—
I'll taunt thee   Politian v 90

Teach
Could teach or bribe me to define
Lake 16

Tear
And, Guy De Vere, hast thou no tear?—
weep now or never more   Lenore 3
To the lov'd object—so the tear to the lid
Stanzas¹ 18
So tear down the temples   Triumph 7

Tearful
Some human memories and tearful lore
Silence 8

Tears
While pettish tears adown her petals run
Al Aaraaf i 69
Unguided Love hath fallen—'mid " tears
of perfect moan   Al Aaraaf ii 181
They remember'd not our tears Ballad 6
Vain, oh! vain, are tears and wailing
Departed 21
For the tears that drip all over
Dream-Land 12
For the tears that drip all over
Fairy-Land 4
As long—as tears on Memory's eye
Irene 44
With tears are streaming wet
Lenore (1843) 16
Weep not! oh, sob not thus!—thy bitter
tears   Politian iv 5
And pour my spirit out in tears
Tamerlane 107
It is not that my founts of bliss are gush-
ing—strange with tears   To M 10
She has seen that the tears are not dry on
Ulalume 42
Perennial tears descend in gems
Valley 27
They wave; they weep; and the tears, as
they well   Valley (1845) 28
In veils, and drowned in tears Worm 4

Teeth
Be always throwing those jewels in my
teeth   Politian ii 48

Tell
No swellings tell that winds may be
City 38
Do tell! when may we hope to make men
of sense out of the Pundits
Experiments 7
And the giddy stars (so legends tell
Israfel 5
They tell me (while they speak
Paean 13
Fair mirror and true! now tell me (for
thou canst   Politian ii 62
I tell thee, holy man   Politian ii 101
Tell me what thy lordly name is on the
Night's Plutonian shore!   Raven 47

On this home by horror haunted—tell me
   truly, I implore   Raven 88
Is there—is there balm in Gilead?—tell
   me—tell me, I implore   Raven 89
Tell this soul with sorrow laden if, within
   the distant Aidenn   Raven 93
I have no words—alas!—to tell
                 Tamerlane 75
T' awake her, and a falsehood tell
         Tamerlane (1827) 289
With Nature, in her wild paths; tell
         Tamerlane (1827) 312
It boots me not, good friar, to tell
         Tamerlane (1827) 349
If I can tell exactly what about
                Tempora 80
But they tell thee I am proud   To⁴ 29

Telling
Came hurriedly upon me, telling
               Tamerlane 49
Of her wond'rous ways and telling bless
         Tamerlane (1827) 313

Tells
On the Future!—how it tells   Bells 29
What at tale of terror, now, their turbu-
   lency tells   Bells 38
What a tale their terror tells   Bells 52
Yet the ear distinctly tells   Bells 61

Tempest
Thro' many a tempest, but she rode
            Al Aaraaf i 108
Whether Tempter sent, or whether tem-
   pest tossed thee here ashore Raven 86
Get thee back into the tempest and the
   Night's Plutonian shore   Raven 98
My spirit with the tempest strove
         Tamerlane (1827) 146

Tempests
With the tempests as they toss
             Fairy-Land 32

Temple
Was a proud temple call'd the Parthenon
           Al Aaraaf ii 215

Temples
There open temples—open graves
           City (1831) 33
So tear down the temples   Triumph 7

Temporary
Near four bright suns—a temporary rest
            Al Aaraaf 118

Tempt
Tempt the waters from their bed
              City 35
Thine eyes are wild—tempt not the wrath
   divine   Politian ii 110

Tempted
Am I not—am I not sorely—grievously
   tempted   Politian v 83
And tempted her out of her gloom
             Ulalume 73
Oh, what demon hath tempted me here
             Ulalume 90

Tempter
Whether Tempter sent, or whether tempest tossed thee here ashore Raven 86

Ten
The pulse beats ten and intermits
             Physician 1
When falsehood wore a ten-fold crime
        Tamerlane (1827) 190
One settled fact is better than ten sages
             Tempora 78

Tenanted
By good angels tenanted   Palace 2

Tenantless
Leave tenantless thy crystal home, and
   fly   Al Aaraaf i 143
Tenantless cities of the desert too
           Al Aaraaf 224

Tenderly
She tenderly kissed me   Annie 73
I lov'd—and O, how tenderly
        Tamerlane (1827) 108

Tenderness
The tenderness of years   Ballad 8

Tent
Videlicet, a tent   Fairy-Land 37

Terminates
To where the prospect terminates—thee
   only   To¹ 27

Terms
Can find, among their burning terms of
   love   Mother 3

Terrible
The terrible and fair   Al Aaraaf i 84
Has abated—the terrible   Annie 33
The wild—the terrible conspire
            Tamerlane 163

Terror
What a tale of terror, now, their turbu-
   lency tells   Bells 38
What a tale their terror tells   Bells 52
To the terror of the lone lake   Lake 12
Yet that terror was not fright   Lake 13
Through the terror-stricken sky   Nis 40
Thro' the terror-stricken sky
             Nis (1836) 38
To the terror of that lone lake
          Tamerlane (1831) 90
Yet that terror was not fright
          Tamerlane (1831) 91
In the terror of my lot   To⁴ 36
In terror she spoke, letting sink her
             Ulalume 56

Terrorless
Render him terrorless: his name's " No
   More."   Silence 9

Terrors
Still think my terrors but the thunder
   cloud   Al Aaraaf i 136
Thrilled me—filled me with fantastic
   terrors never felt before   Raven 14

Test
Of witchery may test Al Aaraaf ii 153

Text
With thy dear name as text, though bidden by thee   To³ 18

Thank
Thank Heaven! the crisis   Annie 1

Theatre
Sit in a theatre, to see   Worm 5

Theme
Be now my theme
     Al Aaraaf i (1831) 4
I have been happy—and I love the theme
        Dreams 28
Such, father, is not (now) my theme
        Tamerlane 2
Shall be an endless theme of praise
        To FSO 7

Thence
Thence sprang I—as the eagle from his
  tower   Al Aaraaf ii 219
For him who thence could solace bring
        Lake 20

Theresaean
Her way—but left not yet her Therasaean
  reign   Al Aaraaf i 158

Thereabout
And every sculptur'd cherub thereabout
       Al Aaraaf ii 32
Thereabout which Time hath said Nis 9

Thereat
Let me see, then, what thereat is, and
  this mystery explore   Raven 34

Thereby
Thereby, in heat of anger, to address
       Politian v 50

Therefore
Is it therefore the less gone
     Dream w. Dream 9
Therefore, thou art not wrong
       Israfel 29
Therefore by that dear name I long have
  called you   Mother 5
Therefore, to thee this night Paean 41
Is it, therefore, the less gone
     Tamerlane (1831) 248

Therein
Of the pale cloud therein, whose hue
     Tamerlane (1827) 320
In dreams of thee, and therein knows
       To F 6

Theses
Employed in even the theses of the school
       Elizabeth 13

Thick
My thick pulses hastily beating
       Departed 5

Thing
Each hindering thing Al Aaraaf ii 93
Over every drowsy thing
       Fairy-Land 24
Like—almost anything Fairy-Land 33
So like a thing alive you know
     Fairy-Land (1831) 16
Hast thou a crucifix fit for this thing
       Politian ii 98
The unsatisfactory and ideal thing
       Politian iv 32
Of nothing which might warrant thee in
  this thing   Politian v 54
Prophet!" said I, "thing of evil!—
  prophet still, if bird or devil
       Raven 85, 91
To while away—forbidden thing
     Romance (1831) 43

In every tuneful thing around
       Sarah 5
From the thing that lies hidden in these
  wolds   Ulalume 100
A blood-red thing that writhes from out
       Worm 27

Things
All Nature speaks, and ev'n ideal things
       Al Aaraaf i 128
Yet silence came upon material things
       Al Aaraaf ii 64
Are the music of things
       Al Aaraaf ii 126
All hindering things
     Al Aaraaf ii (1843) 93
Things past and to come Departed 28
On things around him with a ray
       Dream 7
To the delirious eye, more lovely things
       Dreams 32
Always write first things uppermost in
  the heart   Elizabeth 16
Through all the flimsy things we see at
  once   Enigma 3
Never-contented things Fairy-Land 44
And in an instant all things disappeared
       Helen² 29
And the other listening things
       Israfel 17
All things lovely—are not they
       Nis 5
All about unhappy things   Nis 14
But evil things, in robes of sorrow
       Palace 33
Think of eternal things Politian ii 75
Throw over all things a gloom
       Politian iv 64
To while away—forbidden things
       Romance 19
There are some qualities—some incorpor-
  ate things   Silence 1
Two separate—yet most intimate things
       Tamerlane 126
From the most unpolluted things
       Tamerlane 235
To take things seriously or all in jest
       Tempora 12
That things should stare us boldly in the
  face   Tempora 32
Who alterest all things with thy peering
  eyes   To Science 2
At bidding of vast formless things
       Worm 13

Think
Still think my terrors but the thunder
  cloud   Al Aaraaf i 136
Which I think extravagant
       Fairy-Land 38
I think not so—her infelicity
       Politian ii 19
Think of eternal things Politian ii 75
Think of thy precious soul
       Politian ii 83
Think of my early days!—think of my
  father   Politian ii 84
And mother in Heaven! think of our
  quiet home   Politian ii 85

Think of my little sisters!—think of them
      Politian ii 87
And think of me—think of my trusting
 love   Politian ii 88
And confidence—his vows—my ruin—
 think—think   Politian ii 89
I will think of it Politian v 40
Think not to fly me thus Politian v 85
I think I hear thy voice's sound Sarah 4
Thrilling to think, poor shild of sin
       Sleeper 59
Thou can'st not—would'st not dare to
 think   Tamerlane (1827) 103
I will not madly think that power
     Tamerlane (1831) 3
Yet still I think these worse than them
 a little   Tempora 8
For he does think, although I'm oft in
 doubt   Tempora 79
I think he'll take this likeness to himself
      Tempora 89
I cannot write—I cannot speak or think
       To³ 19
I laugh to think how poor To⁴ 37
And think that these weak lines are
 written by him To MLS 16
By him who, as he pens them, thrills to
 think   To MLS 17

Thinking
 Thinking me dead Annie 18, 94
Thinking him dead D'Elormie
     Bridal Ballad 18
And little given to thinking
      Politian i 53
Fancy unto fancy, thinking what this
 ominous bird of yore Raven 70
I've been a thinking, isn't that the phrase
      Tempora 9
I've been a thinking, whether it were best
      Tempora 11

Thirst
 Torture of thirst Annie 34
That quenches all thirst Annie 38
Of weary pilgrimage and burning thirst
      Coliseum 5
Thirst for the springs of lore that in thee
 lie   Coliseum 6

Thistle
 Waved to the wind, now wave the reed
 and thistle   Coliseum 21

Thither
 And Valisnerian lotus thither flown
     Al Aaraaf i 74
Fly thither with me
    Politian iv 76, 86
And thither and thither fly Worm 11

Thitherward
 Headlong thitherward o'er the starry sea
     Al Aaraaf ii 256

Thorn
 The mock-bird chirping on the thorn
      Sarah 8

Thought
 And here, in thought, to thee
     Al Aaraaf i 110
In thought that can alone
     Al Aaraaf i 111

And this maiden she lived with no other
 thought   Annabel Lee 5
With the thought of the light Annie 101
What a world of solemn thought their
 monody compels Bells 72
Of mine own thought—what more could I
 have seen   Dreams 18
Some gentle wind hath thought it right
      Irene 31
With a wild, and wakıng thought
     Imitation 6
With a thought I then did cherish
     Imitation 20
When from your gems of thought I turn
     Impromptu 1
Whose wild'ring thought could even make
     Lake (1827) 22
In the monarch Thought's dominion
      Palace 5
I thought not of the jewels
     Politian ii 50
'T is strange!—'t is very strange—me
 thought the voice Politian iii 107
But its thought thou can'st not banish
     Spirits 22
Hath ever told—or is it of a thought
     Stanzas¹ 13
Beneath the eternal sky of Thought
     Stanzas² 24
It was but man, I thought, who shed
     Tamerlane 58
On which my every hope and thought
     Tamerlane 90
I had not thought, until this hour
    Tamerlane (1827) 17
Or thought, save of the passing scene
    Tamerlane (1827) 77
We still were young: no purer thought
    Tamerlane (1827) 151
All that I felt, or saw, or thought,
    Tamerlane (1827) 175
'T were folly now to veil a thought
    Tamerlane (1827) 183
That kindling thought—did not the beam
    Tamerlane (1827) 210
There—in that hour—a thought came o'er
    Tamerlane (1827) 234
Who, that had known the secret thought
    Tamerlane (1827) 247
Perforce, a passing thought of one
    Tamerlane (1827) 274
Awake, that I had held a thought
    Tamerlane (1827) 295
As to the seat of thought in man and
 brute   Tempora 74
For that the power of thought attend the
 latter   Tempora 75
Another proof of thought, I'm not mis-
 taken   Tempora 86
A thought arose within the human brain
       To³ 4
Unthought-like thoughts that are the
 souls of thought To³ 12

Thoughts
 Those thoughts I would control
     Imitation 13

Till thoughts and locks are left, alas
                  Irene 7
Where deep thoughts are a duty
                  Israfel 24
They seem to whisper thoughts of love
                  Sarah 10
To guide my wandering thoughts to
  heaven   Sarah 23
Our thoughts, our souls—O God above
                Serenade 24
'Mid dark thoughts of the gray tomb-
  stone   Spirits 2
Now are thoughts thou shalt not banish
                Spirits 19
With thoughts such feeling can command
        Tamerlane (1827) 256
O God! when the thoughts that may not
  pass   Tamerlane (1827) 323
Unthought-like thoughts that are the
  souls of thought   To³ 12
But our thoughts they were palsied and
  sere   Ulalume 21
How many thoughts of what entombed
  hopes   Zante 6

Thousand
A thousand seraphs burst th' Empyrean
  thro'   Al Aaraaf ii 157
Hell, rising from a thousand thrones
                City 52
Upon the upturn'd faces of a thousand
              Helen² 8
A thousand, a thousand, a thousand
         Latin Hymn 1, 2
A thousand, a thousand, a thousand, a
  thousand   Latin Hymn 4
Sing a thousand over again
          Latin Hymn 5
Who knocked over a thousand so fine
          Latin Hymn 8
His cloak, of a thousand mingled hues
             Parody 5
A thousand hearts—losing at length her
  own   Politian ii 24
A thousand leagues within the golden
  west   Politian iv 68
And shouting with a thousand rills
          Tamerlane 144

Thrace
Democritus of Thrace, who used to toss
  over   Tempora 16

Three
Three eloquent words, oft uttered in the
  hearing   Valentine (1849) 15

Threshold
A voice came from the threshold stone
         Tamerlane 217
Threshold of the wide-open gate of
  dreams   To³ 22

Threw
As she threw off her cloak, yon moon
        Fairy-Land (1831) 22

Thrill
O! nothing earthly save the thrill
         Al Aaraaf i 5

Nor thrill to think, poor child of sin
        Sleeper (1842) 60
Or that the thrill of a single kiss
            To M 11

Thrilled
Thrilled me—filled me with fantastic
  terrors never felt before   Raven 14

Thrilling
Had I but heard it with its thrilling tones
           Politian iii 59
Thrilling to think, poor child of sin
           Sleeper 59
To her soft thrilling voice: To part
        Tamerlane (1827) 292
And thrilling as I see upon the right
            To³ 24

Thrillingly
Thrillingly, holily   Experiments 3

Thrills
Thrills with intenser love than I for thee
          Politian iv 17
By him who, as he pens them, thrills to
  think   To MLS 17

Thrive
Nor that the grass—O! may it thrive
            To M 17

Throats
From the rust within their throats
            Bells 77
From their deep-toned throats
         Bells (1849) 14
From the melancholy throats
         Bells (1849) 16

Throb
The mournful hope that every throb
          Octavia 8

Throbbing
With that horrible throbbing Annie 22
Horrible throbbing   Annie 24
To the throbbing of the bells Bells 102
I'd throw me on her throbbing breast
          Tamerlane 106
Some ocean throbbing far and free
            To F 11

Throne
From their pride and from their throne
         Al Aaraaf i 92
A partner of thy throne
        Al Aaraaf i 113
Lo! Death has reared himself a throne
            City 1
Here, where on golden throne the monarch
  lolled   Coliseum 22
Here, where on golden throne the Caesar
  sate   Coliseum (1842) 22
Her bosom is an ivory throne
         Divine Right 5
On a black throne reigns upright
        Dream-Land 4, 54
From thy holy throne above
        Hymn (1833) 4
From moan and groan to a golden throne
  beside the King of Heaven
          Lenore 22
Round about a throne where, sitting,
  Porphyrogene   Palace 21

And vows before the throne
                              Politian ii 93
Tho' not with Faith—with godliness—
  whose throne   Stanzas¹ 30
Amid the jewels of my throne
                              Tamerlane 18
Of flattery round a sovereign's throne
                              Tamerlane 64
A cottager, I mark'd a throne
                              Tamerlane 130
Seem'd to become a queenly throne
                              Tamerlane 152
Shall form the pedestal of a throne
                              Tamerlane 172
And my proud hopes had reached a
  throne   Tamerlane (1827) 348

Thrones
Hell, rising from a thousand thrones
                              City 52
Up thrones—up long-forgotten bowers
                              City (1831) 24
Of more than thrones in heaven
                              Paean 40
From their high thrones in the heaven
                              Spirits 13

Throng
A hideous throng rush out forever
                              Palace 47
An angel throng, bewinged, bedight
                              Worm 3

Throw
Throw over all things a gloom
                              Politian iv 64
And used to throw my earthly rest
                              Romance (1831) 29
I'd throw me on her throbbing breast
                              Tamerlane 106
To gain an empire, and throw down
                              Tamerlane (1827) 243
And, lest the guessing throw the fool in
  fits   Tempora 91

Throwing
Be always throwing those jewels in my
  teeth   Politian ii 48

Thrown
Thrown back from flowers) of Beauty's
  eye   Al Aaraaf i 2
As if the towers had thrown aside
                              City (1831) 45
But when the Night had thrown her pall
                              Lake 7
Against whose portal she hath thrown
                              Sleeper 55
Had thrown her mantle over me
                              Tamerlane 158
But when the night had thrown her pall
                              Tamerlane (1831) 85

Throws
She throws aside the sceptre—leaves the
  helm   Al Aaraaf i 27
And the lamp-light o'er him streaming
  throws his shadow on the floor
                              Raven 106

Thrust
As if the towers had thrust aside
                              City 44

Thule
From an ultimate dim Thule
                              Dream-Land 6

Thunder
Still think my terrors but the thunder
  cloud   Al Aaraaf i 136
From the thunder, and the storm
                              Alone 19
Into a western couch of thunder-cloud
                              Helen² 49
Shall bloom the thunder-blasted tree
                              Paradise 19
With tumult as they thunder by
                              Romance 13
Lay bare, thro' vistas thunder-riven
                              Romance (1831) 15

Thundered
With tumult as they thundered by
                              Romance (1831) 37

Thunders
And the deep trumpet-thunder's roar
                              Tamerlane 48

Thus
But ah! not so when, thus, in realms on
  high   Al Aaraaf i 130
She seem'd not thus upon that autumn
  eve   Al Aaraaf ii 200
Thus, in discourse, the lovers whiled away
                              Al Aaraaf ii 261
And thus the words were spoken
                              Bridal Ballad 20
And thus they said I plighted
                              Bridal Ballad (1837) 19
By the lakes that thus outspread
                              Dream-Land 21
And thus the sad Soul that here passes
                              Dream-Land 49
Thus much let me avow
                              Dream w. Dream 3
In my young boyhood—should it thus be
  giv'n   Dream 11
Thus hums the moon within her ear
                              Irene 25
Peccavimus; yet rave not thus! but let a
  Sabbath song   Lenore 13
And thus are dearer than the mother I
  knew   Mother 12
Thus on the coffin loud and long
                              Paean 29
Thus speaketh one Ferdinand in the
  word of the play   Politian ii 17
Thus endeth the history—and her maids
                              Politian ii 25
To see thee thus   Politian iii 7
As for to leave me thus
                              Politian iii 71, 75, 80, 84
Weep not, oh, sob not thus!—thy bitter
  tears   Politian iv 5
Thou askest me that—and thus I answer
  thee   Politian iv 12
Thus on my bended knee I answer thee
                              Politian iv 13
Should shake the firm spirit thus
                              Politian iv 62
And thus I clutch thee—thus
                              Politian iv 102

To break upon Time's monotone
                Romance (1831) 60
So sweet the hour, so calm the time
                Serenade 1
As dew of the night-time, o'er the summer
  grass   Stanzas[1] 16
Upon the rock-girt shore of time
                Stanzas[2] 12
And mid-time of night   Star 2
I have no time to dote or dream
                Tamerlane 6
The undying voice of that dead time
                Tamerlane 23
In that time of dreariness, will seem
                Tamerlane 204
Ev'n such as from th' accursed time
            Tamerlane (1827) 145
Which knows (believe me at this time
            Tamerlane (1827) 189
For short the time my high hope lent
            Tamerlane (1827) 269
Science! true daughter of old Time thou
  art   To Science 1

Times
Do err at time   Politian v 57
Oh Times! Oh Manners! It is my opinion
                Tempora 1
And as for times, although 't is said by
  many   Tempora 5
The " good old times " were far the worst
  of any   Tempora 6

Timid
A red Daedalion on the timid Earth
                Al Aaraaf ii 244
At least by sight, for I'm a timid man
                Tempora 61

Timour
And who her sovereign? Timour—he
                Tamerlane 173

Tiniest
No mote may shun—no tiniest fly
                Tamerlane 238

Tinkle
How they tinkle, tinkle, tinkle   Bells 4
Give a trickle and a tinkle and a knell
              Valley (1845) 30

Tinkled
Swung by seraphim whose foot-falls
  tinkled on the tufted floor   Raven 80

Tinkling
From the jingling and the tinkling of the
  bells   Bells 14
With a tinkling like a bell
            Fairy-Land (1831) 29

Tint
In its autumn tint of gold   Alone 16

Tinted
My tinted shadows rise and fall
                Irene 40

Tintinnabulation
To the tintinnabulation that so musically
  wells   Bells 11

Tintless
Are tintless of the yellow leaf
            Romance (1831) 62

Tints
With the moon-tints of purple and pearl
                Eulalie 11
With the morn-tints of purple and pearl
            Eulalie (1845) 11

Tiptoe
Where no wind dared to stir, unless on
  tiptoe   Helen[2] 10

Tire
With speed that may not tire
              Al Aaraaf i 96

Tired
So tired, so weary   Physician 7

Titan
And chasms, and caves, and Titan woods
              Dream-Land 10

Titanic
Here once, through an alley Titanic
              Ulalume 10

Titled
From Love to titled age and crime
            Paradise (1835) 29

Tittle
Of which sound doctrine I believe each
  tittle   Tempora 7

To
That shift the scenery to and fro
              Worm 14

Toad
Where the toad and the newt encamp
              Dream-Land 28

To-day
To-day (the wind blew, and) it swung
            Fairy-Land (1831) 14

Together
We have been boys together—school-
  fellows   Politian iii 32
Into the dust—so we descend together
              Politian iv 44
Descend together—and then—and then
  perchance   Politian iv 45
Arise together, Lalage, and roam
              Politian iv 47
And still together—together
              Politian iv 50
We grew in age—and love—together
              Tamerlane 96
We walk'd together on the crown
              Tamerlane 139

Toil
Its steady toil, its loyalty   Physician 4

Toils
Last night with many cares and toils
  oppress'd   Poetry 1

Token
Here is a ring as token
            Bridal Ballad 24
Behold the golden token
            Bridal Ballad 26
But the silence was unbroken, and the
  stillness gave no token   Raven 27
Leave no black plume as a token of that
  lie thy soul hath spoken   Raven 99
Is a symbol and token   Spirits 26

Seemed to have years too many
                    Politian ii 20
Ha! here at least's a friend—too much a
    friend   Politian ii 60
Pause ere too late!—on, be not—be not
    rash   Politian ii 111
Succeeding years, too wild for song
                    Romance (1831) 11
But now my soul hath too much room
                    Romance (1831) 46
Thus, while no single sound too rude
                    Serenade 22
Too cold—too cold for me   Star 11
I read, perhaps too carelessly
                    Tamerlane 149
Too well that I should let it be
                    Tamerlane 153
Too real, to his breast who lives
                    Tameralne (1827) 307
A tale the world but knows too well
                    Tamerlane (1827) 350
I'll mend my manners and my measures
    too   Tempora 40
Of poets, by poets; as the name is a poet's,
    too   Valentine 16

Took
And the cloud that took the form
                    Alone 20

Top
One by one from the tree top   Nis 33
Upon the quiet mountain top
                    Sleeper 6
The wanton airs, from the tree-top
                    Sleeper 20

Toppling
Mountains toppling evermore
                    Dream-Land 13

Tops
As if their tops had feebly given
                    City 46
As if the turret-tops had given
                    City (1831) 47
They wave:—from out their fragrant tops
                    Valley 24

Torch
Whose fervid, flick'ring torch of life was
    lit   Stanzas¹ 4

Tore
I tore it from its pride of place
                    Fairy-Land (1831) 17

Tormented
Of a surf-tormented shore
                    Dream w. Dream 13

Torn
Hast thou not torn the Naiad from her
    flood   To Science 12

Torrent
From the torrent, or the fountain
                    Alone 13
The torrent of the chilly air
                    Tamerlane 60

Torture
That torture the worst   Annie 32
Torture of thirst   Annie 34

Tortures
And of! of all tortures   Annie 31

Torturing
It still remaineth, torturing the bee
                    Al Aaraaf i 58

Toss
On the breezes to toss   Al Aaraaf ii 105
With the tempests as they toss
                    Fairy-Land 32
Democritus of Thrace, who used to toss
    over   Tempora 16
Toss back his fine curls from their fore-
    head fair   Tempoar 51

Tossed
Whether Tempter sent, or whether tem-
    pest tossed thee here ashore
                    Raven 86

Totter
Lets the stars totter in the guilt of man
                    Al Aaraaf i 150

Tottering
These crumbling walls; these tottering
    arcades   Coliseum (1831) 31
Tottering above   Israfel 8
I clamber'd to the tottering height
                    Tamerlane (1827) 352

Touch
Upon me with the touch of Hell
                    Tamerlane 43

Tower
Thence sprang I—as the eagle from his
    tower   Al Aaraaf ii 219
While from a proud tower in the town
                    City 28
The gay wall of this gaudy tower
                    Tamerlane (1827) 15

Towered
And the tall pines that towered around
                    Lake 6
When Hope, the eagle that tower'd, could
    see   Tamerlane 187
And the sultan-like pines that tower'd
    around   Tamerlane (1831) 84

Towering
Of rosy head, that towering far away
                    Al Aaraaf ii 7
And mountains, around whose towering
    summits the winds   Politian iv 71

Towers
There shrines and palaces and towers
                    City 6
Time-eaten towers that tremble not
                    City 7
As if the towers had thrust aside
                    City 44
While from the high towers of the town
                    City (1831) 27
Grey towers are mouldering into rest
                    Irene 11
Afar from its proud natural towers
                    Tamerlane 141
Nightly, from their azure towers
                    Valley 5

Town
On the long night-time of that town
                    City 13

But a tremulous delight   Lake 14;
                    Tamerlane (1831) 92
Let us on by this tremulous light
                    Ulalume 62

Tress
And the life upon each tress
                    Paean (1836) 28
Strange, above all, thy length of tress
                    Sleeper 35

Tresses
And shake from your tresses
                    Al Aaraaf ii 84
They are light on the tresses
                    Al Aaraaf ii 98
Of the tresses of Annie   Annie 72

Trial
A kind which, upon trial   Fairy-Land 13

Trickle
Give a trickle and a tinkle and a knell
                    Valley (1845) 30

Tried
Endymion, recollect, when Luna tried
                    Acrostic 7
Eagerly I wished the morrow;—vainly I
  had tried to borrow
                    Raven (1845) 9

Trifles
Of the trifles that it may   To¹ (1829) 12

Trim
Ah yes! his little foot and ancle trim
                    Tempora 81

Triumphant
Triumphant, o'er the crested palls
                    Sleeper 52

Triumphantly
Triumphantly with human kind
                    Tamerlane 34

Trivialest
The trivialest point, or you may lose your
  labor   Valentine 9

Trod
The last spot of Earth's orb I trod upon
                    Al Aaraaf ii 214
But the skies that angel trod
                    Israfel 23
That haunteth the lone regions where
  hath trod   Silence 14

Troop
A troop of Echoes, whose sweet duty
                    Palace 29

Tropic
Then roll'd like tropic storms along
                    Romance (1831) 12

Trouble
Sit down!—let not my presence trouble
  you   Politian ii 3
Dew in the night-time of my bitter trouble
                    Politian ii 33
Ah, this you'd have no trouble descrying
                    Valentine (1846) 19

Troubled
Dying along the troubled sky
                    Romance (1831) 14

Troublesome
Indeed, she is very troublesome
                    Politian ii 36

Truant
My soul, lest it should truant be
                    Hymn 7

True
Those kisses of true love
                    Al Aaraaf ii 90
And true love caresses
                    Al Aaraaf ii 96
Fair mirror and true! now tell me! for
  thou canst   Politian ii 62
Fair mirror and true! thou liest not
                    Politian ii 71
Thou true—he false!—false!—false
                    Politian ii 74
It is most true   Politian v 22
All this is very true   Politian v 23
Now this is true   Politian v 30
All very true   Politian v 31
It is—it is—most true
                    Politian v 72
So banished from true wisdom to prefer
                    To Margaret 3
Science! true daughter of Old Time thou
  art   To Science 1

Truest
Thou! thy truest type of grief
                    Al Aaraaf (1831) i 26
The truest—the most fervently devoted
                    To MLS 15

Truly
I feel thou lovest me truly
                    Politian iv 52
Sir," said I, " or Madam, truly your for-
  giveness I implore   Raven 20
On this home by Horror haunted—tell me
  truly, I implore   Raven 88

Trumpet
And her, the trumpet-tongued, thou wilt
  not hear   Politian iii 23
And the deep trumpet-thunder's roar
                    Tamerlane 48

Trunk
Twirls into trunk-paper the while you
  con it   Enigma 8

Trust
Trust to the fire within, for light
                    Tamerlane 95
To trust the weakness of my heart
                    Tamerlane (1827) 291
Ah, we safely may trust to its gleaming
                    Ulalume 67
We surely may trust to a gleaming
                    Ulalume 69

Trusting
And thy trusting heart beguiled
                    Ballad 18
And think of me!—think of my trusting
  love   Politian ii 88
Trusting to the mild-eyed stars
                    Valley 4

Trustworthy
Trustworthy and respectful
                    Politian ii 40

Truth
That Truth is falsehood—or that Bliss is
  Woe   Al Aaraaf ii 167
A dream of the truth   Annie 69

How my heart beats in coupling those two
   words   Helen² 27
I see them still—two sweetly scintillant
                    Helen² 65
But when a week or two go by   Irene 45
Through two luminous windows saw
                  Palace 18
Lean over her and weep—two gentle
   maids   Politian ii 26
There is a two-fold Silence—sea and
   shore   Silence 5
Two separate—yet most intimate things
             Tamerlane 127
Embrac'd two hamlets—those our own
       Tamerlane (1827) 222
Instead of two sides, Job has nearly eight
            Tempora 21
Two words—two foreign soft dissyllables
                To³ 7
Said we, then—the two, then: "Ah, can
   it   Ulalume 95

Type
Thou! thy truest type of grief
       Al Aaraaf i (1831) 26
Type of the antique Rome! Rich reliquary
            Coliseum 1
A type of that twin entity which springs
            Silence 3

Types
In myriad types of the human eye
            Valley 21

Tyranny
Usurp'd a tyranny which men
          Tamerlane 66

Tyrant
Where tyrant virtue reigns alone
        Divine Right 6

Ugo
How fares good Ugo?—and when is it to
   be   Politian ii 44
There's Ugo says the ring is only paste
         Politian ii 52

Ulalume
She replied: "Ulalume—Ulalume
          Ulalume 80
'Tis the vault of thy lost Ulalume
          Ulalume 81

Ultimate
From an ultimate dim Thule
        Dream-Land 6
From this ultimate dim Thule
       Dream-Land 56
In the ultimate climes of the Pole
         Ulalume 17

Unaccountable
Some words most unaccountable, in writ-
   ing   Politian v 51

Unassuming
Thy unassuming beauty
       To FSO (1835) 6

Unavailing
Fierce deep grief is unavailing
        Departed 22

Unbelieving
The unbelieving things
      Fairy-Land (1829) 44

Unblest
Far off in a region unblest
        City (1845) 3

Unbroken
But the silence was unbroken, and the
   stillness gave no token   Raven 27
Leave my loneliness unbroken!—quit the
   bust above my door   Raven 100
Shadowy—shadowy—yet unbroken
         Spirits 25

Unburthened
Of gorgeous columns on th' unburthen'd
   air   Al Aaraaf ii 12

Unceasingly
Unceasingly, from morn till even
       Valley (1845) 19

Uncertain
Th' uncertain, shadowy heaven below
         Irene 59
And the silken, sad, uncertain rustling of
   each purple curtain   Raven 13

Unchained
Empyrean splendor o'er th' unchained
   soul   Al Aaraaf i 21

Unchecked
Uncheck'd by sarcasm, and scorn
      Tamerlane (1827) 257

Unclosed
To the weak human eye unclosed
        Dream-Land 46
Forever with unclosed eye
       Sleeper (1842) 43

Undaunted
Desolate yet all undaunted, on this desert
   land enchanted   Raven 87
Albeit he soared with an undaunted wing
        To Science 8

Undefiled
From the most undefiled things
      Tamerlane (1829) 235
From the pure well of Beauty undefiled
       To Margaret 2

Undefined
And a feeling undefined Lake (1827) 15
All was an undefin'd delight
      Tamerlane (1827) 162

Understand
I will not understand   Politian iii 39
If one could merely understand the plot
       Valentine 12

Undimmed
Lustrous in youth, undimmed in age
       Stanzas² 20

Undivided
Shall give his undivided time
       City (1836) 56

Undo
Which one might not undo without a
   sabre   Valentine 11

Undoubtedly
The singer is undoubtedly beneath
       Politian iii 65
'T was a mistake?—undoubtedly—we all
       Politian v 56

Undying
The undying voice of that dead time
       Tamerlane 23

Untangled
A ne'er-to-be untangled mass   Irene 8

Unthought
Unthought-like thoughts that are the souls of thought   To³ 12

Until
Like woman's hair, 'mid pearls, until, afar
    Al Aaraaf i 33
Saw only them until the moon went down
    Helen² 41
I had not thought, until this hour
    Tamerlane (1827) 17
One object—and but one—until
    Tamerlane (1827) 99
Wings until they trailed in the dust
    Ulalume (1850) 57

Untimely
Whispers of early grave untimely yawning
    Politian ii 70
Untimely sepulchre, I do devote thee
    Politian v 60
But should some urgent fate (untimely lot
    Silence 12

Unto
Like unto what on earth we see
    Al Aaraaf i (1831) 17
Unrolling as a chart unto my view
    Al Aaraaf ii 223
Light, brazen rays, this golden star unto
    Al Aaraaf ii 240
Glides, spectre-like unto his marble home
    Coliseum 23
From us, and from all Ruin, unto the wise
    Coliseum 35
Surging, unto skies of fire
    Dream-Land 16
Is due unto that lyre   Israfel (1841) 19
From Hell unto a high estate within the utmost Heaven   Lenore 21
You who are more than mother unto me
    Mother 6
Devoutly singing unto one another
    Mother (1850) 2
Give way unto these humors
    Politian iii 3
Oh! I am sick, sick, sick, even unto death   Politian iii 29
Unto thy friend   Politian iii 38
Does it not? unto this palace of the Duke
    Politian iii 64
Unto the Duke   Politian iii 98
Apology unto the Duke for me
    Politian iii 112
Unto this man, that I, the Earl of Leicester   Politian v 34
Unto the Count—it is exceeding just
    Politian v 36
Even unto death   Politian v 89
Fancy unto fancy, thinking what this ominous bird of yore   Raven 70
They had gone unto the wars   Valley 3

Untrammelled
Of Heaven untrammelled flow—which air to breathe   Politian iv 72

Untrodden
And there, from the untrodden grass
    Irene 51

Untruest
In the falsest and untruest
    Al Aaraaf i (1831) 19

Unusual
Of those unusual strings   Israfel 22

Unveiling
Uprising, unveiling, affirm   Worm 38

Unwonted
With madness, and unwonted reverie
    Al Aaraaf i 59

Upbraiding
At one upbraiding word or token
    Tamerlane (1827) 201

Uplifted
Save but the soul in thine uplifted eyes
    Helen² 38
But Psyche uplifted her finger
    Ulalume (1848) 51

Uplifting
The uplifting of the fringed lid
    Dream-Land 48
But Psyche, uplifting her finger
    Ulalume 51

Upper
To bear my secrets thro' the upper Heaven
    Al Aaraaf i 142

Uppermost
Always write first things uppermost in the heart   Elizabeth 16

Upraise
And I—to-night my heart is light:—no dirge will I upraise   Lenore 25

Upreared
Uprear'd its purple stem around her knees   Al Aaraaf i 49
Uprear'd upon such height arose a pile
    Al Aaraaf ii 11

Upright
On a black throne reigns upright
    Dream-Land 4, 54
Jew, or downright upright nutmegs out of a pine-knot   Experiments 10
For they were childish and upright
    Tamerlane 92

Uprising
Uprising. unveiling, affirm   Worm 38

Upstarting
" Be that word our sign of parting, bird or fiend! " I shrieked, upstarting
    Raven 97

Upturned
Upon the upturn'd faces of a thousand
    Helen² 8
Fell on the upturn'd faces of these roses
    Helen² 11, 14
Fell on the upturn'd faces of the roses
    Helen² 19

Upturns
While ever to her dear Eulalie upturns her matron eye   Eulalie 20
While ever to her young Eulalie upturns her violet eye   Eulalie 21

Urged
Hath without doubt arisen: thou hast been urged   Politian v 49

Urgent
A sacred vow, imperative, and urgent
        Politian ii 95
But should some urgent fate (untimely
 lot   Silence 12

Usage
Logic and common usage so commanding
        Elizabeth 2

Use
They use that moon no more
        Fairy-Land 35
Have use for jewels now Politian ii 56

Used
And used to throw my earthly rest
      Romance (1831) 29
Democritus of Thrace, who used to toss
 over   Tempora 16

Usurped
Usurp'd a tyranny which men
       Tamerlane 66

Usurpingly
I claim'd and won usurpingly
       Tamerlane 29

Utmost
From Hell unto a high estate within the
 utmost Heaven   Lenore 21

Utter
Could hope to utter. And I! my spells are
 broken   To³ 16

Utterance
Beyond the utterance of the human tongue
        To³ 5

Uttered
Nothing farther then he uttered—not a
 fearther than he fluttered Raven 57
A well-known name, oft uttered in the
 hearing   Valentine 15

Utterly
A heaven so calm as this—so utterly free
       Politian v 26
The blotting utterly from out high heaven
       To MLS 3

Utters
"Doubtless," said I, "what it utters is its
 only stock and store Raven 62

Vacant
A vacant coronet Lenore (1843) 19
In vacant idleness of woe
    Tamerlane (1827) 395

Vacuum
A vacuum in the filmy Heaven
      City (1831) 48

Vague
These vague entablatures—this crumbling
 frieze   Coliseum 28
There the vague and dreamy trees
        Nis 35

Vain
Elizabeth, it is in vain you say
       Acrostic 1
In vain those words from thee or L. E. L
       Acrostic 3
Vain, oh! vain, are tears and wailing
      Departed 21
In vain I struggle to forget Octavia 3

Vainly
Eagerly I wished the morrow;—vainly I
 had sought to borrow Raven 9

Vales
Bottomless vales and boundless floods
      Dream-Land 9
Dim vales—and shadowy floods
      Fairy-Land 1

Valisnerian
And Valesnerian lotus thither flown
      Al Aaraaf i 74

Valley
As he sails on his pinions o'er valley and
 sea   Campaign 4
Down the Valley of the Shadow
       Eldorado 21
Lies that valley as the day Nis 3
It is called the valley Nis Nis 7
But "the valley Nis" at best Nis 15
Means "the valley of unrest." Nis 16
That slumber o'er that valley-world
      Nis (1836) 32
Wanderers in that happy valley
       Palace 17
And travellers, now, within that valley
       Palace 41
Into the universal valley Sleeper 8
The sad valley's restlessness Valley 10

Valleys
In the greenest of our valleys Palace 1
Within the valleys dim and brown
      Serenade 11

Vallies
In vallies of the wild Taglay
    Tamerlane (1827) 357

Vampire
And vampire wing-like pannels back
     Irene (1836) 72
Despair, the fabled vampire bat
    Tamerlane (1831) 27

Vampyre
And vampyre-winged pannels back
      Irene 72

Vanish
Now are visions ne'er to vanish
      Spirits 20

Vanished
But they have vanish'd long, alas
     Happiest Day 6

Vanities
Of the hollow and high-sounding vanities
     Politian iii 30
Dim, vanities of dreams by night
     Tamerlane 121

Vapid
While yet my vapid joy and grief
    Romance (1831) 61

Vapor
That the vapor can make Eulalie 10
An opiate vapor, dewy, dim Sleeper 3
Upon the vapor of the dew
     Tamerlane 134

Vapors
Amid empurpled vapors, far away
      To³ 26

Varied
Of varied being, which contain
     Tamerlane (1827) 165

Vast
Vast forms move fantastically Palace 43
At bidding of vast formless things
     Worm 13

Vastly
So pat, agreeable, and vastly proper
     Tempora 47

Vastness
Vastness! and Age! and Memories of Eld
     Coliseum 10

Vatican
Do we not?—at the Vatican
     Politian v 44
In the Vatican—within the holy walls
     Politian v (1835) 47
Of the Vatican   Politian v (1835) 48

Vault
For her may some tall vault unfold
     Sleeper 49
Some vault that oft hath flung its black
     Sleeper 50
Some vault from out whose sounding door
     Sleeper (1842) 58
'Tis the vault of thy lost Ulalume
     Ulalume 81

Veil
Breathe it less gently forth,—and veil
 thine eyes   Acrostic 6
There fell a silverly-silken veil of light
     Helen² 6
'T were folly now to veil a thought
     Tamerlane (1827) 183

Veiled
To gaze upon that veiled face, and hear
     Politian iii 103

Veils
In veils, and drowned in tears   Worm 4

Velvet
Was the velvet violet, wet with dews
     Parody 6
Then, upon the velvet sinking, I betook
 myself to linking   Raven 69
On the cushion's velvet lining that the
 lamp-light gloated o'er Raven 76
But whose velvet-violet lining with the
 lamp-light gloating o'er Raven 77

Vengeance
At me in vengeance shall that foot be
 shaken   Tempora 85

Venom
The venom thou hast pour'd on me
     Happiest Day 11
And my brain drank their venom then
     Tamerlane (1827) 41
Its venom secretly imparts
     Tamerlane (1827) 345

Ventured
That from his marble dwelling ventured
 out   Al Aaraaf ii (1829) 33

Venuses
Venuses, unextinguished by the sun
     Helen² 66

Verdant
No more—no more upon thy verdant
 slopes   Zante 8

Vere
And, Guy de Vere, hast thou no tear?—
 weep now or never more   Lenore 3

Veriest
" Silence "—which is the veriest word of
 all   Al Aaraaf i (1843) 127
I am the veriest coward   Politian v 73
Falling—her veriest stepping-stone
     Tamerlane 171

Veritably
And, veritably, Sol is right enough
     Enigma 9

Vermin
And seraphs sob at vermin fangs
     Worm 31

Verse
Lady! I would that verse of mine
     Stanzas² 1

Very
From a spring but a very few   Annie 41
From a cavern not very far   Annie 43
The very hours are breathing low
     City (1831) 50
My very soul thy grandeur, gloom, and
 glory   Coliseum 9
And loveliness,—have left my very heart
     Dreams 15
Has studied very little of his part
     Elizabeth 9
Is by (the very source of gloom
     Fairy-Land (1831) 34
Were seen no more: the very roses' odors
     Helen² 34
Oh, I am very happy   Politian i 4
When I am very happy   Politian i 10
'T is very strange   Politian i 56
But like—oh, very like in its despair
     Politian ii 22
Indeed she is very troublesome
     Politian ii 36
Very plainly through the window—it be-
 longs   Politian iii 63
'T is strange!—'t is very strange—
 methought the voice   Politian iii 107
Where am I?—'t is well—'t is very well
     Politian iv 103
'T is well, 't is very well—alas! alas
     Politian iv 105
All very true   Politian v 21
All this is very true   Politian v 23
To lisp my very earliest word
     Romance 8
So shake the very Heaven on high
     Romance 12
That very blackness yet doth fling
     Romance (1831) 17
To dream my very life away
     Romance (1831) 55
By notes so very shrilly blown
     Romance (1831) 59
Have nestled in my very hair
     Tamerlane 40
In the tangles of Love's very hair
     Tamerlane 243

Its very form hath pass'd me by
Tamerlane (1827) 100
His very voice is musical delight
Tempora 69
On this very night of last year
Ulalume 86

Vestibules
Gaunt vestibules! and phantom-peopled
aisles   Coliseum (1833) 13

Vestris
And hop o'er counters with a Vestris air
Tempora 52

Vex
To grieve thee or to vex thee
Politian ii 38

Vexed
Too much of late, and I am vexed to see it
Politian i 12
Some ocean vexed as it may be
To F (1842) 11

Vice
No subject vice dare interfere
Divine Right 7

Victory
The battle-cry of Victory   Tamerlane 54
With victory, on victory
Tamerlane (1827) 335

Videlicet
Videlicet, a tent   Fairy-Land 37

Vie
In beauty vie   Al Aaraaf i 85
Can vie with the modest Eulalie's most
unregarded curl   Eulalie 12

View
Which turneth at the view
Al Aaraaf i 88
Spirits in wing, and angels to the view
Al Aaraaf ii 156
Unrolling as a chart unto my view
Al Aaraaf ii 223
Of a demon in my view   Alone 22
May not—dare not openly view it
Dream-Land 44

Vigil
A midnight vigil holds the swarthy bat
Coliseum 19

Vigilance
Which thy vigilance keep
Al Aaraaf ii 119

Villain
Villain, thou art not gone—thou mockest
me   Politian iv 101
Hold him a villain?—thus much, I pry-
thee, say   Politian v 35
Draw, villain, and prate no more
Politian v 57
Ha!—draw?—and villain? have at thee
then at once   Politian v 58
Before all Rome, I'll taunt thee, villain
Politian v 90

Vindictively
Can it be fancied that Deity ever vindictively   Experiments 5

Vine
The viol, the violet, and the Vine City 23

Viol
The viol, the violet, and the Vine City 23

Violate
A traitor, violate of the truth
Tamerlane (1827) 277

Violet
On violet couches faint away
Al Aaraaf i (1831) 15
In violet bowers   Al Aaraaf ii 81
The viol, the violet, and the Vine City 23
While ever to her young Eulalie upturns
her violet eye   Eulalie 21
Clad all in white, upon a violet bank
Helen² 17
Was the velvet violet, wet with dews
Parody 6
But whose velvet-violet lining with the
lamp-light gloating o'er   Raven 77

Violets
Over the violets there that lie   Valley 20

Viper
Thy servant maid!—but courage!—'t is
but a viper   Politian ii 58

Virginal
Virginal Lillian, rigidly, humbily dutiful
Experiments 1

Virginia's
In setting my Virginia's spirit free
Mother 8

Virtue
Where tyrant virtue reigns alone
Divine Right 6
With wisdom, virtue, feeling fraught
Stanzas² 22
In Truth, in Virtue, in Humanity
To MLS 7

Virtues
Virtues that challenge envy's praise
Stanzas² 7

Visage
With a visage full of meaning   Nis 21

Vision
In a vision or in none
Dream w. Dream 8
That vision on my spirit   Imitation 12
The earth reel—and the vision gone
Tamerlane (1827) 97
In a vision—or in none
Tamerlane (1831) 247

Visionary
Flap shadowy sounds from visionary
wings   Al Aaraaf i 129
And donn'd a visionary crown
Tamerlane 156

Visions
In visions of the dark night   Dream 1
The vision of my youth have been
Happiest Day 7
When winged visions love to lie   Irene 3
Now are visions ne'er to vanish
Spirits 20
Richer, far wilder, far diviner visions
To³ 13
How many visions of a maiden that is
Zante 7

Visit
'T is his first visit   Politian i 43

Visitor

" 'T is some visitor," I muttered, " tapping
at my chamber door   Raven 5

'T is some visitor entreating entrance at
my chamber door   Raven 16

Some late visitor entreating entrance at
my chamber door   Raven 17

Now each visitor shall confess   Valley 9

Vista

Gazing, entranced, adown the gorgeous
vista   To³ 23

And we passed to the end of the vista
Ulalume 75

Vistas

Lay bare, thro' vistas thunder-river
Romance (1831) 15

Vital

Flow softly—gently—vital stream
Louisa 1

Vivid

Dreams! in their vivid coloring of life
Dreams 29

Voice

Joy's voice so peacefully departed
Al Aaraaf i 8

She stirr'd not—breath'd not—for a voice
was there   Al Aaraaf i 122

The eternal voice of God is passing by
Al Aaraaf i 131

Silence is the voice of God
Al Aaraaf i (1829) 125

Is not its form—its voice—most palpable
and loud   Al Aaraaf ii 47

And the voice seemed his who fell
Bridal Ballad 10

She, whose voice alone had power
Departed 19

Of his voice, all mute   Israfel 7

That my voice is growing weak
Paean 15

A voice from out of the Future cries
Paradise 10

There is—what voice was that
Politian iii 18

I heard not any voice except thine own
Politian iii 19

It is a phantom voice   Politian iii 25

A lady's voice!—and sorrow in the tone
Politian iii 54

Into my heart of hearts! that eloquent
voice   Politian iii 57

Be still!—the voice, if I mistake not
greatly   Politian iii 61

'Tis strange!—'tis very strange—methought the voice   Politian iii 107

Sweet voice   Politian iii 109

And let me hear thy voice—one word—one
word   Politian iv 95

His very voice is musical delight
Tempora 69

I think I hear thy voice's sound   Sarah 4

Thy lover's voice tonight shall flow
Serenade 18

The undying voice of that dead time
Tamerlane 23

Of human battle, where my voice
Tamerlane 50

My own voice, silly child! was swelling
Tamerlane 51

A voice came from the threshold stone
Tamerlane 217

To her soft thrilling voice: To part
Tamerlane (1827) 292

Comes o'er me, with the mingled voice
Tamerlane (1827) 340

Who has " The sweetest voice of all God's
creatures   To³ 15

Voices

In voices of surpassing beauty   Palace 31

And phantom voices   Politian iii 25

Void

A void within the filmy Heaven   City 47

Volatile

Gay, volatile, and giddy—is he not
Politian i 52

Volcanic

These were days when my heart was
volcanic   Ulalume 13

Volume

Over many a quaint and curious volume
of forgotten lore   Raven 2

Voluminously

What a gush of euphony voluminously
wells   Bells 26

Vow

They have sever'd ev'ry vow   Ballad 2

But, when first he breathed his vow
Bridal Ballad 7

And this the plighted vow
Bridal Ballad 21

An irrevocable vow
Bridal Ballad (1837) 20

There is a vow were fitting should be
made   Politian ii 94

A sacred vow, imperative, and urgent
Politian 95

A solemn vow   Politian ii 96

This sacred vow   Politian ii 99

The deed—the vow—the symbol of the
deed   Politian ii 105

Behold the cross wherewith a vow like
mine   Politian ii 107

Vows

And confidence—his vows—my ruin—
think—think   Politian ii 89

And vows before the throne
Politian ii 93

Witnessed thy vows to me   Sarah 12

Vulture

Vulture, whose wings are dull realities
To Science 4

Waft

But waft the angel on her flight with a
Paean of old days   Lenore 26

Wailing

Vain, oh! vain, are tears and wailing
Departed 21

Waist

And zone that clung around her gentle
waist   Al Aaraaf ii 54

Wait

Shall wait upon thee, and the angel Hope
Politian iv 81

Waiting
I did not know, Jacinta, you were in
waiting   Politian ii 2
Wake
Thy heart—thy heart!—I wake and sigh
To[1] 9
Wakening
Wakening the broad welkin with his loud
battle cry   Campaign 2
Waking
But a waking dream of life and light
Dream 3
Of waking life, to him whose heart must
be   Dream 6
With a wild, and waking thought
Imitation 6
Nothings of mid-day waking life
Tamerlane (1827) 170
Walked
We walk'd together on the crown
Tamerlane 139
Walks
For the spirit that walks in shadow
Dream-Land 41
Wall
Wherein I sate, and on the draperied wall
Al Aaraaf ii 205
More beauty clung around her column'd
wall   Al Aaraaf ii 216
O'er th' horizon's fiery wall   Nis 42
That o'er the floor and down the wall
Sleeper 28
The gay wall of this gaudy tower
Tamerlane (1827) 15
Walls
Up fanes—up Babylon-like walls City 18
But stay! these walls—these ivy-clad
arcades   Coliseum 26
Over ruin'd walls
Fairy-Land (1831) 60
In the Vatican—within the holy walls
Politian v (1835) 47
Wan
Lit by the wan light of the horned moon
Coliseum 24
While the angels, all pallid and wan
Worm 37
Wander
Do I wander on   Departed 4
Do I wander on forever   Departed 11
And we wander on, caressing
Departed 29
Lonely do I wander ever   Departed 38
Wandered
I have wandered home but newly
Dream-Land 55
I wandered of the idol, Love
Tamerlane 232
But as I wander'd on the way
Tamerlane (1827) 364
Wanderer
A wanderer by moss-y-mantled well
Al Aaraaf ii 183
As they pass the wanderer by
Dream-Land 36
The weary, way-worn wanderer bore
Helen[1] 4

Wanderers
The hearts of many wanderers who look
in   Al Aaraaf ii (1829) 42
Wanderers in that happy valley
Palace 17
Wanderest
Where wand'rest thou my soul
Dream (1827) 4
Wandering
The wandering star   Al Aaraaf i 15
Ghastly grim and ancient Raven wander-
ing from the Nightly shore   Raven 46
Of crystal, wandering water   River 2
To guide my wandering thoughts to
heaven   Sarah 23
Who woulst not leave him in his wander-
ing   To Science 6
Wane
Huge moons there wax and wane
Fairy-Land 5
Waned
The night that waned and waned and
brought no day   Al Aaraaf ii 262
Waning
Whose waning is the dreariest one
Tamerlane 208
Want
Much, much, oh much I want
Politian i 29
Wantest
To a becoming carriage—much thou
wantest   Politian i 28
Wanton
From the wild energy of wanton haste
Al Aaraaf ii 52
The wanton airs, from the tree-top
Sleeper 20
Wantonest
The wantonest singing birds   To[1] 2
War
My soul is at war with God
Politian ii 77
Of war, and tumult, where my voice
Tamerlane (1827) 55
Warm
She covered me warm   Annie 80
Warmer
And I said: "She is warmer than Dian
Ulalume 39
Warrant
Of nothing which might warrant thee in
this thing   Politian v 54
Warrior
We, with one warrior, have slain
Latin Hymn 3
Wars
They had gone unto the wars   Valley 3
Wast
Thou wast that all to me, love
Paradise 1
Wasted
It speaks of sunken eyes, and wasted
cheeks   Politian ii 65

Watch
To keep watch with delight
             Al Aaraaf ii 110
To keep watch above the flowers
             Valley 6

Watches
In the sad, silent watches of my night
             Helen[1] 63

Water
I have drank of water   Annie 37
Of a water that flows   Annie 39
How could I from that water bring
   Lake (1831) 20; Tamerlane (1831) 96
Of crystal, wandering water   River 2

Waterfall
Rolling like a waterfall   Nis 41
Rolling, like a waterfall Nis (1836) 39

Waterfalls
Fair flowers, bright waterfalls, and angel
  wings   Al Aaraaf ii 65
Over waterfalls   Fairy-Land (1831) 61
Silent waterfalls   Fairy-Land (1831) 62

Waters
From struggling with the waters of the
  Rhone   Al Aaraaf i 75
The melancholy waters lie   City 11; 25
Tempt the waters from their bed City 35
Their lone waters, lone and dead
          Dream-Land 18; 22
Their still waters, still and chilly
          Dream-Land 19
Their sad waters, sad and chilly
          Dream-Land 23
On the clear waters there that flow
          Irene 57

Wave
Far from upon the wave that sparkued
  there   Al Aaraaf ii 14
Of beautiful Gomorrah! O, the wave
          Al Aaraaf ii 38
The wave—there is a vomement there
          City 43
Waved to the wind, now wave the reed
  and thistle   Coliseum 21
One from the pitiless wave
          Dream w. Dream 22
Death was in that poisonous wave
          Lake 18
But when within thy wave she looks
          River 7
The lily lolls upon the wave   Sleeper 10
And wave the curtain canopy Sleeper 24
Over the lilies there that wave Valley 22
They wave:—from out their fragrant tops
          Valley 24
They wave; they weep; and the tears, as
  they well   Valley (1845) 28

Waved
Waved to the wind, now wave the reed
  and thistle   Coliseum 21
Was the lance which he proudly wav'd
  on high   Parody 10

Waves
Yawn level with the luminous waves
          City 31

The waves have now a redder glow
          City 48
Her beam on the waves   Star 8

Wax
Huge moons there wax and wane
          Fairy-Land 5

Way
Love not "—thou sayest it in so sweet a
  way   Acrostic 2
Its way to Heaven, from garden of a king
          Al Aaraaf i 73
Her way—but left not yet her Therasaean
  reign   Al Aaraaf i 158
In my own country all the way
          Fairy-Land (1831) 30
The weary, way-worn wanderer bore
          Helen[1] 4
Its way to some remember'd lake
          Irene 48
Methinks thou hast a singular way of
  showing   Politian i 5
Give way unto these humors
          Politian iii 3
And hurried madly on my way
          Tamerlane (1827) 300
But as I wander'd on the way
          Tamerlane (1827) 364
Upon the left, and all the way along
          To[3] 25
To bar up our way and to ban it
          Ulalume 98

Ways
Of her wond'rous ways, and telling bless
          Tamerlane (1827) 313
I like your Yankee words and Yankee
  ways   Tempora 10
So with the world thy gentle ways
          To FSO 5

Weak
To the weak human eye unclosed
          Dream-Land 46
That my voice is growing weak Paean 15
Once upon a midnight dreary, while I
  pondered, weak and weary   Raven 1
And think that these weak lines are writ-
  ten by him   To MLS 16

Weakness
My womanly weakness   Politian iv 98
This weakness grows upon me
          Politian v 1
In women's weakness had a part
          Tamerlane 74
So trust the weakness of my heart
          Tamerlane (1827) 291

Weal
Oh! was it weal to leave me
          Ballad 9, 21, 33
Thro' good and ill—thro' weal and woe I
  love thee   Politian iv 15

Wealth
Wretches! ye loved her for her wealth,
  and ye hated her for her pride
          Lenore 8
Pre-eminent in arts and arms, and wealth
          Politian i 49

In wealth and wo among
Politian iii 73, 82, 92
Stored with the wealth of bard and sage
Stanzas² 18

Weapon
Here is no let or hindrance to thy weapon
Politian v 81

Wearied
The wearied light is dying down
Serenade 13

Weariness
To thy weariness shall seem   Spirits 16

Wearing
Wearing its own deep feeling as a crown
Stanzas¹ 32

Wears
Thy looks are haggard—nothing wears
away   Politian i 15
Wears it away like evil hours and wine
Politian i 18

Weary
And there—oh! may my weary spirit
dwell   Al Aaraaf ii 172
Of weary pilgrimage and burning thirst
Coliseum 5
When the weary moon descendeth
Departed 13
The weary, way-worn wanderer bore
Helen¹ 4
So tired, so weary   Physician 7
Weary—I laid me on a couch to rest
Poetry 2
Once upon a midnight dreary, while I
pondered, weak and weary   Raven 1

Weather
My breast her shield in wintry weather
Tamerlane 98
Of a weatherbeaten shore
Dream w. Dream (1829) 11

Wedding
Hear the mellow wedding bells   Bells 15
We'll have him at the wedding
Politian i 43, 46, 50
Thou hast not spoken lately of thy wed-
ding   Politian ii 43

Week
But when a week or two go by   Irene 45

Ween
Of power! said I? yes! such I ween
Happiest Day 5
That blush, I ween, was maiden shame
Song (1827) 9
Redoubling age! and more, I ween
Tamerlane (1827) 336
I still was young: and well I ween
Tamerlane (1827) 353

Weep
While I weep—while I weep
Dream w. Dream 18
At least as long as Love doth weep
Irene 42
And, Guy De Vere, hast thou no tear?—
weep now or never more   Lenore 3
And I must weep alone   Manuscript 2
And weep!—oh! to dishonor   Paean 7
Lean over her and weep—two gentle
maids   Politian ii 26

Weep not: oh, sob not thus!—thy bitter
tears   Politian iv 5
Oh weep not, Lalage,
Politian iv (1836) 6
To weep, as he did, till his eyes were sore
Tempora 14
And weep above a nameless grave
Valley 23
They weep: from off their delicate stems
Valley 26
They wave; they weep, and the tears, as
they well   Valley (1845) 28

Weeping
The sacred sun—of all who, weeping, bless
thee   To MLS 4

Weeps
Where weeps the silver willow
Paradise (1836) 32

Weigh
It would weigh down your flight
Al Aaraaf ii 95

Weighed
How drowsily it weigh'd them into night
Al Aaraaf ii 207
Then sinks within (weigh'd down by wo)
Irene 58

Weight
With the weight of an age of snows
To M 16

Weir
In the misty mid region of Weir
Ulalume 7
In the ghoul-haunted woodland of Weir
Ulalume 9
Nor the ghoul-haunted woodland of Weir
Ulalume 29
This misty mid region of Weir
Ulalume 92
This ghoul-haunted woodland of Weir
Ulalume 94

Weird
From a wild weird clime that lieth, sublime   Dream-Land 7

Well
Zanthippe's talents had enforced so well
Acrostic 4
A wanderer by moss-y-mantled well
Al Aaraaf ii 183
That eve—that eve—I should remember
well   Al Aaraaf ii 202
And my lord he loves me well
Bridal Ballad 6
A soul that knew it well
Happiest Day (1827) 24
Just now so fairy-like and well
Fairy-Land (1831) 3
None sing so wildly well   Israfel 3
Well may the stars be mute   Israfel 39
He might not sing so wildly well
Israfel 48
The former was well known to fame
Lampoon 7
But the latter's well known " to report
Lampoon 8
To a lute's well-tuned law   Palace 20
In state his glory well befitting
Palace 23

Thou art not well   Politian i 11
Sir Count! what art thou dreaming? he's
    not well   Politian i 33
I crave thy pardon—indeed I am not well
    Politian i 35
And know him well—nor learned nor
    mirthful he   Politian i 62
'T is well   Politian ii 93
Daughter, this zeal is well   Politian ii 96
Father, this zeal is anything but well
    Politian ii 97
Surely I never heard—yet it were well
    Politian iii 58
Where am I—'t is well—'t is very well
    Politian iv 103
'T is well, 't is very well—alas! alas
    Politian iv 105
'Tis he—he comes himself! Thou reasonest
    well   Politian v 38
Well   Politian v 40
Shall I be baffled thus?—now this is well
    Politian v 65
If that we meet at all, it were as well
    Politian v (1835) 45
Exceeding well!—thou darest not fight
    with me   Politian v (1835) 66
For I have travelled, friend, as well as
    you   Tempora 42
As such it well may pass   Song 10
The loveliness of loving well
    Tamerlane 76
Too well that I should let it be
    Tamerlane 153
A tale the world but knows too well
    Tamerlane (1827) 350
I still was young; and well I ween
    Tamerlane (1827) 353
I well remember having dwelt
    Tamerlane (1831) 108
As well it might, a dream   To⁴ 2
From the pure well of Beauty undefiled
    To Margaret 2
That must be worn at heart. Search well
    the measure   Valentine 7
A well-known name, oft uttered in the
    hearing   Valentine 15
They wave; they weep; and the tears, as
    they well   Valley (1845) 28
Well I know, now, this dim lake of Auber
    Ulalume 91
Well, I know, now, this dank tarn of
    Auber   Ulalume 93

Wells
To the tintinnabulation that so musically
    wells   Bells 11
What a gush of euphony voluminously
    wells   Bells 26

Welkin
Wakening the broad welkin with his loud
    battly cry   Campaign 2

Went
Went envying her and me
    Annabel Lee 22
Went gloriously away
    Dream w. Dream (1829) 12;
    Tamerlane (1831) 256; To⁴ 24

The pearly lustre of the moon went out
    Helen² 31
Saw only them until the moon went down
    Helen² 41
Where oft—in life—with friends—it went
    Irene 49
And the mystic wind went by   Lake 9
A winged odor went away   Palace 16
I went from out the matted bow'r
    Tamerlane (1827) 299

Wert
Thou wert my dream
    Al Aaraaf i (1831) 2

West
Far down within the dim West   City 3
A thousand leagues within the golden
    west   Politian iv 68

Western
Into a western coach of thunder-cloud
    Helen² 49
Breathes the shrill spirit of the western
    wind   Politian ii 10

Wet
And over the wet grass rippled away
    Fairy-Land (1831) 28
With tears are streaming wet
    Lenore (1843) 16
Was the velvet violet, wet with dews
    Parody 6

Whatever
Whatever it might be   Song 6

Wheeled
Straight I wheeled a cushioned seat in
    front of bird and bust and door
    Raven 68

Whence
Whence sprang the "Idea of Beauty"
    into birth   Al Aaraaf i 31
From the sun and stars, whence he had
    drawn forth   Stanzas¹ 5
The dwindled hills, whence amid bowers
    Tamerlane (1827) 218

Whereat
The bowers whereat, in dreams, I see
    To¹ 1

Wherein
Wherein I sate, and on the draperied wall
    Al Aaraaf ii 205

Whereon
A crucifix whereon to register
    Politian ii 99
Enwritten upon this page whereon are
    peering   Valentine 13

Wherever
Ligeia! wherever   Al Aaraaf ii 112
Wherever they may be   Fairy-Land 21

Wherewith
Behold the cross wherewith a vow like
    mine   Politian ii 107

Whether
Whether Tempter sent, or whether tem-
    pest tossed thee here ashore   Raven 86
I've been a thinking, whether it were best
    Tempora 11
Whether with Heraclitus of your
    Tempora 13

While
But O that light!—I slumber'd—Death,
  the while   Al Aaraaf ii 210
Give me to live yet—yet a little while
                Politian v 8
To while away—forbidden things
                Romance 19
I gaz'd a while   Star 9
Of beauty which did while it thro'
              Tamerlane 136
But pray be patient: yet a little while
              Tempora 38

Whiled
Thus, in discourse, the lovers whiled away
          Al Aaraaf ii 261

Whisper
They seem to whisper thoughts of love
              Sarah 10

Whispered
And the only word there spoken was the
  whispered word, "Lenore?" Raven 28
This I whispered, and an echo murmured
  back the word, "Lenore!" Raven 29

Whispering
Young flowers were whispering in melody
          Al Aaraaf ii 60
The angels, whispering to one another
              Mother 2

Whispers
Whispers of early grave untimely yawning   Politian ii 70

White
Heaving her white breast to the balmy air
          Al Aaraaf i 64
See the White Eagle soaring aloft to the
  sky   Campaign 1
Then here's the White Eagle, full daring
  is he   Campaign 3
White-robed forms of friends long given
          Dream-Land 37
Clad all in white, upon a violet bank
            Helen² 17
Snow-white palace—reared its head
         Palace (1839) 4
What tho' the moon—the white moon
         Tamerlane 201

Whole
To God, and to the great whole
      Tamerlane (1827) 310
But take it generally upon the whole
           Tempora 44

Wide
O! where (and ye may seek the wide skies
  over   Al Aaraaf ii 179
But now, abroad on the wide earth
        Dream (1827) 3
While its wide circumference
         Fairy-Land 18
To haunt of the wide world a spot
  Lake 2; Tamerlane (1831) 80
That I scarce was sure I heard you"—
  here I opened wide the door Raven 23
Threshold of the wide-open gate of dreams
             To³ 22

Wife
By that infinity with which my wife
            Mother 13

Thy wife, and with a tainted memory
         Politian iv 27
My own, my beautiful, my love, my wife
         Politian iv 84

Wild
Of many a wild star gazer long age
          Al Aaraaf ii 43
From the wild energy of wanton haste
          Al Aaraaf ii 52
Or tufted wild spray Al Aaraaf ii 69
Where wild flowers, creeping
         Al Aaraaf ii 136
Its own core my wild heart eating
          Departed 35
From a wild weird clime that lieth, sub-
  lime   Dream-Land 7
'T was once—and only once—and the wild
  hour   Dreams 19
What wild heart-historic seemed to lie
  enwritten   Helen² 42
With a wild, and waking thought
         Imitation 6
None sing so wild—so well
        Israfel (1831) 3
Of a wild lake, with black rock bound
             Lake 5
Leaving thee wild for the dear child that
  should have been thy bride Lenore 16
All wreathed round with wild flowers
        Paradise (1834) 5
Thine eyes are wild—tempt not the wrath
  divine   Politian ii 110
While in the wild wood I did lie
          Romance 9
Succeeding years, too wild for song
        Romance (1831) 11
His naivete to wild desire
        Romance (1831) 25
But I will half believe that wild light
  fraught   Stanzas¹ 11
Bow'd from its wild pride into shame
         Tamerlane 14
Roaming the forest and the wild
         Tamerlane 97
The wild—the terrible conspire
         Tamerlane 163
And beauty of so wild a birth
         Tamerlane 185
O how would my wild heart rejoice
      Tamerlane (1827) 57
A light in the dark wild, alone
      Tamerlane (1827) 233
Of peril in my wild career
      Tamerlane (1827) 242
With Nature, in her wild paths; tell
      Tamerlane (1827) 312
In vallies of the wild Taglay
      Tamerlane (1827) 357
Of a wild lake with black rock bound
      Tamerlane (1831) 83

Wilder
Richer, far wilder, far diviner visions
             To³ 13

Wildered
A wilder'd being from my birth
        Dream (1827) 1

She'd look up in my wilder'd eye
Tamerlane (1827) 132
My wilder'd heart was far away
Tamerlane (1827) 356

Wildering
Whose wild'ring thought could even make
Lake (1827) 22

Wilderness
Along that wilderness of glass   City 37
Light in the wilderness alone
Tamerlane 154
But leav'st the heart a wilderness
Tamerlane 182

Wildly
None sing so wildly well   Israfel 3
He might not sing so wildly well
Israfel 48

Wiles
And laughing at her girlish wiles
Tamerlane 105

Will
Thy will is done, oh, God
Al Aaraaf i 106
O! is it thy will   Al Aaraaf ii 104
In death around thee—and their will
Spirits 9
Find pride the ruler of its will
Tamerlane (1827) 194

Willing
A portion of his willing soul
Tamerlane (1827) 309

Willow
Where weeps the silver willow
Paradise (1825) 32

Wills
So wills its King, who hath forbid
Dream-Land 47

Wilt
Thou wilt—thou must   Politian i 23
Wilt thou, my good Jacinta, be so kind
Politian ii 29
And her, the trumpet-tongued, thou wilt
not hear   Politian iii 23
O, wilt thou—wilt thou   Politian iv 74
Fly to thy Paradise—my Lalage, wilt
thou   Politian iv 79
My all;—oh, wilt thou,—wilt thou, La-
lage   Politian iv 85
A piece of service; wilt thou go back and
say   Politian v 33
Thou wilt not fight with me didst say, Sir
Count   Politian v 64
Dost hear? with cowardice—thou wilt not
fight me   Politian v 91

Wind
A wind blew out of a cloud by night
Annabel Lee 15
That the wind came out of the cloud,
chilling   Annabel Lee 25
Waved to the wind, now wave the reed
and thistle   Coliseum 21
Of a wind-beaten shore
Dream w. Dream (1831) 11
Or spell had bound me—'t was the chilly
wind   Dreams 21
That dream was as that night-wind—let
it pass   Dreams 26

Today (the wind blew, and) it swung
Fairy-Land (1831) 14
Where no wind dared to stir, unless on
tiptoe   Helen² 10
Some gentle wind hath thought it right
Irene 31
And the mystic wind went by   Lake 9
Breathes the shrill spirit of the western
wind   Politian ii 10
These fancies to the wind
Politian iii 96
Stirred by the autumn wind
Politian iv 58
But the night wind   Politian iv 62
'T is the wind and nothing more
Raven 36
Unshelter'd—and the heavy wind
Tamerlane 56
Are—shadows on th' unstable wind
Tamerlane 80
And the black wind murmur'd by
Tamerlane (1831) 87
Of a wind-beaten shore
Tamerlane (1831) 250
Ah, by no wind are stirred those trees
Valley 14
Ah, by no wind those clouds are driven
Valley 17

Window
A window of one circular diamond, there
Al Aaraaf ii 22
Lo! in yon brilliant window-niche
Helen¹ 11
Very plainly through the window—it
belongs   Politian ii 63
Surely," said I, "surely there is some-
thing at my window lattice   Raven 33
This window open to the night
Sleeper 19

Windows
Through two luminous windows, say
Palace 18
Through the red-litten windows see
Palace 42

Winds
And the red winds are withering in the
sky   Al Aaraaf i 132
While the silver winds of Circassy
Al Aaraaf i (1831) 14
Sprang from her station, on the winds
apart   Al Aaraaf ii 235
Around, by lifting winds forgot   City 9
No swellings tell that winds may be
City 38
No heavings hint that winds have been
City 40
The winds ran off with it delighted
Fairy-Land (1831) 20
To the night-winds as they pass   Irene 54
Rich melodies are floating in the winds
Politian iii 47
And mountains, around whose towering
summits the winds   Politian iv 71

Wine
Than all Syria can furnish of wine
Latin Hymn 12

This is a question which, Oh Heaven,
Romance (1831) 26
Such squalid wit to honourable rhyme
To Margaret 4

Witch
The witch, the sprite, the goblin—where
are they   To Science (1841) 14

Witchery
Of witchery may test   Al Aaraaf ii 153

Withal
Than ev'n thy glowing bosom beats withal
Al Aaraaf ii 217

Withdrew
This is a question which, Oh Heaven,
withdrew   Tempora 19

Withered
Upon the Siroc-wither'd plain
Tamerlane 180
Wither'd and blasted; who had gone
Tamerlane (1827) 276
Which have wither'd as they rose
To M 14

Withering
And the red winds are withering in the
sky   Al Aaraaf i 132
To thy withering shall seem
Spirits (1827) 16
Thy withering portion with the fame
Tamerlane 16
Withering at the ev'ning hour
Tamerlane (1827) 91
The leaves they were withering and sere
Ulalume 3
As the leaves that were withering and
sere   Ulalume 84

Witness
Witness the murmur of the grey twilight
Al Aaraaf ii 41

Witnessed
Witnessed thy vows to me   Sarah 12

Wizard
The bodiless airs, a wizard rout
Sleeper 22

Woe
That Truth is falsehood—or that Bliss is
Woe   Al Aaraaf ii 167
The night had found (to him a night of
wo)   Al Aaraaf ii 190
How dark a wo! yet how sublime a hope
Helen² 44
In joy and wo—in good and ill   Hymn 3
Then sinks within (weigh'd down by wo
Irene 58
Though it be rife with woe
Politian ii 64
In wealth and wo among
Politian iii 73, 82, 93
To Lalage?—ah, wo—ah, wo is me
Politian iv 3
Thro' good and ill—thro' weal and woe I
love thee   Politian iv 15
An humbler heart—a deeper wo
Tamerlane 221
In vacant idleness of woe
Tamerlane (1827) 395
Invisible wo   Worm 16

Woes
For the heart whose woes are legion
Dream-Land 39
Even for thy woes I love thee—even for
thy woes   Politian iv 21
Thy beauty and thy woes
Politian iv 22
Beloved! amid the earnest woes   To F 1

Wolds
From the secret that lies in these wolds
Ulalume 99
From the thing that lies hidden in these
wolds   Ulalume 100

Woman
Like woman's hair 'mid pearls, until, afar
Al Aaraaf i 33
And woman's loveliness—and passionate
love   Al Aaraaf ii 230
They are neither man nor woman
Bells 86
In woman's weakness had a part
Tamerlane 74
I knew no woman's heart, alas
Tamerlane (1827) 297

Womanly
My womanly weakness   Politian iv 98

Won
But I know with gold they won thee
Ballad 17
Proud heart, never won   Departed 24
I claim'd and won usurpingly
Tamerlane 29
Farewell! for I have won the Earth
Tamerlane 186

Wonder
On the stars which your wonder
Al Aaraaf ii 74
What wonder? for each star is eye-like
there   Al Aaraaf ii 186
Not all the wonder that encircles us
Coliseum 42
A wonder to these garden trees
Sleeper 33

Wondering
Deep into that darkness peering, long I
stood there wondering, fearing
Raven 25
Wondering at the stillness broken by reply
so aptly spoken   Raven (A. W. R.) 61

Wonderous
Of her wond'rous ways, and telling bless
Tamerlane (1827) 313

Wonders
The night and the wonders here
Fairy-Land (1831) 40

Wont
On desperate seas long wont to roam
Helen¹ 6
Is calmer now than it was wont to be
Politian iii 46
Whom daily they are wont to see
Tamerlane (1827) 262

Wood
While in the wild wood I did lie
Ramance 9
And driven the Hamadryad from the wood
To Science 10

That slumber o'er that valley-world
                    Nis (1836) 32
The world, its cares, and my own lot
                    Sarah 20
And would not, for the world, awake
                    Sleeper 15
The world all love before thee Song 4, 16
The world, and all it did contain
                    Tamerlane 117
Of half the world as all my own
                    Tamerlane 131
Of glory which the world hath known
                    Tamerlane 169
The world with all its train of bright
                    Tamerlane (1827) 160
A tale the world but knows too well
                    Tamerlane (1827) 350
To haunt of the wide world a spot
                    Tamerlane (1831) 80
So with the world thy gentle ways
                    To FSO 5

Worldly
And my worldly rest hath gone
                    Imitation 17
The worldly glory, which has shown
                    Tamerlane (1827) 26

Worlds
What tho' in worlds which sightless cycles
    run   Al Aaraaf i 133
What tho' in worlds which own a single
    sun   Al Aaraaf i 139
And wing to other worlds another light
                    Al Aaraaf i 146
And scowls on starry worlds that down
    beneath it lie   Al Aaraaf ii 193
Of what in other worlds shall be—and
    giv'n   Stanzas¹ 25

Worm
These cheeks, where the worm never dies
                    Ulalume 43
And its hero, the Conqueror Worm
                    Worm 40

Worms
In agony, to the worms—and Heaven
                    Dream-Land (1844) 44
Soft may the worms about her creep
                    Sleeper 47

Worn
The weary, way-worn wanderer bore
                    Helen¹ 4
That must be worn at heart. Search well
    the measure   Valentine 7

Worry
The sweet airs from the garden worry me
                    Politian ii 80

Worse
Or worse—upon her brow to dance
                    Irene 5
Yet still I think these worse than them a
    little   Tempora 8

Worship
I'd worship Kings and kingly state
                    Divine Right 10
Which we worship in a star
                    Israfel 28

And worship thee, and call thee my be-
    loved   Politian iv 83
Nearest resembles worship—oh, remember
                    To MLS 14

Worshipper
Her worshipper resembles   River 10

Worst
That torture the worst   Annie 32
Where the good and the bad and the worst
    and the best   City 4
The worst ill of mortality
                    Tamerlane (1827) 305
The "good old times" were far the worst
    of any   Tempora 6

Worthy
Or one more worthy Italy, methinks
                    Politian v 17
O, she was worthy of all love
                    Tamerlane 86
Yet more than worthy of the love
                    Tamerlane 112

Wouldst
Command me, sir! what wouldst thou
    have me do   Politian iii 9
I knew thou wouldst not go
                    Politian iv 99
I knew thou wouldst not, couldst not,
    durst not go   Politian iv 100
I know what thou wouldst say—not send
    the message   Politian v 39
Thou can'st not—wouldst not dare to
    think   Tamerlane (1827) 103
Thou wouldst be loved?—then let thy
    heart   To FSO 1
Who wouldst not leave him in his wan-
    dering   To Science 6

Wounded
For the wounded spirit in Gilead it is
    there   Politian ii 32

Wrangling
And the wrangling   Bells 63

Wrapped
I wrapp'd myself in grandeur then
                    Tamerlane 155

Wrapping
Wrapping the fog about its breast
                    Sleeper 11

Wrath
The storm, the earthquake, and the ocean
    wrath   Al Aaraaf i 137
Thine eyes are wild—tempt not the
    wrath divine   Politian ii 110

Wreath
A wreath that twined each starry form
    around   Al Aaraaf i 40
And the wreath is on my brow
                    Bridal Ballad 2

Wreathed
Whose wreathed friezes intertwine
                    City 22
All wreathed with fairy fruits and flowers
                    Paradise 5

Wreathing
Wreathing for its transparent brow
                    Irene 52

In years, but grey in fame
                    Politian i 47
Seemed to have years too many
                    Politian ii 20
Of late, eternal Condor years
                    Romance 11
Succeeding years, too wild for song
                    Romance (1831) 11
The hallow'd mem'ry of those years
                    Tamerlane (1827) 136
When, a few fleeting years gone by
                    Tamerlane (1827) 268
That years of love have been forgot
                    To² 3
Hath palsied many years   To M 12
Within the lonesome latter years
                    Worm 2

Yellow
Up rose the maiden in the yellow night
                    Al Aaraaf i 151
As sprang that yellow star from downy
    hours   Al Aaraaf i 155
Here, where the dames of Rome their
    yellow hair   Coliseum (1833) 22
Till the yellow-haired young Eulalie be-
    came my smiling bride   Eulalie 5
Or a yellow Albatross   Fairy-Land 34
The life upon her yellow hair, but not
    within her eyes   Lenore 18
Banners yellow, glorious, golden
                    Palace 9
Are tintless of the yellow leaf
                    Romance (1831) 62

Yells
And he dances, and he yells   Bells 95

Yield
Blest with all bliss that earth can yield
                    Stanzas² 27

Yields
The faithful heart yields to repose
                    Physician 6

Yon
Adorn yon world afar, afar
                    Al Aaraaf i 14
Now happiest, loveliest in yon lovely
    Earth   Al Aaraaf i 30
And greener fields than in yon world
    above   Al Aaraaf ii 229
As she threw off her cloak
                    Fairy-Land (1831) 22
Lo! in yon brilliant window-niche
                    Helen¹ 11
Is dripping from yon golden rim
                    Irene (1836) 4
Above yon cataract of Serangs
                    Irene (1836) 15
Which we worship in yon star
                    Israfel (1831) 27
See! on yon drear and rigid bier low lies
    thy love, Lenore   Lenore 4
Yon heir, whose cheeks of pallid hue
                    Lenore (1843) 15
To look upon the face hidden by yon lat-
    tice   Politian iii 102

Yonder
Proceeds from yonder lattice—which you
    may see   Politian iii 62

Of yonder trees methought a figure past
                    Politian iv 54
Laden from yonder bowers!—a fairer day
                    Politian v 16

Yore
Like those Nicean barks of yore
                    Helen¹ 2
In there stepped a stately Raven of the
    saintly days of yore   Raven 38
Fancy unto fancy, thinking what this
    ominous bird of yore   Raven 70
What this grim, ungainly, ghastly, gaunt
    and ominous bird of yore   Raven 71
Whether with Heraclitus of yore
                    Tempora 13

Young
The Sephalica, budding with young bees
                    Al Aaraaf i 48
The birth-place of young Beauty had no
    more   Al Aaraaf i 154
And nursled the young mountain in its
    lair   Al Aaraaf ii 15
Young flowers were whispering in melody
                    Al Aaraaf ii 60
Young dreams still hovering on their
    drowsy flight   Al Aaraaf ii 158
Upon a mountain crag, young Angelo
                    Al Aaraaf ii 191
Oh! that my young life were a lasting
    dream   Dreams 1
In my young boyhood—should it thus be
    giv'n   Dreams 11
Than young Hope in his sunniest hour
    hath known   Dreams 34
Till the yellow-haired young Eulalie be-
    came my smiling bride   Eulalie 5
While ever to her young Eulalie upturns
    her violet eye   Eulalie 21
An anthem for the queenliest dead that
    ever died so young   Lenore 6
A dirge for her the doubly dead in that
    she died so young   Lenore 7
That did the death the innocence that
    died, and died so young   Lenore 12
With young hope at her side
                    Lenore (1843) 34
With young Hope at her side   Paean 22
Young hope! thou didst arise
                    Paradise (1834) 8
A man quite young   Politian i 46
"She died full young"—one Bossola
    answers him   Politian ii 18
And so, being young and dipt in folly
                    Romance (1831) 27
Of young passion free   Song (1827) 6
Might envy; her young heart the shrine
                    Tamerlane 89
Pure—as her young example taught
                    Tamerlane 93
Young Love's first lesson is—the heart
                    Tamerlane 102
Nightly their dews on my young head
                    Tamerlane (1827) 40
We still were young: no purer thought
                    Tamerlane (1827) 151
To leave her while we both were young
                    Tamerlane (1827) 236